Bedding Plants IV

A Manual on the Culture of Bedding Plants As a Greenhouse Crop

Fourth edition, edited by

E. Jay Holcomb

Published by

Ball Publishing

Batavia, Illinois USA

Sponsored by

Pennsylvania Flower Growers

Ball Publishing
335 North River Street
P.O. Box 9
Batavia, Illinois 60510-0009 USA

Printed in the United States of America
98 97 96 95 94   5 4 3 2 1

Illustrations: Within text and color insert, except where noted, the chapter authors provided illustrations.

Library of Congress Cataloging-in-Publication Data

Bedding plants IV : a manual on the culture of bedding plants as a
  greenhouse crop / edited by E. Jay Holcomb. — 4th ed.
     p. cm.
  "Sponsored by Pennsylvania Flower Growers."
  Rev. ed. of: Bedding plants III. 3rd ed. 1985.
  Includes bibliographical references and index.
  ISBN 1-883052-05-X
  1. Bedding plants—Handbooks, manuals, etc. 2. Bedding plant
industry—United States—Handbooks, manuals, etc. 3. Greenhouse
management—Handbooks, manuals, etc. I. Holcomb, E. Jay.
II. Pennsylvania Flower Growers. III. Bedding plants III.
IV. Title: Bedding plants 4. V. Title: Bedding plants four.
SB423.7.B44 1994
635.9'62—dc20   94-19177
                                                            CIP

Front cover: *(starting upper right)* Dreams Mix petunias; Rally Lilac Cap pansies; *(lower left)* Rally Light Blue with Blotch pansies, all from PanAmerican Seed Co., West Chicago, Illinois, and Cirrus dusty miller, Ball Seed Co., West Chicago, Illinois.

CONTENTS

PREFACE

This fourth edition of the Penn State Bedding Plant Manual continues a tradition established by John Mastalerz in 1966, the year that the Pennsylvania Flower Growers published the first edition of *Bedding Plants*. During the early 1960s Cornell, Ohio State, and Penn State published several crop production manuals since the techniques needed to produce those crops were rapidly changing, and growers had few other sources of the new cultural information. The researchers and Extension people of that time saw a need and did an excellent job in filling that need.

Since 1966 the amount of information about bedding plants has exploded. The first edition had 121 information-packed pages. The second edition, published in 1976 (only 10 years later), had almost five times as much information, and the third edition, published in 1985, about the same as the second. Over the past four decades not only has the amount of technical information and the size of the grower audience increased dramatically, but the breadth of the issues facing growers has increased as well.

Bedding plant growers in 1966 were concerned about basic issues like bedding plant culture and growing structures. By 1976 the growers needed to know about material handling and operational analysis in the growing structure, and by 1985 they needed to know about computers. In 1966 there was general cultural information about bedding plants, by 1976 the information had been divided by important crops like petunia and sun and shade plants. By 1985 bedding plant growers were growing more perennials, and a chapter was added on perennials.

Scientific, technical, and business information about bedding plants continues to expand because the bedding plant growers' concerns continue to span a broad spectrum of issues from cultural to financial to marketing. However, modern growers have a great deal of information available to them in books, magazines, conferences, and Extension publications. What today's bedding plant grower needs is in-depth information plus the latest technological and business developments. Thus the overall objective of this manual was to provide growers concise, in-depth information on basic bedding plant issues as well as the latest technological and business developments.

The manual begins with the status of the industry, then marketing and use of bedding plants. A section on bedding plant culture includes a chapter on plugs. Environmental factors and their effects on bedding plant culture are thoroughly discussed, and a special section features nutritional deficiency diagnosis. Information on greenhouse design and material handling is included, since growers are still involved with these problems.

Pest problems are always a concern, and these topics are treated in detail by leading experts. Costs and pricing are, of course, important as well as people management. Vegetable transplants, asexually propagated plants and perennials, all of which are important to bedding plant growers, receive special emphasis. Post-production handling and breeding complete the manual.

In summary, the topics most needed by bedding plant growers are included, and the most recent information available on each topic is presented, so that modern bedding plant growers are current on all aspects of bedding plant production.

Authors

Gale L. Arent, Professional Plant Growers Association, Lansing, Michigan

Allan M. Armitage, Professor of Horticulture, University of Georgia, Athens, Georgia

James R. Baker, Extension Entomologist, North Carolina State University, Raleigh, North Carolina

James Barrett, Department of Environmental Horticulture, University of Florida, Gainesville, Florida

John Bartok, Extension Specialist, University of Connecticut, Storrs, Connecticut

David J. Beattie, Associate Professor of Ornamental Horticulture, Pennsylvania State University, University Park, Pennsylvania

Bridget K. Behe, Assistant Professor of Horticulture, Auburn University, Auburn, Alabama

Thomas A. Brewer, Professor of Agricultural Economics, Pennsylvania State University, University Park, Pennsylvania

Robin G. Brumfield, Extension Farm Management Specialist, Rutgers University, New Brunswick, New Jersey

William Carpenter, Professor of Environmental Horticulture, University of Florida, Gainesville, Florida

James Corfield, President of S&G Seeds Inc., Downers Grove, Illinois

Richard Craig, Professor of Plant Breeding, Pennsylvania State University, University Park, Pennsylvania

John E. Erwin, Assistant Professor and Extension Floriculture Specialist, University of Minnesota, St. Paul, Minnesota

William C. Fonteno, Professor of Horticultural Science, North Carolina State University, Raleigh, North Carolina

Ralph N. Freeman, Extension Floriculture Specialist, Cornell University, Riverhead, New York

Winand Hock, Professor of Plant Pathology and Extension Pesticide Specialist, Pennsylvania State University, University Park, Pennsylvania

E. Jay Holcomb, Professor of Floriculture, Pennsylvania State University, University Park, Pennsylvania

Mark P. Kaczperski, University of Georgia, Athens, Georgia

Meriam Karlsson, Associate Professor of Horticulture, University of Alaska, Fairbanks, Alaska

Larry Kuhns, Professor of Ornamental Horticulture, Pennsylvania State University, University Park, Pennsylvania

Robert Langhans, Professor of Floriculture, Cornell University, Ithaca, New York

Roy A. Larson, Professor of Floriculture, North Carolina State University, Raleigh, North Carolina

David G. Lemon, New Product Development Manager, Oglevee, Ltd., Lompac, California

Ria T. Leonard, University of Florida, Gainesville, Florida

Richard K. Lindquist, Professor of Entomology, Ohio State Agricultural Research and Development Center, Wooster, Ohio

Ted Marston, President, Ted Marston Associates, Kirkland, Washington

Gary W. Moorman, Professor of Plant Pathology, Pennsylvania State University, University Park, Pennsylvania

Terril A. Nell, Professor and Chairman of Environmental Science, University of Florida, Gainesville, Florida

Paul V. Nelson, Professor of Horticultural Science, North Carolina State University, Raleigh, North Carolina

Ellen Paparozzi, Associate Professor of Urban Horticulture, University of Nebraska, Lincoln, Nebraska

Charles C. Powell, President, Plant Health Advisory Services, Worthington, Ohio

William J. Roberts, Director of Center for Controlled Environmental Agriculture, Extension Specialist, Rutgers University, New Brunswick, New Jersey

Charles Vavrina, Agricultural Research and Education Center, University of Florida, Immokalee, Florida

Alvi O. Voigt, Professor Emeritus of Agricultural Economics, Pennsylvania State University, University Park, Pennsylvania

Marcia L. Voigt, Professional Plant Growers Association, Lansing, Michigan

Dennis J. Wolnick, Associate Professor of Floriculture, Pennsylvania State University, University Park, Pennsylvania

CHAPTER 1

Bedding Plant Industry

Ralph N. Freeman

This chapter presents an historical overview of the bedding plant industry, from the beginning of plant culture to the development of an emerging and growing bedding plant industry, and ends with a view of what the future holds. As Vic Ball stated in 1976, it was a slow start, with "centuries of painstaking, slow progress." Recently, however, the industry's development and production are gaining momentum at an increasing pace.

The past

Horticulture's beginnings are documented sporadically in the literature. It is not easy to locate the entire history in one volume; however, a good overview is found in a feature article by Vic Ball entitled *Early American Horticulture* [3]. Perhaps the article's most important aspect is its positive vision of gardeners, growers, breeders, engineers, and many others who contributed to the industry.

Horticultural history began on the third day of creation when "God said, Let the earth bring forth grass, the herb yielding seed, and the fruit tree yielding fruit after his kind, whose seed is in itself, upon the earth and it was so. And the earth brought forth grass, and herb yielding seed after his kind, and the tree yielding fruit, whose seed was in itself, after his kind: and God saw that it was good" [1]. The next record dates back to 500 B.C., when Romans built forcing houses for plants. By 100 B.C. their forcing-house walls were made of translucent mica sheets with heat ducts built into the walls [3].

1

Prior to the 1850s, greenhouses were framed with wood that had portable sashes similar to what growers know today as sash-houses [9]. The glass was small and heavy. Heating was supplied by coal- or wood-burning stoves or by placing cow manure under benches or under the soil in growing beds to emit heat throughout the long winters. Ventilation procedures were crude, and temperature control was not sophisticated; yet crops were propagated, and the warmer spring and summer temperatures helped improve the plants' growth and development.

First glass-roofed greenhouse

"About 1855, Frederick A. Lord, founder of the firm Lord & Burnham, erected in Buffalo, NY what is said to be the first permanent glass-roofed greenhouse. This construction met with favor with the few men of that period interested in flower-growing, and several houses similar to Mr. Lord's were soon built. This was a beginning, but the houses of that period were very crude and primitive. The framework was of large dimensions, the glass small in size, heavy and thick. Interior light conditions were correspondingly poor. Still they were a vast improvement over sash houses, and from the crude greenhouses of that period the present-day modern house has been evolved" [9]. Since that time we have seen many glass and plastic greenhouse manufacturing firms develop and many disappear. Lord & Burnham is one that is no longer in business.

Throughout these developmental times plants also were grown out-of-doors in beds and cold frames. (In fact, gardeners continue to produce in this fashion.) These plant growing methods, and this knowledge, experience, and wisdom stimulated today's modern technology.

In the late 1800s and early part of this century, the U.S. floriculture industry began developing near metropolitan areas, including Boston, New York, Philadelphia, Washington D.C., Chicago, Pittsburgh, St. Louis, San Francisco, Los Angeles and San Diego. The primary reason for locating in these areas was proximity to market. The only transportation was by horse and wagon or train.

Frequently, growers who didn't own motorized or horse-drawn vehicles would have to transport their product, usually cut flowers, in wooden crates on long, flat wheelbarrows to the train station and ship their product to the flower market; only a small amount of product was purchased for use by local retail florists. The distant wholesaler would ship the empty crates back to the grower for reuse. Perhaps this was the advent of "recycling."

Bedding plant production begins

Bedding plant production as we know it today began at the turn of the century primarily by private estates and emerging commercial growers. Production numbers then were not what they are today; bedding plants were produced in small quantities by individual growers.

Bedding plant production began as a major force in the late 1940s. Geraniums, marigolds, petunias, vinca, pansy, begonias, lantana, *Dracaena indivisa*, dusty miller, coleus, bulbs, tomatoes, lettuce, and cabbage were the mainstay of the bedding plant industry. Primary usage included home gardens, cemetery urns, and planting boxes. Geraniums, begonias, and numerous other crops were propagated by seed or cuttings, usually in the early fall, planted in 2¼-inch (5.6 cm) clay pots after the seedlings developed and then transplanted into 4-inch (10 cm) clay pots in early January and February. Growers hoped a few plants would be ready for Easter and Mother's Day sales, but Memorial Day was the only big holiday for bedding plant sales.

Vegetable bedding plant and some flowering plant production was accomplished by sowing seeds in flats. Seedlings were transplanted or pricked-off from the seedling flat into other flats of soil, grown until the seedlings were 6 to 12 inches (15 to 30 cm) tall and then were considered ready for sale. Total growth time was usually four to six months prior to sale.

The sales routine also differed from the one we are accustomed to today. Customers would frequently visit production sites, retail-growers, or even local hardware stores to decide which plants they wanted and how many. The sales clerk would cut the individual plants out of the flats or beds with a flat trowel and wrap them in newspaper for the customer to carry home. Some plants were available in clay pots, too, but the majority were not.

Merchandising and display techniques were also crude at that time. The plants were always on the ground, generally outside the greenhouse or store. Although a rather inefficient method of growing, displaying, and selling plants, it was considered advanced at the time.

Progress slow

During the post-World War II period, new varieties were introduced and different methods of growing bedding plants were developed. Paper pots were used instead of clay and special paper or tar-paper-type dividers were inserted in flats to keep roots separate and intact. Many of these new ideas were not accepted by growers. They still produced their plants the old way. Progress was slow.

Research has been conducted at the United States Department of Agriculture and many of the land-grant universities throughout the United States since the 1930s. Scientists were learning why plants grow, how they grow, why and how they respond to light, temperature, gases, fertilizers, different types of soil, fungicides, insecticides, and many more areas of interest to growers.

The literature was beginning to explode with information for the industry. Papers reporting research results appeared in professional journals, books written by numerous professors, and industry trade magazines such as *Florists' Review, The Florists' Exchange,* and *Southern Florists' and Nurserymen.* Additionally, nearly every state florists' organization published a "Bulletin" packed with cultural information for the grower. Much of this information was recognized by the professional community as an official publication, and many professors were editors and/or publishers in cooperation with the states' grower organizations.

Geo. J. Ball, Inc. began publishing a monthly magazine, *GrowerTalks*, in 1937. *GrowerTalks* was a handy, pocket-sized publication with grower information, sowing schedules, how-to instructions for specific crops, and other items of interest. In 1982, the publication was updated, and circulation continued to grow. An international trade magazine, *FloraCulture International*, was begun by Ball in 1990. Other international trade magazines followed. *Greenhouse Manager* and *Greenhouse Grower* began publishing in May 1982 and January 1983, respectively.

Industry contributions

Major milestones in the bedding plant industry include:

The 1940s:
- Chemical fumigants for soil and air, DDT, and chemical weed control
- Automatic watering and subirrigation
- Bench construction
- Floriculture extension agents
- Christmas begonia production takes six months
- Cuttings effectively propagated
- Parathion aerosol for pest control
- Photoperiod concepts for flowering plants year-round
- Vermiculite

The 1950s:

- Flash flame soil sterilizer
- Systox and methyl bromide
- Mist propagation
- Plastic greenhouses as production facilities
- Polyethylene air inflation for greenhouses (developed by Bill Roberts, Rutgers University)
- Polyethylene, mylar and fiberglass as greenhouse coverings
- Mercury products in greenhouse paints phytotoxic
- Agricultural chemical safety emphasis
- Market packs, plastic flats and packs, Jiffy Products
- First automatic planter
- Flat and pack labeling
- Hanging baskets
- Urea-formaldehyde nitrogen fertilizer
- Screening greenhouses for thrips control
- Soil testing
- Crop nutrition and pest control for growers
- Gibberellins, Cycocel, and B-Nine chemical growth regulators
- Out-of-season crop forcing
- Wet evaporative pads for cooling greenhouses

The 1960s:

- Peat-lite mix from Cornell
- *Silent Spring* by Rachel Carson
- Bedding Plants Inc.
- Foliage plants, the No. 1 crop
- Four-inch annuals
- One-half of bedding plant sales in chain stores
- Bedding plants, the No. 2 crop
- Plugs for field crops (George Todd); plugs introduced to the bedding plant market
- Waffle flat from Blackmore
- Hanging baskets
- Early work on seedling storage
- Aisle eliminators
- Crop manuals
- Carbon dioxide use
- Automatic tube watering
- Culture-indexed geraniums
- Soil depth and aeration emphasis
- Foliar analysis

The 1970s:

- Oil crisis
- Heat screens, efficient boilers, and heat distribution systems for energy conservation
- Low pressure storage
- Virus-free geraniums
- DuPage Horticulture School, West Chicago, Illinois
- Hanging baskets increase
- Balcony gardening
- Controlled release fertilizers
- Double-deck benching
- Roll-out benching
- Fricke automatic seeder
- Four-inch pots
- High intensity discharge (HID) lighting
- Bedding plants, No. 1 crop
- Computers

The 1980s:

- Vegetable sales increase
- Polycarbonate and acrylic panels
- Northeastern growers save money with coal furnaces
- Dutch begin shipping heavily to United States
- Greenhouse expansion increasing
- Computers accepted by some growers
- Geranium petal shattering a problem
- Transportable benching important
- Focus on operation/marketing efficiency
- Environmental laws/regulations impacting producers
- Mass markets/chains important market outlets
- International imports causing competition
- Bar coding
- Ebb and flood irrigation
- Age of automation: automatic transplanters, seeders and label machines
- DIF

The 1990s:

- Stiffer environmental laws/regulations
- Worker Protection Law
- Many pesticides no longer available
- Integrated Pest Management employed by industry
- Foliage plant production dropping off
- Bedding plants, the No. 1 crop
- Most growers using computers
- Bar coding used for over 60% of bedding plants

- Cut flower imports very strong
- Storage of plugs
- Greenhouse expansion slowing down slightly
- Mass marketers selling nearly 60% to 75% of plants and flowers
- Ebb and flood irrigation

Crop trends

The history of floriculture is most interesting. Over time hundreds of crops have been grown. Crop selection was based on usage, needs of the day, and tastes of the consumer. H.L. Bailey's work, which was reported by White [9], Bahr [2], Laurie and Poesch [6], Laurie and Kiplinger [5], Post [7], Seeley [8], and many others, reveals that many of these crops have been used over a long period of time and will continue to be important. For example, roses, carnations, gardenia, cut violets, chrysanthemums, cineraria, and calceolaria, have been popular for many decades but their market share fluctuates. Some crops, such as the sweet pea, freesia, and orchids, were heavily in demand at one time but have never returned to favor.

A major turning point in the bedding plant industry occurred in the 1960s. Cut flowers had been the principal crop for many years. Then potted plants (flowering and tropical) and bedding plants suddenly became important. In the mid-1960s, cut flower growers experienced marketplace resistance. They had to adjust or go out of business. Most growers began to emphasize potted plants or bedding plants, which required a tremendous financial investment to retrofit greenhouses, purchase new and different equipment and supplies, and also to hire and train additional workers.

Several key growers of bedding plants and groundcovers identified a need for a national trade organization to disseminate and share production and marketing information. As a result, Bedding Plants, Incorporated, was born in 1969. The organization's name was changed to Professional Plant Growers Association, Inc. in 1988, to better reflect the industry's professional image.

In the mid-1970s, an energy crisis hit the country. Fuel prices increased from a few cents per gallon to nearly $1 per gallon. Prices of some products increased as well, forcing growers to recognize inefficient practices and begin conserving resources. Labor-saving mechanization and automation became increasingly cost-efficient. Double-layer greenhouse coverings were introduced, which reduced heat loss and improved efficiency over traditional, single-pane glass.

New, efficient boilers were installed, increasing combustion efficiency from 40% to 50% to 70% to 90%. Some growers installed heaters capable of burning either gas or coal to gain a price advantage when one fuel decreased in price. New heat distribution systems were also installed. The impact of the crisis was most felt by growers in the northeastern and north-central United States, although costs for cooling greenhouses in the southern United States increased at the same time.

New crops developed

From the 1970s to the 1990s, new crops were developed to stimulate consumer interest. Some of these include New Guinea impatiens, seed and vegetative geraniums, miniature poinsettias, kalanchoes and perennials. Over the last 20 years a move-towards-nature trend and the field production of cut flowers has become important again (a big crop in the early 1900s), along with herbs of all kinds.

As technology in breeding, biotechnology, and numerous other scientific fields advanced, the development of different crops, even different colors occurred at a faster pace than ever before. Consumer demand increased for bedding plants in 3- to 4½-inch (7.5 to 11.2 cm) containers, flats/packs, hanging baskets, and, most importantly, for smaller, shorter, and more compact plants.

The industry continues to grow and change. In spite of competition, growers remain dependent and interdependent upon each other. For example, if a heating system fails, several growers will usually offer help and equipment. There is a great openness and sharing of information; everyone wants to learn and improve. These attributes are not often seen in other industries; truly, the horticultural field is unique.

The future

Floriculture has been and continues to be a profitable industry for many people. Even during the Great Depression of 1929, World War II, and other crisis periods, growers and retailers found their businesses profitable, contrary to economic trends. We expect this economic stability to continue.

At present, large mass marketers and chain stores merchandise nearly three-fourths of our products with surprising efficiency by keeping consumer prices affordable. Producers who are pressured by mass marketers into a commitment to a low contract purchase price must be creative to produce the product for a profit. Pressures are also being exerted upon the middle-sized producer and the small mom and pop operations, where the lower sales volume increases the need for a higher per-unit profit.

As we look to the future, large producers will probably increase in size to better serve their clients with efficient and creative marketing and the introduction of new ideas and new products. The large producer, however, may not be able to adequately service garden centers and small retailers. This ensures a need for the middle- and small-sized growers, who may not be as efficient as the large grower, but are able to deliver 20 or 30 product units to a small retailer. The per-unit cost may be higher, but the consumer is willing to pay a little extra for the enhanced product and service. (The large producer will have to deliver truck- or trailer-load quantities to be cost-effective.)

Roadside and garden center marketing will remain a strong retailing method. The consumer's desire to get to the farm or to the country to browse, relax, and receive personalized service from the staff will continue to support this part of the industry.

Gardening remains a prime activity

Mechanization will grow with continual refinements. New varieties and new plants will be introduced to meet consumer needs. All industry phases will adapt to consumer purchase patterns; growers must provide new cultivars, new display, marketing, and distribution techniques that will be attractive to buyers.

Direct selling from producer and/or marketer to consumer via electronic ordering will also grow as communications systems improve. Gardening will remain a major leisure-time activity. The impact of plants and flowers on people's lives is positive, and consumers desire to have their dream garden.

Due to university and extension system budget constraints, information to growers will not continue to be free. Already there are charges for bulletins, books, education programs, seminars, and special services. Most programs will be funded by growers interested in the information. Faculty and extension staff will be reduced, and the number of quality horticultural specialists will not equal that of the past.

Information will be privatized and made available to growers on a subscription basis or on request by private consultants, universities, Cooperative Extension, and various supply companies at a fee. Some of this has already occurred with two crop interest groups: Roses, Inc. and the Poinsettia Growers Association. Growers who desire detailed information, full service, research results and recommendations will have to join these various interest groups.

Is there a bright and profitable future ahead? Definitely, but the industry faces significant changes and adjustments.

References

[1]   *Holy Bible.*
[2]   Bahr, F. 1922. *Fritz Bahr's commercial floriculture*. New York: De La
      Mare Co.
[3]   Ball V. 1976. Early American horticulture. *GrowerTalks* 40(3): 1-58.
[4]   Laurie, A. and L.C. Chadwick 1934. *Commercial flower forcing*.
      Philadelphia: Blakiston.
[5]   Laurie, A. and D.C. Kiplinger. 1944. *Commercial flower forcing*.
      Philadelphia: Blakiston.
[6]   Laurie, A. and G.H. Poesch.1939. *Commercial flower forcing*.
      Philadelphia: Blakiston.
[7]   Post. K.A. 1949. *Florist crop production and marketing*. New York:
      Orange-Judd.
[8]   Seeley, J.G. 1979. Advancements in commercial floriculture during
      the past 75 years. *HortSci* 14(3): 364-368.
[9]   White, E.W. 1920. *The principles of floriculture*. New York: Macmillan.

CHAPTER 2

All-America Selections, Fleuroselect, and FloraStar Trials

David G. Lemon

As competition among flower and vegetable seed breeders becomes more intense, it is very important to have organizations like All-America Selections, Fleuroselect, and FloraStar that are devoted to the independent testing of new varieties on a nationwide or worldwide basis.

All-America Selections

When All-America Selections [1] was conceived back in 1932, what few trial grounds that existed for flower or vegetable seeds around the country were all at seed company locations. W. Ray Hastings acted as the organization's first chairman and later became executive director, a position he held for many years. He was really the father of the organization. Ray was able to obtain small donations from the Southern Seedsmen's Association and the American Seed Trade Association and started with 20 trial locations. Only new, previously unsold varieties could be entered in the trials. Each judge was instructed to evaluate the varieties strictly on their performance at his or her location.

I well remember his visits back in 1965 to 1972 when I worked at Ferry-Morse Seed Company. He would always come unannounced to make sure we were doing a good job. For many years we just had the outdoor flower and vegetable trials.

In 1986, a bedding plant category was added. These plants are grown in flats and flowered before they go to the field. Minimum point scores are required in both the flat and outdoor trials to gain this award. Because this is a very difficult test, there tend to be fewer winners than in the outdoor flower trials.

All-America Selections is currently directed by a nine-member board of directors. Nona Wolfram-Koivula is the executive director.

Today AAS has 33 outdoor flower trials, 21 bedding plant trials and 26 vegetable trials located at seed companies, universities, and botanical gardens. Breeders from around the world are invited to submit new varieties before November 1 each year. Photographs and descriptions are required upon acceptance of entry seeds. The AAS office codes all entries to provide anonymity. Entries and comparisons are reviewed by comparison committees to ensure that all entries are distinct.

Judges look for the following characteristics in flowers:

- Color
- Insect tolerance
- Attractiveness
- Uniqueness

- Disease resistance
- Prolonged flowering
- Uniformity
- Fragrance

In the bedding plant category, appearance in the flat is also noted.

In the vegetable trials, these points are evaluated:

- Flavor
- Appearance
- Disease resistance
- Nutrition

- Yield
- Texture
- Production and space efficiency
- Novelty value

Currently, two types of medals are awarded—the Gold and the regular winner award. Gold medals are rarely awarded and are given to varieties of exceptional merit.

Once a variety is designated a winner, the breeder/producer is required to have sufficient seed on hand, or "in the bag" to satisfy North American marketplace requirements. When the board is satisfied about seed quantity, the award is granted, and the variety is announced for the following year. The AAS office sends out publicity to various seed companies, magazines, newspapers, and other garden communicators. Media coverage is extensive, and the resulting publicity is very helpful in promoting the winners. Because these varieties have been judged by panels of experts, great credibility is given the winners.

Recent All-America Selections winners are:

Outdoor flower category

1989   Early Sunrise coreopsis—Gold Medal   Golden Gate French marigold
         Telstar Picotee F$_1$ dianthus   Clown Mixture torenia

	Tango F$_1$ impatiens	Sandy White verbena
1990	Summer Pastel achillea	Jolly Joker pansy
	Castle Pink celosia	Scarlet Splendor F$_1$ zinnia
1991	Red Plume *Gaillardia pulchella*	Padparadja pansy
	Freckles geranium	Pretty in Rose vinca
1992	Tropical Rose canna	Peaches and Cream verbena
	Lady in Red salvia	
1993	Mont Blanc nierembergia	Imagination verbena
1994	Lady lavendar	

Bedding plant category

1989	Orchid Daddy F$_1$ petunia	Novalis Deep Blue verbena
1990	Polo Burgundy Star F$_1$ petunia	Polo Salmon F$_1$ petunia
1991	Maxim Marina F$_1$ pansy	Parasol vinca
1992	Ideal Violet F$_1$ dianthus	Pretty in White vinca

Vegetable category

1990	Derby bean	Cream of the Crop F$_1$ squash
	Super Cayenne F$_1$ pepper	Sundrops F$_1$ squash
1991	Kentucky Blue bean	Golden Crown F$_1$ watermelon
	Tivoli F$_1$ squash	
1992	Thumbelina carrot	Fernleaf dill
1993	Baby Bear pumpkin	Husky Gold F$_1$ tomato
1994	Fanfare F$_1$ cucumber	Big Beef F$_1$ tomato

Fleuroselect

Fleuroselect [2], founded in 1970, is an association of flower seed breeders and trading companies. The concept is very similar to All-America Selections, but Fleuroselect has membership and stages a convention each July in Europe. There are 23 trial grounds throughout Europe, from Finland in the north to Italy in the south. Pack trials were added to the outdoor trials in 1989.

Many well-known flower-seedsmen have served as president of Fleuroselect and on the board and committees. Current president is Bill Scott of PanAmerican Seed Co., West Chicago, Illinois, the first American to serve in this capacity. Marcel Bartels is executive director and his office is in Noordwijk, the Netherlands.

Fleuroselect recognizes breeders in three ways:

Gold Medal: awarded to the varieties with the highest points in the trial. It is given for exceptional breeding work on new colors, longer flowering periods, more uniformity, disease resistance, etc. Gold Medal winners are promoted for five years.

Quality Mark: a certificate of merit for new flower varieties that are better than existing varieties.

Novelty Register: a register of new and distinct flower seed varieties that are guaranteed variety protection by all Fleuroselect members.

Recent Fleuroselect medal winners are:

1989	Early Sunrise *Coreopsis grandiflora*	Disco Orange *Tagetes patula*
	Telstar Crimson *Dianthus hybrida*	Espana Mix *Tagetes patula*
	Compliment Scarlet *Lobelia speciosa*	Orange Jacket *Tagetes patula*
	Disco Golden Yellow *Tagetes patula*	
1990	Garden Sun *Gazania splendens*	Jolly Joker *Viola wittrockiana*
1991	Pin Up *Begonia tuberosa*	Dalli *Eschscholtzia californica*
	Sonata *Cosmos bipinnatus*	Orange Appeal *Pelargonium hortorum*
	Color Magician *Dianthus hybrida*	Imperial Gold Princess *Viola wittrockiana*
	Raspberry Parfait *Dianthus chinensis*	Padparadja *Viola wittrockiana*
	Strawberry Parfait *Dianthus chinensis*	
1992	Starlight Rose *Callistephus chinensis*	Safari Tangerine *Tagetes patula*
	Mega Orange Star *Impatiens walleriana*	Peaches and Cream *Verbena hybrida*
		Lady-in-Red *Salvia coccinea*
1993	Forever Gold *Limonium sinuatum*	Imagination *Verbena speciosa*
	Mont Blanc nierembergia	Imperial Frosty Rose *Viola tricolor*
1994	Robella *Bellis perennis*	Florence White *Centaurea cyanus*
	Florence Pink *Centaurea cyanus*	Velour Blue viola

FloraStar

FloraStar [3] is a program designed to find and award outstanding new potted plants. Organized in 1988 by the Professional Plant Growers Association, it has a nine-member board of elected directors along with the past president of FloraStar and the president of the Professional Plant Growers Association. The current executive director is Michael Novovesky. FloraStar has 19 trial locations in the United States covering a wide range of geographic and climatic areas.

FloraStar differs from All-America Selections and Fleuroselect by including cultivars propagated from vegetative cuttings, bulbs, corms, and tubers, as well as seed.

All winners must be superior to older varieties, and entries are solicited from domestic and international breeders.

There are two seasonal trials per year. Fall test varieties include seasonal plants such as chrysanthemums, poinsettias, and cyclamens. Spring and summer trials include seasonal plants such as cutting geraniums, lilies, New Guinea impatiens, and tuberous begonias.

Every entry is paired with a commercially available comparison variety, and the judges look for improvements that will benefit the consumer such as plant habit, form, color of flower and foliage, ease of culture, uniformity, resistance to disease and insects, longevity, ease of care in the home or office, and overall appearance.

Winning varieties are:

Grace floribunda geranium	Majestic kalanchoe
Judy floribunda geranium	Burgundy Clown torenia
Marilyn floribunda geranium	Blue and White Clown torenia
Blue Lisa eustoma	Thalia streptocarpus

Fig. 2.1. FloraStar winner Blue Lisa eustoma.

Fig. 2.2. Judy floribunda geranium, FloraStar winner.

TABLE 3.2

Bedding plants' commercial floriculture share, 1992

| | 32 states | |
	1992 (x $1,000)	Share (%)
Bedding plants	1,111,774	40.4
Cut flowers	458,272	16.7
Foliage	426,858	15.5
Pot flowers	753,854	27.4
Totals	**2,750,758**	**100.0**

Source: 1992 Floriculture Crops Summary, National Agricultural Statistics Service, USDA.

(table 3.2). The industry has changed significantly in the last 22 years; perhaps the most important change has been the strong, steady advance in bedding plant sales, which are keeping step with the nation's one outdoor leisure activity: gardening.

A broad bedding plant mix

Detailed reporting of bedding plant production and sales by the United States Department of Agriculture began in 1985. Prior to 1985, bedding plants were reported as flats sold and were categorized as flowering/foliar or as vegetable type bedding plants. No differentiations were made for potted bedding plants, hanging baskets, garden chrysanthemum, or pot size. Geraniums were classified as flowering potted plants rather than bedding plants. These and other USDA program aspects made comparisons of sales and production volumes difficult, and sometimes impossible, during the 1980s.

More detailed USDA reporting since 1985 indicates that geraniums comprised 21% of the total bedding plant business wholesale value in 1985, declining to a 13.8% share in 1992 (table 3.3). Of the 13.8% share, geraniums in flats accounted for 2.9%, zonal (cutting) geraniums in pots were 7.2%, and seed geraniums in pots were 3.7%.

Also in 1992, the geranium share was 13.8%, flowering bedding plants accounted for 62.2% (40.5% were grown in flats and 21.7% in pots), vegetable bedding plants accounted for 8.4% (7.0% flat grown

TABLE 3.3

Bedding plant sales and share, 1985, 1992

	1985 ($)	Share (%)	1992 ($)	Share (%)	All 1992 floriculture shares (%)
	(x $1,000)				
Geraniums, flats	24,517	5.0	31,847	2.9	1.2
pots (cutting)	57,171	11.7	80,472	7.2	2.9
pots (seed)	20,424	4.2	41,056	3.7	1.5
Total, geraniums	**102,112**	**21.0**	**153,375**	**13.8**	**5.6**
Flowering bedding plants					
flats	195,986	40.2	450,408	40.5	16.5
potted	59,367	12.2	241,085	21.7	8.8
Total	**255,353**	**52.4**	**691,493**	**62.2**	**25.1**
Vegetable bedding plants					
flats	54,536	11.2	78,149	7.0	2.8
potted	3,855	0.8	15,287	1.4	0.6
Total	**58,391**	**12.0**	**93,436**	**8.4**	**3.4**
Flowering hanging baskets	44,880	9.2	122,136	11.0	4.4
Garden chrysanthemums	26,553	5.4	51,334	4.6	1.9
Grand totals	**487,289**	**100.0**	**1,111,774**	**100.0**	**40.4**

Source: 1992 Floriculture Crops Summary, National Agricultural Statistics Service, USDA.
Note: 1992 data included 36 states' growers with $100,000 or more sales, whereas 1985 data reported 28 states' growers with annual sales greater than $10,000.

and only 1.4% pot grown), flowering hanging baskets were 11.0%, and garden chrysanthemums were 4.6%.

Flowering versus vegetable plants

The 1970 census data showed that U.S. flowering bedding plants enjoyed a 72.7% wholesale market value share versus a 27.3% share for vegetable bedding plants. In 1979, census data indicated the vegetable share had increased to 39.3% versus 60.6% for flowering bedding plants. Vegetable gardening gained impetus during the 1970s due to high inflation, escalating energy costs, higher food costs, and economic uncertainty.

USDA data from the 28-state *Floriculture Crops* report indicated

TABLE 3.7

Bedding plant crop mix, 1988, 1991, 1992

Bedding plants	1988	1991	1992
	(% of total)		
Flowering			
Ageratum	2.0	1.0	1.6
Alyssum	2.0	2.0	2.3
Asters	1.0	1.0	1.0
Begonia	5.0	5.0	6.0
Browallia	1.0	1.0	1.0
Celosia	1.0	1.0	1.6
Coleus	1.0	1.0	1.6
Dahlia	1.0	1.0	1.6
Dianthus	1.0	1.0	2.3
Dusty miller	2.0	1.0	2.3
Geraniums, seed	8.2	7.3	7.0
Geraniums, cutting	11.4	12.7	10.0
Garden mums	1.0	NA	1.0
New Guinea impatiens	NA	3.0	3.0
Impatiens, other	12.2	14.0	14.0
Lobelia	1.0	1.0	1.6
Marigold	7.0	6.0	6.0
Pansy	3.0	3.0	1.6
Petunias	9.7	9.0	9.0
Phlox	1.0	1.0	1.0
Portulaca	2.0	1.0	1.6
Salvia	2.0	3.0	2.3
Snapdragon	2.0	2.0	1.6
Verbena	1.0	1.0	1.6
Vinca	2.0	4.0	3.0
Zinnia	1.0	1.0	1.6
Flowering total	**81.5**	**84.0**	**85.2**
Vegetables			
Cabbage	2.0	1.0	1.0
Peppers	2.0	3.0	2.3
Tomatoes	4.0	5.0	4.0
Vegetable total	**8.0**	**9.0**	**7.3**
Strawberries	1.0	NA	NA
Others [a]	10.0	8.0	8.0
Grand total	**100.5**	**101.0**	**100.5**

Source: 1988, 1991, 1992 Annual Surveys, Professional Plant Growers Association.

[a] Most of 'others' would be flowering bedding plants.

Census). The 1988 total flowering plant share was 91.4% (Census) and a similar percentage for PPGA (85.2% plus most of "others," 8%). It is contrasted with the 1979 60.6% flowering plant share.

Geraniums were the top bedding plant in 1988 with almost one-fifth (19.3% Census of which zonals or cuttings were 12.6% and sccd geraniums 6.7% versus 19.6% PPGA of which zonals were 11.4% and seed geraniums 8.2%), followed by impatiens (9.4% Census, 12.2% PPGA), petunias (6.5% Census, 9.7% PPGA), marigolds (4.5% Census, 7.0% PPGA), begonias (4.2% Census, 5.0%).

From 1979 to 1988 geraniums have dominated, and impatiens have gained a greater foothold. However, by 1991 geraniums had a 20% share versus impatiens' 17%; and in 1992, geraniums and impatiens were tied at 17% (table 3.7). This decline in geraniums' popularity is also documented in the USDA *Floriculture Crops* (table 3.3) where geraniums steadily lost market share from 1985 (21.0%) to 1992 (13.8%).

In contrast, impatiens have been PPGA's reported best-selling bedding plant for the last 10 years (table 3.4). Geraniums lost strength from 1986 as a best-selling bedding plant, and petunias moved into second place in 1990 through 1992 after a 1970 to 1979 decline in market share. Begonias, pansies, and vinca also gained. In general, a wider flowering bedding plants and perennials selection is now available.

Geographic distribution and description

Bedding plant production is not concentrated in a small number of states as are foliage plants and fresh cut flowers. Ten top states enjoyed 66.2% of the total wholesale value reported by 36 states in 1992 (table 3.8). California seemed far in front of the pack with 16.7%. However, California's higher population (29,126,000) means that the 1992 per capita wholesale bedding plant value of $6.38 is actually below Michigan's $9.57 and Washington's $8.23 value per capita.

The average for the top 10 states was $5.56 per capita. The remaining 26 states averaged $3.62, and all 36 states averaged $4.71. Bedding plant surplus-producing states—Michigan, Washington, Ohio, Florida, California, Texas, and North Carolina—have production above $5 per capita. States producing less than the demand could be defined as below $4 per capita—Illinois, Pennsylvania, and New York—as well as some states among the other 26 reporting (all 26 averaged $3.62 per capita) and, of course, some of the remaining 14 unreported states. Market proximity apparently is an advantage in some areas over lower cost production.

Factors affecting the status (increase/same/decrease) of bedding plant emphasis include: attractive urban development value for green-

TABLE 3.8

Top 10 states' bedding plant sales, 1976-1992 [a]

	(x $1 million)					1992 share of 36 states (%)	Share of state's floriculture value (%)	1990 est. population (x 1,000)	1992 wholesale value per capita ($)
	1976 Value	Rank	1981 Value	Rank	1992 Value	Rank				
California	14.6	3	37.0	1	185.9	1	16.7	27.9	21,126	6.38
Texas	5.0	8	14.4	5	90.1	2	8.1	60.2	17,712	5.09
Michigan	17.3	1	31.9	2	88.9	3	8.0	70.0	9,293	9.57
Florida	3.2	13	8.3	9	83.5	4	7.5	15.9	12,818	6.52
Ohio	16.8	2	28.8	3	71.4	5	6.4	55.6	10,791	6.62
New York	9.8	4	18.3	4	64.0	6	5.8	27.8	17,773	3.60
Pennsylvania	6.0	6	12.6	6	44.6	7	4.0	50.6	11,827	3.77
Washington	2.6	18	5.6	20	38.3	8	3.4	57.1	4,657	8.23
Illinois	5.3	7	9.2	8	35.5	9	3.2	54.9	11,612	3.06
North Carolina	2.9	15	7.7	11	34.0	10	3.1	44.2	6,690	5.09
Totals	83.5	—	173.8	—	736.2	—	66.2	34.7	132,299	5.56
Other 26 states					375.5		33.8	50.9	103,603	3.62
All 36 states					1,111.8		100.0	38.8	235,902	4.71

Source: 1976-1992 Floriculture Crops Surveys, National Agricultural Statistics Service, USDA.
Note: 1976 and 1981 surveys included 28 states; 1992 report covered 36 states.
[a] Includes bedding plants in flats, pots, flowering baskets, hardy mums, and geraniums.

house properties; bedding plant "fit" with other crops and retail-growing operations; a state's emphasis corresponding with its large but dispersed population (especially Michigan, Ohio, New York, Pennsylvania, North Carolina); the entry ease for new bedding plant entrepreneurs coupled with (or without) outside income and appropriate direct-to-consumer marketing advantages; astute producers who can buy less expensively than they can grow; and major discount chains that require greater supplies than can be obtained locally or statewide.

For instance, Florida's fourth place bedding plant share is only 15.9% of its floriculture value, partly due to Florida's huge foliage industry, which has suffered from a soft market the last several years. Note also California's 27.9% bedding plant share is due to exceptionally large, varied non-bedding plant floricultural businesses—as well as mild climate, production advantages, and market opportunities.

Other than Florida and California, bedding plants' importance as a share of all floriculture for the remaining states varied from 27.8% for New York to 70.0% for Michigan. Illinois was an obvious deficit producer (only $3.06 per capita) and Michigan a surplus producer ($9.57 per capita). Bedding plants had a 34.7% share of all floriculture (table 3.8).

Price variation: geraniums

Geranium prices are noted in table 3.9. All reported states averaged $9.33 wholesale per geranium flat in 1992, increasing from $8.91 in 1991. For convenience, the top 10 states in 1992 are ranked for total wholesale geranium value. The price differential can be attributed to supply and demand conditions. Those states and markets with lower volumes of geraniums for sale usually get higher prices, and states with greater quantities find weaker prices.

Price ranges are also provided in table 3.9. The highest average geranium price per flat in 1992 was registered in Oregon ($13.64); next was Wisconsin ($12.71). The lowest average geranium flat price in 1992 was in Massachusetts ($5.55); next was Pennsylvania ($7.15). The range was more than double. In 1991, the average geranium price per flat ranged from $7.31 (Alabama) to $11.37 (Oregon), and the range was $4.06. Geraniums in flats, a relatively variable phenomenon, reflect wide product quality, size, and market variability.

Potted zonal (cutting) geraniums' average price differed significantly from potted geraniums grown from seed. All reported states averaged $1.23 wholesale for zonals in less than 5-inch (12.5-cm) pots in 1991, and ranged from $.90 (other) to $1.59 (Alabama) in 1991. For zonals in 5-inch (12.5-cm) pots and larger, the range was $1.25 (Florida) to $5.62 (Indiana) in 1991; $1.30 (Florida) to $4.33 (Iowa) in 1992. Zonal price ranges were more than triple from low to high prices.

For potted geraniums from seed, the price range was less than double for smaller than 5-inch (12.5-cm) pots but more than four times for 5-inch or larger pots. Price variation is extreme for larger-sized geraniums, whether cutting or seed-propagated, perhaps due to larger sizes being sold more often by traditional industry marketers (garden centers, landscapers, retail growers) than nontraditional outlets (discount stores, supermarkets, home centers). Less price variability is evident in the smaller than 5-inch sizes for seed geraniums and cutting-propagated geraniums.

Retail level prices

Price variations are quite wide also at the retail level. Nontraditional outlets, however, have shoppers who aren't aware of value differences

TABLE 3.9

Geraniums average wholesale prices, 1991, 1992

State (Rank)	Flat 1991	Flat 1992	Pot, cutting — less than 5 inch 1991	1992	Pot, cutting — 5 inch or more 1991	1992	Pot, seed — less than 5 inch 1991	1992	Pot, seed — 5 inch or more 1991	1992
AL	$7.31	$8.06	$1.59	$1.30	$3.01	$2.34	$1.09	$.91	$3.00	$3.11
AR [a]	—	—	1.24	1.11	4.10	3.06	—	—	2.27	1.61
CA [a]	—	11.90	—	—	—	—	1.03	.82	—	2.30
CO	10.20	—	1.40	1.70	3.45	3.70	.96	.96	—	—
CT [a]	—	—	1.49	1.54	3.81	3.43	—	—	—	—
FL [a]	—	—	1.15	1.00	1.25	1.30	.65	.60	1.00	1.65
GA	8.46	8.01	1.03	1.27	2.25	3.21	.66	.97	2.10	2.98
HI [a]	—	—	—	—	—	—	—	—	—	—
IL (7)	8.92	9.22	1.31	1.39	3.32	3.23	.73	1.05	—	2.97
IN	11.19	10.51	1.33	1.28	5.62	4.10	.82	.98	4.62	4.59
IA	11.45	11.35	1.22	1.32	4.74	4.33	.89	.87	—	—
KS	9.83	11.99	1.33	1.48	2.66	3.21	.81	.87	2.74	2.05
MD [a]	—	—	1.54	1.67	3.26	3.13	—	—	—	—
MA [a]	9.54	5.55	1.43	1.85	2.77	2.98	—	—	—	—
MI (1)	7.90	7.80	1.35	1.35	3.10	3.65	.70	.70	—	3.40
MN (10)	10.37	7.33	1.32	1.39	3.20	3.34	.95	.91	—	5.00
MO	11.26	11.39	1.15	1.16	3.77	3.17	.93	.88	1.40	1.68
NJ	8.70	7.77	1.19	1.21	1.51	1.62	.75	.75	1.50	1.20
NY (2)	10.51	7.37	1.18	1.11	2.70	2.66	.81	.83	2.22	3.33
NC (9)	8.11	8.23	1.27	1.03	3.15	2.41	.70	.70	2.92	2.50
OH (3)	8.87	8.71	1.17	1.24	2.80	2.99	1.00	.98	1.89	2.00
OR	11.37	13.64	1.21	1.26	2.51	3.06	.86	.99	—	—
PA (5)	9.68	7.15	1.20	1.21	2.35	2.78	.84	.68	2.20	2.52
TN	7.95	7.68	1.11	1.30	2.63	2.15	.76	.73	2.45	2.33
TX (4)	9.27	12.08	1.18	.99	2.16	2.10	.77	.76	1.27	2.09
VA [a]	8.52	10.40	1.47	1.59	3.36	3.67	—	—	—	—
WA (6)	10.86	12.46	1.32	1.26	2.76	2.82	.96	.82	—	1.16
WI (8)	9.73	12.71	1.28	1.40	4.85	3.39	1.18	1.19	—	—
Other	8.25	8.82	.90	.81	2.40	2.40	.65	.88	2.22	2.57
Average 28 states	$8.91	$9.33	$1.23	NA	$2.43	NA	$.80	$.80	$2.24	$2.42
Average 36 states	NA	$9.39	NA	$1.27	NA	$2.45	NA	$.80	NA	$2.40
Price range	$7.31 (AL) to $11.37 (OR)	$5.55 (MA) to $13.64 (OR)	$.90 (other) to $1.59 (AL)	$.81 (other) to $1.85 (MA)	$1.25 (FL) to $5.62 (IN)	$1.30 (FL) to $4.33 (IA)	$.65 (other, FL) to $1.18 (WI)	$.60 (FL) to $1.19 (WI)	$1.00 (FL) to $4.62 (IN)	$1.16 (WA) to $5.00 (MN)

Source: 1992 Floriculture Crops Summary, National Agricultural Statistics Service, USDA.
Note: Eight states—Arizona, Kentucky, Louisiana, Mississippi, New Mexico, Oklahoma, South Carolina and Vermont—were added in 1992.
[a] Included in other states to avoid disclosure of individual operations.

TABLE 3.10

Bedding plant prices, 1992

	Prices ($)			Compact differential	
Bedding plant type	36-state average price	36-state price range	Compact price range[a]	($)	(%)
Flats:					
Geranium	9.39	5.55 (MA)—13.64 (OR)	7.77 (NJ)—12.08 (TX)	4.31	55
Flowering/foliar	7.10	5.35 (MI)—8.90 (CO)	6.30 (PA)—8.24 (TX)	1.94	31
Vegetable	7.01	5.50 (MI)—8.55 (CO)	5.97 (IN)—7.60 (CA, OK, WA)	1.63	27
Pots:					
Garden chrysanthemum					
less than 5-inch	0.83	0.60 (SC)—1.44 (NY, VA)	0.77 (MO, WA)—1.08 (OH)	0.31	40
5-inch and greater	1.84	1.38 (TX)—2.58 (MO)	1.53 (WA)—2.29 (WI)	0.76	50
Pot geraniums					
Cuttings—					
less than 5-inch	1.27	0.65 (AZ)—1.85 (MA)	1.11 (AZ, NY)—1.59 (VA)	0.46	43
5-inch and greater	2.45	1.30 (FL)—4.33 (IA)	2.15 (TN)—3.43 (CT)	1.28	60
Seed—					
less than 5-inch	0.80	0.60 (FL)—1.19 (WI)	0.75 (NJ)—0.98 (OH, IN)	0.23	30
5-inch and greater	2.40	1.16 (WA)—5.00 (MN)	2.00 (OH)—3.11 (AL)	1.11	56
Other potted flowering					
less than 5-inch	0.70	0.40 (OK)—0.63	0.63 (LA, PA)—0.99 (OH)	0.36	57
5-inch and greater	1.93	0.25 (AZ)—3.53 (NY)	1.60 (FL)—2.82 (MA)	1.22	76
Potted vegetable plants					
less than 5-inch	0.63	0.20 (OK)—1.20 (GA)	0.46 (OR)—0.84 (NM)	0.38	83
5-inch and greater	1.73	1.00 (MO)—3.07 (IL)	1.37 (NC)—2.02 (MN)	0.65	47
Flowering hanging baskets:	5.45	3.40 (FL)—10.21 (WAS)	4.68 (NJ, TX)—7.18 (MN)	2.50	53

Source: 1992 Floriculture Crops Summary, National Agriculture Statistics Service, USDA.
[a] Compact price range reduces the 36-state price range from the highest price and lowest price to a range of the 6th highest and 6th lowest, which removes some extreme pricing. For example, for geraniums in flats, the dollar differential is $4.31 ($12.08 minus $7.77 = $4.31) and percent differential is 53% ($12.08 divided by $7.77 = 55%).

in geraniums. Traditional producers and marketers with reputation and knowledge tend to have stable, strong prices with better product quality and probably more customer loyalty.

Consumer education might result in enhanced geranium garden performance and aid the geranium/bedding plant/gardening industry by strengthening the market price for those offering better quality

CHAPTER 4

Finding a Market

Bridget K. Behe

As a professional bedding plant producer, you are most likely concerned with making your seeds or plugs grow into salable plants. The person who will buy those plants is not often given much consideration during the plant production process. However, you should have a good understanding of who will buy your plants **before** you sow the first seed or plant the first plug.

Finding a market for bedding plants can present a real challenge for some businesses. Over the past 10 years, the bedding plant market has been expanding, and it is easier to find a market for plants. However, your long-term, important marketing consideration is to find customers to buy your products and manage how quickly that number grows each year.

What is a market?

A market is simply defined as a gathering of people for buying and selling things. Markets bring together buyers and sellers to make an exchange of something of value to both parties. Markets can be one or more people or clients.

For example, a retail establishment has a market of consumers who will visit the retail location to make purchases. For commercial producers, the market may consist of one or more wholesale companies and several large chain stores. For other professional producers, the market may be a mix of landscape contractors and retail garden centers. The market can be a person or a company to which the producer sells bedding plants and related services.

New businesses need to make an extra effort to develop their market plans before planting any seeds or plugs. They need to examine the market carefully to determine who they will serve this year and how they can expand for the following year. For established businesses, finding a market may be easier, but market analysis is still necessary to determine which are the most profitable markets to serve. Both new and established businesses need to go through these same three steps to find a market:

1. **Analyze potential customers/clients,**
2. **Analyze potential products/services,**
3. **Select target markets.**

Businesses that go through each of these steps will complete what marketers refer to as **market segmentation** and **product targeting**.

Step 1: Analyze potential customers/clients

More and more businesses are finding it increasingly difficult to offer numerous, diverse products and services to meet everyone's needs. They have discovered how hard it is to be all things to all people. Most commercial plant producers must make choices to decide which clients or customers they will cater to with the products and services they offer.

Market segmentation

Dividing the entire market of potential clients or customers into smaller, more easily identified groups is **market segmentation**. Market segmentation takes the market as a whole and divides it into groups based on one or more similarities. You no longer approach the market as a whole, rather in selected parts.

There are several ways to segment a market, and your creativity is the only limit as to how you define your markets. Geography, demography, and benefits are some of the more common ways to segment a market area.

Geographic segmentation. Markets can be defined by geographic boundaries. State or county lines are good examples of geographic boundaries that define markets, but the boundaries can be as simple as a railroad track, river, or mountain range. Supermarkets often have very geographically small markets because potential customers don't want to travel great distances to go to the grocery store. Markets may also be defined by a particular interest. Some mail-order catalogs have international markets because they bring together potential customers for products and services related to sports or art.

A commercial bedding plant producer may want to limit the market initially by geography. This may be a 50-mile (80-km) radius from the business or a one-hour drive time. Other businesses may limit their market to one city or county. Still others may need to choose a market of several portions of a state if they are near those geographic borders.

Demographic segmentation. Demographic characteristics are people's attributes such as age, gender, race, income, and eye color. Some demographic characteristics are used more often to define markets than others. Markets can be defined by the age of potential clients (children, teenagers, or senior citizens), household income (above or below $40,000 annual income), or home ownership (renter versus owner).

Dividing markets into groups based on demographic characteristics is a common basis for market segmentation, but it is not always the best choice. However, as a basis for market segmentation, demographic characteristics are more easily measured than other variables.

Product use segmentation. Customers or clients buy plants for different reasons, and these reasons can be used to group them into different market segments. For example, *Organic Gardening* magazine commissioned National Family Opinion Research to conduct a comprehensive study of American gardeners [1]. They divided gardeners into four segments: Dabblers, Decorators, Cultivators, and Masters.

Dabblers comprised 61% of American gardeners and were described as people who spent an average two hours weekly in the garden and relatively less money on plants. As the name suggests, they are dabbling in gardening as a hobby.

Decorators accounted for 19% of the gardeners and were described as people who spent more time—an average five hours weekly in the garden—and money on this activity. As their name suggests, they may be interested in gardening as a way to improve the look of their homes and landscapes.

Cultivators accounted for 18% of the sample and spent 10 hours weekly in the garden and more money on gardening than Decorators. The name Cultivator suggests that these individuals are more interested in the fruit and vegetable crops they grow rather than in the beauty of the garden alone.

The smallest segment, **Masters**, was only 3% of the sample and was a group of highly experienced gardeners to whom others turned for advice and information. Each of these groups derived different benefits from nearly the same plants and activities.

Another example of product use segmentation would be by type of business purchasing the plants. Many bedding plants are sold to other businesses before they are planted in commercial and residential landscapes. Wholesalers, garden centers, professional landscapers, mass-marketers, supermarkets, florists, and other greenhouses are types of businesses that could purchase bedding plants from a commercial producer. They would have different needs and derive different benefits from similar plants. Landscape contractors might need bedding plants in larger containers to provide more immediate landscape color. Garden centers or other greenhouses may want smaller plants so that they could finish the plants themselves. Mass marketers and supermarkets may dictate the size of the plant, minimum number of flowers, and/or container size to insure sales area uniformity.

Regardless of how you segment your market, it is important that you divide it into manageable parts. Your imagination and creativity are the only limits to the kinds of market segments you can develop for your business.

Step 2: Analyze potential product and service

Just as you need to analyze all the potential customers or clients you may serve, you will need to consider all the types of products and services you could offer to customers. You will need to narrow your product and service mix because it would be impossible to offer all potential products and services to everyone.

- **First, make a product analysis.** For a commercial bedding plant producer, this may seem to be a relatively easy task. Which species will you offer for sale? Which cultivars of those species will you grow? What container sizes will you market? Will you market plugs? Which size flats? Mixed baskets? Will you include care tags and bar codes?
- **Next, consider services.** Delivery is a service. Will you deliver plants, or will you require customers to pick plants up at the greenhouse? What about credit terms? If everyone can't or won't pay cash, you will need to decide credit terms, who is eligible for credit, and how to collect from delinquent customers. Will you offer telephone or catalog sales? Will you guarantee plants for any length of time?

The most helpful way of conducting this analysis is to make a list of products and services, broadening the mix as you go. For example, you may decide to grow flats of bedding plants. Start listing plants grown in flats by flat size: begonias and impatiens in 32-count flats, marigolds and zinnias in 48-count flats. Your list may become quite long, but in the next step you will narrow it to a more manageable size.

Step 3: Select target products and markets

With all the customer segments you listed and all the products you could market, you will need to make some decisions as to what to grow and market first. These are usually the most profitable products or products that you can sell large quantities of while making a smaller profit. How do you know where to start? A customer/product matrix is helpful.

The **customer/product matrix** is a diagram—a set of boxes representing market segments and products that could be targeted to those segments. There are three steps to making a matrix.
- First, list the potential customers across the top of the page.
- Second, list the potential products and services your firm could offer to any potential customer along the side of the page.
- Third, determine which product(s) and market(s) the company would like to target first.

1. Listing potential customers should not be difficult after the business manager has done a customer analysis. The manager should have a good idea of the types of businesses and residents in the market area. Creativity in listing these potential targets will be the only limitation. Divisions can be made as small as practical for the business because market segments do not have to be large to be profitable.

2. Listing potential products should not be difficult for the business manager either. Again, divisions can be as small as practical. The list for many greenhouse companies could be as large as several hundred products and services initially listed on the product side of the customer/product matrix. The only limitation will be the manager's creativity in listing what potential products could be marketed.

A customer/product matrix with some potential products and customers is shown in table 4.1. The grower is considering marketing plug flats of begonias and impatiens, 48-count flats of marigolds and zinnias, 10-inch (2.5-cm) baskets of mixed annuals, and 4-inch (10-cm) containers of marigolds. The grower has listed five potential market segments: garden centers, landscape contracting firms, mass-marketers, home owners, and other commercial greenhouses.

3. Identifying the market potential of each product/customer target will be more difficult. As you evaluate each product/customer target, ask yourself this question: how much of a demand does this customer have for this product? The answer will tell you whether or not it is a target worth investigating. The market potential for the listed products

CHAPTER 5

Promotion and Advertising

Ted Marston

Promotion is the art of bringing a product to the consumer's attention, but whose responsibility is it to promote bedding plants for market-building purposes or to increase brand-name recognition or sales at specific retail outlets? Typically, the bedding plant industry has avoided addressing this issue. Or it has pointed to another level in the marketing chain as being responsible for promotion. With the exception of some outstanding efforts by individual companies, there has been a tendency at the wholesale level to focus on production, customer service, delivery, etc., and overlook product promotion.

The heavy production orientation and uncertainty in using unfamiliar marketing techniques, such as promotion, to build market share or brand loyalty inhibit many wholesalers. Fortunately, the bedding plant market has increased over the years in spite of neglecting promotion. Well-planned advertising and promotion, however, can benefit everyone in the bedding plant industry.

The marketing chain

Bedding plant promotion begins with the plant breeder and continues throughout the marketing chain to the consumer, who is encouraged to plant a wide variety of plant material to beautify the home landscape. A number of specialized markets serve the consumer; breeders, brokers, and growers recognize these intermediate markets as important niches and direct specialized advertising and promotion to them as well as to the home gardener. Breeders often advertise in publications directed to niche markets—landscapers, golf course superintendents, and other high volume consumers. Specialized publications read by mass market buyers are also used to help build brand awareness.

Plant breeders

Many bedding plant breeders promote service, reliability of supply, and other attributes (image), but most often select specific cultivars to promote in the trade press. Major bedding plants classes, such as impatiens, geraniums (both cutting and seed), petunias, marigolds, pansies, and others, support a high degree of marketplace competitiveness, which makes it desirable for breeders to build brand awareness to differentiate their product from competitors' similar cultivars. A variety of techniques are available, including advertisements in grower trade magazines, trade show booths, and promotional literature of all kinds, from posters, calendars, statement stuffers, and inserts in card deck mailings to logo gimmicks such as pens, T-shirts, and knives. Contests with various prizes are also offered to growers to help gain brand recognition.

Controversy exists over the value of brand awareness; many feel that bedding plants become an undifferentiated product (a white petunia is a white petunia is a white petunia) in the marketplace. However, successful marketing of similar products, segments of the produce industry for example, indicates that when name recognition is carefully promoted, extra sales can be generated for a specific item (at even a higher price) provided the product is sufficiently differentiated in the buyer's mind.

Some breeders are strongly committed to cultivar identification and spend considerable money on promotional strategy. Recent examples include PanAmerican Seed Co.'s point of purchase program to support two new pansy series.

For a number of years Goldsmith Seeds has provided retailers with color literature on specific cultivars for distribution to home gardeners. More recently, Goldsmith has worked with Benjamin Moore & Co. to coordinate paint and bedding plant colors. This approach has been used at several trade shows and a summer-long garden show in Columbus, Ohio. Goldsmith has cooperated in developing literature to be used in stores and bedding plant outlets and for the past several years, Goldsmith has also sponsored joint promotions with retailers featuring Goldsmith cultivars.

Several breeders have active public relations programs that provide information and photographs to consumer magazines, newspapers, and radio and TV stations, featuring their proprietary cultivars along with general gardening information.

Breeders are usually eager to work with retailers in disseminating cultivar-specific information. Brokers, growers, retailers, and retail growers should inquire about services and materials a breeder can supply for developing a promotional program for bedding plants. Mail-order garden catalogs are a public relations vehicle as well as a market for breeders. Featured cultivars become familiar to mail-order customers, and many consumer publications refer to commercial catalogs as an information source in preparing garden articles.

Retailers/retail growers

Retailers can definitely see the results of their advertising and promotion if they do an effective job. Store traffic will increase and sales blossom. As part of the marketing mix, advertising, public relations, and sales promotion are powerful tools to help generate sales volume. Most retailers establish a budget as a percentage of their gross sales to be spent on promotion and allocate expenditures among the various segments. The percentage varies but usually ranges between 2% and 10% of sales.

To aid in planning your promotions, establish a calendar with all the promotions, selling emphases, and product specialties for the entire year. Then develop a comprehensive program that allocates your time and money to adequately carry out your promotions. It is important, however, to maintain some reserves of both of time and budget for unexpected contingencies.

Trade associations

National, regional, state and local trade groups have developed promotional programs to benefit bedding plant sales. The Professional Plant Growers Association has actively promoted bedding plants in the past through point-of-sale material and public relations activities. Normally, they develop a market-building public relations media kit that is sent to editors for preparing articles and broadcast segments, and supply photos of annuals and perennials in a variety of garden settings. PPGA also has a color booklet detailing the landscape uses of annuals that can be purchased singly or in quantity.

The Society of American Florists has a very active promotional program, supported by members' contributions, primarily devoted to flower arrangement promotion and flowering pot plant sales.

Regional, state, and local organizations have varying promotional programs. If you are not a member, you should inquire specifically about programs that benefit bedding plant sales. An effective program can be established to promote bedding plants at the local market level, whether you're a wholesale grower or a retailer. A consistent publicity program is vital to success; only continuous activity will grasp the consumer's attention. This can often be achieved cooperatively if a growers' group has paid executive secretary, or if someone skilled in publicity is employed—another way of saying that cash expenditures will benefit the program greatly.

Mobilizing a local program

Plant related businesses tend to concentrate on production and direct sales, ignoring or underutilizing other marketing techniques that can enhance product distribution. A wholesale grower whose only market is the discount merchandiser finds it difficult to finance promotional campaigns independently. Margins are often so tight that profits are minimal. Techniques can be developed, however, to enhance product sales.

Different or unique container packaging is an example, and dressing the containers is an extension of this. Develop coupon specials or participate in joint advertising. Publicity that enhances the image of all bedding plants and market growth is worthwhile for any wholesale or retail grower; although since the wholesale grower is a step removed from the ultimate consumer, this may not be as easily recognized.

A local market or community beautification program that includes the widespread use of annuals can directly impact sales and have a far-reaching benefit enhancing the awareness and use of annuals by the entire community. Enthusiasm for annuals might spread to parks, the business community, and residential neighborhoods. A beautification program is best mobilized by involving the community leaders, media, city government, and parks department in planning and implementation.

A community beautification program can be used by schools and churches to create a new awareness about gardening and bedding plants. Growers initiating such a program usually benefit the most, although other area growers may see sales increase as well.

Many communities have a grower organization that can work jointly with growers to organize a publicity program to enhance bedding plants' role. Supplying plants for local TV stations can result in broad product exposure and may get favorable on-the-air comments. Work with local garden writers to promote bedding plant coverage. Contacts with newspapers, magazines, and radio stations can have the same effect. Gardening contests offering prizes usually attract media support and widespread publicity. Sponsoring lectures and demonstrations by prominent bedding plant experts may enhance media coverage (as well as attendance at the lectures, too).

Most communities now have active Master Gardener programs given by Cooperative Extension Service. Growers/retailers could work with them to expand bedding plant knowledge and provide new ideas on gardening and landscaping.

Effective publicity programs can be developed without large money expenditures, especially when growers donate plants generously. Although it costs to donate plants, it's easier—psychologically—for many growers to give product rather than cash.

In-store sales promotion

Sales promotion can be defined as promotional tools that aren't media related. These include special events, signage, and point-of-sale programs. Plan special events when you want to increase store traffic. Begin early in the season to get people in the mood to buy before the weather is settled. Many retailers hold educational seminars, using either their own staff or outside experts to lecture and demonstrate good garden ideas. Later in the spring, schedule a special event to extend the heavy selling period.

Molbaks, a well known retailer outside Seattle, holds a "2 for 1 Sale" in early July that has become a major draw. Plan a special event in the autumn to stimulate sales of fall planted annuals and perennials, particularly with the increase in interest in pansies during the fall. Because of the heavy demands on staff and high volume of business, don't schedule special events during prime bedding plant sales weeks.

Good signage also contributes to store sales. The more information available to customers, the better. Color identification and care labels and signs and posters are available nationally from suppliers, and many retailers make their own. Customer service kiosks manned by an expert to answer garden questions has also become an important part of many retail operations.

Advertising

Advertising is paid promotion through local media with newspaper ads and radio and television commercials. It includes billboards and direct response pieces distributed to customers by mail or other means. Advertising can be used to establish a retailer's image, as well as sell specific products. The advertising style, its look and feel, allows customers to evaluate the business. Advertising's artfulness makes it more effective in getting results.

Most retailers will hire an advertising agency to prepare the advertising, contract with the media, and take care of the on-going program. Larger operations may hire staff for this. In either case, a retail operation will usually develop a year-round advertising program for seasonal specialties. In most parts of the country, bedding plants get special attention during the spring (and increasingly in the fall for pansies and other fall bedding plants). Seasonal advertising creates an opportunity to merchandise tie-ins such as fertilizers, containers, and other sell-with items.

Many independent retailers will not mention price in their advertisements, leaving price wars to chains and mass marketers, and concentrate on wide selection and other features where they have a competitive advantage. Other retailers feature special prices or other promotion such as a "2 for 1" sale, particularly at season's end. Ads are also used to announce special events and promotions within the store.

The best advertising is always done from the customer's point of view. What appeal will make this person a customer? What kind of service? What are current preferences in color and style? The nature of your retail operation must be defined before developing successful advertisements, but preparing ads helps to sharpen your business' focus.

Publicity

Publicity, as an integral part of the marketing plan, can be an extremely valuable tool in building a business. Get to know the regional media. Even the smallest towns have weekly newspapers. As the size of the community increases, so will your options for exposure. Publicity can be as valuable as advertising; it has increased credibility because it appears in editorial columns and draws attention like a news event.

Find out who the editors are. Many newspapers have a full or part-time garden editor. Even weekly newspapers in small towns will run garden information, although you may have to write it yourself. Many radio and television stations run gardening editorials, sometimes news-like, sometimes presented by gardening personalities. In some areas, extension personnel provide information for garden columns, public television and radio broadcasts. Don't overlook the burgeoning cable channels and local cable access channels. Depending on the region, local magazines are also a potential for business information.

With high consumer interest in gardening, you have good leverage in getting the newspaper editor's attention, but you are competing with many other hobbies. You'll find that garden editors are looking for detailed information to make their own material more timely. The garden writer also wants to make sure that a plant or product is available locally. Invite editors to visit your business and keep in touch with them on a regular basis so that you will become a valuable resource.

Find newsworthy ways to get into print. What's newsworthy and what's not varies from editor to editor. Some ideas might include an open house, a tour of local "showplace" gardens, unique promotions, or a feature story on your operation—its history, expansion, or other item of interest. New plant cultivars are always interesting to gardeners and a feature on All-America Selections provides both a national and local angle. If no one is publicizing local gardening activities, become the media gardening expert.

To do all of this takes time. Many retailers hire an agent who specializes in preparing and placing media publicity material. Publicity can also be handled by the agency preparing your advertisements, although the paid/free space distinction must always be kept clear.

These and other ideas contribute to the educational and promotional process of selling bedding plants. Bedding plant sales' dramatic growth in the last 20 years has been profitable for most growers and retailers. Use of advertising, publicity, and other promotional tools may be even more essential in the future to continue market growth.

CHAPTER 6

Merchandising Bedding Plants

Dennis J. Wolnick

Merchandising covers a wide variety of coordinated activities that bedding plant retailers use to promote bedding plant sales. Merchandising also helps to increase the value of one firm's selection of bedding plant products over another firm's in a highly competitive marketplace. Merchandising generates consumer awareness and interest in bedding plants and turns it into sales.

Retailer merchandising

Retailers add value to bedding plant products through providing the consumer with convenience—convenience of **product**, **place**, **price**, and **promotion**. That is, retailers try to provide the kinds of products demanded by consumers in the "right" quantities and sizes, at the "right" time, in a convenient location, and at prices that are acceptable to consumers.

Today's bedding plant industry offers a large number of plant species and cultivars for sale through a wide variety of sales outlets, from retail greenhouses and high-end garden centers, to supermarkets, large chain stores, and even tents set up temporarily in parking lots.

In this competitive atmosphere the management of individual retail firms must have clear and focused business objectives and extensive marketing know-how to succeed. This means they must have a thorough knowledge of the many products they sell, they must understand their customers' needs and diversity, and be able to communicate effectively with them.

The quality bedding plant

Effective merchandising begins with high quality products considered desirable and useful to consumers. These products would have many features that can be promoted in advertising, in store displays, and in personal sales.

Let's look at a plant product example. An impatiens, consistently popular with industry professionals and consumers, seems to be an ideal bedding plant—both desirable and useful. A high quality impatiens plant will just fill its container with healthy roots at time of sale. The proper container is large enough to support plant health and vigor throughout the marketing process. The ideal plant will be full and symmetrical and not too tall for the container. The plant will be well covered with medium to dark green leaves that are free of hidden and obvious disease symptoms or insects with their associated injuries.

The quality impatiens plant will have several vigorous branches rising from the plant base, suggesting considerable flowering potential in the garden. At least one flower will be open or showing some color, and there will be numerous buds ready to open. Leaves and flowers will look firm and fresh with no mechanical damage. Any old flower petals have been removed. The plant has been properly fed, watered, and acclimatized during production to prevent stalling of growth and deterioration during the marketing process, particularly when the delivery or the retail store environment is less than optimum.

The impatiens described looks great and is "conditioned" to survive adverse marketing conditions. It might sell itself on sight with no further effort. But it must be seen. Consumers need to know that such plants exist, where the plants are, and why they are such a good value. Enter merchandising.

Adding value—the "packaged" bedding plant

Bedding plants are not yet placed in neat cardboard or plastic cartons or shrink-wrapped. Nevertheless they are packaged or enhanced in various ways to increase their value to consumers. Packaging might start with the grower who selects bedding plant containers that are first chosen for consumer preferences and retail needs, and then for production requirements. Color, shape, and size become more important than production needs.

For example, packs containing six connected, 3-inch-square (7.5 cm) dark green plastic pots may be chosen as the production container unit because retailers and consumers find these packs convenient, durable, appealing, and supportive of good plant growth. These six-packs are designed to fit nicely into larger flats that retailers and growers find easy to handle. The number of plants and pots in the flat can be reconfigured, customizing plant size and number per flat to a specific customer without changing the overall space occupied per flat in the greenhouse. Without a retail consumer orientation, the grower might choose a entirely different container—perhaps determined only by cost and production requirements for good plant growth.

Labels

Plant breeders and seed companies go to great lengths to give names to bedding plants that will appeal to customers and distinguish one plant type from another. Using plant names in advertising and connecting positive, descriptive words to the plants in advertising such as "vigorous," "healthy," "beautiful," "sprightly," "dependable," or "ever-blooming" are examples of merchandising where value is added to a plant by giving it an identity.

Research studies confirm that a label that clearly identifies a plant by name is the first information customers seek when they make buying decisions. The astute merchandiser knows that adding a pleasing label to each flat, pack, or pot of bedding plants increases the plant's value to consumers. Greenhouse and retail suppliers and industry trade associations provide colorful, ready-made and custom-made labels for almost any bedding plant. It's also a common practice for growers to place labels, sometimes custom-made for a particular retailer, in the flats or pots before shipping as an added service to their retailers. In this way the grower makes the plants more valuable to the retailer and contributes to the merchandising effort.

At some point bedding plant consumers begin to expect the label to be a standard part of the bedding plant package. When this happens, the label's presence loses its merchandising punch—all good plants have labels. Now, the amount and type of label information and the label's look become important ways of distinguishing one retailer's products from another. Competition for consumer dollars, changing industry standards, and consumer experience combine to raise the ante and force retailers and growers to develop additional merchandising strategies.

Individual retailers can be very creative in packaging bedding plant products to differentiate them from their competitors. Decorative containers, gift accessories, cultural instructions, planting plans, and other items grouped with the plants are intended to increase the plants' perceived value to the consumer. The items become part of the bedding plant package and improve the merchandising effort.

Merchandising also includes packaging ideas or concepts with plants. A mixed group of bedding plants in a decorative container described as an "instant garden," "instant color," or perhaps a "patio pleaser," creates a much broader image or concept. Displaying a wide variety of these "instant gardens" develops a merchandising concept.

Products with services

It's true that fresh, brightly blooming and nicely displayed bedding plants may sell themselves by visual appeal alone, especially during the spring season. But merchandisers recognize that consumers appreciate service with the plants they buy and are really buying bedding plants to satisfy a variety of needs.

Services would include activities the retailer provides that are naturally associated with the plants such as information about the plants, guaranteed plant replacement, wide selection, convenient store location and hours, even delivery to a customer's home, or at least carry-out to the customer's car.

Consumer needs and benefits

Needs. The needs consumers seek to satisfy with bedding plants could go beyond the simple need to have colorful plants in the garden. Some consumers will look for the newest varieties or the most unusual. Some seek plants that fill a special need such as shade tolerance or drought resistance. Others want the convenience of already-planted "gardens" in decorative containers, window boxes, and baskets. Still other consumers may desire creative ideas and would welcome planting plans, imaginative employees, advice on best cultivars, color mixes, and numbers of plants to use in a certain design.

Personal experience may tell a consumer that while a particular bedding plant is very appealing visually, it has not performed well for them in the past. So this customer may need a substitute that will work better. Consumers may not know what they want until they see it, or they may have fairly strict color and price guidelines but would be open to alternatives offered by a creative retailer.

Benefits. The consumer benefits of bedding plant ownership may go beyond gardening pleasure to include abstract concepts such as a beautiful landscape, improved self-esteem, increased social standing in the neighborhood and among friends and business associates, even environmental stewardship.

The "complete" bedding plant

In bedding plant merchandising, the product is more than the plant itself. The final product includes associated services, creative ideas, and consumer benefits. The levels of associated services provided by each retailer and the ways in which each firm presents its bedding plant products and benefits to consumers are unique merchandising expressions.

Merchandising for profit

It is important to remember that a primary merchandising purpose is to increase your firm's sales and profits. The choice of items to be bundled with bedding plants plus other merchandising to increase the perceived value of the plants, must be carefully planned. Success in merchandising is no accident.

Promotion and presentation

Promotion and presentation are two essential aspects of merchandising. Promotional activities, including paid advertising and unpaid publicity, are typically used beyond the store to reach potential customers and are intended to generate consumer awareness, interest, and action related to the products a store has to offer.

Effective merchandisers pay attention to consumers' reading habits, interests, income levels and lifestyles, and physical and social needs. They design their merchandising programs to include interesting and exciting promotions; they create displays with great visual appeal and include messages that highlight their associated services and the benefits of bedding plants.

Advertising-merchandising at a distance

Newspaper, radio, TV, direct mail, and other advertising is almost essential for bedding plant retailers to announce product availability, introduce new products, cut through the noise of competitive ads, and create special and positive consumer recognition for the store. Advertising is used to directly stimulate sales of your products and services and to mold your business image, indicating to consumers what they can expect from you as a professional. Keep your advertising goals simple and honest. You advertise to *attract attention*, to be *understood*, to be *believed*, and to be *remembered*.

Advertising tips

Advertise regularly. Especially advertise when timing is important, and the products are seasonal. Advertise based on consumer plant shopping patterns. Advertise heavily in the spring months when most consumers are thinking about plants and gardening and are out shopping. Advertise on your busiest sales days—probably Friday through Sunday—and every day of a special promotion.

Direct your ads. The consumers are exposed to hundreds, even thousands, of promotional messages every day. Your ads about bedding plants need to be directed to the right audience. They need to be attractive and precise enough to break through other promotional noises enticing consumers to act.

Do your homework. Determine by survey who your customers are, what they need, what they like and buy, and how they live. Advertise using direct mail, the newspapers they read, the radio stations they listen to, and the TV stations they watch. Advertise enough so you know you are heard and recognized. Consider advertising in two or more media at once to reinforce your promotional message in different forms.

Use your advertising to educate and inform. Tell potential customers about the wide variety of plants they can choose at your store. Tell them about the All-America varieties you have and what that means. Tell them about the planting and design information you provide, and definitely mention special values available, such as quantity discounts.

Use descriptive and meaningful words in advertising. "High quality," "fresh," "new," "improved," "special," "unique," and "beautiful" are words widely used, attractive, and exciting to consumers. Create simple word pictures to help consumers envision what your bedding plants would look like in their gardens.

Emphasize price in ads only when it's a special feature. Unless consumers are familiar with local prices for bedding plants, which is not common in the marketplace yet, price advertising is meaningless. A percentage price reduction like 10% or 25% off could be mentioned instead, and consumers who are not familiar with actual prices might see it as valuable.

Always include and emphasize your business name and location in ads. Offer service information—phone number, hours, acceptance of bank cards, even a small map or directions to your store. Choose a style for your advertising that enhances your business image. Use that style consistently in all your ads.

Keep ads simple. Stick to one main theme in each ad, and use frequent ads to cover all the information. Use simple, accurate illustrations and simple, consistent type styles and borders.

Capitalize on industry promotions and promotional materials. Horticultural marketing and trade organizations produce all kinds of advertising copy and publicity designed to generate consumer enthusiasm and highlight good bedding plant cultivars. Take advantage of the wide variety of pre-printed promotional materials including clip art, ad slicks, ad copy, point-of-purchase display signs and labels, even tear-off planting instructions, which are available from commercial firms and trade associations. These materials are well-designed and successful. They could save you time and money compared to preparing materials in-house and from scratch.

Encourage opportunities for positive publicity about the business. Publicity generated through sponsorships, community projects, or benevolence creates a good image for your business in the community and encourages interested shoppers to visit.

Maintain design control. Above all, stay in charge of your advertising and strive for accuracy and consistency in illustrations and text. Advertising is critical to the success of all bedding plant retailers in a competitive environment. It is the advertisements' creativity, their frequency, placement and content with some request for action that distinguishes merchandising from advertising.

Presentation

Presentation is by far the most influential part of a merchandising program. It involves everything about promoting the product's qualities and appearance, its packaging, displays, store appearance and layout, and even the attitudes, behavior, and creativity of store personnel.

Once consumer interest in bedding plants is generated through advertising, by word of mouth, or from the pull on gardeners that accompanies the arrival of spring, consumers will act. They shop, collecting additional information about bedding plants, comparing one product to another, and comparing one store to another looking for the best value. When consumers visit in search of bedding plants, **presentation merchandising** really pays off.

Store layout and product displays

Consumers need to see and experience bedding plants' life, freshness, and beauty. If advertising has done its job, consumers will visit the store to shop and see the live plants at their best. When excited consumers come to your store they shouldn't be disappointed. Remember that your business is the place for bedding plants and garden ideas (you suggested or specifically said so in your ads). The way the store is laid out and the exciting ways plant products are displayed should capitalize on the positive images and interest already created through good advertising. (See Chapter 7 for store layout and display.)

Personal sales and merchandising

Beautiful and well displayed plants and flowers often seem to sell themselves. Displays provide customers with ideas, they entertain and educate with minimum active employee involvement. Still, many consumers go from initial interest to purchase as a result of pleasant and rewarding interaction with a store employee.

Though display areas are well marked with signs, prices are reasonable and clearly marked, displays are full, and the atmosphere is attractive, customers still want personal attention. It can be little more than a simple courteous greeting or perhaps assistance with heavy items at checkout or in the parking lot. For one customer it may be a knowledgeable recommendation about plant use. For another customer it might be the skillful handling of a complaint. In any case, customers are more likely to shop with some degree of loyalty where friendly, helpful, and knowledgeable employees are commonplace.

Consumers expect courtesy and friendliness where they shop. Indifference and surliness from store employees are the biggest reasons that consumers give for taking their business to a different store. Assuming a friendly and courteous attitude is expected from your store, true merchandising goes beyond simple courtesy to provide customer service. The following suggestions for interpersonal techniques are proven winners in personal sales. They should be part of employee training programs, company philosophy, and a measure of management success. Certainly they will build a positive image for your business.

Be attentive and friendly, not overbearing to customers. Offer a friendly greeting whenever possible as customers enter the store, and greet the customer by name. In many cases a prompt greeting is sufficient initial contact. If you wish to say more, it is helpful to point out current promotions and special merchandise, referring to current advertising as necessary. Give customers a chance to adjust to the store's atmosphere and explore on their own.

Offer and provide assistance as needed. Assure customers with a look or statement that a salesperson will be available to help them when needed. Train salespeople to read faces, looking particularly for signs of confusion or excitement, or perhaps a question. Customers really want *personal service* and *professional information.* Provide these through a well informed, friendly, efficient sales staff. Be sure your employees are easily identified with shirts, hats, jackets, aprons, name tags, or other identification.

Stress customer service and satisfaction to all salespeople. Remember, a truthful, knowledgeable salesperson can easily add many dollars in sales simply by matching the customer's needs to the products available.

Ask the right questions. Teach salespeople to ask questions that require more than a yes or no answer. Answers to questions beginning with *how*, *when*, *where*, *what*, and *why* will provide salespeople with more information to serve customers better and will convince customers of the firm's personal interest in them.

Determine customer's knowledge level. It is especially important to encourage interest in first-time customers and get some idea of their general gardening knowledge. Don't underestimate a customer's intelligence, but at the same time don't overestimate their knowledge about plants and gardening.

Employees must know the products. Sales personnel should be knowledgeable professionals and feel comfortable talking about and using the store's products. Employees should be regularly trained in horticulture to remain current. They should understand horticultural terminology but be able to express terms in simple language a non-horticulturist or new gardener would understand. They should read industry trade magazines, attend seminars on new products and concepts, and pay attention to how bedding plants are used in the garden and community.

Know store policies. Be sure your employees understand store policies so they can deal with customers honestly. A complaint that goes unresolved or a service that is not performed satisfactorily or fairly can reduce your business' credibility.

Handle complaints quickly, honestly, and privately. The retailer is on the firing line with the customer. If the bedding plants perform badly, it is the retailer who often shoulders the blame, fairly or unfairly. Always try to turn each complaint into a benefit.

Give feedback to the supplier and store management. Consistent complaints about a cultivar, a method of production, or a service should be reviewed and a solution found. Perhaps it is the seed company or propagator who should be informed so corrections can be made. If the problem is internal in production or marketing, a change in suppliers, some procedure or company policy may help. In any case, analyze complaints and act on them.

Cultivating customers is a continuous job. Repeat business is important. A satisfied customer will return and recommend your business to others. Large sales should be followed up with a phone call to see how the plants are doing. Develop a mailing list of customers for special promotions. Try to greet customers by name and remember special things about them. Provide special purchase opportunities for your favored customers, or involve them in evaluating some new products you might like to sell.

Merchandising is as merchandising does

Merchandising must go beyond the minimum standards customers expect from your type of business and bedding plant products. Merchandising is the skillful bundling of bedding plants with services, features, and benefits that are important to consumers and that add value and desirability to products. Merchandising is a wide variety of activities that make customers feel good about you and your business.

Merchandising helps to create joy, stimulate excitement, and promote the educational value of a shopping trip to your store. It enhances your business image as a positive force in the community. Successful merchandising is profitable for the bedding plant retailer and can also guarantee a steadily increasing demand for bedding plants for years to come.

CHAPTER 7

Layout and Display

Dennis J. Wolnick

"Your store's layout, its displays, and its merchandise are all closely tied to your business image and how customers perceive your store. The physical sensations you provide with space, signs, colors, sounds, and smells are often what create favorable impressions among patrons [1]."

Designing the sales environment for bedding plant sales and displaying bedding plants with sales appeal are two vital parts of an organized merchandising effort, an effort that also includes product development, advertising, personal salesmanship, and customer service.

Store design and displays that generate excitement and sales appeal result from a retailer's merchandising strategy, knowledge of consumer behavior, and the uses of plant products; proper plant product maintenance in a retail environment; space available; market competition; creative design ability; and thoughtful and ongoing planning by management and staff.

Planning a retail layout

The major objectives for a successful garden store layout are:
- Safe and convenient parking;
- Smooth customer traffic flow through the sales areas from entrances to checkouts;
- Maximum visibility for customers and store personnel outside and inside the store, from the highway, from the parking lot, and in the sales area;
- Indoor and outdoor sales areas that are well organized, well-lighted, protected from bad weather, and that have hard-surfaced and spacious aisles;
- Neat, uncluttered display areas full of attractive plant products;

- Well-maintained, fresh plants;
- Well-designed, creative, and visually appealing displays;
- Display area flexible to change orientation and type of display;
- Effective, accent lighting to highlight merchandise;
- Clear, simple, and informative signs; sales areas not cluttered or obscured with signs;
- Clearly marked prices;
- Easily maintained and restocked displays that are easily shopped by customers;
- Easy to identify and friendly store personnel;
- Easy to find, efficient checkouts.

Organizing retail space

The entire store and its sales areas can be systematically organized to have the greatest sales impact. Keeping the layout objectives in mind, here are some of the different ways to look at layout organization in retail garden stores.

Layout organized by activities

Major activities in a garden retail center can suggest ways to organize the store's layout:
- plant sales (the most important);
- associated sales of related garden products;
- service activities related to the plants, including landscape design, educational seminars, plant problem diagnosis, and parking;
- product storage and preparation;
- management activities (clerical, finance, planning);
- employee facilities.

Newer garden stores and chain stores will probably have all of these activities under one roof, although that roof may be an all-season one, a glass or plastic greenhouse roof, the wood lath or saran fabric of an outdoor shaded area, or a combination of structures and roofing materials.

Organizing by departments

The sales environment can be further divided into departments containing related items that require the same environment and support such as house plants (warmth), fresh cut flowers (refrigeration and design facilities), greenhouse flowering and foliage potted plants (sunlight, moderate temperatures), bedding plants and other outdoor plants such as perennials, trees and shrubs that need less protection, require regular watering, and can be particularly messy.

Organizing layout by space requirements

The plant display space is a major part of the store's sales environment, but not all. The store also requires aisle space between and within the various sales areas, some on-site storage, a checkout area, service areas, and, of course, parking. Sales space assigned to bedding plants will also depend on stock requirements such as turnover, restocking time, product support (maintenance) available, and contribution to sales.

Parking. A parking lot should be organized and safe, provide enough space to accommodate the number of cars on a better than average sales day, and have a strategy to turn over parking spaces as rapidly as possible.

Parking often requires more area than the total area devoted directly to sales. Three or 4 square feet (.3 or .4 m^2) of parking for each square foot (.1 m^2) of sales space is a common design requirement for shopping centers. About 350 square feet (31.5 m^2) is needed to park a car, including backup space.

Layout patterns and traffic flow

Remember, customers won't buy what they don't see. They must have easy access to the entire sales area so they will see everything you have to offer and learn enough about the plants to make their buying decisions.

The arrangement pattern of aisles and displays is very important to customers in the store and in outdoor display areas. A well-organized store layout has four objectives:
- to make it easy for customers to find the goods they need or have seen advertised;
- to lead the customer past everything that is on display in the store;
- to provide quick and easy checkout when the time comes;
- to provide safe and convenient loading of bulky items.

Space distribution patterns:

1. Grid layout pattern. One of the most common layout patterns is the *grid*, which employs a network of wide and narrow aisles placed at right angles to one another—like the layout of city streets in a block pattern. One or more major central aisles lead away from the main entrance and enclose the checkout area. The large entrance aisle serves as a feeder aisle to distribute customer traffic throughout the store by means of smaller aisles leading away in each direction.

In the grid it is easy for customers to change direction using the many side aisles that intersect. Even the narrowest aisles are wide enough to accommodate two people passing with baskets or carts without a collision.

Major aisles must be wide enough to accommodate people moving in two directions, maybe with carts. In all cases the narrowest aisle should be 5 feet (1.5 m) wide, major aisles should be at least 8 feet (2.4 m) wide or wider, and any aisle intended for motorized vehicles should be at least 6 feet (1.8 m) wide.

The grid layout is popular and is the pattern favored by the large chain stores because it allows the largest amount of merchandise to be displayed. This arrangement of aisles and displays is functional, simple to organize and maintain, and customers are familiar with it.

2. Curvilinear layout pattern. A second general layout pattern, more typical of department stores and boutiques, is the *curvilinear* pattern. In this pattern aisles are gradually curved and may actually radiate from a central point in concentric circles or maybe squares.

Areas of merchandise are set off in boutique fashion along the curved aisles. Displays may be island-like through the area, and the flavor of the layout is sophisicated.

Although less merchandise can be displayed using a curvilinear pattern compared with the standard grid pattern, the curvilinear pattern has great potential for a garden plant display because it is more like a garden in appearance and regains some of the intimacy lost in large open stores.

Within the curvilinear pattern, other patterns can be used depending on the merchandise sold. For example, mass displays of pesticides, fertilizers, pots, or even the plants themselves can be arranged according to the grid pattern, but be part of a larger, circular, or curved arrangement that involves the entire store.

3. Peninsular layout pattern. A third layout pattern used particularly in display greenhouses is the *peninsular* pattern. The peninsular layout consists of a wide central aisle with several short, dead-end aisles located at right angles to either side. Display benches surround the short side aisles on three sides and provide more bench space while opening the display area to easy access by customers and employees. The peninsular pattern does not allow display of the largest amount of merchandise but is used to enhance the image and add extra quality or value to the merchandise displayed.

Traffic flow. The traffic flow concept considers the overall ease of customer movement from arrival at your greenhouse or garden center to departure. No matter what pattern is used, aisles must first be designed to distribute and direct customer traffic. In general, the overall traffic flow should be somewhat circular, either in a clockwise or counterclockwise direction. The direction will depend on where the entrance is located and how the aisles are arranged. The circular trip should end at the checkout area and exit to the parking lot. A counterclockwise direction may be somewhat favored over a clockwise because people entering the store are less likely to block those leaving.

The best way to get a feel for traffic flow is to go into several department stores, supermarkets, and other retail garden stores and greenhouses to watch the general flow of customers as they enter the store and circulate. Determine also how each store is laid out to encourage the movement of people in an organized way.

In large multi-department stores, departments that attract a lot of attention are generally located to the back and sides of the store. A garden department with bedding plants is an excellent example of a department generating large seasonal demand. Customers are subtly forced to pass by lesser demand but profitable impulse items on their way to desired merchandise (bedding plants). Supermarkets distribute their high-demand produce, dairy, and meat departments around the store's perimeter and more recently down the center aisles to encourage customer traffic to move throughout the store.

Display benches and fixtures

More flexibility is added to the sales area when it is designed to allow display units to be arranged in as many configurations as needed. Movable and modular display fixtures can be readily expanded and contracted with changing inventory.

Display bedding plants on raised benches that are flat or slightly angled. The best height for raised benches is 3 to 3½ feet (.9 to 1 m) above the floor. Plants are easier for customers to see and reach and easier for employees to water and groom. Bedding plants displayed on raised benches are less likely to be stepped on, kicked, or tripped over by customers or employees, and plants are more visible to consumers.

Make raised benches narrow enough so the salesperson or customer can reach the back of a 3½ to 4-foot-wide (1 to 1.2 m) one-sided display or to the center of a 6-foot-wide (1.8 m) display bench that can be approached from both sides.

Simple benches constructed of 2 x 4s and turkey wire placed on construction blocks or other sturdy supports provide flexible height, support, and the necessary drainage. Build the benches to standard lengths of 6, 8, or 10 feet (1.8 m, 2.4 m, or 3 m), and they can be put together in any combination to provide aisle space in all directions. Of course, more elegant benches made of wood, concrete, or metal can be used to add a special touch. Build display benches with raised edges on all four sides to keep plants secure.

Structures and product support systems needed

Plant product needs will dictate the display environment, and costs of protective structures, plant support systems, and display fixtures. The retail store building with year-round climate control is most expensive to construct per square foot. Other less expensive structures are greenhouses and covered but unheated outdoor structures such as lath and saran shade structures.

Greenhouses. The best structure for bedding plant display is the greenhouse. Glass, fiberglass, rigid polycarbonate or acrylic plastic double layer panels, and polyethylene films are all suitable greenhouse coverings. For the retail store a glass or rigid plastic greenhouse provides a look of permanence and class, and the covering will last many years before it needs replacing. Plastic films appear less permanent, and, in fact, they need replacing every few years. In a greenhouse, plants receive plenty of natural light and are protected much like they were during production.

Lath and saran structures for overhead protection. In warm sections of the country with stable weather conditions, bedding plants can be displayed outdoors in a protected area. A lath or saran-covered area protects plants from sudden storms and shades plants from hot sun. The amount of shade can be controlled by the density of the material used. Bedding plants displayed in full sun dry out rapidly and quickly deteriorate unless frequently watered. A lath or saran cover will shade the plants, reduce water loss, and keep the blooms fresher and more colorful.

Air temperatures in bedding plant displays should be maintained between 45 F and 85 F (7.2 C and 29.4 C) to avoid desiccation from heat and chilling or freeze damage from cold. Provide shading to reduce day temperature. Walled structures and even microfoam or other plastic insulating covers can prevent frost damage.

Watering plants in displays. Place design plants near a water supply and provide adequate drainage for water. Bedding plants on display will require regular, gentle watering to maintain their high quality.

Automatic systems, using individual watering tubes, tend to get disorganized as customers pick up and replace plants. There is little labor savings from automated watering if tubes must be continually replaced, or if plants dry out.

Capillary watering systems, used widely in Europe, show some promise for maintaining pot plants in retail displays, but are not yet commonly used in the United States.

As local water use regulations become more stringent in the 1990s, drip and capillary mat irrigation systems and other water-conserving systems will need to be installed to replace hand watering and overhead sprinkling. Stores should consider water containment and recycling from plant displays in addition to drainage.

Crowding. Do not crowd plants on a bench. Crowding encourages disease, stretching of stems, and mechanical damage, and quality plants will decline rapidly under these conditions. Though it is tempting to place plants on shelves in order to accommodate more plants on display, you should avoid this practice. Plants on low shelves will not get enough light, they are likely to be underwatered or overwatered, and air circulation is poor. It is also difficult for customers to see the plants, and it is harder for employees to groom plants.

Grooming. Healthy plants come from clean displays. Bedding plant displays should be constantly observed and groomed to remove any bad foliage and flowers, or to remove diseased plants and those in broken containers. Constant observation will help employees detect problems early, before they become serious.

Employees can carry pruning shears and wear large pocketed work aprons where they can keep dead flowers and plant debris until they can find a waste can.

Light. Outdoors, under shade structures, and in greenhouses, natural light is ideal and usually adequate. It is also balanced to show true flower colors. Under poor light conditions on cloudy days and perhaps at the end of relatively short days in spring, color-balanced electric lighting may be needed in the store or display greenhouse as a supplement to natural daylight. But electric light is a poor substitute for natural light. Bedding plants grown in sunny greenhouses will not last long under low light conditions and must be sold rapidly.

Signs. Signs should serve a definite purpose. Keep them helpful, clear, simple, and to the point. Many times good ideas for signs come from questions that customers frequently ask. Be brief: Use simple words and only a few of them. Seven words is a good average for simple signs. Display cards giving one or two benefits from a product or suggesting tie-ins are also good.

All signs should be clear with large, uniform, easy-to-read letters. Avoid elaborate script styles; use bold letters instead. Black letters on yellow backgrounds, green or red letters on white, and black letters on white are easiest to see and read. Handwritten signs are fine if they are neat and artistic. An employee may have an artistic flair and be happy to do the lettering job. Signs will look better if they are done in a professional, consistent style.

All signs should be moisture-resistant or waterproof and be done in fade-resistant ink. Greenhouses have too much water, humidity, and light to keep delicate signs attractive. They will warp, run, peel, and fade. Consider carefully using old signs unless they are still in very good condition, or can be neatly touched up. Signs shouldn't interfere with the merchandise being sold—at the same time, signs should be conspicuous if they are going to be read.

Signs and labels with color pictures of the plants are very helpful to customers, when the plants they are buying are not yet in bloom. A substitute could be larger pots of the same variety in full bloom, scattered throughout the displays. Don't be surprised, though, if a customer asks to buy the blooming display plants!

If the sales layout is somewhat confusing, signs can help guide customers to specific areas. Signs should be simple and carefully worded to avoid confusion. A good layout is planned carefully to avoid confusion and reduce the need for directional signs.

Use signs to reinforce newspaper and radio advertising and to indicate store services, special offers, and promotions such as local beautification contests. Signs can sell the plants quietly and quickly.

Plant labels and price signs. Certainly all plants should be labeled with cultivar name, care information, and price—if prices are not uniform or clearly displayed elsewhere. Use a labeling system that allows rapid sorting of plants into categories by color, growth habit, variety, or use. Each unit, whether a pot, pack, or flat, should have its own price and identification label.

Crossed-out prices on signs are commonly used to suggest a bargain or sale, but fresh signs with new prices are probably better for maintaining your high quality, organized image. Clear, permanent price coding is important for salespeople and cashiers. Simplify pricing so cashiers and customers don't have to remember several prices for similar items.

Displaying bedding plants

Major display objectives are to:
• generate sales for bedding plants;
• maintain or improve the quality of the plants you display;
• provide customer satisfaction and value;
• provide ideas for customers.

Bedding plant displays should be a great source of ideas for the customers. Simple displays of massed bedding plants in a garden setting or in the sales area have excellent sales appeal. Good sales appeal is also present in displays of blooming container gardens using pots of many sizes or planted window boxes.

Apply design principles to store displays

Store displays, whether simple or elaborate, are compositions that can benefit from artistic design principles.

Unity and centers of interest. A good display is unified by a dominant theme, color or group of colors, eye flow, texture, and focal point or major center of interest. A French marigold display may feature several cultivars in yellow or a petunia display may focus on several cultivars from lightest pink to darkest red. The display could feature one idea—plants for a sunny area, a shady area, a terrace, a border, or a window box. Each display needs a dominant theme to pull it together and make it simple for the customer to understand.

Contrast. Contrast is used primarily to attract attention and make merchandise stand out. Red flowers on a grayish-green or grayish-blue background are examples of color contrast. Blue and green are used for backgrounds in flower photography to bring out flower colors. Light, warm colors like yellow, orange, and beige are good background colors. In general, pastels and grayed colors are good for background and complement the merchandise. Green foliage also works well. For good visual balance use brightest colors in smallest amounts. For unusual effects consider contrasts in texture (rough and smooth), size (large and small), natural versus man-made (plants and containers), and shapes (round and triangular).

Balance. Any good display will look visually balanced. It doesn't look top or bottom heavy, and it gives the feeling that everything is in the right place. Balance is considered in terms of objects' symmetry or their visual weight. Balance may be symmetrical or asymmetrical. With symmetrical balance, also called formal balance, objects in equal numbers, sizes, and visual weights are located on each side of the display's vertical center line. Stacks of canned goods and horizontally massed flats of bedding plants are examples of symmetrical balance. Asymmetrical balance is also known as informal or natural balance. More objects or larger sizes are placed on one side of the center line and balanced by fewer objects placed at a greater distance from the focal point on the other side. The result is visual stability, although the two sides don't look the same.

Visual weight. The visual weight of specific objects is another aspect of balance. Visual weight is influenced by an object's size, color, texture, and density. Objects that are dark or bright, highly textured, large, or very dense tend to look heavy. Light colored, smooth, porous objects appear light. Iron will look heavier than silver or gold; red will look heavier than pink; burlap will look heavier than silk; and bowling balls look heavier than balloons of the same size. Try to achieve balance in every display with merchandise of different sizes, colors, textures, and styles.

Gradation, transition and repetition. Gradation means varying the size, color, texture, and location of objects in some regular or gradually changing pattern. Gradation of size, color, or texture creates transition and, in turn, unity. The eye flows smoothly from one part of the display to another, top to bottom, side to side, and front to back. Gradation also creates depth. Any pattern can be repeated, which creates unity. Repetition can be impressive—a towering display of canned goods or a sea of blooming bedding plants. Repetition can also be boring, especially if the customer craves that one-of-a-kind item. You can't avoid repetition, but use it purposefully in displays for best effect.

Line. Lines are vital to composition—they have direction and character. A display will appear either horizontal or vertical because of the major line underlying its structure. For best harmony, the parts of the display should follow the major line of the display. Lines may be diagonal, straight, curved, wavy, bold, subtle, simple, and intricate, and each type of line has its own character. Straight lines are formal. Curved lines are informal and graceful. They are pleasing when used in walkways or flower bed edges. Vertical lines are formal, while horizontal lines are informal and restful. Diagonal and zig-zag lines are bold and modern. Consider carefully the placement of merchandise and props to produce lines that lead the eye to the display's focus. Be sure none of the pathways created by line lead the viewer's eye out of the display.

Space and form. Space is just as important as solid objects in a display, and it is a critical element of landscape designs. Extra space will lighten a heavy looking display and give it extra class. You will notice in magazines and window displays that expensive products such as jewelry and glassware are given lots of space to emphasize their importance and value. Be cautious using space, however, because too much space can give a feeling of limited choice and availability of merchandise.

Color. When it comes to customer appeal, color may be the most powerful tool you have to work with. Color has great emotional impact, and we use expressions like "we are green with envy," "he is yellow," "I've got the blues," and "she sees red." Green means go and is a very 1990s natural color. Red means stop. It also stimulates the appetite and creates restlessness. Yellow means caution but is also known for its cheerfulness.

Shades and tones are considered visually receding or can be depressing. Tints and bright colors are visually advancing and uplifting. Tints mean spring, bold colors are summer and fall, shades and tones signify winter.

Combine colors according to the principles of design, and avoid color combinations that appear loud, dull, or cheap. Colors in the blue, green, purple, and red families are often associated with high class and high fashion. Yellows and oranges, especially in signs, might suggest bargain or sale and yet are among the most visible colors. Just remember, it is impossible to please everyone when it comes to color.

Putting displays together

A display's sales effect depends on whether or not it appeals to a customer's need for the products displayed, and also the care with which the display has been created and maintained. One-third or more of all the purchases made on a shopping trip are impulse buys made merely because the shopper saw the merchandise displayed.

Locate major displays at points where people are likely to stop. Good places for special displays are at the end of aisles, across from a service or information desk, inside the main entrance, near the entrances to departments, and near checkouts. Locating special displays at intervals throughout the sales area will lead customers from one place to another. Be sure to have special, easy-to-find displays of any advertised merchandise.

Don't hide the merchandise, but hide the clutter. Customers are likely to think you take care of your plants in a sloppy way. Although some customers may be careless housekeepers, they expect better of you.

Self-service is commonly used in garden centers and greenhouses. Beware of the display that is so perfect that the customer is afraid to remove anything. Some retailers will actually remove one item from such a display just to encourage customers to do likewise.

Merchandise size

Customers should be able to reach to the back of the display bench or shelf easily, or at least to the middle, if the plants can be reached from both sides. Waist-high benches that are 4 to 6 feet (1.2 to 1.8 m) wide are ideal. Customers shouldn't have to bend down too far or reach up too high for their selections. Benches may even be tilted toward the customer for a better view like supermarkets do in displaying produce.

What messages are being sent?

When you sell not just plants, but beauty and benefits, you add value to your products. Attempt to sell ideas. Customers translate good ideas into personal benefits, thus increasing the value of the product and your business. The one thing all displays should have in common is sales appeal. If displays don't sell the products and ideas they show, they are ineffective.

Stocking and restocking displays

Restocking can be a problem particularly on busy days. Plan the display locations so they may be restocked efficiently with minimum inconvenience to customers or employees. Where no replacement stock is planned, consolidate merchandise into new displays to maintain a well-stocked look.

Empty spaces in displays created by removing plants should be filled regularly or consolidated. Systems that allow employees to transport many bedding plants at once can speed up restocking and reduce effort. If all display parts are easy to reach, employees will be more likely to maintain displays properly. Well-organized displays save employee time and are easier to maintain.

Displays should be kept fully stocked throughout the bedding plant season although the actual products may change. The merchandise needs to be seen to be sold, and the bedding plant sales season lengthens each year.

Take advantage of vertical spaces that are otherwise wasted. Hanging baskets take advantage of vertical space and enhance the overall display area appearance. Use simple pyramids or racks made of pipe or wood to hang several layers of baskets securely and attractively. Even the vertical support posts for greenhouses and lath structures may be decorated with baskets or container gardens. Hang baskets in interesting patterns that create unusual design effects. Place hanging baskets in areas beside the aisles, not over the aisles. Dripping baskets or those hung too low over aisles are inconvenient, even dangerous.

Just like home. If your retail nursery or garden center has several different departments, consider laying out the sales area like a private home where visitors enter the front door from the parking area, pass through the store, enter the greenhouse or a covered patio area, then finally end up in the outdoor garden. Place suitable plants along the way to give the customer a homey feeling.

Keep up a good front and back. Although there seems to be a back to every store and display area, it should not be a place to store uninteresting, slow-to-move merchandise and discards. Such a setup is sure death to good traffic flow. Avoid the "backside" problem with the circular layout that plant conservatories and botanical gardens often use.

Home-grown image. Customers are attracted to the idea of "home grown" or "locally grown," and nothing promotes this idea more than having plants displayed in a greenhouse. The greenhouse structure, to make a good impression, must be kept clean and in good condition. The retail greenhouse should be considered primarily for its display value and sales appeal rather than its production efficiency. The greenhouse also provides a better place for maintaining bedding plants, reducing the effects of damaging storms and cold weather, and providing enough light.

Sell gardens, not just plants. Remember that you will get great results from selling ideas in addition to plants. The sales area should be like a garden—attractive and full of interesting ideas for bedding plants. Never underestimate the entertainment and educational value of a shopping trip to a well-stocked greenhouse or garden center. Take advantage of the natural interest customers have in plants and gardening. You want the buying experience, however, to be as efficient as possible. An effective layout will get customers into the store easily, allow them to see everything with minimum effort, and then get them out through checkout as quickly and as painlessly as possible.

Seasonal attraction. As a department, the bedding plant section will attract a lot of attention in the spring and can be made slightly less accessible to draw customers through other parts of the store. People will find it anyway. At the same time it is desirable to distribute some bedding plants and related merchandise throughout the sales area to provide continuity, to stimulate the desire for flowers, and to lead the customers from one area to another. Besides, blooming bedding plants are spectacular to look at and should be very visible.

Summary

When deciding layout and display, consider how the customer thinks and behaves. Customers are generally aware of what you have to offer and are prepared to purchase something. They are seeking information, weighing possibilities, looking for personal service and reassurance about their purchases. Customers also have a good eye for freshness and quality.

Good signage, attractive layout and friendly salespeople help to service customers efficiently and assure them that they are making the best purchase decisions. Welcome customers quickly, and help them feel they have plenty of time to consider their purchases carefully.

The careful way that merchandise is handled in displays and by salespeople can have great impact on the image you create with your customers and will determine not only what and how much they buy, but whether they will return for more and tell their friends in the process.

References

[1]   Carpenter, E.D. 1986. Designing your store to have a selling personality. *Amer. Nursery*. Dec. 15:81-83.

CHAPTER 8

Landscaping

Gale L. Arent and Marcia L. Voigt

Annual flowers are unique above all other plants. They allow you to "redecorate" your outdoor living spaces each year by changing your landscape's color scheme and texture. Several characteristics have made bedding plants popular with both professional landscapers and home gardeners alike:

Instant color. Annuals are often planted at the first-flower stage of development, giving you instant gratification from your purchase and instant color in your landscape.

Season-long color. Bedding plants can bring continuous color to your landscape, blooming from early spring through late fall and well into the winter in milder climates.

Changing landscape effects. Annuals bring variety. Each year you can give your landscape a new look by changing colors, flower types, foliage textures, and planting patterns.

Versatility and movability. Container-grown annuals, such as hanging baskets, window boxes, and patio containers, can enhance the effect of flower beds or introduce season-long color to landscapes where flower beds are not possible.

Bedding plant use has been increasing throughout North America for the past four decades. Initially, this trend resulted from expanding suburban lifestyles. As rural families moved to the city, they wanted to replicate the backyard vegetable and cut flower gardens so characteristic of their former environment. Planting annual flowers in home landscape designs eventually became common and resulted in the expanded use of bedding plants. Today, two primary classes of bedding plant consumers exist:

Professionals. This group includes those who landscape public places such as parks, community entryways, civic buildings, and streetscapes, as well as private sector landscapers who use bedding plants to enhance retailing areas, housing complexes, golf courses, and the image and uniqueness of private businesses.

Homeowners. These fall into two broad categories, the "yardners" and the "gardeners." Yardners are homeowners who use bedding plants because they wish to have attractive yards. They are, however, likely to seek good results with minimum effort. Yardners look for familiar plants that are known to do well under their landscape conditions. Gardeners, on the other hand, are serious students of flowering plants who are likely to seek new varieties, All-America winners, and unique types. Gardeners demand a knowledgeable retail source. An elaborate retailing network that includes mass markets, garden centers, and retail-growers has developed to supply the homeowner market. Serious gardeners also fuel innovation and creation of niche-markets within the bedding plant industry.

The successful growing and selling of bedding plants is linked to a deep appreciation for the dramatic effects that annuals can achieve in landscapes and the diversity represented by the industry's present customer base.

Making decisions

Before planting, determine what you want your landscape to do for you. Annuals can create an outdoor living space, providing respite from the the busy world. They can be focal points, accents, or ribbons of living color to tie together other landscape elements such as shade trees, evergreens, flowering trees, shrubs, and perennial flowers. Besides adding aesthetic value, annuals can also highlight special areas, camouflage problem spots, and even direct foot traffic. In newly planted landscapes, annuals can fill in the gaps until shrubs and permanent ground covers mature.

Design possibilities

When you think about coloring your landscape with flowering annuals, let your imagination run wild. You can plant annuals almost anywhere: along driveways, in front of buildings, around patios, under signs, at the base of flagpoles, in raised planters, in parking lots, along fences, at the edges of ponds, as accents to statuary, by entrances, in night-lighted areas, next to benches... anywhere within the reach of soil, light, and water.

Consider how your plantings will be seen. If you must limit planting due to space, light, or budget, stick to areas that are on view. Take into account existing and immovable features such as buildings, fences, and trees as well as topography. Think beds, borders, focal points, and practical effects as you include flowers in the overall design.

Beds. Beds are accessible from all sides, like an island planting centered in a turfed area. Plant beds in proportion to their surroundings. A large bed can overwhelm a small grassed area.

Berms. These mounds of soil give plantings height and perspective where the ground is flat.

Borders. Borders edge an area, such as a lawn, walkway, driveway, foundation, shrub planting, or fence. Since borders can usually be worked from one side only, keep them narrower than 5 feet (1.5 m), or maintenance will be difficult. Up to that size, borders can be as wide as space and design permit.

Companions. While annuals are magnificent used alone, they can also be planted effectively with perennials, summer bulbs, dwarf shrubs, and trees. Annuals bring variety and new interest to your permanent plantings.

Containers. Lack of ground space does not mean you have to do without color. By using containers, you can locate color wherever you want it—in planters, window boxes, and hanging baskets—then take it away if you change your mind. This is one of the easiest ways to bring color into the landscape with minimal time and cost.

Color—ways to mix and match

Color, which reflects the personality of a home or business, has more impact than any other aspect of flower bed design. Which color scheme you choose is up to you; just be sure to select one and stick to it.

Rules of thumb from the color wheel:
- Single color masses have great impact.
- Adjacent colors go well together, for example, yellow with orange.
- Opposite colors are compatible, for example, violet and yellow.
- White can separate two incompatible colors, mixes well with any one color, and makes an outstanding border color.

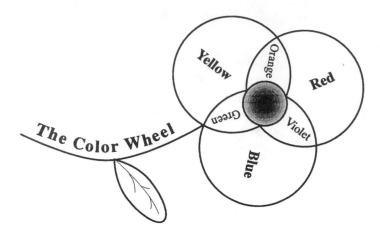

Fig. 8.1. A color wheel is useful in making color decisions.

- White, silver, and gray foliage plants, such as dusty miller, follow the same rules as white-flowered annuals.
- Split complementary colors are on either side of opposite colors, such as red with blue or red with yellow.
- Analogous color harmony uses three colors in a row on the wheel, such as yellow, yellow-orange or gold, and orange.
- Monochromatic design uses different tones or pastels of the same color (pink/red).

Create a mood or feeling. Warm colors—yellow, gold, orange, and red—create excitement and attract attention. Warm colors make a planting appear to be smaller than it is. Cool colors—blue and violet—create a tranquil, soothing mood. Cool colors used in small spaces make them appear larger.

Finally, keep it simple. More than two or three colors can make your planting busy and unattractive. Decide on a primary color, and use it alone or with one secondary and possibly a third. If you like the idea of a rainbow of colors, you can still maintain design simplicity by planting many colors using the same plant. Zinnias, impatiens, dahlias, and celosia are each available in a wide range of colors.

Shapes and sizes—ways to mix and match

Once you've set the mood with color, it's time to consider design. The size and shape of a particular plant and its flowers affect how it will look in proportion to the surroundings.

The tall and the short:
- Small beds or edgings along low hedges or beneath foundation plantings call for a low-growing choice such as ageratum or alyssum.
- In larger areas, vary the height to make the effect more interesting, especially if the ground is flat.
- In a free-standing bed, place taller plants in the center, stepping down to small ones in the front.
- For a border against a fence or a wall, use the tallest plants in the back and work down toward the front.
- For a mixed bed or border, choose three sizes of plants for best results. Either combine three varieties of the same plant, such as zinnias or marigolds, in different heights; or combine three different plants, such as tall spider flowers and medium-sized dahlias edged with a carpet of short petunias.
- In containers, as with beds, you may either plant in one variety, or combine plant forms. An upright plant in the center of a large container with trailing stems cascading over the sides is a popular design choice. Foliage plants can be added for interest and texture.

Unlimited options. Annuals also grow in a multitude of plant shapes and styles with a variety of foliage colors and textures. Mixing these can make an attractive bed, but give careful consideration to each plant's uniqueness and how it will look when combined with others.

- Spiked snapdragons
- Mounded begonias
- Ground-hugging lobelia
- Upright, bushy African marigolds
- Open, informal cosmos
- Plumes of celosia
- Globes of gomphrena
- Fuzzy ageratum
- Single, daisy-shaped gerberas
- Double, frilled petunias
- Round, ruffled calendula
- Petite, sweet alyssum
- Large, graceful hibiscus
- Paisley-shaped coleus

Combination versus mass plantings. Although combinations of shapes are attractive and interesting close up, mass plantings of one variety in one shape and color can be equally appealing. It depends on the effect you want to create. A mass planting looks sleek, modern, and impressive, especially when viewed at a distance.

Rotations. Rotating annuals gives you color all season or throughout the year in warm areas. Start in spring with pansies or other cool-temperature plants, followed by any of a large selection of summer annuals, and end the season with another cool favorite such as flowering mums or ornamental cabbage or kale.

Design details

Shaping the planting area. Geometric designs present a formal appearance, while sweeping lines following contours offer a more relaxed feeling. Don't limit your thinking to just linear beds. If you're not comfortable with visualizing design concepts in your mind's eye, take a garden hose and lay out various shapes around buildings and permanent landscape plants. Experiment with moving the hose until you've found the perfect design for your new flower bed.

Drawing the plan. Before you plant, create a planting guide that lays out the bed's shape and size. The easiest way to do this is on graph paper with the plan drawn to scale. Each square on the paper represents 1 square foot (.09 m²) of the planting. Your plan should also show the location of each type of plant. Table 8.1, a landscape flower selection and spacing guide, will be invaluable for selecting the annuals to use.

Calculating the area. After your design is complete, calculate the area of your plantings to help determine how much fertilizer to apply and how many plants you will need. If you use graph paper, just count the squares to arrive at the total area (fig. 8.2). If you do not use graph paper, calculate the area mathematically.

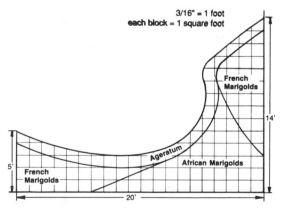

Fig. 8.2. Graph paper can be used to create a scale planting guide.

TABLE 8.1

Landscape flower selection and spacing guide

Flower	Spacing (inches)	Maintenance	Height (inches)	Light	Moisture	Temp.	Hardiness
African daisy	8-10	Medium	10-12	S	D	C	H
Ageratum	5-7	Low	4-6	S, PSH	A-M	A	HH
Amaranthus	15-18	Medium	18-36	S	D	H	HH
Aster	6-18	High	6-30	S, PSH	M	A	HH
Balsam	10-15	Low	12-36	S, PSH	M	H	T
Begonia, fibrous	7-9	Low	6-8	S, PSH, SH	A	A	HH
Begonia, tuberous	8-10	Low	8-10	PSH	M	C	T
Black-eyed Susan vine	12-15	Medium	72	S, PSH	M	A	HH
Browallia	8-10	Low	10-15	SH	M	C	HH
Calendula	8-10	High	10-12	S	M	A-C	H
Candytuft	7-9	Low	8-10	S	D	H	H
Canna	9-24	Medium	18-48	S	M	A	T
Celosia	6-8	Low	6-15	S	D	H	HH
Clarkia	8-10	High	8-24	LSH	A	C	H
Coleus	8-10	Low	10-24	SH, PSH	A	A-H	T
Cornflower	6-12	Medium	12-36	S	A-D	A	VH
Cosmos	16-18	Medium	18-30	S	A-D	A	HH
Creeping zinnia	5-7	Medium	5-6	S	A	ANY	H
Dahlberg daisy	4-6	Low	4-8'	S	A-D	H	HH
Dahlia	8-10	High	8-15	S, PSH	M	A	T
Dianthus	7-9	Low	6-10	S, PSH	A	ANY	H
Dusty miller	6-8	Low	8-10	S, PSH	D	H	T
Flowering cabbage/kale	15-18	Low	15-18	S	M	C	VH
Forget-me-not	8-12	Low	6-12	S, PSH	M	C	H
Fuchsia	8-10	High	12-48	PSH, S	M	A	T
Gaillardia	8-15	Medium	10-18	S, LSH	M	H	H
Gazania	8-10	High	6-10	S	D	ANY	HH
Geraniums	10-12	High	10-15	S	M	A-H	HH
Gerbera	12-15	Medium	12-18	S	M	A-H	HH
Gloriosa daisy	12-24	Low	18-36	S	M	H	H
Gomphrena	10-15	Medium	9-30	S	D	A	H
Hibiscus	24-30	Medium	48-60	S, LSH	M	A-H	H
Impatiens	8-10	Low	6-18	PSH, S	M	A	HH
Impatiens, New Guinea	10-12	Medium	10-12	S, LSH	M	A	T
Ivy geranium	10-12	Medium	24	S	M	A	T
Kochia	18-24	Low	24-36	S	D	H	HH
Lantana	8-10	Medium	10-12	S	A	A	T
Lisianthus	8-10	Medium	10-15	S	A	A-H	HH
Lobelia	8-10	Low	3-5	S, PSH	M	C	HH
Marigold, African	12-15	High	18-30	S	A	A	HH
Marigold, French	3-6	High	5-10	S	A	A	HH
Monkey flower (Mimulus)	5-7	Low	6-8	SH	M	C	HH
Nicotiana	8-10	Low	12-15	S, PSH	M	A-H	HH

TABLE 8.1 continued

Flower	Spacing (inches)	Maintenance	Height (inches)	Light	Moisture	Temp.	Hardiness
Ornamental pepper	5-7	Low	4-8	S, PSH	M	A-H	HH
Pansy	6-8	Medium	4-8	S, PSH	M	C	VH
Petunia	10-12	Medium	6-12	S	D	A	H
Phlox	7-9	Low	6-10	S	M	C	H
Portulaca	6-8	Low	4-6	S	D	H	T
Primrose	4-6	High	6-8	PSH	M	C	H
Salpiglossis	10-12	Medium	18-24	S	M	C	HH
Salvia	6-8	Low	12-24	S, PSH	A-M	A-H	HH
Scabiosa	8-12	High	12-24	S	M	A	HH
Snapdragon	6-8	Medium	6-15	S	A	C	VH
Spider flower	12-15	Low	30-48	S	D	A-H	HH
Statice	12-14	Medium	12-36	S	D	ANY	VH
Stock	10-12	High	12-24	S	M	C	H
Strawflower	7-9	Medium	15-24	S	D	H	H
Sweet alyssum	10-12	Low	3-5	S, PSH	A-D	A	VH
Verbena	5-7	Medium	6-8	S	A	A-H	HH
Wishbone flower (Torenia)	6-8	Low	8-12	SH	M	C	HH
Vinca	6-8	Low	12-14	S, PSH	ANY	H	T
Zinnia	4-10	High	4-36	S	A	A-H	T

Light:
  S = sun, full, day-long exposure to sun
  SH = shade, sheltered from sun exposure throughout the day
  PSH = part shade, a few hours of protection from the sun, particularly in the heat of the afternoon
  LSH = light shad
Moisture: A = average   D = dry   M = moist
Temperature: A = average   H = hot (> 85 F)   C = cool (< 70 F)
Hardiness:
  VH = very hardy; will actually stand frosts*
  H = hardy; will stand light frosts with little damage*
  HH = half hardy; stands cold weather but no frost
  T = tender; does poorly in cold weather; susceptible to frost
Note: Both hardy and very hardy plants often winter through in milder climates.

If the planting beds are free-form, separate them into individual rectangles, squares, or triangles. Calculate the area of each, and add the total together to obtain the square footage.

Area of a rectangle = length x width
Area of a triangle = ½ base x height
Area of a square = length x width or side²
Area of a circle = pi x radius² (pi = 3.14)

Determining the number of plants needed. Once you have determined the total area, refer to table 8.1, the landscape flower selection and spacing guide, for recommended spacing. Use the larger spacing figure in the chart in areas with long, hot growing seasons; use the smaller spacing figure in areas with short, cool seasons or where instant effect is needed.

Determine your plants per square-foot factor using the chart below:

Spacing (inches)	Plants per square-foot facto r	Spacing (inches)	Plants per square-foot factor
4	9.0	12	1.0
6	4.0	15	.65
8	2.3	18	.45
10	1.4	24	.25

To determine the number of plants needed, multiply the plants per square-foot factor by the number of square feet in the area you've allocated for this particular plant. For example: Total area = 116 square feet (10.4 m²)

Ageratum—(4-inch/10-cm spacing) = 24 square feet (2.1 m²) x 9.0 = 216 plants

French Marigold—(6-inch/15-cm spacing) = 50 square feet (4.5 m²) x 4.0 = 200 plants

African Marigold—(12-inch/30-cm spacing) = 42 square feet (3.7 m²) x 1.0 = 42 plants.

Selecting plants. Although many factors contribute to successful use of bedding plants, selecting the right plant for your landscape conditions will get you off to a good start.

When choosing plants for containers, select those that are compact, long-blooming and in proportion to the container (table 8.2).

Plants for special places and uses

Heavy shade. Impatiens, begonias, coleus, browallia, monkey flower, fuchsia, wishbone flower.

Light shade. Lobelia, nicotiana, salvia, pansy, ageratum, dahlia, dianthus, dusty miller, ornamental pepper, sweet alyssum, vinca, black-eyed Susan vine.

For hanging. Impatiens, begonias, browallia, petunias, lobelia, verbena, creeping zinnia, sweet alyssum, coleus, portulaca, vinca, fuchsia, black-eyed Susan vine, ivy geraniums.

Cool climates. Stock, monkey flower, salpiglossis, primrose, pansy, forget-me-not, browallia, calendula, lobelia, snapdragons, dianthus.

Hot spots. Amaranthus, wax begonia, ornamental pepper, vinca, celosia, dahlia, Dahlberg daisy, kochia, petunia, portulaca, salvia,

TABLE 8.2

Container flower selection guide

Flower	Hanging basket	Tub or 2- to 5-gallon container	Large container, 8- to 12-inch pot	Small container 4- to 6-inch pot	Full sun	Part shade	Full shade	High yield	Transplant	Water sparingly
Ageratum			X	X	X	X			X	
Sweet alyssum	X			X	X	X				
Aster			X		X	X			X	
Balsam			X		X	X			X	
Begonia	X			X		X	X			
Browallia	X			X	X	X			X	
Calceolaria				X			X	X	X	
Calendula			X		X	X			X	
Candytuft				X	X	X			X	
Carnation			X		X	X			X	
Clarkia				X	X	X			X	X
Coleus	X			X		X	X		X	
Creeping zinnia	X		X		X					
Daisies (many types)			X		X	X				
Dianthus				X	X	X			X	
Forget-me-not				X	X	X				
Fuchsia	X						X		X	
Gazania			X	X	X	X			X	X
Geranium	X	X	X		X	X			X	X
Impatiens	X		X			X	X		x	
Lobelia				X	X	X			X	
Marigold			X	X	X	X			X	
Morning glory	X				X	X				X
Nasturtium	X				X	X				X
Nicotiana			X		X	X			X	
Pansy	X			X	X	X			X	
Petunia	X			X	X	X			X	
Phlox			X		X	X				
Portulaca	X			X	X	X				X
Salvia			X		X	X			X	
Snapdragon			X		X	X			X	
Stock			X		X	X			X	
Sweet peas	X				X	X				
Torenia						X	X		X	
Vinca	X				X	X			X	x
Zinnia		X	X		X	X				x

creeping zinnia, dusty miller, triploid marigolds, verbena, zinnia, gazania, coleus, nicotiana, gerbera.

Moist areas. Monkey flower, wishbone flower, pansy, ageratum, browallia, calendula, flowering cabbage and kale, impatiens, lobelia, nicotiana, ornamental pepper, phlox, salpiglossis, salvia, stock, sweet alyssum.

Alkaline soil. Aster, dianthus, scabiosa, strawflower.

Dry and drought conditions. Amaranthus, African daisy, vinca, Dahlberg daisy, gazania, kochia, sweet alyssum, portulaca, salvia, creeping zinnia, dusty miller, candytuft, celosia, petunia, spider flower, strawflower, zinnia.

Hardy annuals. (Those that will tolerate light frosts.) Pansies, cornflower, flowering cabbage, kale, primrose, snapdragon, statice, and sweet alyssum. These "annuals" are really tender perennials that can survive the winter in mild climates.

For fragrance. Dianthus, sweet alyssum, stock.

For cut flowers. Zinnias, marigolds, stock, snapdragons, dahlia, calendula, salvia, aster, gerbera, cornflower, ageratum, cosmos, spider flower, statice, daisy, lisianthus.

Turning your design into reality

Preparation

Soil is the foundation of your planting. Preparing it properly in advance will pay off in healthy, beautiful flower beds. Good garden soil should hold plants securely and retain moisture like a sponge, allowing surplus water to drain away rapidly. To determine your soil type, take a generous handful of soil from a flower bed and squeeze it. If it is:
- *Sandy*—the soil will be very light and run through your fingers. The addition of organic matter to retain soil moisture is usually desirable.
- *Loam*—the soil will be loose, not compacted, but heavy enough to stay in your hand without forming a ball. This is an excellent planting medium.
- *Clay*—the soil will be heavy and tend to form chunks or a ball. This soil needs to be lightened with sand or organic matter to give plant roots air and drainage.

When creating a new flower bed. Pay special attention to the soil. If it has been in turf or wild a long time, it will need considerable improvement, if not total replacement, due to the build-up of salt and other road service chemicals from rain run-off, snow plowing, and ice-melting applications.

Soil test. Soil for most annuals should be slightly acid to neutral with a pH of 5.5 to 7.0. Have it tested at your county extension office, taking special care to test soil along driveways, walkways, and parking lots, which are prone to salt and chemical build-up. A soil test will determine whether your soil needs lime to raise the pH or sulfur to lower it—or if a high salt/chemical residue requires total soil replacement. Soil testing also determines the availability of major plant nutrients.

Soil additives. Most soils benefit from incorporating organic matter such as peat moss, leaf mold, or compost at a rate of about 25% of soil volume into areas where the roots will be growing, approximately the top 8 inches (20 cm). Organic matter will improve moisture retention and drainage. Wetting agents can help achieve similar results.

   Fertilizer should also be mixed in; choose one where the ratio of N-P-K is 1:1:1 or 1:2:1, and apply according to label directions. Normal rate of application on new beds is 1 to 2 pounds (.4 to .8 kg) of 5-10-5, 10-10-10, or similar amount of another fertilizer analysis per 100 square feet (9 m^2). On established beds, 1 pound (.4 kg) of fertilizer per 100 square feet (9 m^2) is normally sufficient, unless your soil test results indicate corrective measures. Spade, rototill, or otherwise mix well until all additives are uniformly incorporated.

Reduce weeding. Apply a pre-emergent herbicide labeled for ornamental use just before or immediately after planting. In general, these herbicides should be left undisturbed on the surface, but read all label recommendations before use and follow the instructions carefully. Professional landscapers who care for large beds should check annually with their state extension service for herbicide recommendations.

When using herbicides, remember:
• Thoroughly read the label, and follow all directions.
• Test a trial plot the first time herbicides are used prior to treating the entire area.
• If herbicides are spilled on skin, wash thoroughly with soap; if swallowed, in contact with eyes, or absorbed to the point of showing poisoning symptoms, call a doctor immediately.
• Since environmental conditions vary, herbicides do not always exhibit similar results from year to year.

Other methods of weed prevention include spreading organic mulches 2 to 3 inches (5 to 7.5 cm) thick to shade the soil and reduce weed seedling survival, pulling weeds regularly while they are small, and using a physical barrier such as a black plastic film, which may be covered with a thin layer of decorative mulch. Be sure to punch numerous holes into the plastic with a garden rake to ensure adequate water penetration.

Containers. Soil is too heavy for containers and can harbor pests and diseases, so use a soilless medium of peat moss or bark with perlite and/or vermiculite. Fill to about one-half inch of the rim and water well before planting. If your container has no drainage holes and none can be made, cover the bottom with a thick layer of gravel to prevent water-logging the roots.

Timing. Do not work beds in early spring when the soil is still saturated, or you will damage its texture. Ideally, beds should be worked and turned the previous fall or in spring just prior to planting.

Discard. Any plants that may have reseeded themselves from last season should be discarded. They'll be less vigorous and probably will not resemble their hybrid parents.

Planting

Wait. Don't jump the gun on planting! Most annuals can't be planted until after the danger of frost has passed; refer to the *Landscape Flower Selection and Spacing Guide* (table 8.1) for "hardy" exceptions to this rule.

Protect. If it's not possible to plant right away, keep your annuals in a lightly shaded spot, and be sure to water them as needed. If possible, plant them on a cloudy or overcast day or late in the day to reduce transplanting shock.

Mark beds. When planting time has come, mark the flower beds based on specified planting distance and your design plan.

Remove carefully. Just prior to planting, water the plants in their containers; moist plants are easier to remove from a container without disturbing the root ball. Lift plants from cell packs or pots carefully, keeping the root ball intact. If the container is pliable, gently squeeze or push up the bottom of the container, otherwise turn it upside down to let the plant fall into your hand. If the plant does not slide out easily, tap the bottom of the container with a trowel. If roots are extremely compacted, loosen them gently before planting. Occasionally you will find plants in a tray without individual cells. If so, separate the plants gently by hand or with a knife just prior to planting so the roots don't dry out. For plants in individual peat pots, either peel most of the pot away or be sure the top of the pot is below soil level after planting.

Plant. Dig a hole slightly larger than the root ball, set the plant in place at the same level at which it was growing, and carefully firm soil around the roots.

Water. Ideally, the garden bed should be moist when planting. If the soil is dry, be certain to thoroughly water plants immediately after planting.

Fertilize. Apply soluble fertilizer high in phosphorus after planting. A fertilizer such as 10-52-17 mixed at the rate of 1 pound (.4 kg) per 100 gallons (380 l) of water will cover 400 square feet (36 m²). Do not apply fertilizer to dry soil.

Mulch. Adding a 2- to 3-inch (5 to 7.5 cm) layer of mulch is optional— but it does add a decorative "finished" look as it reduces weeds and conserves soil moisture for better growth. The best mulches are organic, such as bark, chips, pine needles, shredded leaves, peat moss or hulls. The following year, mix in the mulch to enrich the soil before planting. Additional mulch can be added each spring, improving soil structure as years pass. Apply a high nitrogen fertilizer such as ammonium nitrate at the rate of 1 to 2 pounds (.4 to .8 kg) per 100 square feet (9 m²) when adding fresh mulch. This will compensate for the nitrogen used during mulch decomposition.

Keeping it colorful

Fertilizer

Most annuals do not require high levels of fertilizer, but will do much better if adequate nutrients are available. Notable exceptions are nasturtium, spider flower, portulaca, amaranthus, cosmos, gazania or salpiglossis, which thrive in poorer, infertile soils. With these, the fertilizer added at planting time is adequate.

With other annuals, you can fertilize once or twice more during the growing season with 5-10-5 or similar at the rate of 1 to 2 pounds (.4 to

.8 kg) per 100 square feet (9 m²). As an alternative, you may use a soluble fertilizer such as 20-20-20 mixed at a rate of 1 pound (.4 kg) per 100 gallons (380 l) and applied every four to six weeks.

Too much fertilizer causes a build-up of soluble salts that can damage plant roots. Test soil regularly to check soluble salt levels.

Water

New plants need to be watered well after planting and frequently thereafter until they are established and new growth has started. Deep, infrequent watering is generally better than frequent, light watering, since the former encourages deep root growth. Don't allow plants to remain for extended periods in puddles of standing water, however, since this encourages disease and overwatering symptoms such as yellow leaves.

Water your annuals about as often as you water your turf. Refer to the individual plant descriptions to see which plants like more or less moisture than average. When annuals need less water than the surrounding turf, raised flower beds will improve drainage and reduce the chance of overwatering.

Annuals' foliage should be kept dry during watering. Soaker hoses work best. However, if you must use overhead sprinklers, water disease-prone annuals (zinnias, calendula, stock, and grandiflora petunias in particular) as early as possible in the day so the foliage will dry off before night, lessening the chance of disease.

When using annuals for cut flowers, do not water them overhead, if at all possible, to prevent water damage to the blooms. Where dry soil and dry skies prevail and irrigation is not possible, choose drought-resistant annuals such as celosia, cosmos, sunflower, amaranthus, candytuft, dusty miller, gazania, spider flower, sweet alyssum, or vinca.

Maintenance

Many annuals—chiefly begonias, impatiens, alyssum, ageratum, lobelia, vinca and others—are self-cleaning and require little additional care. Their flowers fall from the plant after fading and do not need to be manually removed.

Deadheading. Other annuals, such as marigolds, geraniums, zinnias, calendula, and dahlias will need to have faded flowers removed. This is known as "deadheading" and not only keeps plants attractive, but also discourages disease and keeps them from going to seed so they will produce more flowers. Deadheading can be done with pruning shears or sometimes with the fingers.

CHAPTER 9

Scheduling Crops

Seeding, Germination, and Seedling Production

William Carpenter and E. Jay Holcomb

Bedding plant marketing has changed over the past few years, requiring growers to carefully evaluate their bedding plant production schedule. The goal for growers is to have bedding plants in prime condition when the consumer wants them. This requires growers to develop a plan.

The first step is to determine market trends, including those genera, species, and cultivars having the greatest demand. Next, you must establish plant container target size: packs, pots, or some other container; and the best stage of development for marketing: flowering or green. Finally, consider what production procedures to follow.

Bedding plants can be started from seed, then transplanted to packs for sale; seeds can be sown directly in packs; seeds can be sown in plug trays and the plugs can be transplanted; seedlings or plugs for transplanting can be purchased. The option chosen usually depends on greenhouse space, transplanting labor, types of facilities, other crops being grown, and the quality of the seedlings or plugs available from specialist propagators.

Develop a production schedule

Once you make these decisions, you can develop a production schedule for each crop. Published schedules can be used as guidelines; however, many environmental factors can influence a schedule. Differences in local weather conditions mean that you should maintain accurate records for future schedules.

Carlson and Rowley [6] recommend listing the following information:
(1) the number of pots, packs, and/or flats of each cultivar grown;
(2) the number of plants dumped;

(3) the number of pots or packs planned;

(4) the quantity of seed needed;

(5) the quantity of good seed on hand (if it is last year's seed, is it still viable?);

(6) how much seed is on order;

(7) the source of the seed.

In addition to these items, make notes giving the dates when seedlings from each sowing were ready to transplant and when the transplants were ready for sale. Also include comments about the crop's uniformity as well as any problems that developed. This information may be helpful in deciding what adjustments to make in next year's schedule.

Keep your schedule on a weekly basis so that all planning is related to what must be done each week [2]. In all probability, a weekly schedule is precise enough to manage labor efficiently and complete all of the necessary tasks. Working out a budget to estimate income and expenses is also recommended [2].

Prior to preparing your seed order, take inventory of leftover seeds (storage techniques are discussed later in the chapter). Viability may deteriorate during storage; it is wise to run a germination test on a small sample of stored seed. The germination test should be conducted at the optimum temperature, moisture, light, and oxygen levels for the species.

Carlson and Rowley [6] suggest that if the stored seed's germination percentage is below 60%, discard the seed. Plan to compensate when sowing for germination percentages between 60% and the standard for the crop. Once you have determined how much seed you have on hand and the number of plants you can expect that seed to produce, you can determine the amount of seed you need to order.

Sowing seed

Seed, flats, media, tools, and work areas must be clean prior to sowing. The growing media should be steam-treated to kill insects, diseases, and weed seeds. It may be beneficial to treat the seeds with a fungicide prior to sowing. Carlson and Rowley [6] recommend that Thiram, captan, chloranil, or dichlone be added to the seed packet. They indicate that 3 mm on the end of a knife will treat an entire seed packet. Be sure to shake the seed packet well to coat all seeds uniformly with fungicide. If seeds have already been coated with a fungicide by the seed company, do not add additional fungicide.

Direct sowing

Direct sowing involves germinating seeds directly in the final sales container to eliminate the need for transplanting. However, the ability to sow seeds thinly and uniformly by hand is a difficult skill to perfect; so, many growers use seed sowing machines. These are very valuable for direct sowing of plants and are essential if plugs are being used. Most seeders work by a vacuum pickup. A pump creates a vacuum and the equipment holds one or two seeds per station. The station is moved over the flat and, when the vacuum is released, seeds drop into place. If only one seed were placed in each location in a flat or plug tray, the germination rate would have to be 100% to produce a full flat. Very few seeds currently available have that rate of germination; therefore, it may be necessary to sow two or more seeds per location. It is common to sow three to five seeds of alyssum or portulaca per location.

Manual transplanting is required to fill blank locations and replace seeds failing to germinate, so that flats are full and salable. Replacing many plants per flat is time consuming and uneconomical. Direct sowing also requires more germination space than broadcasting seeds for transplanting. Ball [2] suggests that alyssum, celosia, portulaca, and other crops that do not need thinning can be direct sowed. Using a seeding machine to direct sow bedding plant seeds is a practical procedure.

Broadcasting

Broadcasting is defined as spreading the seeds uniformly over the growing medium surface. To broadcast seeds, fill the flat or pack with a moist growing medium; then carefully tap the seed packet with your index finger so that seeds will drop one or two at a time. Slowly move the packet over the entire flat or pack so that seeds are evenly spread over the entire surface. Ideally, seeds should be placed with the same amount of space around each seed. In reality, sow thinly so that the seedlings will not be too crowded and stretch and become spindly. The advantages of sowing thinly are improved aeration, huskier transplants, reduced tangling of roots among transplants which lessens root damage, and reduced transplant shock [14].

If seeds are the size of petunia seed or smaller, Dietz [14] recommends sowing 1,000 to 1,200 seeds per 11- x 22-inch (27.5 cm x 55 cm) flat. If seeds are larger than marigolds, then sow 750 to 1,000 seeds per flat. After sowing, cover seeds larger than petunias with a thin layer of growing medium.

In general, seeds should be covered to a depth of twice the diameter of the seed. Very small seeds, such as begonias and petunias, need no covering. The flat should be watered, preferably by subirrigation or with a fine, gentle mist. Do not use a mist with droplets large enough to wash fine seeds off the surface. Once the medium has been thoroughly watered, move the flat to the germination area.

Sowing in rows

Growers may see an increase in soil-borne diseases in flats if plants are sown too close together and the roots become entangled. To prevent this, sow seeds in rows. Although rows can be made lengthwise in the flat, it is preferable to position rows crosswise of the flat.

First, fill the flat with moist medium, then make a depression between one-eighth- and one-fourth inch (.4 cm and .6 cm) deep using something like a label edge. Sow as thinly as possible within the row and cover if the seed is large. Apply water and handle like flats with broadcast seed.

Seed viability

Seed viability means that the seed is alive and capable of germinating to produce a "normal" seedling under proper environmental conditions. Seed viability is highest at maturity, but seed dormancy usually prevents germination then. After physiological maturity, seed viability gradually declines, with longevity dependent on environmental conditions during seed storage.

The seed industry uses the term seed vigor when evaluating seed viability and seed quality. Seed vigor is defined as "those seed properties which determine the potential for rapid germination, uniform emergence, and development of normal seedlings under a wide range of field conditions" [1]. Seed vigor includes the total germination percent, speed of germination, uniformity of germination and seedling development, normal seedling morphological development, and capacity for seed storage under favorable or adverse environmental conditions.

A number of factors affect seed viability and vigor, including proper seed development before harvest, seed damage during harvest, improper seed storage, and seed aging. Seed companies are required to determine the germination percentage of the seed lot being sold and to make that information available to their customers. Carry-over lots must be retested in subsequent years, prior to sale. Factors most important to growers are the storage and aging of their seed.

Seed storage

Bedding plant seeds are stored for varying periods after harvest. Seed viability after storage depends on the plant species, the methods of production and seed handling, and the rate of seed deterioration during storage. The rate of change or aging of seed during storage varies with the crop and the environmental conditions of storage, primarily temperature and relative humidity. The interaction of temperature and relative humidity during seed storage of phlox cultivar Light Salmon is shown in fig. 9.1.

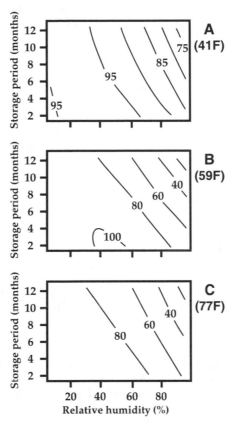

Fig. 9.1. Contour plots for total germination percentages for Light Salmon phlox seeds germinated at 68 F following storage at 41 F (A), 59 F (B), or 77 F (C) and 11% to 95% relative humidity for three to 12 months [11].

Control of the seed's moisture content is probably the most important factor in seed longevity during storage. Most bedding plant seeds demonstrate the best storage at a moisture content below that at harvest. Further moisture reduction is gained by drying in the field or by using heat under controlled conditions. Moisture in seeds is in proportion to the storage container's ambient relative humidity. An increase in relative humidity increases seed moisture content.

Although low moisture content generally enhances seed storage life, desiccation tolerance is highly variable among important ornamental species. Amaryllis [7] and aster seeds contain 29% and 11% moisture respectively at harvest, but both are tolerant of seed moisture levels below 4% during storage. Delphinium, primula, salvia, and vinca seeds have 9.5% to 12% moisture levels at harvest, but all have reduced total

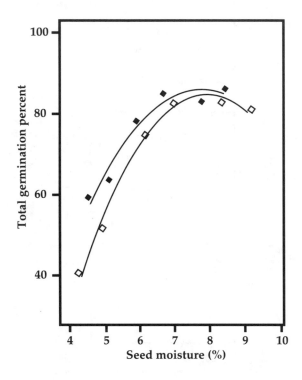

Fig. 9.2. Relationship between seed moisture content during storage and the subsequent total germination percent of Magic Fountains Lavender and Magic Fountains Lilac delphinium [9].

germination when seed moisture content during storage is below 7% (fig. 9.2).

These species also have delayed and irregular germination following storage at less than 7% seed moisture content. Seed storage temperatures of 40 F to 50 F (4.4 C to 10 C), and relative humidity from 15% to 40% have been found best for storing bedding plant seed (fig. 9.1). Seed physiological deterioration accelerates during seed storage at relative humidity higher than 50% (fig. 9.1), and the integrity of cell membranes is reduced at levels below 10%.

Seed aging

Seed vigor and viability decline as seeds age. The slowest decline occurs for seeds at low moisture contents stored at low temperatures. Reduced total germination percentages, a slow germination rate, and greater variability among seeds during germination are signs of reduced seed vigor resulting from seed aging. This aging frequently becomes evident only when unfavorable conditions, such as heat or water stress, occur during germination or seedling growth; otherwise the seeds appear to develop normally. The cellular and metabolic changes that occur during seed aging are not well understood.

If you keep surplus seed from one season to the next, store seed at the proper temperature and humidity levels to maintain viability. Home refrigerators maintaining 41 F temperatures and a 40% to 45% relative humidity are appropriate. Seeds stored in a refrigerator in non-sealed containers generally have 7% to 12% moisture content, which is ideal for many species. Seeds tolerant of storage at very low moisture content, such as asters, phlox, and vinca, should be dried to ± 4% moisture and placed in glass vials with screw caps before storing in the refrigerator.

Never store seed in the greenhouse or headhouse without refrigeration, because fluctuations in temperature and humidity cause rapid seed aging. If you use stored seed, conduct a germination test prior to sowing to see if the seeds have adequate viability, germinate rapidly and uniformly, and produce normal seedlings.

Germination and environmental factors

Germination begins after absorption increases the seed moisture level during storage from 4% to 12% to 70% to 100% of full hydration. To germinate, storage tissue containing carbohydrates, fats, and proteins must be hydrolyzed and degraded into simpler, mobile chemical forms, which are translocated to the embryo's growing points and resynthesized into new tissue. Some of the hydrolytic products also are utilized in the respiration process. Since oxygen is involved, it is known as oxidation, and the end products are CO_2, water, and energy.

Cell division and enlargement begins only after food digestion and translocation are underway, first in the radicle or embryonic root and slightly later in the plumule or embryonic shoot. Cell division and enlargement cause the seed to enlarge, crack, and the radicle to extend through the seed coat into the medium. Soon after, the plumule pushes through the surface of the medium, the cotyledons or seed leaves expand, followed by the first true leaves. The germination process is then complete, and the seedling can manufacture its own food by the process of photosynthesis.

Water and oxygen

Water absorption, the entry of water through the seed coat causing hydration of the seed interior, is essentially a process that promotes germination. Water uptake by a seed during germination has four major phases:

Phase 1 is characterized by increased imbibition of water into initially a dry seed (fig. 9.3). Enzyme activity begins within hours (Phase 2). Activation results from reactivation of stored enzymes formed during the embryo's development, and, in part, from the new enzymes' synthesis as germination begins. The rate of water uptake is unchanged during Phase 2 and is controlled by the cellular membranes. Seeds

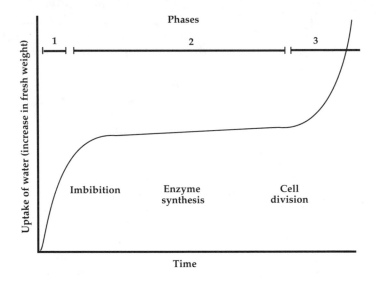

Fig. 9.3. Water uptake level by a dry seed has four phases: Phase 1, imbibition of water into the seed; Phase 2, enzyme activation; Phase 3, initiation of cell division and enlargement, and Phase 4, (not shown) root emergence. (Adapted from Bewley and Black, [3]).

achieve full hydration during Phase 2 of water uptake if the substrate medium contains adequate moisture.

The rate of water uptake progressively increases during Phase 3 when seeds swell and the embryo's cell division begins, and during

Phase 4 when roots emerge from the seed. Seeds of some bedding plant species require a relatively high moisture level in the medium; others prefer less moisture. Verbena seeds require a relatively dry medium with little or no water in the non-capillary pores (free-water). Research has shown that verbena seeds absorb excessive water during Phase 2 of water uptake when germinating in a moist or wet medium [8]. The excessive cellular hydration at this stage of germination probably interferes with enzyme synthesis and stored food digestion.

Seed germination requires the breakdown of stored food reserves and the utilization of large amounts of energy. The energy needed becomes available to living tissues through respiration, a physiological process that requires oxygen. Therefore, seed germination media must provide adequate water and oxygen. The germination medium's physical structure must provide contact between seeds and water films surrounding the particles, and replace water absorbed. Medium particles that are too large reduce the water content available for absorption, while particles that are too small reduce the oxygen level by filling pores with water.

Low soluble salts. Both the water and germination medium should have very low soluble salts contents. Germinating seeds do not need fertilizer until seedlings emerge and are actively growing. During germination, high to excessive levels of soluble salts restrict water absorption by osmotic action. If the water used for germinating seeds contains a high level of soluble salts, then the seed's water absorption will be restricted or even prevented.

Problems from high salt levels increase as the germination medium becomes dry, particularly at or near the surface where seeds are germinating. Use care in selecting a medium for germinating seeds. When preparing a germination medium, avoid using components having high soluble salts levels, such as vermiculite, which contains 3% to 5% K_2O.

Best seed germination occurs in media providing adequate water and oxygen to meet each particular bedding plant species needs. A continuous water supply is critical after seeds germinate. Since seeds are germinated on the surface or in the upper layers of the medium where the greatest moisture fluctuations occur, constant care is needed. Moisture fluctuations can be reduced by deeper covering of seeds not requiring light, frequent misting with low or high pressure systems, or by covering or enclosing seed flats after sowing and irrigation.

Temperature

Temperature is the most important environmental factor governing seed germination rate, and the capacity of seeds to germinate (table 9.1). Each bedding plant species has a range of temperatures at which seed germination will occur. Some seeds germinate over a wide range of temperatures, while others have rather narrow limits. Within that range is an optimum temperature at which the highest percentage of seeds germinate most rapidly.

TABLE 9.1

Temperature effect on non-primed pansy seed germination[a]

		Germination	
Temp. (F)	G (%)	T_{50} (days)	$T_{90}-T_{10}$ (days)
50	75	11	15
59	85	5	6
68	90	4	4
77	84	4	4
86	56	4	5
95	10	5	6

Source: Data from W.J. Carpenter and J.F. Boucher, 1991, Proper environment improves the storage of primed pansy seed, *Hort.Sci.* 26:1483-1485 [8].

[a]Majestic Giant Yellow pansy seed.

The seed germination range for Majestic Giant Yellow pansy is shown in table 9.1. Maximum total germination of 90% was achieved at constant 68 F (20 C). At this temperature, 45% (50% of the 90% total germination) of the seeds germinated within four days of sowing (T_{50}), and the number of days between 10% and 90% (9% and 81%) germination was four days ($T_{90}-T_{10}$). Total germination percentages and germination rate decreased as germination temperature increased or decreased from the optimum 68 F (20 C).

A study conducted over a much longer period than 28 days would demonstrate total germination percentages more similar among temperatures. Table 9.1 shows that the primary effect of temperature during seed germination controls the rate of germination (days required).

Temperature during germination also controls the seeds' capacity to germinate. At a constant 95 F (35 C) germination temperature, only 10% of pansy seed had the capacity to germinate (table 9.1). Similarly, a low total germination percent probably would have resulted if pansy seed had been germinated at constant 35 F to 40 F (1.7 C to 4.4 C). Seeds imbibed in water and germinated at highly unfavorable temperatures for long periods (one to two weeks) lose their capacity to germinate by becoming dormant.

This is commonly referred to as "stress dormancy," "induced dormancy," or "secondary dormancy." Highly irregular seed germination would result if seeds are later germinated at favorable temperatures.

Keeping imbibed seeds requiring light in total darkness for long periods or allowing seeds to become dehydrated during the latter stages of germination also can induce stress dormancy.

Light

The need for light during seed germination varies with the bedding plant species, frequently with the cultivars within a species, and among seeds of the same cultivar. Some seeds have an absolute light requirement, for other seeds light inhibits germination, and some seeds germinate equally well in light and darkness. Impatiens seed germination is reported to require light, but 18%, 19%, 25%, 57%, 77% and 90% germination was achieved in total darkness for cultivars Lipstick, Accent Orange, Accent Pink, Super Elfin Coral, Red Velvet, and Accent Red, respectively [12].

Cathey [13] has classified petunia cultivars according to their seed germination light requirement. Phytochrome, a photochemically reactive pigment found in seeds, is responsible for light sensitivity. The seed's outer living layers, including the seed coat, nucellus, or endosperm, that adjoin the embryo are the locations of the physiological active tissue for light reception [18].

For seeds requiring light, germination is promoted when sunlight or incandescent light is received. Sunlight or incandescent light can delay or prevent the germination of seeds requiring darkness during germination. Cool white and "Wide Spectrum Gro-Lux" fluorescent lamps are equally effective for promoting germination.

The duration and intensity needed to induce germination in seeds requiring light has received only limited study. Bewley and Black [4] reported that short-term exposure of imbibed seeds to light for seconds or minutes does not inhibit or promote germination, rather light or darkness is needed for many hours. However, Maytime petunia seed germination has been promoted by a single 10-minute light treatment, and begonia and primula seeds by four 10-minute lighting periods daily [13]. The light period duration needed to promote the germination of impatiens Accent Orange seed depended on the light intensity. Seeds receiving constant 10 foot-candles (.1 klux) of incandescent light required three days of lighting to achieve maximum total germination (85% to 90%), while at 100 or 500 f-c (1.1 or 5.4 klux) intensities, two or one days of light, respectively, were needed (table 9.2).

Light intensity. Light intensity and the hours of light received daily during germination influenced the germination percentage of impatiens Accent Orange (table 9.3). Highest total germination occurred when seeds received 10 f-c (.1 klux) of light for six hours daily (92%) or

TABLE 9.2

Influence of light intensity and days of light on impatiens seed germination[a]

Light (f-c)	Number of days of light			
	1	2	3	4
	Germination (%)			
10	59	79	87	90
100	72	85	88	91
500	86	89	91	90

Source: Data from W.J. Carpenter, E.R. Ostmark, and J.A. Cornell, 1994, Light governs the germination of *Impatiens wallerna* Hook f. seed, *HortSci.* 29 (in press) [12].
[a]Accent Orange impatiens seed.

100 or 1,000 f-c (1.1 or 10.7 klux) for 1 hour daily (88% and 95%, respectively). These results indicate a possible relationship between the light energy level needed to terminate the impatiens seeds' photodormancy and total seed germination.

At all light intensities, total germination declined as the duration of the daily lighting periods increased from 12 hours to 24 hours (table 9.3). The reduction rate in total germination increased when the lighting intensities were increased (table 9.3).

TABLE 9.3

Percent seed germination as a function of light and hours of light[a]

Light (f-c)	Hours of light per day				
	1	6	12	18	24
	Germination (%)				
10	79	92	87	78	73
100	88	91	78	63	47
500	95	88	80	58	20
	Days for 50% germination (T_{50})				
10	4.4	4.1	4.3	4.4	4.7
100	3.7	4.1	5.0	5.8	6.8
500	5.0	6.6	8.0	8.3	8.7

Source: Data from W.J. Carpenter, E.R. Ostmark, and J.A. Cornell, 1994, Light governs the germination of *Impatiens wallerna* Hook f. seed *HortSci.* 29 (in press) [12].
[a]Accent Orange impatiens seed.

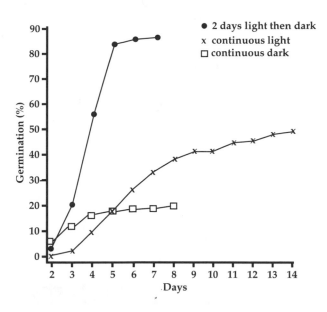

Fig. 9.4. Cumulative germination curves of impatiens seeds at 77 F in continuous dark-ness, continuous light, or two days in light, then darkness.

Continuous darkness. The total germination percentages of impa-tiens Accent Orange seeds germinated in continuous darkness, contin-uous light at 100 f-c (1.1 klux), and two days of continuous light at 100 f-c (1.1 klux) followed by continuous darkness are compared in figure 9.4. Only 19% of the seed germinated in continuous darkness, indicat-ing that they lacked a dormancy requiring light for termination (photodormancy). Forty-seven percent germination occurred from con-stant 100 f-c (1.1 klux) of light during 14 days, which increased to 63% after 28 days.

Seeds receiving two days of light at 100 f-c (1.1 klux) followed by continuous darkness had 86% germination within seven days. These results show that light to satisfy light-requiring seeds' photodormancy is needed only during the first stages of germination. The higher the intensity of light imbibed seeds receive, the shorter the period (hours or days) of light needed to terminate the photodormancy.

Seeds should be germinated in continuous darkness after the light requirement has been met. The slow rate and highly irregular germi-nation of impatiens seeds receiving continuous light is the result of delayed emergence of the root from the seed, caused by light received during the latter stages of germination.

The retarded root emergence could result from light delaying the onset of cell division in the radicle, or from reduced enlargement of cells in the radicle. Based on these results, commercial producers should initially provide light to the seeds of those species and cultivars requiring light, and then place the seeds in darkness.

Germination-inhibiting light. Light (incandescent, fluorescent, or daylight) may inhibit or prevent the germination of calendula, centauria, phlox, statice, or vinca seeds. Research shows that the total germination percentages of phlox seed receiving zero to six days of light before continuous darkness were similar (92% to 96%). These results indicate that the early stages of phlox seed germination probably proceed at similar rates at 68 F (20 C) in both light or darkness, but seeds receiving light during the latter stages of germination have delayed emergence of the seed root and plumule (table 9.4). The action of light in delaying the root emergence for phlox is probably the same as impatiens.

TABLE 9.4

Light delays germination phlox seed rate[a]

| Lighting period before darkness (days) | Germination | | |
	Total (%)	T_{50} (days)	$T_{90}-T_{10}$ (days)
0	94	4.0	3.8
1	93	4.3	3.8
3	92	5.9	5.1
5	93	7.5	6.7

Source: Data from W.J. Carpenter, E.R. Ostmark, and J.A. Cornell, 1993, The role of light during *Phlox drummondii* Hook seed germination, *HortSci.* 28:786-788 [11].
[a]Lighting Light Salmon phlox seed had no effect on germination percentages but delayed rate (T_{50}) and increased irregular ($T_{90}-T_{50}$) germination.

Ten f-c (.1 klux) or higher intensities during the latter germination stages can delay impatiens root emergence, while delays occurred at 1 f-c (10.7 lux) for phlox [11]. Light received during the latter stages of seed germination may delay root emergence in all bedding plant species regardless of their present light response classification during germination. If this is correct, then all bedding plant species seeds should be in darkness during the latter stages of germination, with light exposure at seedling emergence.

Seed priming and enhancement

Increased production of bedding plants by direct seeding in plug trays or flats has placed a premium on the use of seed producing high total germination that germinates rapidly and uniformly. Seeds treated by new techniques—enhancement, priming, or hydration—are now available for many flower and vegetable cultivars. These seeds have been partially hydrated for short periods to hasten germination after sowing. Seed priming reduces the effect of unfavorable temperature or other environmental stresses during seed germination. Primed pansy seeds (table 9.5) have higher total germination, germinate faster, and seedlings are more uniform than those germinated from nonprimed seeds (table 9.1). Seed priming benefits become greater under less favorable germination temperatures. Remember that primed seeds are less tolerant of storage at low seed-moisture content. As primed seed moisture content declines below 9% during storage, total germination percentage also declines [8].

TABLE 9.5

Temperature's effect on primed pansy seed germination[a]

Temp (F)	Germination		
	Germ. (%)	T_{50} (days)	$T_{90}-T_{10}$ (days)
50	84	6	8
59	87	4	5
68	91	3	3
77	88	3	3
86	84	3	3
95	51	4	5

Source. Data from W.J. Carpenter and J.F. Boucher, 1991, Proper environment improves the storage of primed pansy seed, HortSci. 26:1483-1485 [8].
[a]Majestic Giant Yellow pansy seed.

Commercial seed producers have developed specialized handling and seed preparation techniques including seed precision grading, sizing, coating, checking for cracks or other damage, removal of non-viable seeds, and careful selection of seed stock to improve seed performance. Companies have established trade names for their treatments and handling procedures. Examples are GelCoat, Genesis, Ultra Seed, Seed Enhancement, Quick Kote, Super Frax, Split Pil, Quick Pil, Hytech Seeds, and High Energy Seeds. Growers can frequently become confused by the large number of seed treatments available. Seed catalogues and sales representatives can assist by providing information regarding each process and whether it will improve the germination of the flower and vegetable species you are producing.

Growing environment for seedlings

Light

Light is the driving force behind a plant's growth. Its effect on plants is a result of either intensity or photoperiod, or a combination of the two. Once germination is complete, the extent of seedling elongation depends on light intensity. Low light levels produce seedlings that are tall, thin, and very weak. This type of seedling is difficult to transplant and recovers from transplanting very slowly. If seeds are germinated in a growth chamber under artificial light, the seedlings may need to be acclimatized to the sun's intensity in the greenhouse. To acclimatize seedlings, move them to the greenhouse and reduce the light by covering with saran for a week or so before exposing to full sun.

Supplementary light. Generally the need is not to reduce light, but to increase it. Does it pay to provide supplementary light for bedding plants? Graper and Healy [17] reported that petunia growth increased as total light received by the plant increased. This means a grower can use a lower light level for a longer period, or a higher light level for a shorter time.

It is also important to provide light in the early stages of growth when the plants are close together. Graper and Healy [16] reported that HPS lighting of begonia for only a 10-day period increased growth. Kessler et al. [19] confirmed that lighting for periods as short as two to four weeks accelerated seedling growth. Lighting during the seedling stage is relatively efficient because a great many plants can be concentrated in a small area.

Norton [20] indicated that lighting a crop to reduce bench time may be more economical than extending the production period. The final consideration is determining which crops should be lighted. Norton [20] reported that petunia, salvia, lobelia, snapdragon, and geraniums were very responsive to high-intensity illumination. Tomatoes, lettuce, ageratum, and aster have an intermediate response, while verbena, alyssum, and impatiens were the least responsive to supplementary high-intensity illumination.

Photoperiod. The second factor associated with light is photoperiod. When bedding plants are started in January or February, the days are naturally short. The days lengthen through March, April, and May with the longest day occurring in June. Does this changing photoperiod affect plant growth? Carlson and Rowley [6] indicated that alyssum, balsam, begonia, gomphrena, impatiens, French marigold, pansy, vinca, carnation, lobelia, tomato, pepper, and cabbage are day neutral; so the changing photoperiod throughout the spring will have no effect.

African marigold, zinnia, salvia, basil, coleus, celosia, cleome, cosmos, dahlia, morning glory, perilla, and rudbeckia were reported to be short-day plants. Phlox, verbena, snapdragon, centaurea, feverfew, gaillardia, gypsophila, hollyhocks, nicotiana, scabiosa, salpiglossis, and ageratum were reported to be long-day plants. Carlson and Rowley [6] also emphasize that these statements are generalizations, and all cultivars do not respond in the same way.

Temperature

Temperature for optimum seedling growth will vary with species, but some generalizations apply. In general, warm air temperatures will encourage soft, succulent growth. Dreesen and Langhans [15] reported that impatiens plugs were taller when grown at high temperatures. It may be beneficial to reduce temperatures to produce a slightly harder, stockier seedling that will withstand transplanting a little better. Higher night- than day-temperatures (negative DIF) have been reported to keep seedlings short; however, seedlings grown under those conditions are often very chlorotic. Generally the chlorosis clears up when the seedlings are returned to a positive DIF environment.

Research has also been conducted on the effect of soil temperatures on plant growth. Shedlosky and White [21] reported that soil warming was beneficial for the nine bedding plant species they tested. Many growers are converting to warm floors and placing the flats right on the floor. These growers have reported improved growth of young plants, leading to the conclusion that warm soil temperatures (around 70 F) (21.1 C) improve and accelerate plant growth. As the crop matures, soil heat may not be necessary.

Water

Seedlings can be irrigated with a mist system or by subirrigation. A hose with a nozzle may propel too forceful a water stream and knock seedlings over, making transplanting more difficult. If a mist system is used, the mist must be on long enough to wet the medium thoroughly to the bottom of the flat. If irrigation is not thorough, root growth may be shallow and/or soluble salts may begin to build up. Subirrigating seedlings is an effective way of thoroughly irrigating the medium.

Transplanting

Carlson [5] defined transplanting as "the procedure for transferring seedlings from seed flat to production container." Most bedding plants are transplanted to save space in the germination area. The germination area is generally warmer than the production area, thus, the germination area is more expensive to heat, and it should be used as efficiently as possible.

Seedlings should be transplanted as soon as the first true leaves begin to develop and the seedlings can be handled. At this stage of growth, the proportion of roots to top growth is greater than it will be later. By transplanting as early as possible, most of the root system will be retained, and even if some of the roots are lost in lifting the seedling, the balance of root to shoot remains in favor of the root system. Even when done with extreme care, transplanting is a stunting operation. Early transplanting reduces transplanting shock to a minimum.

In contrast, plugs can be transplanted much later in the seedling growth cycle. Each seedling's roots are growing in an individual cube of soil, seedlings have more space and receive more light energy, fertilization programs can be started, and removing the plug from its container for transplanting does not result in any appreciable disturbance or root loss. However, growers should recognize that seedlings growing in plugs can become overcrowded once the leaves begin to touch, and although there is more leeway in getting the transplanting job done, it is possible to check growth and reduce the finished plants' quality if plugs are not transplanted soon enough.

References

[1] Association Official Seed Analysts. 1980. Rules for testing seeds. *J. Seed Tech.* 12(3).
[2] Ball, V., ed. 1975. All about growing bedding plants. Chap. 1 in *Ball redbook*. 13th ed. West Chicago, Ill.: Geo. J. Ball, Inc.
[3] Bewley, J.D., and M. Black. 1978. *Physiology and biochemistry of seeds.* Vol. 1. New York: Springer-Verlag.
[4] ———. 1982. *Physiology and biochemistry of seeds.* Vol. 2. New York: Springer-Verlag.
[5] Carlson, W.H. 1976. Transplanting vs direct seeding. Chap. 2 in *Bedding plants.* Ed. J.W. Mastalerz. University Park, Penn.: Pennsylvania Flower Growers Assn.
[6] Carlson, W.H., and E.M. Rowley. 1980. Bedding Plants. In *An introduction to floriculture.* Ed. R.A. Larson. New York: Academic Press.

[7]   Carpenter, W.J., and E.R. Ostmark. 1988. Moisture content, freezing, and storage conditions influence germination of amaryllis seed. *HortSci.* 23:1072-1074.

[8]   Carpenter, W.J., and J.F. Boucher. 1991. Proper environment improves the storage of primed pansy seed. *HortSci.* 26:1483-1485.

[9]   ———. 1992. Temperature requirements for the storage and germination of *Delphinium* x *cultorum* seed. *HortSci.* 26:1469-1472.

[10]   Carpenter, W.J., and S. Maekawa. 1991. Substrate moisture level governs the germination of verbena seed. *HortSci.* 26:1469-1472.

[11]   Carpenter, W.J., E.R. Ostmark, and J.A. Cornell. 1993. The role of light during *Phlox drummondii* Hook seed germination. *HortSci.* 28:786-788.

[12]   ———. 1994. Light governs the germination of *Impatiens wallerana* Hook f. seed. *HortSci.* 29 (in press).

[13]   Cathey, H.M. 1964. Control of plant growth with light and chemicals. *The Exchange* 141(11):31-33; 141(12)33-35.

[14]   Dietz, C.F. 1976. Sowing schedules. Chap. 8 in *Bedding plants.* Ed. J.W. Mastalerz. University Park, Penn.: Pennsylvania Flower Growers Assn.

[15]   Dreesen, D.R., and R.W. Langhans. 1992. Temperature effects on growth of impatiens plug seedlings in controlled environments. *J. Amer. Soc. Hort. Sci.* 117(2):209-215.

[16]   Graper, D.F., and W. Healy. 1990. Synergistic acceleration of *Begonia semperflorens* development using supplemenal irridance and soil heating. *Acta Hort.* 272:255-260.

[17]   ———. 1992. Modification of petunia seedling carbohydrate partitioning by irradiance. *J. Amer. Soc. Hort. Sci.* 117(3):477-480.

[18]   Hartmann, II.T., D.E. Kester, and F.T. Davies, Jr. 1990. *Plant propagation: principles and practices.* 5th ed. Englewood Cliffs, NJ.: Prentice Hall.

[19]   Kessler, R., A.M. Armitage, and D.S. Koranski. 1991. Acceleration of *Begonia* x *semperflorens-cultorum* growth using supplemental irradiance. *HortSci.* 26(3):258-260.

[20]   Norton, R.A. 1979. Commercial lighting of bedding plants. *Florists' Review* 163(4231):24-25, 60-62.

[21]   Shedlosky, M.E., and J.W. White. 1987. Growth of bedding plants in response to root zone heating and night temperature regimes. *J. Amer. Soc. Hort. Sci.* 112(2):290-295.

CHAPTER 10

Traditional versus Plug Production

Allan M. Armitage and Mark P. Kaczperski

The bedding plant industry has grown steadily over the past half century. Along with this growth has come competition and the need for production efficiency. The last few decades have seen vastly improved materials handling methods, greenhouse automation explosion, more efficient benching designs, and an enormous improvement in cultivars. However, the greatest improvement to date in bedding plant production has been the development of the single cell transplant or "plug method."

Early bedding plant production simply involved digging transplants from the field, wrapping them in newspaper, and selling the product to the consumer. As production moved to the greenhouse, especially after World War II, seeds were direct sown into containers and grown until ready for sale. Over time, growers realized that efficiency could be improved if large numbers of seeds were started in a seed flat. Seedlings were maintained in the seed flat until two or three true leaves developed. They were then carefully removed from the seed flat and transplanted to the finishing flats or pots (table 10.1).

Traditional method

This method, known as the traditional method of production, increased the finished product's quality and uniformity and legitimized bedding plants as profitable items. As an additional benefit, heating expense was reduced during germination, since seed germination was confined to fewer initial flats.

Numerous disadvantages of the traditional method slowly became obvious. While in the seed flat, seedlings quickly become crowded, and stretch as they compete for light and space. It is essential when seedlings are ready to transplant that the job be done without delay. One or two days postponement of transplanting can cause thin, spindly

TABLE 10.1

Traditional and plug method production phases

Production phases	
Traditional	Plug
Germination. Occurs in open seed flat. In general, a single environment is maintained for the entire germination phase. Seedlings remain in open flat until two to four true leaves appear, after which time they are transplanted to the final container. A modification made by some growers is to direct sow in the final container.	**Germination.** Occurs in a many-celled plug tray. Germination phase is separated into Stage 1 germination phase and Stage 2, and the transition between the two stages is closely monitored. The optimum environment may be different for Stage 1 and Stage 2.
Time. Approximately 10 to 21 days, however, highly dependent on climate, species, and cultivar.	**Time.** Approximately three to five days for Stage 1, seven to 14 days for Stage 2, depending on species and cultivar.
Growing-on. The phase of young seedling growth from transplanting until flower buds are barely visible. Growing-on occurs in the final container.	**Growing-on.** The phase of young seedling growth until they are ready to be transplanted to the final container. The growing-on phase is divided into Stage 3 and Stage 4. The optimal environment may be different for Stage 3 and Stage 4, depending on species. Flower buds are seldom visible at the end of this phase. Growing-on occurs in the plug tray.
Finishing. The time from visible bud to sale (usually anthesis). The greenhouse environment is modified to prepare plants for the retail environment. Finishing occurs in the final container.	**Finishing.** The time from transplanting to the final container until sale (usually anthesis). The greenhouse environment is modified to prepare plants for the retail environment. Finishing occurs in the final container.

Source: Adapted from A.M. Armitage, 1994, Ornamental bedding plants, in *Ornamental production science in horticulture 2,* Wallingford, U.K.: C-A-B International [3].

seedlings that will depress the finished crop's value. Even when care is used in removing the seedling from the seed flat, root system damage is common. Disturbance to the root system can result in significant transplant shock to the seedling, causing a decrease in growth and development after transplanting.

Several variations of the traditional method exist, although all are based on manually sowing seeds over a greenhouse soil, then transplanting individual seedlings after initial growth into the finishing pot or flat. Containers for germination and early growth vary; standard open flats, smaller market packs, or specialized flats with preformed rows are used. Regardless of the container, seedlings produced by the traditional method often quickly crowd each other and must be removed at an early age to reduce transplant shock.

Plug method

In the late 1970s and early 1980s, the plug method of seedling production was developed. In plug production, seeds are sown in specialized plug trays that are partitioned into individual cells, ranging from 50 to 800 cells per tray. The seedling produced in each cell is called a plug. Four maturity stages of seedling growth have been defined to reflect physiological changes from germination to transplanting from the plug tray [11]. The first stages occur during germination and early seedling growth, the last two occur as seedlings actively grow and mature (table 10.1).

Plug trays approximate a standard finishing flat's dimensions, although depth may vary from as little as one-fourth inch up to 2 inches depending on individual plug size. The plug method provides several advantages over the traditional method. One of the most important is the separation of root systems of each individual seedling; each root system is segregated, root competition is absent, and seedlings can develop strong root systems. Damage to the rootball is minimal, the root ball remains intact, and little or no transplant shock occurs. Early plant growth continues after transplanting with no setback.

The plug method's second major advantage is the ability to grow plants in plugs for a longer time before seedlings must be transplanted. Seedlings may remain as plugs for six weeks longer than comparable seedlings grown under the traditional method [4]. There is no urgency to immediately transplant plug-grown seedlings like there is with traditionally grown seedlings. The ability to grow seedlings in the plug container for a longer time allows greater flexibility in scheduling crops. If necessary, plug-grown seedlings can be placed in cold storage to hold the plants for longer time periods [7, 8].

Plug production is a rapidly evolving technology, and the plug method requires unique growing techniques. Irrigation, fertility, media, and cultivar selection need greater attention. Specialized equipment and competent operators are also necessary for plug production.

Although production is more complex with plugs than with traditional methods, production efficiency is greatly increased. In the United States, at least 75% of the bedding plants sold are grown from plugs and represent about 1.5 billion plants [5].

Plug usage

The plug seedling production method has spawned new categories of growers within the bedding plant trade (fig. 10.1). Plug growers may be specialists who produce plugs for sale to growers who finish them, or they may produce plugs for their own finishing. The finisher may purchase plugs from the plug specialist to finish the majority of crops.

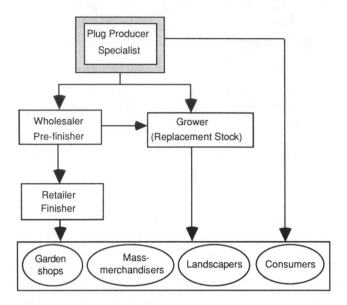

Fig. 10.1 Plug distribution chain.

Many growers utilize a combination of methods; for example, a grower may produce some crops by the traditional method and purchase plugs of more difficult to germinate species.

All growers benefit from this type of arrangement; the plug producer concentrates on producing a transplantable plug, and the finisher avoids the equipment requirements as well as production problems associated with the early stages of growing plugs. In addition, a finisher can purchase plugs to replace seedlings lost to mishandling or disease during the production process or totally eliminate in-house production of seedlings.

Converting from the traditional to the plug method

Converting from the traditional to the plug method requires effort on the producer's part. The producer must obtain proper equipment and must also alter or abandon many of his growing practices to develop a new protocol for seedling production. A plug tray's limited soil volume is much less forgiving than a seed tray's higher volume. Problems of drying out, high soluble salt levels, and overwatering can quickly occur if growers are not vigilant. Early attempts at plug production often ended in disaster.

Once plug production rudiments have been mastered, the entire operation's efficiency can increase. A more accurate inventory of seedlings for transplanting may be maintained when plugs are used; the number of empty cells can be quickly estimated, allowing an accurate determination of viable seedlings. Estimating the number of seedlings in a traditional flat is considerably more time consuming. Plug trays are also easier to handle with less damage when they must be moved. The large soil volume in a traditional flat can be quite heavy compared to the lighter plug tray.

Space utilization differences

Another primary difference between the two methods is space utilization. Costs of production are often calculated as cost per square foot per week. Overhead expenses per plant can be reduced if the number of square feet required in the greenhouse or the time spent in the greenhouse can be reduced. Overall, the plug system reduces both space and time requirements per plant, and the faster turnover allows for increased production.

The plug method does, however, require more space in the germination area, and the number of seedlings per plug tray may be less than in traditional seed flats. Number of seedlings per plug tray varies with plug size, but averages 128 to 400 seedlings. Seed trays planted according to the traditional method may have more seedlings per tray, yet occupy the same square footage of germination area. Space savings are gained in other areas of production when plugs are used.

The plug method reduces overall space and time requirements because seedlings remain in the plug tray longer than seedlings in a flat. Traditionally grown seedlings must be transplanted to the finishing container at an early age, or they crowd each other. Thus, they occupy their finishing space (i.e. maximum space) very early in the crop cycle. Plug-grown seedlings are held much longer in the plug trays, and a smaller area is required to produce the same number of plants for several weeks of the crop cycle. Because plugs are confined to a smaller area for a longer period of time, heating large sections of greenhouse space may be delayed, reducing overhead costs significantly.

Many tasks involved in producing a bedding plant crop can be performed more economically while the plugs occupy a smaller space. Watering, fertilizing, insect and disease control, and growth regulator applications can be accomplished with less effort in a smaller space. More efficient fungicide applications are also possible.

Growth enhancement techniques

Growth enhancement techniques that are not economical with traditional seed flats can be used successfully in plug production. Supplemental lighting of bedding plant crops such as seed geraniums reduces time to flower and improves plant quality [1]. Supplemental light is most effective when plants are young. The cost to install supplemental lighting in production houses for young plants grown by the traditional method is usually prohibitive, but with plugs, a smaller production area needs to be illuminated. By reducing equipment costs and cost per plant, supplemental lighting can be a profitable technique.

Carbon dioxide fertilization lends itself more easily to plug production for the same reasons. Elevating carbon dioxide in the plug production area can reduce time to transplant and time to flower by several weeks [9, 10]. Many large growers accomplish plug production in growth rooms, at least for a part of the life cycle, where temperature can be maintained without outside ventilation. Elevated CO_2 levels can easily be maintained under these conditions. As little as two weeks of supplemental CO_2 at 1,000 ppm can reduce overall time to flower.

In all areas of the country, CO_2 fertilization in the greenhouse is much more profitable with plugs than with traditional production; in the South, however, where ventilation occurs even during the winter months, it is more difficult to realize additional plant quality than in the North.

Differences in equipment

No special equipment is required to sow seeds in traditional flats. The grower's greatest concern is to sow the seeds in even rows across the flat or pack.

Seeds are easily sown by shaking the open seed packet over the soil surface. Sowing can be facilitated by using vibrating seed troughs or simple seed shakers, which are a minimal cost. With exceptionally small seeds, such as begonias or petunias, sand can be mixed with the seed allowing an easily monitored seed application rate.

Sowing seed into plug trays requires specialized equipment. A seeder is very important and costs from several hundred to several thousand dollars. Most seeders employ some type of manifold with a series of nipples using a vacuum source and compressed air to transfer seeds from a seed trough to the plug tray. While the equipment is more expensive, seeders are faster and more precise than hand sowing, which saves labor cost and reduces waste.

Individual manifolds can be expensive and increase plug production equipment costs. A different set of manifolds are required for each plug tray density used with most seeders. Seed size also influences the number of manifolds required. Small seeds, such as petunias or begonias, require a manifold with very small openings while larger seeds require larger openings, enabling the vacuum to lift the heavier seed.

The plug tray selection is also important. Trays must be compatible with the seeder to ensure proper seed placement; the number of plug cells per tray varies and density may range from 50 to 800 cells per plug tray. Premium plants such as seed geraniums are produced at low densities to preserve each seedling's quality. Easier to grow seedlings (for example, lobularia) may be sown at higher densities to conserve space. Traditional seedling flats can be used for any crop produced and are often cleaned and reused during the crop cycle finishing phase. Only plug trays specific to the seeder and to germination can be used to grow the plugs.

The traditional seedling method does not rely on specialized equipment; it can be performed in any convenient location. Usually seeds are sown in the immediate germination area, reducing handling of seed flats. Costly automatic seeders, however, can be affected by dust and high humidity found in the germination area and should be housed in a protected place. Protection is important—an entire sowing and subsequent production schedule is easily upset when a seeder is down for repair. A remote location increases the handling of the planted plug trays.

Seed requirement differences

Handling tiny or odd shaped seed is a problem, regardless of production method. Uniform sowing of such seeds is difficult because seeds may clump together, especially under high humidity, causing several seeds to be sown in the same location. This can occur during hand sowing and even when the proper manifolds are used on seeders.

Non-uniform sowing is a more serious problem in plug trays because a high-quality plug flat cannot have empty cells or cells with three to four seedlings. Adjusting plug flats is costly and time consuming.

To alleviate problems associated with very small seed, many seed companies offer pelleted seed—seeds coated with an inert substance that dissolves after sowing. Coated seeds are larger and more uniform in shape and can be handled by a seeder more efficiently. Other seeds, such as marigolds, may be sold as de-tailed seed, which permits easier handling by a mechanical seeder.

High germination percentage is more important for plug production than for traditional seedling flats. In the traditional method, up to 1,000 seeds may be scattered over the seed flat and unless germination is exceptionally low, non-germinating seeds are not easily detected. In plug production, seeds are singled out to individual cells. At 90% germination, a 406-plug tray will have 40 empty cells per tray and will be considered poor quality.

The seed industry was forced to improve seed for use in automatic seeders and has developed higher quality seed (hi-tech, refined seed, primed seed) to provide better uniformity of germination than standard seed. Plug production has resulted in better seed technology, superior seed quality, and far better quality control by seed producers. The seed industry might not have advanced so quickly without the plug producers' demands.

Differences in irrigation

Of the many problems encountered in bedding plant production, those associated with irrigation are constant. Flats used for traditional seeding have a much larger soil volume than the standard plug tray, which provides a cushion against rapid changes in soil moisture content. The small soil volume in plug trays is vulnerable to a greater damage risk if watering practices are not closely monitored.

In traditional seedling flats, water is absorbed over the large surface area and has less runoff than plug trays. The dry and wet areas left by an inexperienced irrigator are more likely to equalize within the flat due to capillary action through the soil. Irrigation is less frequent because the soil volume has a significantly greater water holding capacity compared with a plug cell.

Watering a plug tray requires a more experienced technique. The small amount of soil calls for more frequent irrigation, with less water volume. If soil moisture levels are not closely watched, seedlings can easily dry out. Seedlings produced in plugs are especially vulnerable to improper watering during the critical time between germination and early development.

During these early growth phases, overall plant growth can be permanently reduced if the seedlings receive too little or too much water. Uneven water application is of special concern with plugs; since the seedlings are growing in separate cells, water cannot move from cell to cell by capillary action. As a result, one seedling can be dry to the point of wilting while the seedling immediately adjacent to it may be waterlogged.

Apply water as evenly as possible to reduce this problem. Areas that dry out can be carefully re-watered, but it is difficult to avoid soaking already moist areas surrounding dry seedlings. Lack of attention to detail is most obvious in the plug irrigation area, and its importance cannot be over-emphasized.

Water application. Many water application means are used. The cheapest and potentially poorest method is overhead irrigation where water is applied from a hose equipped with a fine mist nozzle. This can be detrimental for both plug and traditional production systems—seeds can be washed away under high water pressure or coarse mist.

In traditional flat systems, seeds can be washed together to one area of the flat, overcrowding seedlings. In a plug tray, seeds may be washed out of individual cells into others, so that several seedlings will emerge from a single cell. This, of course, defeats the purpose of using the plug method in the first place.

Overhead watering does not have to be detrimental in plug production; in fact, many well respected growers do nothing but hand watering. If you use overhead watering, exercise care in equipment selection and water placement to avoid disturbing the planted seeds. Take the greatest care, however, in selecting the person controlling the hose.

Automated watering. An automated watering system provides uniform irrigation. One example is the boom system, consisting of a series of fine nozzles attached to a water source that is mechanically drawn at a predetermined rate over the plug flats. Each boom waters plugs of the same age, growing in similar cell densities.

When water is applied by hand, some areas inevitably receive more water than others, resulting in wet and dry spots. Because boom movement is motor driven and maintained at a constant velocity, water is applied at the same rate to all plug trays, practically eliminating problem areas on the bench.

However, human attention is still required when using a boom system, since someone must decide when to turn the boom on, as well as keep it in good running order. An obstructed nozzle, kinked hose, or misplaced plug tray can defeat the built-in efficiency of a boom system. Although a boom system provides excellent results for most plug irrigation, it is an expensive piece of equipment for many growers.

Boom waterers are useless on a bench where plugs of different ages and/or densities are growing. Fog systems and overhead sprinklers are also used to irrigate plugs, with similar benefits and shortcomings.

Subirrigation. Subirrigation systems are also successful with plug trays. Water is applied from below the flats so that the seeds are not disturbed. Flood benches are commonly used, where seed trays are placed on water-tight benches after sowing. When irrigation is required, the bench is flooded with water to a level below the tray surface. Water then moves into the cells through capillary action. After sufficient time, water is removed from the bench, and the seed trays are allowed to drain excess water.

Subirrigation can be used with either traditional seedling flats or the plug method, although the plug system really lends itself to this type of irrigation. The small soil volume works as an advantage for capillary action. The lower profile also allows water to move into the plug tray at a faster rate. Capillary matting, moist sand, or some other media that can deliver sufficient water to seed tray base can also be used successfully.

There is a cost associated with developing a subirrigation system. Special benches are required if flooding is to be used, and capillary matting or some other absorptive surface must be applied to existing benches. This type of application significantly reduces the hazards of such overhead watering as uneven moisture levels across a plug tray.

Watering practices. As plugs germinate and grow, watering practices must be adjusted to meet the developing plants' changing needs. Since plug trays dry out more easily than traditional flats, carefully observe germinating seedlings to prevent tender seedlings from desiccating. As seedlings mature, reduce watering to harden the seedlings prior to transplanting. Water application is a critical factor for bedding plant growers, regardless of the production method.

Water quality. Water quality has a significant impact on growth and development of any greenhouse crop, but is specially relevant to plug production. Due to the small soil volume, seedlings are not well protected from extremes in pH, soluble salts, or other water properties. Plants grown in traditional flats with larger soil volume, although still affected by water quality, are better buffered. It is essential to test water quality before starting a plug production program.

Improper watering practices can lead to disease problems regardless of production method. Many of the water molds common to bedding plants thrive in wet conditions and can quickly decimate a crop. Plug-grown seedlings are more isolated from each other, so the spread of disease is slower, resulting in fewer infected seedlings.

Media differences

Media used for germination and seedling growth is a critical concern in producing plugs. The mix must be sufficiently fine-textured to ensure even cell filling, but sufficiently coarse to allow drainage and aeration. The small cell volume in plug trays introduces a greater risk of error. Good water-holding capacity is necessary to prevent the seedlings from drying out too quickly. Sphagnum-based medium is a good choice but requires screening to remove any clumps or small sticks. Specially prepared soils are available for use in plug production, or homemade mixtures may be preferred.

The cell density in a plug tray has a major influence on the media properties. Fonteno [6] showed that the same medium's water container capacity and aeration significantly differed as the plug density increased. When density was increased from 288 to 648 cells per flat, the aeration in each cell decreased from 8.8% to 4.1% when coarse vermiculite was used. When the medium was 3:1 vermiculite:peat, aeration dropped from 2.9% (288 cells) to 0.6% (648 cells).

Fertility differences

Traditionally grown seedlings are removed from the seed flat and transplanted at an early age to the finishing container. Fertilization is usually initiated after transplanting. Slow growing seedlings, such as begonias, may require one or two light applications of fertilizer to spur growth. High fertilizer applications to the seed flat could be detrimental by introducing high soluble salts levels or by accelerating growth to the point that the seedlings become overcrowded or too lush.

Plug-grown seedlings benefit from a balanced fertilization program while still in the plug stage. Without an adequate nutrient supply, the seedlings can become stunted, delaying flowering and reducing overall quality. Use caution in plug production to ensure soluble salts do not reach levels injurious to seedlings. The small soil volume is susceptible to soluble salt level fluctuations.

Height control differences

Growth regulator applications are usually not made until traditionally grown seedlings have been transplanted and are vigorously growing. When grown in plug trays, seedlings often benefit from one or more light growth regulator applications, usually at a more dilute concentration than applied to a transplanted seedling. The treated seedlings are more likely to remain compact and sturdy, facilitating their handling during transplanting.

Because of the frequent water requirements of plug grown seedlings, an experienced grower can alter the irrigation schedule for some degree of plug height control. Water can be an effective growth retardant if applied properly; however, previous experience and careful observation are important when using this form of control, because seedlings are easily damaged or killed if water is applied improperly.

The success or failure of height control using day/night temperature

References

[1]   Armitage, A.M. 1988. Supplemental lighting of plugs: basic questions and answers. *Greenhouse Grower* 6(2):48-49.

[2]   ——. 1993. *Bedding plants: prolonging shelf performance*. Batavia, Ill.: Ball Publishing.

[3]   ——. 1994. Ornamental bedding plants. In: *Ornamental production science in horticulture 2*. Wallingford, U.K.: C-A-B International.

[4]   Carlson, W.H., M.P. Kaczperski, and E.M. Rowley. 1992. Bedding plants. In: *Introduction to floriculture*. 2nd ed. Ed. R.A. Larson. San Diego: Academic Press, San Diego.

[5]   Dill, R. 1993. Powerhouses of the plug industry. *Greenhouse Grower* 11(11):10-11.

[6]   Fonteno, W.C. 1988. Know your media, the air, water and container connection. *GrowerTalks* 51(11):110-111.

[7]   Heins, R.D., and N. Lange. 1992. Development of systems for storage of bedding plant plugs. Research report #F-056. Bedding Plant Foundation Incorporated.

[8]   Kaczperski, M.P., and A.M. Armitage. 1992. Short-term storage of plug-grown bedding plant seedlings. *HortSci.* 27:798-800.

[9]   ——. 1993. Preconditioning plug-grown geraniums with temperature and fertility before storage. *HortSci.* 28:572 (Abst.).

[10] Kessler, J.R., and A.M. Armitage. 1993. Effects of carbon dioxide, light and temperature on seedling growth of *Begonia* x *semperflorens-cultorum. Hort Sci.* 68:281-287.

[11] Koranski, D., and P. Karlovich. 1989. Plugs: problems, concerns and recommendations for the grower. *GrowerTalks* 53(8):28, 30, 32, 34.

CHAPTER 11

Growing Media

William C. Fonteno

There is no one growing medium that is best for producing bedding plants. Plants have evolved with the ability to grow in almost any medium and in a multitude of environments. It is precisely this ability that allows growers to manipulate plant growth for specific markets and conditions. Bedding plants can be successfully produced in a wide variety of growing media or substrates. The selection of a substrate is dependent on component and equipment availability, the growing operation size, the operator expertise, and irrigation management. The keys to proper substrate management are: (1) the attitude of the grower and (2) the people involved in selection, use, and handling of materials.

The grower's attitude is important. In the 1950s, one mark of a good grower was the soil mix that he or she made. In fact, many of the cultural problems encountered by growers in that era could be traced to problems in blending their mix. In the 1960s, the Cornell and University of California soilless mixes eliminated many of the problems associated with low aeration and over-watering. However, today, growers still have many misconceptions about substrates.

Substrate functions

A substrate must serve four functions: 1) to provide water, 2) to supply nutrients, 3) to permit gas exchange to and from the roots, and 4) to provide support for the plants. Unfortunately, some have thought that these properties are immediately present after the components are blended. The only function that is guaranteed after blending is plant support. The other three are still grower-controlled. Otherwise, why would the same mix perform differently for different growers?

A more successful approach to substrates is to think in terms of creating and managing the bedding plant's subsurface environment. This environment is created by: 1) selecting the components, 2) blending these components and additives, 3) filling flats and/or pots, and 4) initial watering of flats after transplanting.

A useful way of thinking about this process is to envision steps of a staircase (fig. 11.1). Creating this subsurface environment is done by climbing each step in order until you reach the top. The subsurface environment is not set until the bedding plants are placed in the greenhouse and watered-in. Once the environment is set, however, it is not constant. It changes as roots grow and explore the substrate. Even during the day, the environment can change hourly as water is removed by the plant and replaced by the grower.

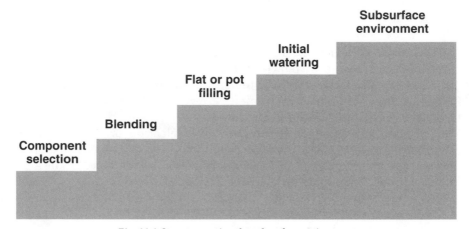

Fig. 11.1 Steps to creating the subsurface environment

Desirable substrate properties

Substrate properties are defined as:

A *substrate* is any material or combination of materials used to provide support, water retention, aeration, or nutrient retention for plant growth. This is the standard term today. Other similar terms are: medium (plural = media) and mix.

A *component* is a single material that is combined in volumetric proportions with other components to achieve a desired air, water, nutrient ratio for plant growth. Examples are peat moss, pine bark, perlite, vermiculite, etc.

Total porosity is the percent volume of a substrate or component that is comprised of pores or holes. This is the volume fraction that provides the water and aeration in a substrate. *Total porosity + percent solids = 100% of the substrate volume.*

Container capacity is the percent volume of a substrate or component that is filled with water after the substrate is saturated and allowed to drain. It is the maximum amount of water (or capacity) the material can hold. Since drainage is influenced by the substrate height, *this property depends on container size.* The taller the container, the more drainage it will cause and the less substrate capacity to hold water.

Air space is the percent volume of a substrate or component that is filled with air after the material is saturated and allowed to drain. It is the minimum amount of air the material will have. Air space is affected by container height in reverse fashion to container capacity— the taller the container, the more drainage and therefore more air space. *For a given density and moisture content, air space = total porosity – container capacity.*

Bulk density is the ratio of dry solids mass to the substrate bulk volume. The bulk volume includes the volume of solids and pore space. The mass is determined after drying to constant weight at 105 C (221 F), and volume is that of the substrate in the container. Values are expressed as pounds/cubic feet or grams/cc.

Unavailable water (PWP) is the percent volume of a substrate or component containing water that is unavailable to the plant. This is also called the permanent wilting percentage (PWP). This is defined as the amount of water remaining at 1.5 mPa (approximately -15 atmospheres). This property is a measure of the substrate's inefficiency to provide water to the plant.

Moisture content is the percent moisture found in a substrate/component sample on a wet mass basis. This is calculated by: *[(wet weight – dry weight)/wet weight] x 100.* This is the common format for most data. It denotes how much water a particular sample is comprised of.

The pH is a measure of hydrogen ion (H+) concentration found in the substrate and controls the availability of all essential plant nutrients. The pH range is from 0 to 14, with pH 7 being neutral; below 7 is acid and above 7 is alkaline. The pH is the logarithm of the reciprocal of the H+ ion concentration. This means that a pH value of 6 has 10 times more H+ ions than a pH value of 7, and a pH value of 5 has 100 times more H+ than pH 7.

Soluble salts are mineral salts that are found in the substrates. They come from fertilizers, impurities in water sources, and organic matter, such as manures and substrate components. They are the basis of nutrition in substrates.

Cation exchange capacity is the substrate's ability to regulate the supply of certain nutrients to the plant. It is defined as the sum of the exchangeable cations (positively charged nutrients) that a substrate can absorb per unit weight. For field soils this is usually expressed as milligram equivalents per 100 grams of substrate, but for soilless mixes it expressed as milligram equivalents per 100 cubic centimeters (meq/100 cc).

Bedding plant substrates should have a light bulk density to ease handling and shipping. For this reason, organic matter is usually a large percentage of the final mix. The organic matter must persist throughout the crop, not cause significant volume changes, and must be chemically stable to prevent a crop's nitrogen depletion. Initial nutrient content (soluble salts) should be low so it won't damage sensitive young plants and seedlings. Cation exchange capacity should be high for ample nutrient reserves (6 to 15 meq/100 cc). The pH should range from 5.4 to 6.0 for soilless mixes and 6.2 to 6.8 for substrates that contain mineral soil at volumes plus or minus 20%. Air and water volume are not properties of the substrates alone but are affected by container size, handling and flat filling, and watering practices.

TABLE 11.1

Substrate components and formulations[a]

Material	Solid fraction	Total porosity	Container capacity	Air space	Available water	Bulk density wet[b]	Bulk density dry[c]
Soil (sandy clay)	53.3	46.7	43.9	2.8	37.5	106.0	85.3
Sand (concrete grade)	59.3	40.7	39.7	0.9	35.3	107.1	87.8
Sphagnum peat moss	15.4	84.6	81.4	3.2	59.4	53.7	22.0
Vermiculite (Progro #2)	17.3	82.7	58.7	14.0	36.7	46.1	31.1
Pine bark (aged, >³/₈")	20.7	79.3	66.5	12.7	36.5	50.6	32.7
Perlite (Krum, hort grade)	36.9	63.1	45.3	17.9	40.3	32.1	20.8
Polystryene beads	64.6	35.4	19.0	16.4	14.0	7.5	1.6
Rockwool (Pargro, medium)	8.9	91.1	76.0	15.2	71.6	54.4	16.5

[a] In a 48-cell pack bedding plant tray.
[b] Bulk density of components at container capacity.
[c] Bulk density at permanent wilting percentage (-15 atmospheres).

Substrate components

Substrates are made up of two or more components. Common components are mineral soil, sand, sphagnum peat moss, vermiculite, pine bark, perlite, polystyrene beads, and rockwool. The physical properties of these materials are listed in table 11.1.

Soil-based and soilless substrates. Substrates are generally divided into two groups. Soil-based substrates contain some portion of field mineral soil, such as a sandy-loam. In 1963, Drs. James Boodley and Raymond Sheldrake introduced the Cornell peat-lite mixes which contained no mineral soil. Equal quality plants can be produced from soil-based and soilless mixes. However, the irrigation and fertility regimes are markedly different.

The peat-lite mixes are generally more uniform, light weight, drain more quickly, provide better aeration, and hold more water and nutrients than soil-based mixes. Although soil-based mixes are still used, the majority of growers use peat-lite mixes they either blend themselves or buy commercially.

Pore space. A major difference between soil-based and soilless mixes is total pore space. Most mineral soils have approximately 50% solids and 50% pore space by volume. Most organically-based substrates will have between 75% and 85% pore space. This increased pore space improves the substrate's water and air holding capacities in containers. It also makes these soilless mixes more susceptible to mishandling during blending and flat or pot filling.

Water content. Another major difference between soil-based and soilless mixes is the unavailable water content. When water is applied to a substrate, a thin film of water binds so tightly to the substrate particles that the root cannot pull it from the soil, and it is not available to the plant. Mineral soils and soil-based mixes generally having only 5% to 10% of the substrate volume contain water unavailable to the plant. However, soilless mixes have 20% to 25% of their volume filled with water the plant cannot see. Because total porosity and unavailable water in soilless substrates are vastly different from soil-based mixes, growers must not treat them similarly but need a fundamentally different approach when using soilless substrates.

Suggested formulations

A formula for a typical peat-lite mix is listed in table 11.2. Most commercially available mixes are variations on this formula. While the

TABLE 11.2

Cornell Peat-lite Mix A for seedlings, bedding plants, and potted plants.

Materials	Cubic yard	Bushel
Sphagnum peat moss	0.5 cubic yard (13 bushels)[a]	0.5 bushel
Horticultural grade vermiculite #2 (germination) #2 or #3 for transplanting	0.5 cubic yard (13 bushels)[a]	0.5 bushel
Superphosphate	1 to 2 pounds	20.5 to 41.0 grams (1 to 2 tablespoons)
or Treble superphosphate[b]	0.5 to 1 pound	10.3 to 20.5 grams (0.6 to 1.2 tablespoons)
Ground dolomitic limestone[b]	5 to 10 pounds	103 to 206 grams (5.2 to 10.4 tablespoons)
Gypsum[b]	2.0 pounds	41 grams (2.5 tablespoons)
Calcium nitrate	0.5 pound	10 grams (1.2 tablespoons)
Potassium nitrate	0.5 pound	10 grams (1.2 tablespoons)
Trace element material (Use only one)		
Esmigran, Perk or	4.0 pounds	81 grams (4.0 tablespoons)
Micromax	1.5 pounds	31 grams (1.7 tablespoons)
Wetting agent (Use only one[c])		
Aqua-Gro 2000 granular or Aqua-Gro 2000 • L liquid[d]	1.0 pound 5 fluid ounces or 3 fluid ounces	0.5 level teaspoon

Source: Adapted from Table 8.1 of The Commercial Greenhouse by James W. Boodley, and Table 3 of *1989 Cornell Bedding Plant Guidelines for New York State,* T.C. Weiler, ed.

[a] A cubic yard equals 27 cubic feet, or approximately 22 bushels. A 15% to 20% shrink occurs in mixing. Therefore, an additional 5 cubic feet or 4 bushels are used to obtain a full cubic yard. For the bushel of mix, make a proportionate increase.

[b] If treble superphosphate is used, gypsum is added to supply sulphur. If only 5 pounds of limestone are used for pH control, then add the gypsum, which supplies calcium and sulphur.

[c] The granular Aqua-Gro is preferred.

[d] 5 ounces per yard for bedding plants and pot plants; 3 ounces per yard for germination and seedlings.

TABLE 11.3

Soil-based media formulations

1 part field soil	1 part sphagnum peat moss	1 part coarse vermiculite or perlite
2 parts silty clay soil	1 part sphagnum peat	
1 part sandy soil	2 parts muck peat	
1 part sandy soil	1 part sphagnum peat moss	1 part muck peat
1 part sand soil	2 parts sphagnum peat moss	
2 parts muck peat	1 part perlite calcined clay or	
	expanded polystyrene	

component complement may change among commercially available mixes, the resulting physical and chemical properties will be similar.

Soil-based formulations are listed in table 11.3. These formulations should be tested on a small portion of the crops to be grown to determine proper fertility and watering practices. All field soil must be decontaminated before blending. Pasteurization (preferably with aerated steam) gives the best results. Chemical cleaning with methyl bromide will work but should not be used with sensitive crops, such as carnation, snapdragon, and salvia. Remember, the keys to producing a successful mix is the grower's attitude and the people who handle, mix, and fill the flats.

Mixing options

Growers can prepare their own formulation or obtain a commercially prepared mix. To mix or purchase the substrate is a management and economic decision. In addition to the cost of mixing equipment and raw materials, growers must factor skilled labor, consequences of mixing errors, and quality control testing into the cost of making their own mixes. When deciding on a commercial mix, choose a reputable company with a well-developed quality assurance program and technical assistance for trouble shooting, rather than a particular product.

Generally, it is less expensive for growers with less than 50,000 square feet of greenhouse space to purchase commercial mixes rather than mix their own. Growers with over 100,000 square feet who are willing to commit time and resources to quality control may find some economic advantage in mixing their own, although the price of commercial mixes decreases as order volume increases.

mix will drain, the less water the mix can hold, and the more the air space will increase.

Air space in bedding plant flats should range from 5% to 10%, while plug flats should range from 2% to 5%. The air and water content of four substrates in 6-inch (15 cm) pots, 4-inch (10 cm) pots, a 48-cell bedding plant flat, and a 512-cell plug tray are shown in table 11.4. For example, in 6-inch (15 cm) pots, the soil-based mix had only 7% air space while the soilless mixes had 19% to 23%. As container size decreased, all mixes decreased in air space and increased in water content. When air space decreases, the chance of plant damage due to overwatering increases. Generally, greater air space in these ranges enhanced root growth and promoted a better start for seedlings and transplants.

Air/water relationships

Pot and flat filling also influences a substrate's air and water relations. Compaction's effect on a peat:vermiculite mix is shown in table 11.5. For a 48-cell bedding plant flat, air space dropped from 9% to 2% with increasing packing density, while unavailable water content rose from 21% to 30%. Substrate compaction reduces air space, increases the chance of overwatering, and reduces the mix's ability to provide water and nutrients to the plant.

Whether done by hand or by machine, flats and pots should be filled to excess, then brushed or scraped level to the container's top. Take care not to stack pots or flats directly over one another, as this increases compaction.

Excessive shrinkage in the container after initial watering is caused by low moisture content in the substrate, not from light container packing. If excessive shrinkage is a problem, increase the water content in the substrate prior to filling the container—do not pack more substrate into the container. Maximum effect will occur when the moistened substrate is allowed to equilibrate overnight and is agitated just prior to container filling.

Summary

The best subsurface environment will be created by:
- Acquiring an attitude of creating the subsurface environment;
- Using well-trained personnel for blending, container filling, and transplanting;
- Following the steps in fig. 11.1.

References

[1] Baker, K.F., ed. 1957. *The UC system for producing healthy container-grown plants.* Manual 23. Berkeley: Univ. of California Agri. Exp. Sta. and Ext. Ser.

[2] Boodley, J.W., and R. Sheldrake, Jr. 1982. *Cornell peat-lite mixes for commercial plant growing.* Ext. Inf. Bul. 43. NY State College of Agri. and Life Sci.

[3] Bunt, A.C. 1988. *Media and mixes for container-grown plants.* London: Unwin Hyman.

[4] Fonteno, W.C. 1991. *A common misconception about substrates.* N.C. Comm. Flower Growers' Bull. 36(3):1-4.

[5] Fonteno, W.C. 1991. Media considerations for plug production. In *Proceedings,* Plug Symposium, International Floriculture Industry Short Course, July 13, 1991.

[6] White, J.W. 1985. Growing Media. In *Bedding plants III: A Penn State manual* Ed. J.W. Mastalerz and E.J. Holcomb.

[7] Milks, R.R., W.C. Fonteno and R.A. Larson. 1989. Hydrology of horticultural substrates: III. Predicting air and water content in limited-volume plug cells. *J. Amer. Soc. Hort. Sci.* 114:57-61.

[8] Nelson, P.V. 1991. *Greenhouse operation and management.* 4th ed. Englewood Cliffs, N.J.: Prentice Hall.

CHAPTER 12

Irrigation

Robert W. Langhans and Ellen T. Paparozzi

Irrigation controls plant growth, plant size, timing, and quality, so it is necessary to use the best practices. In the past, bedding plants were commonly irrigated daily and with relatively large quantities of water. Today, growers must account for water and avoid excessive use.

Seed germination

Water imbibition is the first process in seed germination. It is critical during this stage to ensure no drying out, or the sprouting seedling will be lost. Most seeding is done in areas where the relative humidity is high and danger of drying out is reduced (see Chapter 9 for more details on various seed germination systems). Correct moisture content of the medium is critical for the success of any seed germination system. Some seeds do best in rather wet conditions and others do not; be sure to check each species' requirements.

Asexual propagation

The only way for water to enter a vegetative cutting is through the cut end of the stem. This restricts the amount of water taken up. Thus, cuttings must be protected from excessive water loss. Mist or fog systems accomplish this well by keeping the leaves cool and by increasing the relative humidity of the surrounding air, both of which reduce transpiration. (See Chapter 28 on asexual propagation).

Growth

Water is absorbed from the medium around the roots and moves up the stem via the xylem and into the leaves. Most of the water is lost to the air through the stomata (small openings on the leaf surface) by transpiration. A small portion of water is retained by the cells and creates pressure. This pressure allows the cells to enlarge, and consequently the whole plant grows. This pressure (turgor) gives the stems and leaves support. When water is limited, the pressure is diminished, and the plant wilts.

A smaller quantity of water is used in the photosynthesis process, which produces sugars and serves as the energy source for most plant growth. For most bedding plants, the water usage ratio would be 100 water units for transpiration, 1 water unit for the plant growth, and 0.1 water units for photosynthesis.

Transpiration is important because leaves are cooled as water evaporates from the stomata. The transpiration stream also moves dissolved nutrients (nitrogen, phosphorus, potassium, calcium, iron, etc.) from the media solution to plant cells. During some stages of propagation it is beneficial to limit transpiration, but for most growth stages, transpiration is necessary for plant temperature control, carbon dioxide uptake, and nutrient supply.

Withholding water reduces plant growth and is sometimes used as an inexpensive growth regulator. Experienced growers may know when to withhold water to reduce growth without negatively affecting plant quality; however, the inexperienced grower may overdo the process, resulting in poor plant quality. When withholding water to control growth consider that: 1) time and greenhouse space cost money, and withholding water slows growth and increases bench time; and 2) plant quality is of prime importance. Most growers supply sufficient water at all times and use other growth regulation methods to adjust plant size.

Withholding water is also used to harden plants or make them more resistant to transplant shock. This is a difficult point to define or describe, and most inexperienced growers overdo the hardening off process resulting in plant quality loss.

Watering systems—general problems

Uniformity. Devising a watering system for bedding plants that applies water quickly and uniformly is difficult. Pot watering systems are usually very uniform and quick. Problems include the challenge of providing adequate water to more than one species and/or plant size in an area. High density is common, and if the whole greenhouse floor is covered, accessibility to individual plants is limited. The solution is to apply enough water to the driest area (consequently overwatering the other areas), and adjust the watering frequency.

Wet foliage. A general rule for most floricultural crops is *do not wet the foliage*. Bedding plant operators ignore this rule and, in most cases, the disease incidence is not great. Subirrigation systems avoid wetting the foliage, but currently most operators use some form of overhead watering.

Rapid change in plant size and requirements. Watering schemes are complicated by plants that are closely spaced and rapid growing. In a few weeks they grow from small seedlings with a small water requirement to large plants that transpire large amounts of water. The bedding plant season spans the dark days of late winter and the bright days of late spring.

Media volume. Another complication is the volume of medium to plant ratio. When plants are ready for sale, the container's volume or water holding capacity may be too small for the plant's size. Make sure plants are irrigated frequently enough to adjust for the small water reservoir and large water loss of the plants.

Even the best irrigation system has compromises—a lack of uniform watering; overhead watering systems may wet the foliage and cause disease problems. Frequent irrigation is necessary for a small volume of medium.

Water stewardship

The public, government regulations, and regulatory organizations have made the greenhouse industry conscious of problems associated with runoff water from agricultural establishments. At one time, growers were concerned with pesticides contaminating runoff water, but research at Cornell University indicated no pesticides were found in greenhouse leachate. However, this research did show high fertilizer levels in the leachate.

What can we do to reduce or prevent this problem? The subirrigation watering method, where water is recirculated, is very effective. A judicious use of water and fertilizer will also help. A grower must be conscious of water runoff and consider ways to avoid potential problems.

Researchers at Cornell and other universities are working on such concepts as artificial wetlands, where the water is run through an artificial wetland in a greenhouse to remove nutrients before the water is released outside. In a zero runoff wetland, the leachate's nutrients are absorbed by plants, excessive nitrogen is denitrified, and water is transpired into the atmosphere.

When building a new greenhouse, consider using a plastic sheet under the greenhouse to retain all leachate. Leachate can drain into a storage basin and either be reused for watering plants or disposed of properly. Currently no regulations describe a correct solution to the problem.

Watering systems

There are five commonly used watering systems in the bedding plant industry: 1) hose, 2) overhead irrigation, 3) spray stakes, 4) automatic watering rigs or booms and 5) subirrigation.

Hose

The most common method used by a small operator is hose watering. It requires minimal capital outlay and can be successful when used by a competent person. It is probably the most expensive method because of labor costs involved. An untrained or careless employee can do a lot of plant/seedling damage by over or underwatering. Hose watering is time consuming, and on warm days it may be difficult to prevent plant damage from drying out.

Overhead irrigation

Water is applied to plants in a circular pattern by permanently installed flat spray nozzles. A number of different nozzles can be used. The common design is a series of nozzles that cover a 10- to 20-foot (3- to 6-m) diameter circle. The design depends on the greenhouse configuration and water pressure and volume. Height is usually not a consideration, as nozzles are placed overhead out of the way.

Nozzle selection is a series of compromises. Uniform application, a major consideration, is the most difficult to achieve. The spray pattern is a full circle, which means the four corners may not be reached. The water quantity from the nozzle (center of the circle) to the edge of the spray pattern will vary. Usually the plants closest to the nozzle receive the greatest quantity of water. Each overhead spray system must be custom designed, so it's best to work closely with the manufacturers' specifications and instructions.

After the system is installed, test the water distribution by placing coffee cans in a line along the circle radius, extending from the nozzle to the outer edge of the spray pattern. Turn the system on for five minutes, then measure the quantity of water in each can.

Adjusts according to those measurements to ensure an adequate amount of water to the driest area and not too much in the wettest. For example, if the average amount of water measured in the cans was 125 ml (4.4 oz.) and the area of each can was one-fourth square feet (0.025 m), an average 500 ml (17.6 oz.) of water was applied per square foot in five minutes. This is equal to about one pint (.4 l) per square foot (.1 m).

If there was a great variation in the measurements, the system may have to be altered. If the can under the nozzle contained 250 ml (8.8 oz.)

Fig. 12.1 Spray stakes for watering petunias.

of water and a can further away contained only 75 ml (2.6 oz.), the plants under the nozzle would be overwatered and the outer plants underwatered. The manager should determine the amount of water to apply to each pack or each square foot and add extra for leaching (5% to 10%). A pint (.4 l) per square foot (.1 m) is a good estimate for most artificial mixes that have not been allowed to get too dry. Each grower must make his or her own measurements.

Spray stake

The spray stake system is a 360-degree flat spray nozzle installed on top of a stake (fig. 12.1). Each stake is usually fed with a large diameter spaghetti tube, which is fed from a header. The system is relatively inexpensive to install and is flexible. A 6-foot spray pattern is usual, and the spacing of stakes and frequency of watering are determined by compromises. Individual nozzles can be turned off, an added advantage.

Automated watering rigs/booms

Uneven watering patterns of the above irrigation systems can be corrected by a moving overhead spray rig (fig. 12.2). The mechanism moving the rig is placed on a trolley over the greenhouse center walk, and

Fig. 12.2 An example of an automated watering boom.

the spray booms are placed wall to wall, usually 20 to 30 feet (6 to 9.1 m) wide. The nozzles on the spray boom are adjustable to improve water uniformity. The rig is propelled back and forth the length of the greenhouse by an electric or gasoline engine. The attached hose is dragged down the center aisle. Quantity of water applied is determined by calibrating the rig's speed over the ground, the water pressure, and nozzle type. The system can be automated, but most managers assign a person to watch the system, which is uniform and quick watering. The system is costly, however, and requires maintenance.

Subirrigation

Watering from below keeps leaves dry and allows more uniform watering of each container. When watering from above, leaves may deflect water away from the container.

Major problems associated with subirrigation are the logistics of setup and cost. Most bedding plants are grown on the greenhouse floor, which creates a problem. If plants are bench grown, the ebb and flow system works very well, and this same system can be used in off-season to water pot plants. When the crops are grown on the ground, the solution is more complex.

One solution is to concrete the greenhouse floor area and make it waterproof. The concrete must be carefully installed so that all containers are flooded (subirrigated) to the same level (about 1 inch [2.5 cm] deep) and when drained, no wet spots remain. The drained water is collected in a reservoir and reused for the next watering time or the next house in a series. The rule of thumb for the capacity of the reservoir is about three times the capacity needed to flood one area.

The operating system is simple. A float valve for the reservoir opens when the reservoir level goes down. The incoming water is supplemented with the proper fertilizer amount. The water is pumped (flooded) onto the greenhouse floor where packs of bedding plants are grown.

For example, it may require about 15 minutes to flood the floor; the water remains for another 15 minutes to irrigate the plants and then is drained back into the reservoir. About one-third to one-half of the flooded water will be retained in the packs (depending on the medium's dryness). The system floods the second greenhouse area as soon as it drains from the first. The water is ultimately returned to the reservoir.

Because this system eliminates runoff, it may become the common system in the future. Each grower should evaluate this system's potential implementation carefully. The most convenient and least expensive time to install this subirrigation system is during new construction. Retrofitting a greenhouse is more costly, particularly if greenhouse areas are a distance apart or if the ground level is uneven.

When to irrigate

When to water is an important question. The technical answer can be determined accurately by measuring the amount of water available in the medium. The practical answer is not that easy. Most growers use their experience to determine when to water. This is based on many considerations: weather (sunlight, temperature, relative humidity), crop size, medium, cultivar, work loads, etc.

When mineral soil was the major medium component, overwatering was a common problem. Today with the wide use of artificial mixes, overwatering is much less of a problem. Most media are designed to avoid overwatering. As a general rule, if the container has adequate drainage so water can't accumulate, overwatering is not a problem. During the peak season most plants should be watered daily.

Plant size to medium volume ratio is important, particularly for plug production. Plugs are a boon to the bedding plant industry but require a very careful watering program. Plant size as compared to volume of medium just before transplanting a plug can be very large. A sheet of plugs, just before transplanting, may need more watering than once per day. There is a very little water reserve and a large mass of roots in the plug medium.

Most growers anticipate watering needs by watering once a day. A grower can look at a plant and see it is flagging or wilting, pick up the pack and feel that it is light and know water is needed. This, however, is at a later stage of plant growth, and water should have been consistently applied before this stage.

The problem of deciding when to water is more complicated for bedding plant growers because they are working with many species, cultivars, and stages of growth (from seedling to flowering plants ready to sell). Each plant group has a different water requirement. The biggest plants with the greatest need must be watered frequently enough to prevent damage, and the youngest plants must not be overwatered. Again, artificial media drain quickly, so overwatering of even small seedlings is not common.

Controls for automatic watering

All watering systems, except the hose method, can be automated. On/off is operated by a solenoid valve placed in the water line to control a section's watering. The controller can range from a simple time clock to a computer. The time clock turns the system on and off, usually once a day for a determined on-time. The other end of the controller spectrum allows the watering control to be determined by an accumulation of light or evaporation of water. The computer then waters the whole greenhouse in sequence. The manager can also program the individual sections to adjust to the size of the plants, etc.

Water quality

Water quality can be a major problem, and a grower must inspect the water supply for potential problems, such as high soluble salts, excessive hardness, toxic ions, or other pollutants.

Soluble salts/electric conductivity

Soluble salts or electric conductivity (EC) measures the amount of salts dissolved in water. Some salts are needed as a mediator of fertilizer availability. The lower the EC reading, the less salts are dissolved in the water. Water diffuses into the roots by a process called osmosis, where water molecules move from a higher water concentration to a lower water concentration. Normally there exists a higher water concentration in the medium after irrigation, as water moves into the root system. However, if the irrigation water has a high soluble salt/EC reading, the salts concentration is higher in the media solution than inside the root. So, the water concentration is opposite (higher inside the root), and water moves out of the plant. The result is dehydration,

TABLE 12.1

Electrical Conductivity (EC) or soluble salts in water supply

EC readings (mS)	Suitability for irrigation
0-0.25	Excellent
0.26-0.6	Good
0.61-1.5	Fair
1.5+	Poor

and ultimately the plant dies. The EC water readings should be used as an indicator of irrigation requirements (table 12.1).

Fertilizers added to irrigation water increase the soluble salts content. Fertilizer added to the medium also increases the soluble salts. To avoid excess accumulation, the medium must be leached with clear water to remove salts and reduce the readings (table 12.2).

The instrument to measure the soluble salts/EC is easy to use. The probe contains two equal electrodes, and the instrument measures electrical conductance between the electrodes. The more salt in solution, the greater the current flow. This instrument should be calibrated to specific salt concentration. Every grower should have an EC meter as there are many questions or problems that can be easily solved with its use.

TABLE 12.2

Electrical Conductivity (EC) in soil and peat-lite mixes

Mineral soils	Peat-lite mixes		
(mS)		Interpretation	
2.0+	3.5+	Excessively high	Plants may be severely injured.
1.76-2.0	2.25-3.5	Very high	Plants may grow adequately, but range is near danger zone, especially if soil dries.
1.26-1.75	1.76-2.25	High	Satisfactory for established plants. May be too high for seedlings and cuttings.
0.51-1.25	1.0-1.76	Medium	Satisfactory for general plant growth. Excellent range for constant fertilization program.
0.0-0.50	0.0-1.0	Low	A low EC does no harm, but may indicate low nutrient content.

Note: Soil EC is tested using one part of dry soil to two parts of water. Peat-lite is tested using a level teaspoon of dry mix to 40 ml of water.

CHAPTER 13

Fertilization

Paul V. Nelson

This chapter addresses fertilization in all stages of bedding plant production, from plugs through the finish flat/pot stage. The Iowa State University production stage classification system that is used is defined as: Stage 1—from sowing to the point when the radicle (root) has emerged and bent downward; Stage 2—from bent radicle to first appearance of a true leaf; Stage 3—from initial perception of a true leaf to the point when the plug can be transplanted to a finish flat or pot; Stage 4—the time during which finished plugs are held prior to transplanting (this stage does not exist when finished plugs are planted immediately); Finish Stage—from transplanting of bare root or plug seedlings into the finish flat up to the time of retail market sale.

Bedding plants are generally classified in the lightly fertilized category; however, that does not reduce fertilization's importance. Fertilization is more difficult for bedding plants than for any other crop category. No single fertilizer scheme covers all species of bedding plants grown. Even within a bedding plant species, fertilizer rate and formulation must be altered according to growth stage, desired growth rate, and shifts in substrate pH level.

Substrate pH level will be carefully considered. When pH level is maintained within the prescribed range more than half of all greenhouse nutritional problems are prevented. Water quality will be considered first since it impacts the fertilization program, then fertilization program with the three dimensions of pre-plant fertilizers in the substrate, post-plant liquid fertilizer application, and the alternative of slow-release fertilizers in the substrate, and finally nutritional monitoring with the three ramifications of substrate testing, tissue testing, and visual observation.

A note of caution is in order for bedding plant fertilization recommendations. Research is in its infancy for plug fertilization and is far from complete for finish stage production. The precise timing of substrate sampling, substrate standards, most tissue standards, many nutrient disorder symptoms, and the concentration-frequency relationship for complete fertilizer application to meet individual species needs requires further study.

Take much of the information in this chapter as a guideline or a starting point. By keeping records you can match plant response with fertilizer practices and develop your own fertilization program.

Water quality

Be sure to test a sample of your irrigation water annually. The results can forecast many nutritional problems and suggest preventive strategies. Eight important water analyses are described, and the maximum acceptable levels of six analyses are presented in table 13.1.

TABLE 13.1

Maximum acceptable water quality indices for bedding plants

	Plug production	Finish flats and pots
pH [a] (acceptable range)	5.5 to 7.5	5.5 to 7.5
alkalinity [b]	1.5 me/l (75 ppm)	2.0 me/l (100 ppm)
hardness [c]	3.0 me/l (150 ppm)	3.0 me/l
EC	1.0 mmho/cm	1.2 mmho/cm
ammonium—N	20.0 ppm	40.0 ppm
boron	0.5 ppm	0.5 ppm

[a] pH level is not very important by itself; alkalinity level is more important.

[b] Moderately higher alkalinity levels are acceptable when lower amounts of limestone are incorporated into the substrate during its formulation. Very high alkalinity levels require acid injection into the water source.

[c] High hardness values are not a problem if calcium and magnesium are balanced and the soluble salt level is within the tolerable range. When hardness values are 3 me/l and above, the calcium and magnesium concentrations should be carefully checked.

pH

Water's pH is a measure of hydrogen ion concentration. Acidic water (low pH) has a high hydrogen ion concentration, and alkaline water (high pH) has a low concentration. The pH level of water by itself is not terribly important. A range of pH levels from 5.5 to 7.5 can be tolerable under the right circumstances. Unbuffered water at pH 7.5 will not affect substrate pH, but highly buffered water at pH 7.5 will adversely raise the substrate's pH level.

Alkalinity

Alkalinity, which is a measure of the water's buffering capacity, is more important than the pH level. The most prevalent sources of alkalinity in irrigation water are bicarbonate and carbonate. Carbonate is not present unless the water pH level is 8.3 or higher. Bicarbonate is important because it removes hydrogen ions from the soil solution and raises the substrate's pH level. The more alkaline the irrigation water, the more bicarbonate there is to consume hydrogen ions in the substrate, and consequently, the higher the pH level will become in the substrate. Adding alkaline water to a crop is equal to applying limestone.

You can have two water sources with the same pH level but with different alkalinity levels. One pH 7.5 water source could have a low alkalinity level with little impact on substrate pH while the other could have an intolerably high alkalinity level that rapidly raises substrate's pH level.

Alkalinity level categories

Alkalinity levels should be at or below 1.5 me/l (milliequivalents per liter of water) for plug production and 2.0 me/l for finish plant production. We can think of alkalinity in one of four categories. The low category just defined requires no action.

The negative effects of the next category, from 1.5 or 2.0 me/l to 4 or 5 me/l, can be prevented by incorporating less limestone into the substrate. Since the negative effect of this alkalinity level is a rise in the substrate's pH level, one can start with a lower substrate pH level to offset it. If an initial 6.0 pH level is desired in soilless substrate, it could be formulated instead to an initial 5.4 level. With an additional 0.6 units of permissible pH rise, the substrate pH level might not climb to an adverse level by the end of the crop.

Do not lower limestone to the point where active plant growth takes place at a substrate pH level below the minimum recommended range. However, plug substrate can be formulated at a lower than recommended pH level. The pH level of the plug cells' small substrate volume rapidly rises in response to water alkalinity before the seedling has formed. Some growers with very high water alkalinity apply no limestone to their plug mix.

The third category is a higher alkalinity level than can be compensated by reducing the substrate limestone level. Here it is necessary to

TABLE 13.2

Acid required to lower pH level [a]

Acid	Amount of acid to add for each me/l of alkalinity		Nutrient concentration from 1 fl. oz. of acid per 1,000 gal. water (from 1 ml per 1,000 l)	
phosphoric acid (75%)	7.3 fl oz./1,000 gal.	(54.75 ml/1,000 l)	6.60 ppm P_2O_5	(0.88 ppm P_2O_5)
sulfuric (96%)	4.0 fl oz./1,000 gal.	(30.00 ml/1,000 l)	3.10 ppm S	(0.41 ppm S)
sulfuric (35%)	11.0 fl oz./1,000 gal.	(82.50 ml/1,000 l)	1.13 ppm S	(0.15 ppm S)
nitric (67%)	6.8 fl oz./1,000 gal.	(51.00 ml/1,000 l)	1.64 ppm N	(0.22 ppm N)

[a] Fluid ounces of various acids to inject into each 1,000 gallons of irrigation water (ml to inject in 1,000 l of water) to lower the pH level to below 6.0 and the concentration of nutrients provided by 1 fluid ounce of each acid per 1,000 gallons of water (by 1 ml of acid in 1,000 l of water).

inject acid into the water source. One of three acids can be used—phosphoric, nitric, or sulfuric. The application rate for each depends on the number of alkalinity milliequivalents in a liter of irrigation water (table 13.2).

A good sulfuric acid source is battery acid, which is 35% sulfuric acid. It is inexpensive, available from auto parts companies, free of toxic levels of impurities, and safer to handle than the 96% concentrated sulfuric acid alternative. Phosphoric acid has been commonly used, but plug growers may not be able to use it exclusively because it will provide more than the desired phosphorus level prescribed in their fertilizer formulation.

Sulfuric acid then is the acid of choice because it is safer to handle a 35% formulation, and high sulfate levels in the substrate are relatively safe. If nitric acid is used, be sure to determine the nitrate amount applied and reduce it in the fertilizer by an equivalent amount. Neutralization of very alkaline waters with nitric acid may result in nitrogen levels too high for plug production.

The fourth category occurs when water alkalinity levels are so high that the water's electrical conductivity level is intolerable. Reverse osmosis units are used to remove the alkaline calcium and magnesium bicarbonates as well as other salts from the water. It is highly effective but expensive.

Hardness

High alkalinity alerts us to look at the water's hardness level. Hardness is a measure of the water's combined calcium and magnesium, which are the main ions balancing carbonate and bicarbonate in water. An exception is found in areas with high sodium content soils, such as the southwestern United States, where sodium balances much of the carbonate and bicarbonate.

When hardness levels are above 3 me/l (this is equivalent to 150 ppm of calcium carbonate equivalent since 1 me/l = 50 ppm), there is the potential for water to supply much or all of the calcium and magnesium needed by the crop. Appropriate alterations can then be made in the fertilization program. It is also important to note the relative calcium and magnesium concentrations in water. A high concentration of either nutrient will reduce uptake of the other nutrients, leading to a possible deficiency.

Calcium and magnesium

Precise calcium to magnesium ratios in water have not been worked out for greenhouse crops. However, a ratio of 3 to 5 ppm calcium to 1 ppm magnesium appears to be a safe range. If ratios outside of this range are experienced, correct the balance by incorporating additional calcium or magnesium into the fertilization program.

EC (soluble salts)

Water's salt content is generally determined by measuring water's electrical conductivity (EC). The result is reported as millimhos per centimeter (mmho/cm) or as milliSiemens per centimeter (mS/cm), which are equal. Good water does not exceed 1.0 mmho/cm for plug production and 1.2 mmho/cm for finish flat and pot production.

Water that has a higher than desired salt level is remedied by:

1. Accepting the poor quality level and managing salt levels in the substrate by avoiding excessive substrate drying. As substrate dries, its salt concentration increases. Plants are injured when substrate salt concentrations become equal to or higher than salt levels inside the plant root. When this happens, water will not enter the root and the plant desiccates. Salt levels are also managed by not applying high fertilizer concentrations. Apply only the minimum fertilizer amount and in small, frequent doses.

2. Removing the salts, which is an expensive procedure. Some greenhouse firms clean irrigation water through reverse osmosis. Weigh carefully the cost of cleaning water against the next alternative.

3. Using a new water source, such as city water, which is usually free of excessive salt but is usually expensive. Farm ponds with rain water may harbor disease organisms from neighboring agricultural lands, which could mean injecting chlorine into the water.

Always check with your area state hydrologist to determine the salt content of water from different strata below your location. Changing the depth of wells can solve serious problems.

Boron

Boron levels in water are generally low except in the southwest United States. A level of 0.5 ppm is safe. Water containing 1 ppm is unsatisfactory for crops. Boron's solubility decreases with increasing pH or calcium application. It is tied up as insoluble calcium borate. Where boron toxicity is a problem, raise the root medium pH to the highest safe level for the crop. Heavy use of gypsum in the substrate also helps to alleviate boron toxicity without raising the pH level.

Fluoride

Fluoride can injure plants. Tips and margins of older leaves burn as fluoride reaches toxic levels at the ends of leaf veins. The burn starts as a gray or water-soaked discoloration that gives way to tan or orange-brown necrosis. Natural fluoride water levels are rarely a problem as toxic levels usually result from fluoride additions to drinking water to prevent tooth decay. The general application level is 1 ppm fluoride, which is not sufficiently high to injure most of the traditional bedding plant species. There are, however, a number of sensitive ornamental plants, many belonging to the Liliaceae and Marantaceae plant families.

Because plug technology has recently expanded to the production of seedlings of many other categories of greenhouse crops as well as plant rooting in plug trays, sensitive plants that could be injured by fluoridated water include (highly sensitive) *Chlorophytum* (spider plant), *Cordyline terminalis*, and *Dracaena deremensis* (mainly cultivars Janet Craig and Warneckii); (sensitive) *Dracaena fragens* (corn plant), *Maranta leuconeura erythroneura* (red nerve plant), *Maranta leuconeura kerchoviana* (prayer plant), *Spathiphyllum* (most species), *Yucca elephantipes* (spineless yucca), *Ctenanthe oppenheimiana*, *Ctenanthe amabilis* and *Chamaedorea elegans*; (probably sensitive) *Chamaedorea seifrizii*, *Aspidistra elatior*, *Calathea insignis*, *Calathea makoyana*, *Dracaena marginata*, *Dracaena sanderana*, and *Pleomele thalioides*.

Fluoride is a non-volatile element that will not dissipate from water. It can be precipitated as calcium fluoride. The best prevention is to raise the substrate pH level to which high fluorine content water will be applied. A 6.5 pH level will usually prevent toxicity. When a high pH level cannot be tolerated, a heavy neutral salt gypsum (calcium sulfate) application can be made to the substrate to tieup fluoride.

Chlorine and chloride

Chlorine and chloride have very different plant responses. Chlorine is used as a microbicide in municipal water at 1.5 to 2.0 ppm concentrations. These concentrations are not believed injurious to plants growing in solid root substrates. However, our studies show that a 0.7 ppm chlorine concentration kills chrysanthemum and rose plant root tips in hydroponic solution. Chlorine rapidly evaporates (in a matter of hours) after which the water is safe for plant growth. Perhaps chlorinated water is safe in substrates because of a rapid gas exchange or because organic matter mediated conversion to chloride.

Chloride is found in soil, water, and in some fertilizers. Its adverse effect occurs when present in exceedingly high levels and is mainly a high soluble salt problem. Concentrations of 5 to 10 me/l (175-350 ppm) in water are required before toxicities are seen.

Fertilization program

Preplant fertilizer

Growers are responsible for providing 12 essential plant nutrients—six macronutrients and six micronutrients. Ten nutrients can be supplied in the substrate prior to planting in quantities that will last for the whole crop period. This makes a postplant liquid fertilization program much easier.

Preplant nutrients fall into four categories: pH adjustment, phosphorus, micronutrients, and nitrogen plus potassium (table 13.3).

pH adjustment. Recommended substrate pH levels for bedding plants are given in table 13.1. Typical rates of limestone addition for soil-base and soilless substrates are given in table 13.3. The soilless substrates referred to have a peat moss or pine bark base. Hardwood barks have a higher pH level than pine bark. Substrates based on hardwood bark may not require any limestone.

Dolomitic limestone is preferred for incorporating into substrates because it supplies magnesium and calcium rather than just calcium as in regular calcitic limestone. When irrigation water contains a high

TABLE 13.3

Preplant nutrients [a]

Nutrient source	Rate per cubic yard (per m³)			
	Soil-base substrate		Soilless substrate	
To adjust pH and provide calcium and magnesium	(lb)	(kg)	(lb)	(kg)
dolomitic limestone	0-10	0-6	5-10	3-6
To provide phosphorus and sulfur				
superphosphate (0-20-0)	3.0	1.8	4.50	2.7
or				
superphosphate (0-45-0)	1.5	0.9	2.25	1.3
+ gypsum (calcium sulfate)	1.5	0.9	1.50	0.9
To provide micronutrients: iron, manganese, zinc, copper, boron, and molybdenum				
Esmigran or	5	3	5	3
Micromax or	1	0.6	1	0.6
F-555HF or	3 oz	112 g	3 oz	112 g
F-111HF	1	0.6	1	0.6
To provide nitrogen and potassium (optional)				
calcium nitrate	1	0.6	1	0.6
+ potassium nitrate	1	0.6	1	0.6

[a] Nutrient sources and rates commonly incorporated during formulation of substrate for finish bedding plants crops. For plug substrate use the full liming material amount and half of the rates of all other nutrient sources.

magnesium level relative to calcium, use calcitic limestone in the substrate to correct this imbalance. If the proper calcium to magnesium ratio is initially established, these two nutrients will adequately supply plant growth as long as the pH level stays in the desired range. Abnormally low pH levels generally forecast a calcium and/or magnesium deficiency.

A required substrate pH adjustment after the crop is growing may be made in two ways. Use an acidic or alkaline fertilizer (as discussed in the postplant fertilization section). Or make a single application of an acidic or basic material.

The pH level can be lowered by 0.5 to 1.0 units by the applying two pounds of ferrous sulfate per 100 gallons of water (2.4 g/l) as a single normal watering. Plants should be rinsed immediately to avoid burning. Raise the substrate pH level by watering the crop with a flowable limestone at the label rate.

Phosphorus. Phosphorus can be incorporated into the substrate at levels that will last for most if not all of the crop. Rates for superphosphate addition (as well as sulfur) are given in table 13.3. Regular (20% P_2O_5) superphosphate contains calcium phosphate as well as calcium sulfate. Because triple superphosphate (45% P_2O_5) contains only calcium phosphate, the table calls for the addition of calcium sulfate (gypsum). Nearly all commercial substrates contain phosphorus unless otherwise stated. Some contain sulfur, which is a desirable feature.

If water and a fertilizer solution are applied to the top of the tray, flat, or pot, and the leaching percentage is light (10% to 20% of applied liquid), these phosphorus and sulfur substrate components may last for the whole crop cycle. With heavier leaching percentages they probably won't. Monitor crops through substrate and tissue tests to determine if you deplete these nutrients later in the crop cycle. If they do run out, adjust the continuous liquid fertilization program to contain the problem nutrient or nutrients. (See also postplant fertilization section.)

You won't need to have phosphorus in the substrate initially; however, if it is not in the substrate, it is important to use a phosphorus-containing fertilizer in the liquid program when seedlings are transplanted.

Micronutrients. The quantity of micronutrients needed for a crop depends on the substrate's pH level. Soilless substrates at and below 6.0 and soil-based substrates at and below 6.5 have modest micronutrient needs. Micronutrients contained in commercial fertilizers or in commercial substrates will probably meet the crop needs.

At higher substrate pH levels, all micronutrients except molybdenum are less soluble and less available to plants. Additional micronutrients are important at these levels. Additional micronutrients might come from the two combined sources in the fertilizer and in the substrate.

When even higher substrate pH levels are found at or above the upper recommended substrate pH range, it may be necessary to increase to a third micronutrient level as found in special fertilizers marketed for soilless substrates. Some of these products are identified as "Peat-Lite Special" or "Plus." Sources and recommended micronutrient addition rates for substrate formulation are given in table 13.3. Most commercial substrate formulations contain micronutrients, but some do not, and they are labeled. Most water soluble greenhouse fertilizers contain micronutrients, and these are listed on the label.

Some bedding plant species have unusual micronutrient problems. Substrate pH level adjustments are recommended for these problems (table 13.1). Seed geraniums and African marigold are very efficient accumulators of iron, manganese, zinc, and copper micronutrients, and they will take up toxic levels of one or more of these nutrients (figs. 13.1, 13.2). Uptake is reduced by growing these species at higher substrate pH levels than other bedding plant species. Pansy, petunia, snapdragon, and vinca have difficulty in taking up iron. To prevent an

Fig. 13.1. Micronutrient toxicity symptoms brought on by low substrate pH levels. African marigold symptoms begin on the recently fully expanded leaves and include chlorosis in a variety of patterns followed quickly by numerous bronze, necrotic pinpoint spots across the leaf blade that resemble sand sprinkled on the leaves, and finally by death of these leaves, often from the margin inward.

Fig. 13.2. Seedling geranium symptoms of micronutrient toxicity start with interveinal chlorosis of mid- and older leaves, followed by small brown necrotic spots across the chlorotic leaves, and finally by necrosis of the affected leaves from the margins inward.

iron deficiency, these crops are grown at a lower substrate pH level than other bedding plant species.

Nitrogen and potassium. Adding these nutrients during substrate formulation is optional. Nitrogen and potassium are incorporated into most commercial substrates; the amount is small and designed to last only for a few weeks as a supplement to the regular fertilization program. Some growers incorporate the two nutrients into the substrate and start off a little lighter with the continuous fertilization program. If desired, these nutrients can be supplied by incorporating equal parts of calcium nitrate and potassium nitrate into the substrate during its formulation.

When nitrogen and potassium are not contained in the substrate, begin the liquid fertilization program at seedling planting time. If these nutrients are contained in the substrate, the liquid fertilization program can begin on the day of planting or at the next watering. Initially incorporating nitrogen and potassium into the substrate is a matter of personal choice based on experience.

Postplant fertilization

Rate and frequency. The exact fertilizer concentration to use depends on: stage of growth, plant species, desired rate of growth,

TABLE 13.4

Postplant fertilizer rate and frequency [a]

N conc. (ppm)[b]	Frequency	Production stage
50-75	as needed	plug—late Stage 2 through early to mid-Stage 3
100-150	as needed	plug—remainder of Stage 3
100-200[c]	each watering	finish flats or pots
200-300[c]	weekly	finish flats or pots
450-500[c]	every two weeks	finish flats or pots

[a] Fertilizer concentrations to use for various bedding plant production stages. Concentrations given are for nitrogen. The phosphorus and potassium concentrations depend on the selected fertilizer's ratio.

[b] Exact fertilizer application concentration and frequency depends on the plant species, the desired growth rate, and the leaching percentage. During the plug stages fertilizer may be applied at each watering for heavily fertilized, rapid growth crops or at every third or fourth watering for lightly fertilized crops.

[c] These are three alternative fertilization programs. Use only one or a concentration of two.

leaching percentage, and frequency of fertilizer application. General fertilizer rate and frequency guidelines are given in table 13.4.

Young seedlings are sensitive to fertilizer salts and have a very low total requirement. Postplant fertilization begins in late Stage 2, after cotyledons have emerged for such slow-to-develop species as begonia. For faster growing species that reach Stage 3 in seven days, such as marigold, fertilization begins at the start of Stage 3. Nitrogen concentrations for this early growth period (late Stage 2 through early to mid-Stage 3) range from 40 to about 100 ppm, usually 50 to 75 ppm. As the seedling grows larger, it removes nutrients faster from the plug cell. A higher fertilizer concentration is needed to meet this increased removal rate. The range of nitrogen concentrations used in this second period (from early or mid-Stage 3 to the end of Stage 3) extends from 75 to about 225 ppm, but 100 to 150 ppm are most common.

During the Finish Stage (from transplanting of plugs or bare root seedlings into finish flats or finish pots until retail market), the highest fertilizer rates are used. Some growers prefer to fertilize at every watering at a 100 to 200 ppm nitrogen concentration. Others fertilize once per week at a 200 to 300 ppm nitrogen concentration, and a few growers fertilize every two weeks at a 450 to 500 ppm nitrogen concentration.

Either the fertilizer concentration or the application frequency must be varied for bedding plant species because species have very different nutrient requirements. Crops with light needs, such as broccoli, cabbage, cauliflower, impatiens, and pansy, are often fertilized at or below the low concentrations listed in table 13.4. These crops may be fertilized, in the plug stages at every second or third watering. Crops requiring heavy fertilizer, such as begonia, dusty miller, portulaca, verbena, and vinca, should be fertilized at the high end of the recommended ranges in table 13.4. If median levels are used, fertilizer should be applied at every watering.

The desired seedling development rate can vary. During a dark, rainy period it may be necessary to retard growth to prevent stretching.

Fig. 13.3. Two flats of impatiens grown in compact form by withholding fertilizer. The flat on the left recently received a single application of 500 ppm nitrogen from 20-10-20 fertilizer to green it up and prepare it for market, while the flat on the right is still being held for later sales.

When the market does not open up as rapidly as anticipated, it may be necessary to hold a plug or finish crop back. Or the market could develop faster than expected requiring accelerated growth.

Fertilizer concentration and frequency is one tool for controlling growth rate. No fertilizer, or low fertilizer concentrations, or standard concentrations at low frequencies such as every third or fourth watering are used to reduce growth rate (fig. 13.3). Applying fertilizer with every watering can be used to hasten growth. It is easiest to use one fertilizer concentration for all bedding plant species, varying the application frequency according to the species or the desired growth rate.

Leaching percentage is a more important factor than most people realize. A grower who practices a low leaching percentage such as 10% to 15% will be successful using a low concentration of fertilizer. The grower who uses a 50% leaching fraction may need to use double the fertilizer concentration.

In a 10% leaching percentage system, 90% of applied water or fertilizer is retained in the substrate while 10% leaches from the flat or pot's bottom. It is nearly impossible to define a fertilizer rate/frequency specification for a grower who varies the leaching percentage.

When developing a fertilization program, be sure to select a level of leaching and adhere to it. The big problem with variability comes when two or more people are assigned to watering or fertilizing a crop.

Subirrigation systems, including ebb-and-flow and whole floor recirculation are becoming popular. These systems use much lower fertilizer concentrations because no nutrients are leached. Exact rates have not been well defined. In general, you should use half of the fertilizer rate you would normally use in an open system where fertilizer is applied to the flat or pot's top and allowed to leach from the bottom.

pH control. Although the substrate pH level is correct at the start of a crop, it may change over time. Alkaline water will raise it. Heavy watering or fertilization may dissolve the limestone prematurely, lowering the pH level. And fertilizers applied may either raise or lower the pH level. Postplant pH levels can be controlled through fertilizer selection.

Thirty-five commercially available fertilizers are listed in table 13.5 along with their potential acidity or basicity. Some are very acid, such as 21-7-7, with a potential acidity of 1,700 pounds (770.9 kg) of calcium carbonate (limestone) equivalent. This suggests that it would require 1,700 pounds of limestone to neutralize the acidity caused in the substrate by the addition of 1 ton (900 kg) of this fertilizer.

One of the brands of 20-0-20 is neutral—it has no effect on substrate pH level. The most alkaline fertilizer in the list is 13-0-44 with a potential basicity of 460 pounds (209.9 kg) of calcium carbonate equivalent. Applying this fertilizer has the effect on substrate pH of applying 460 pounds of limestone.

You can lower, hold constant, or raise the substrate pH level by selecting the proper fertilizer. A fast, moderate, or slow decline in substrate pH can be obtained by using 20-18-20 (610 pounds acidity), 20-10-20 (422 pounds acidity), or 15-16-17 (215 pounds acidity) fertilizers respectively. A slow, moderate, or fast pH rise can be achieved with 17-0-17 (75 pounds basicity), 13-2-13 (200 pounds basicity), or 15-0-15 (420 pounds basicity) fertilizers respectively.

Ammonium versus nitrate nitrogen. Acid fertilizers tend to contain higher amounts of ammoniacal nitrogen while alkaline fertilizers contain primarily nitrate nitrogen. Ammoniacal nitrogen fertilizers would be used to lower the substrate pH level through fertilizer selection. To avoid the use of high proportions of ammoniacal nitrogen in a situation of chronically rising substrate pH, use less limestone initially in the substrate.

Fig. 13.4. All impatiens plants were fertilized with the same nitrogen concentration but with different ammonium to nitrate proportions. From left to right, the percentage in the ammoniacal form was 0%, 25%, 50%, 75%, and 100% with the remaining nitrogen in nitrate form. Maximum growth occurred at 25% and 50% ammoniacal nitrogen.

Ammoniacal nitrogen results in larger and softer amounts of plant growth. Longer internodes and larger leaves are developed. This occurs when the nitrogen proportion in the ammoniacal form is 25% and higher, and the remaining nitrogen is nitrate.

High nitrate proportion fertilizers are used to keep plants compact. High ammonium proportion fertilizers are used to stimulate rapid growth. See figure 13.4 for the effects of ammonium to nitrate ratio on impatiens growth.

High rates of ammoniacal nitrogen can cause plant injury. The exact proportion of ammoniacal nitrogen that causes injury varies. If less than adequate total nitrogen is applied, a high proportion of the total nitrogen can be in the ammoniacal form, possibly even 100%. Once an adequate amount of nitrogen is applied to the crop, the proportion of ammoniacal nitrogen needs to lessen as the level of total nitrogen application to the crop increases.

It is advisable not to apply more than 50% of total nitrogen in the ammoniacal form. Ammonium sensitivity increases with cooler substrate temperatures in winter and in northern latitudes.

Lower substrate pH levels increase crop sensitivity to ammonium. Under cool and low substrate pH conditions, ammonium is not converted as rapidly to nitrate by bacteria. Under northern winter conditions, it should not exceed 40%.

Nitrogen to potassium ratio. Most bedding plants grow well when nitrogen (N) and potassium (K_2O) are equally concentrated in the fertilizer. In the crop's earlier stages, apply both of these nutrients in fairly equal concentration. Later in the crop other ratios may be necessary. Substrate or tissue analyses will indicate the need to shift the ratio to correct nutrient imbalance.

TABLE 13.5

Commercial fertilizer nutrients [a]

Fertilizer	NH$_4$ [b] (%)	Potential acidity [c]	Potential basicity [d]	Ca (%)	Mg (%)	S (%)
21-7-7 acid	90	1700				
21-7-7 acid	100	1560		—	—	10.0
20-2-20	69	800				
20-18-18	73	710		—	—	1.4
24-7-15	58	612		—	1.0	1.3
20-18-20	69	610		—	—	1.0
20-20-20	69	583				
20-9-20	42	510		—	—	1.4
20-20-20	69	474				
16-17-17	44	440		—	0.9	1.3
20-10-20	40	422				
20-10-20	38	393				
21-7-7 neutral	100	369				
15-15-15	52	261				
17-17-17	51	218				
15-16-17	47	215				
15-16-17	30	165				
20-5-30	56	153				
17-5-24	31	125		—	2.0	2.6
20-5-30	54	118		—	0.5	—
20-5-30	54	100				
15-11-29	43	91				
15-5-25	28	76		—	1.3	—
15-10-30	39	76				
20-0-20	25	40		5.0	—	—
21-0-20	48	15		6.0	—	—
20-0-20	69	0	0	6.7	0.2	—
16-4-12	38		73			
17-0-17	20		75	4.0	2.0	—
13-2-13	11		200	6.0	3.0	—
14-0-14	8		220	6.0	3.0	—
15-0-15	13		319	10.5	0.3	—
15.5-0-0 cal. nitrate	6		400	22.0	—	—
15-0-15	13		420	11.0	—	—
13-0-44 pot. nitrate	0		460			

[a] A list of some commercially available fertilizers along with the percent of total nitrogen that is in the ammonium plus urea form, the potential acidity or basicity of each, and the percentage of calcium (Ca), magnesium (Mg), and sulfur (S) where greater than 0.2%.

[b] NH$_4$(%) is the total nitrogen percentage that is in the ammonium plus urea forms; the remaining nitrogen is nitrate.

[c] Pounds of calcium carbonate limestone required to neutralize the acidity caused by using 1 ton of the specified fertilizer.

[d] Application of 1 ton of the specified fertilizer is equivalent to applying this many pounds of calcium carbonate limestone.

Phosphorus. The greenhouse industry probably uses far more phosphorus than needed. Preplant phosphorus incorporated into most substrates should be adequate to produce a bedding plant crop. Heavy leaching and low substrate pH levels increase the rate at which phosphorus washes out of the substrate. When this occurs, a fertilizer with a low phosphorus concentration, such as 2% to 5%, will keep phosphorus above the minimum critical substrate level. If no phosphorus is initially incorporated into the substrate, a fertilizer with half as much phosphorus as nitrogen will provide more than an adequate phosphorus amount throughout the crop. Such fertilizers include 20-9-20 and 20-10-20.

Calcium and magnesium. The main calcium and magnesium sources are found in the dolomitic limestone incorporated into the substrate and in alkaline water. As long as the substrate pH level is in the desired range, generally calcium and magnesium are sufficient for crop needs. At low pH levels, these two nutrients may be deficient. If both nutrients were well balanced in the substrate prior to the pH drop, then both may become deficient.

If calcium was high relative to magnesium, then magnesium may become deficient first. This latter situation might result from the use of calcitic rather than dolomitic limestone in the substrate, or if the water source contains an abnormally high proportion of calcium relative to magnesium.

A magnesium deficiency can be corrected by applying 2 pounds of Epsom salts (magnesium sulfate) in 100 gallons of water (2.4 g/l) once as a normal watering. Apply half of this rate to plug seedlings. A calcium deficiency can be cured by switching the nitrogen source to calcium nitrate if you formulate your own fertilizers or by using 15-0-15 if you purchase complete fertilizers. Many fertilizers contain calcium and/or magnesium (see table 13.5). Various proportions of these two nutrients can be applied by selecting the proper fertilizer from table 13.5.

Calcium and magnesium are antagonistic toward each other. A high level of either relative to the other will cause a deficiency of the nutrient in low supply. A grower who continuously uses the brands of 15-0-15 fertilizer that contain 11% calcium and no magnesium may eventually develop a magnesium deficiency.

Sulfur. Substrates and fertilizers are composed of purer nutrient sources than years ago. The likelihood of sulfur deficiency is greater today than in the past. If you make your own substrate, incorporate sulfur as recommended in table 13.3. Some commercial substrates contain sulfur, which is desirable.

TABLE 13.6

Commercial fertilizer formulations [a]

Fertilizer	NH4 + urea (%)	N and K₂O concentrations (ppm)						
		50	100	200	300	400	500	600
20-20-20 [b]	70	3.3 c	6.7	13.3	20.0	26.7	33.4	40.0
15-15-15 [b]	52	4.5	8.9	17.8	26.7	35.6	44.5	53.4
15-0-15	13	4.5	8.9	17.8	26.7	35.6	44.5	53.4
13-2-13 (-6 Ca-3 Mg) [b]	11	5.1	10.3	20.5	30.8	41.0	51.3	61.5
14-0-14 (-6 Ca-3 Mg)	8	4.8	9.5	19.0	28.6	38.1	47.6	57.1
17-0-17 (-4 Ca-2 Mg)	20	3.9	7.8	15.7	23.5	31.4	39.2	47.0
20-10-20 b, 20-9-20 [b]	40 to 42	3.3	6.7	13.3	20.0	26.7	33.4	40.0
ammonium nitrate	36	1.4	2.9	5.7	8.6	11.4	14.3	17.1
+ potassium nitrate (23-0-23)		1.5	3.0	6.1	9.1	12.1	15.2	18.2
calcium nitrate	0	3.0	6.0	12.0	18.0	24.0	30.0	36.0
+ potassium nitrate (15-0-15)		1.5	3.0	6.0	9.0	12.0	15.0	18.0
ammonium nitrate	40	1.2	2.5	4.9	7.4	9.9	12.3	14.8
+ potassium nitrate		1.5	3.0	6.0	9.0	12.0	15.0	18.0
+ monoammonium phosphate (20-10-20) [b]		0.5	1.1	2.2	3.2	4.3	5.4	6.5
potassium nitrate	0	1.5	3.0	6.1	9.1	12.1	15.2	18.2
+ calcium nitrate		1.8	3.5	7.0	10.5	14.1	17.6	21.1
+ magnesium nitrate (13-0-13-6.6 Ca-3.3 Mg)		1.8	3.6	7.2	10.8	14.4	18.0	21.6

[a] Quantities of fertilizers or fertilizer salts to dissolve in 100 gallons of water to make solutions containing concentrations of 50 to 600 ppm each of nitrogen (N) and potassium (K₂O) and the percent of total nitrogen that is in the ammonium plus urea forms.

[b] These formulations also contain phosphorus (P_2O_5).

[c] 1 oz. in 100 gal. is equivalent to 0.075 g in 1 l.

A sulfur deficiency can be corrected by watering once with 2 pounds of Epsom salts per 100 gallons of water (2.4 g/l). Use half the rate for plug seedlings. Some commercial greenhouse fertilizers contain sulfur (table 13.5), which provides a good insurance policy against sulfur deficiency.

Fertilizer formulations. Some commercial fertilizer formulations and formulas for make-your-own fertilizers are listed in table 13.6. Also listed are the quantities of each fertilizer to dissolve in 100 gallons (370 l) of water to make solutions with 50 to 600 ppm nitrogen concentrations.

Slow-release fertilizer

Some bedding plant firms incorporate slow-release fertilizers into the substrate for finish flats and pots. These fertilizers are used as a base but not the sole source of nitrogen, phosphorus, and potassium. Infrequent liquid fertilizer applications are then made as indicated by the crop color or rate of growth. This dual source of fertilizers greatly reduces the number of fertilizer applications and saves considerable labor.

Firms rarely try to meet the entire crop needs for nitrogen and potassium through preplant incorporation of slow-release fertilizer into the substrate. Once the slow-release fertilizer is in the substrate it cannot be removed, even by leaching. If the weather should turn cloudy or the desired market date should be delayed, a lower than normal nutrition level would be desired. Slow-release fertilizers are added at a rate to meet this lower than normal level throughout the crop period.

When faster growth is required, supplemental liquid fertilizer applications are made. Slow-release fertilizers are rarely used in plug substrates because of a problem in distributing fertilizer particles into every plug cell. There is also be a problem of controlling fertilizer availability over the extremely wide range in plug production.

Some slow-release fertilizers and the rates used in bedding plant finish crops are: Osmocote (14-14-14), which is a commonly used formula. It has a 3- to 4-month release period at a 70 F (21.1 C) substrate temperature. Rates of application range from 3 to 8 pounds per cubic yard of substrate (1.8 to 4.7 kg/m^3). A similar encapsulated product line is Nutricote. The 14-14-14 and 16-10-10 formulas are available in a variety of release periods. The 70-day release period is used for finish bedding plants at rates of 2.5 to 5.0 pounds per cubic yard (1.5 to 3.0 kg/m^3) while the 100-day release period products are used at rates of 3.5 to 7.5 pounds per cubic yard (2.0 to 4.4 kg/m^3). MagAmp, a slowly soluble 7-40-6 slow-release fertilizer is often used. The medium-size grade has a release period of three to four months and is used at rates of 6 to 10 pounds per cubic yard (3.6 to 5.9 kg/m^3).

The exact usage rate of the slow-release fertilizers listed depends on two factors. One is the proportion of the total fertilizer need that will be met by the slow-release fertilizer, and the second is the crop's rate of nutrient demand. The high end of each rate range listed will meet all of the crop fertilizer needs under poor to moderate growing conditions or for lightly fertilized species under any conditions. Each range's lower end would allow for several liquid fertilizer applications and give the grower more control. These lower rates are also better suited to northern winter conditions.

Deficiency symptoms of various bedding plant crops

Plate 1. Nitrogen—petunia. *The entire lower leaf blades are yellow. Plant is severely stunted. Later the entire plant will become yellow, and the lower leaves will die [1].*

Plate 2. Nitrogen—begonia. *Lower leaves are affected first, turning yellow with reddish margins. Upper leaves will be bright red in severe deficiency. Plant will become severely stunted [1].*

Plate 3. Nitrogen—marigold. *Lower leaves turn yellow, followed by a red discoloration of the leaf margins. The yellowing progresses toward the top of the plant. Plant is severely stunted [1].*

Plate 4. Phosphorus—petunia. *A phosphorus-deficient plant beside a normal plant. The deficient plant is deeper green than normal and severely stunted. Later, chlorosis followed by necrosis will appear on the lower leaves and spread up the plant.*

Plate 5. Phosphorus—begonia. *Lower leaves are dull olive green with a purplish tint around the edges. Upper leaves are dark purplish red. Plant is severely stunted [1].*

Plate 6. Phosphorus—marigold. *Lower leaves remain green, but a red discoloration appears on the margins and expands inward; symptoms move upward on the plant over time. Plant is severely stunted [1].*

Plate 7. Potassium—petunia. *Necrosis is the major symptom. It begins as marginal necrosis or spots usually near the lower leaf margins. Necrosis may spread inward in severe cases. Upper leaves remain dark green. Entire plant is stunted [1].*

Plate 8. Potassium—begonia. *Necrosis begins as tan spots near lower leaf margins. Spots enlarge rapidly and merge to form larger necrotic areas with the original spots still distinguishable. Lower leaves are light green while upper leaves are slightly darker than normal. Considerable stunting occurs [1].*

Plate 9. Potassium—marigold. *Leaves cup downward and have short petioles. The plant has a bushy appearance [1].*

Plate 10. Calcium—petunia. *Necrosis appears between petal lobes just as the flower expands fully.*

Plate 11. Calcium—begonia. *Necrosis begins at lower and middle leaf tips and progresses toward the petiole. The growing point is often totally inhibited but doesn't die. Severe plant and root stunting will occur [1].*

Plate 12. Calcium—marigold. *Necrosis begins at the leaf tip and spreads inward; this necrosis will ultimately involve the entire leaf. Roots are short, stubby, and highly branched [1].*

Plate 13. Magnesium—petunia. *Well defined interveinal chlorosis develops on the lower leaves and spreads up the plant.*

Plate 14. Iron—petunia. *Interveinal chlorosis appears first on young leaves and then spreads down the plant. Young leaves may eventually become totally yellow and finally necrotic.*

Plate 15. Manganese—petunia. *Interveinal chlorosis occurs first on young leaves. In the advanced stage of deficiency, tan necrotic spots can be seen in the chlorotic areas between veins.*

Plate 16. Boron—petunia. *Symptoms seen on this plant as they occur are leaf chlorosis, thickened leaves, short stem internodes, bud abortion, orange brown necrosis over leaf veins, and more general leaf necrosis.*

Deficiency symptoms

Plate 1. Nitrogen–petunia

Plate 2. Nitrogen–begonia

Plate 3. Nitrogen–marigold

Plate 4. Phosphorus–petunia

Plate 5. Phosphorus–begonia

Plate 6. Phosphorus–marigold

Plate 7. Potassium–petunia

Plate 8. Potassium–begonia

Plate 9. Potassium–marigold

Plate 10. Calcium–petunia

Plate 11. Calcium–begonia

Plate 12. Calcium–marigold

Plate 13. Magnesium–petunia

Plate 14. Iron–petunia

Plate 15. Manganese–petunia

Plate 16. Boron–petunia

Nutritional monitoring

Three different systems can be used for monitoring bedding plant crops' nutritional status: substrate testing, tissue testing, and visual observation. Because some visual symptoms are irreversible, substrate and tissue testing are the preferred methods used to prevent nutrient disorders from starting. Unique features of substrate testing are the pH level measurements, soluble salts level, and the nitrogen forms available to the plant. Tissue analyses, however, offer the advantage of accurate tests for all essential nutrients. Both substrate and tissue tests should be used.

Substrate testing

Substrate test results can be highly variable, depending on the point in the fertilization cycle when the sample is gathered. High nutrient levels will appear in a sample taken after a fertilization versus low levels in a sample drawn after a watering. The variation becomes even greater after a second or third consecutive watering.

Even when samples are drawn only after fertilizations, variations can occur due to differences in the applied fertilizer concentration. Be consistent in drawing substrate samples at the same point in the fertilization cycle. The best time is within a few hours after applying fertilizer.

Expect nutrient levels to vary considerably even with samples are drawn consistently after fertilization. Substrate from a crop that is fertilized at every watering with a dilute fertilizer solution will have relatively low salt and nutrient levels. Substrate from a crop being fertilized once per week with a high concentration fertilizer will have high salt and nutrient levels. Recommended ranges for substrate pH and soluble salts are given in table 13.7. Interpretative values for some essential nutrients are tabulated in table 13.8. The acceptable range in the Michigan State University guidelines can be used for plug substrates and the optimum ranges in both sets for the finish bedding plant crops (table 13.8). These salt and nutrient levels are just estimates since exact standards have not been developed for plug or finish bedding plant crops.

Growers should sample representative bedding plant species continuously over successive plantings. By associating plant response to the substrate nutrient concentrations, the grower can learn what each crop's optimum ranges are and refine the standards in table 13.8. Representative species could include petunia for its popularity and intermediate fertilizer requirement, impatiens for its low fertilizer

| | + | High calcium levels can result in potassium, magnesium, and boron deficiencies. |

Magnesium   –   The first symptom is lower leaf interveinal chlorosis. In some crops, the interveinal chlorosis occurs across the leaf blade, while in others it begins in the leaf blade center. Necrotic spots may then form in the chlorotic areas between the veins. Symptoms spread toward younger foliage.

                       +   High magnesium levels may cause calcium deficiency.

Sulfur   –   All plant leaves turn pale green. Plants with normally bronze, red, or pink leaves develop a light pink pigment in the leaf interior and pale green margins.

Iron   –   Interveinal chlorosis of young leaves. As the interveinal chlorosis moves down the plant, the youngest leaves become totally yellow and later necrotic.

                       +   An excess of iron invariably leads to manganese deficiency.

Manganese   –   Interveinal chlorosis occurs on young leaves. On heavily chlorotic leaves light tan, sunken spots one-thirty-second to one-eigth inch in diameter (1 to 3 mm) develop randomly between the veins, which sets manganese deficiency apart from iron deficiency.

                       +   Necrosis develops at tips of older leaves or as spots across older leaves. High manganese levels also cause iron deficiency.

Boron   –   At first the foliage is dark green. Young leaves develop thicker than normal with a leathery feel. Leaves may curl downward from end to end, giving a wilted appearance; however, they are turgid. Young leaves become chlorotic. Rusty brown to orange necrotic spots appear across young leaves. These leaves then become crinkled or develop puckered surfaces. Stem internodes become shortened. The terminal shoot aborts, and later the lateral shoots abort. This often leads to a cluster of stems known as a witch's broom. Brown necrotic notches of missing cells may occur in leaf petioles, stems, and flower stems.

+ Boron toxicity results in reddish-brown to orange-brown necrosis along older leaf margins.

Copper – Interveinal chlorosis occurs on young leaves, but unlike iron deficiency, the leaf tips remain green. More severe deficiencies result in leaf blade tissue collapse as it expands. This results in very small leaves, which appear to have been burned back due to desiccation. The burning symptom will affect a few leaves and then stop. After a few nearly-normal leaves appear, the burn can occur again. In severe deficiencies, veinal chlorosis can occur.

Zinc – Chlorosis of young leaves occurs somewhat in an interveinal pattern. Internodes are very short. Leaves are greatly reduced in size. Shoot tip abortion occurs in severe situations.

Ammonium + Leaves in the mid- and lower portion of the plant become chlorotic and possibly thickened. Leaves curl to give a wilted appearance or simply become distorted. Older leaf necrosis then follows, usually from the margin inward; however, in a few species it may occur as spots across the leaf blade. Root tips take on an orange-brown color as they die.

References

[1] Hansen, R., D. Krauskopf, and L. Ewart. 1983. Bedding plants deficiency digest. *Greenhouse Grower* 9:45-48.
[2] Jones, J.B., Jr., B. Wolf, and H.A. Mills. 1991. *Plant analysis handbook.* Athens, Ga.: Micro-Macro Pub., Inc.
[3] Warnecke, D.D., and D.M. Krauskopf. 1983. Greenhouse growth media: *Testing and nutrition guidelines.* Bul. E-1736. Michigan State Univ. Agr. Ext.

CHAPTER 14

Bedding Plant Containers

James Corfield

In the '90s, as never before, growers' decisions as to which container to use are being driven by mass merchandising retailers. The wholesale grower selling to these retailers knows clearly which size and style of flat and pack is expected. Today a retailer/grower has to think seriously about how to differentiate his product from the mass merchants'.

Consolidation and focus

It's important to consider the changes in bedding plant marketing that have occurred and will continue to occur during the next decade. The decision-making process that each grower uses to choose containers will be influenced by this ongoing wave of consolidation, concentration, and focus.

Ten years ago, mass merchants sold roughly 35% of our bedding plants. Today, that number is at least 70%. At the same time, these retailers have reduced their number of suppliers; thus forcing the creation of very large, multi-acre production facilities that are capable of supplying the retailers' needs efficiently and economically. Industry and general business data confirm this swing (table 14.1).

The data show that the Consumer Price Index has grown 35% in eight years, while the average wholesale price of a bedding plant flat has increased only 30%.

Producer efficiency and cost management are central issues to performance and business survival in the '90s. Growers who ship to mass merchant retailers are required to provide products with increased durability and shelf life, more point of sales aides, just-in-time deliveries, and a host of other alliance-driven services. This translates into an improved value product being sent to the retailer and, ultimately, to the consumer.

TABLE 14.1

Industry changes, 1984-1992

	1992	1984
No. of producers of flowering plants [a]	2,048	3,378
Average flats per producer [a]	28,400	9,700
Average sales per producer [a]	$202,000	$53,000
Average price per flat [a]	$7.10	$5.45
Consumer Price Index [b]	140.3	103.91

[a] *Floriculture crop summaries*, 1984 and 1992. U.S. Dept. of Agriculture.

[b] *Economic indicators*. May 1993. U.S. Government Printing Office.

Mass merchant expectations

In recent times, mass merchant retailers have begun to mandate the container styles that their vendors may use in shipping plants to them. These decisions are based on marketing strategies that differ among retailers. One company may emphasize improved shelf life, which translates into less merchandise shrinkage for them but also provides a larger, better quality, faster growing product for the home gardener. Another may choose to differentiate through the use of brand identification. Yet another may have an absolute ceiling on the retail price point. Solutions to these challenges have led to the creation the flat and pack styles that we see today at K-Mart, Wal-Mart, Home Depot, Frank's Nursery and Crafts, and similar stores.

Growers must accurately anticipate their customers' requirements, regardless of production scale. However, supplying the mass merchant involves a greater risk of loss if you misjudge a particular season's trends. There is no single, uniform market for bedding plants. Retailers in diverse regions of the country have their own particular needs and expectations. In some states, retailers have specific demands for container style, rather than for particular species or cultivars.

The variety of expectations, combined with the mass merchants' own niche requirements, places increasingly complex demands on wholesale growers, and raises serious questions. Can you grow the product in two or more types of containers at one time? Can you adjust various planting and growing schedules to satisfy the requirements of several mass market customers? Can you afford to dedicate your entire production to a single customer to avoid misjudging the demand?

Today's flat and pack preferences

Keep in mind that the marketplace is highly fragmented, even confused, in terms of what constitutes a better container.

Jumbos. One of the main growth areas recently is the jumbo pack system. This system usually uses six packs per flat with four or six individual cells per pack. East of the Rockies, this system is in the more traditional 1020 size flat, while on the West Coast and some areas of the Southwest, the flat size is 17- x 17-inch. In either case, the packs are about 3 1/8 inches deep versus a standard pack at 2³/₈ inches deep. The jumbo system provides 25% to 30% more soil volume than the traditional depth pack. This is the system of choice for retailers who are looking to lengthen shelf life, reduce their economic loss due to shrinkage, and give the customer a better plant.

Some jumbo or deep systems have eight packs or even 18 packs per flat and are designed to be used with standard height flats. Deep flats are often used with jumbo six-packs to provide greater stability in shipping and handling. There are even jumbo sixes available with built-in handles. Variety is the name of the game and is seemingly endless.

Standards. The 11- x 21-inch flat continues to be the industry standard. Often referred to as a 1020 flat, it varies in both length and width from manufacturer to manufacturer. Eighteen packs per flat with one to four cells per pack is the norm. The 1803 with a triangular-shaped cell has been very popular, but an 1803 with rectangular cells is gaining ground as one merchandiser brand identifies the product it sells. This rectangular or strip arrangement has two rows of nine packs filling a flat to allow for the insertion of a branded plant tag into each pack. With the triangular arrangement, there are three rows of six packs each. The center row is not easily accessed for sticking a tag, either manually or mechanically. Some markets still want 12 packs per flat with three, four or six cells per pack while others demand an eight-pack series.

Economy series. In 1993-94, a few growers began growing in a downsized (from standard) flat to achieve two goals: 1) to hold steady the price per flat charged to their mass merchant customers, thus allowing the mass merchants to hold their retail price; and 2) to increase the number of flats produced without increasing greenhouse space required.

These economy systems also vary in size, depending on the manufacturer and the grower who worked with them to develop the unit's specifications. The resulting flat dimensions are, for example, 10¹/₂- x

21-inch or an actual 10 x 20 inches. A standard unit could be 10⅝ x 21⅛ inches. The difference of as little as one-eighth, one-fourth, or one-half inch, multiplied by a large number of flats, allows additional flats to fit into an existing greenhouse or bench area. Every time a crop turns in that space, more units are produced than with standard flats. Considering an entire bedding plant production season, it might then be possible to produce 10% to 15% more finished flats.

In terms of production inputs, the grower may see some slight reduction in the flat and pack costs. There will be savings in growing media used per unit and in transportation costs resulting from lowered weight per unit and more units shipped per rack and truck. Capital investment in greenhouse and logistical infrastructure adjustments may be high initially.

Containers for non-mass markets

Our discussion has been limited to plastic flats and packs. The vast majority of markets readily accept these containers. For the retail grower or wholesaler producing for resale to the traditional market, there is little risk associated with this type of container.

Defining markets, developing a plan

If your production focus is on the more traditional retail market, you must clearly identify competing products in your trading area, understand your own production capabilities or retail needs, and develop a plan that allows you to create a niche that promotes success. Differentiating your products by means other than price is a critical issue.

As an independent retailer, there is little justification for you to compete with the low price points that most mass merchants are likely to create. Instead:
- Differentiate the quality and appearance of your product.
- Think of the containers you use as part of your product's packaging.
- Set a goal of creating packaging that encourages potential customers to buy and existing customers to buy more.

Generally speaking, growing fewer plants per flat is a good first step toward setting your bedding plants apart from others. Larger soil volume, combined with quality growing techniques, should produce plants that are larger, more vigorous, and ready to give quick gratification in the home garden or commercial landscape.

Distinct packaging alternatives

Unique styles of flats and packs are available from a number of manufacturers and distributors that will let you create a distinct packaging look to attract consumers. Here are a few examples:

- Flats or trays with some number (eight, 10, 12, or 18) of pockets designed to hold thin walled pots (either individually or in sheets). Allows free spacing of plants and holds them in place for improved retail display.
- A deep system pack called the Handle Pack. There are six cells in each of three packs filling a flat. Each pack has a built-in handle that the grower buttons together above the grown plants. This is a customer convenience item, making it easier to pick up and carry a unit (fig. 14.1).
- The Magic Planter is an instant color flat. Two flats nest together, each flat holding nine 4-inch type plants (fig. 14.2). When nested together, 18 plants fit in a standard flat size for initial growing. To

Fig. 14.1 The Handle Pack is a deep system pack with built-in handles for customer convenience.

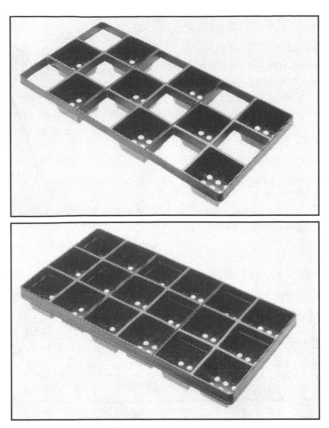

Fig. 14.2 The Magic Planter is two flats that nest together and holds 18 4-inch plants.

space plants, the flats are conveniently separated. To plant in a landscape, you just place the individual flat on top of level ground and let the bedding plants grow.

• Nu Pots and Nu Trays are units combining 12, 16, or 25 pots in 13- x 17½-inch (12 pots) or 13- x 13-inch (16- and 25-pot) trays. The pots are 3¼ inches deep and are widely used by growers of perennials and herbs (fig. 14.3).

Hanging baskets, especially the 10-inch size, have strong consumer demand. Several innovative designs are available, offering styling alternatives and improvements in saucer and hanger design. Fiber- or moss-lined wire baskets in larger sizes continue to be dependable traffic builders for retail growers and garden centers.

Mass merchants have developed a thriving trade in 3½- to 4-inch individually potted plants (especially seed geraniums), which are delivered to them and displayed in carrying trays that hold 14, 15, or 18

Fig. 14.3 Nu Pots and Nu Trays combine 3¹/₄-inch-deep pots in two sizes of trays.

pots. Retail growers can produce a broad array of plant material in 4-, 4¹/₂- and 6-inch pots and use similar carrying trays to attract customers. Four-inch and 4¹/₂-inch sizes are increasingly sought by landscapers. The 6-inch is a true instant color item that provides an immediate show in the home garden. It's a great way to extend the growing, selling, and income season beyond late spring and well into the summer months.

Ecological impacts

All of the flats and packs manufactured and sold across North America are constructed of recycled raw material. Recycled polystyrene plastic is preferred for many products, for ecological concerns, material availability, and cost. West Coast manufacturers are beginning to use materials other than polystyrene, particularly polyethylene and PET, for this type of container. Cost plays a significant role in this choice, as does the durability of the manufactured product.

There are several businesses devoted to collecting and recycling horticultural containers and other greenhouse products. The transport cost from collection points to the recycling centers is substantial, which often makes it impractical for used materials to be returned. The solutions may be additional specialized recycling centers or local community curbside pickup of all types of plastic.

Alternatives to plastic do exist, but they are in minor use. Molded fiber pots and packs have played a part in bedding plant growing for at least four decades and remain popular in some micro-markets. Paper manufacturers are now experimenting with producing several smaller sizes of pots for horticultural use, but it is too early to tell if a serious trend will develop.

Look and plan

Use a thorough problem-solving approach to analyze your container needs. Identify and understand the market in which your business functions. Know your business's strengths and weaknesses, especially relative to competitors. Keep a customer-driven focus to all of your packaging decisions and be willing and ready to change your product mix from one season to the next if that's what it takes for you to remain in step with your customers' wants and needs.

Manufacturers and their distributors have descriptive literature available and are always willing to provide reasonable samples. With a wide array of products available from a large number of sources, you must take the time and make the effort to familiarize yourself with what is available as you identify your choices and needs.

CHAPTER 15

Light, Temperature, and Carbon Dioxide

Meriam Karlsson and Roy Larson

Light

Much of the bedding plant season occurs during the time of year when weather conditions are less than ideal for plant production in the United States. Light intensity is a limiting factor for optimum plant growth. Short days also can limit growth. Crowded conditioms can affect light quality perceived by adjacent plants, and thin, spindly growth can result when bedding plants and spring holiday crops compete for space. Light intensity, duration, and quality are important factors that must be considered in bedding plant production.

Light intensity

Growers once just accepted the fact that light often would be lacking during the bedding plant season's early portions. There were no satisfactory supplemental light sources or systems. Now there are several options to increase light intensity in the greenhouse. Light sources are continuously being improved, thus specific bulb or tube types and their spectral distribution will not be discussed. However, the cost of adding supplementary light is an important issue, and 1993 prices for a few lamps are:

- 400 watt High Pressure Sodium lamp $248
- 250 watt High Pressure Sodium lamp $247
- 1,000 watt High Pressure Sodium lamp $385
- 400 watt Metal Halide lamp $251

You need to determine, however, if the benefits obtained from installing such lamps would justify the investment. In some regions of the country, sunlight is adequate to achieve good growth, and the benefits could be negligible. In regions where light is limited, such lamps could make the production of high quality bedding plants an easier task.

Most lighting systems have lamps that remain stationary, with the consequences that many lamps are needed to cover the area. Some greenhouse firms have installed movable or roving lights, and the results were comparable to stationary lamps. Devices similar to boom irrigators, with lamps attached, work satisfactorily. Frequency and rate of movement can be determined to ensure effective performance.

Importance of light

Light is important in all phases of bedding plant production, beginning with the seed. Seed of some species only will germinate in light, others only will germinate in darkness, and some will germinate under either condition. Seed size often is indicative of the best treatment. Seed size and light requirements of some bedding plants are shown in table 15.1. The light requirement was determined by which seed should be covered according to a seed supplier's catalog. Seed sizes, which are based on the number of seeds per ounce, were obtained from the same source.

Cultivars of the same species can vary greatly in the effects of light or darkness on germination. An example of this variation is shown in table 15.2.

In some instances seed are covered to prevent desiccation, rather than to fulfill the dark requirement.

TABLE 15.1

Light/dark germination requirement and seed/oz.

Dark (seeds/oz.)	Light (seeds/oz.)	Either condition (seeds/oz.)
Dianthus (25,000)	Ageratum (200,000)	Amaranthus (44,000)
Pansy (20,000)	Alyssum (90,000)	Aster (12,000)
Verbena (10,000)	Begonia (2,000,000)	Dahlia (4,500)
Vinca (21,000)	Browallia (125,000)	Geranium (6,000)
Zinnia (2400 to 4000)	Celosia, crested (34,000)	Gerbera (7,000)
	Celosia, feathered (39,000)	Gomphrena (11,500)
	Coleus (100,000)	Marigold (9,000)
	Dusty Miller (90,000)	
	Impatiens (50,000)	Broccoli (9,000)
	Lobelia (1,000,000)	Cabbage (9,000)
	Nicotiana (200,000)	Pepper (9,000)
	Petunia (275,000)	Tomato (9,500)
	Portulaca (280,000)	
	Salvia (7500)	
	Snapdragon (6500)	
	Celery (72,000)	
	Lettuce (25,000)	

TABLE 15.2

Germination percentages of 12 impatiens cultivars

	Germination percentage	
Impatiens cultivar	Light	Dark
Rose Star	95	96
Super Elfin Lipstick	98	92
Accent Pink	97	80
Accent Salmon	89	61
Super Elfin Orchid	85	71
Super Elfin Orange	90	66
Accent Rose #1	94	64
Accent Rose #2	95	52
Impulse Rose	68	62
Super Elfin Red	86	42
Super Elfin Coral	98	25
Super Elfin Pink	96	26

Source: Data from D. Koranski and P. Karlovic, 1989. Plugs: problems, concerns and recommendations for the grower, *GrowerTalks*, 53(8):28-34.

The influence of light on seed germination can be very dramatic. Shoemaker and Carlson [18] reported that Scarlanda begonia seed did not germinate in three weeks when seed were kept in the dark, but did germinate when seed were exposed to just 10 seconds of light.

Light intensity continues to be an important factor after transplanting the germinated seedlings. Recent research by Graper and Healy [9, 10] has focused on the influence of irradiation on photosynthesis, carbohydrate partitioning, and other growth processes. They reported positive results when the Photosynthetic Photon Flux (PPF) was increased. Doubling the PPF for Red Flash petunia increased carbohydrate partitioning by 60%, increased seedling dry weight by 30%, and accelerated the growth rate by 25%. They concluded that PPF had a greater impact than temperature on petunia development.

Lighting and plugs

Plug culture has become a vital part of bedding plant production and several researchers have investigated the benefits of lighting on plug growth. Plugs' economic value have made investment in sophisticated growing rooms feasible. Dreesen and Langhans [4] estimated a crop value of $10 to $12 per square foot for bedding plant plugs.

They compared plant growth at light intensities ranging from 700 to 3,500 foot-candles (7.5 to 37.6 klux) and reported that dry weights of seedlings subjected to 3,500 f-c (37.6 klux) was three times more than those grown at 700 f-c (7.5 klux) after 19 days in growth chambers. Tall, stocky seedlings were produced at the highest intensities. They recommended a minimum light intensity of 1,500 f-c (16.1 klux).

Results of one plug experiment are shown in table 15.3. Seedlings of the highest quality were produced at the highest light intensity (3,500 f-c/37.6 klux).

Dreesen and Langhans [4, 5] have shown the close relationship between light intensity and temperature. Impatiens plug seedlings' shoot dry weight decreased at higher light intensities if the plug medium's temperature was less than 75 F (23.9 C).

TABLE 15.3

**Dry weight, plant height, and quality index
for Accent Red impatiens plugs [a]**

Light levels (f-c)	Dry weight (mg)	Height (mm)	Quality index [b]
700	12	19	6
1,100	19	21	9
1,600	22	18	13
2,300	26	18	15
3,500	35	20	18

Source: Data from D.R. Dressen and R.W. Langhans, 1989, Let there be light (and heat). *Greenhouse Grower,* 7(8):62-64.

[a] Plug seedlings were exposed to five light intensities for 19 days.

[b] Quality index represents dry weight (mg) divided by height (cm).

There are times when storage of plug seedlings could be very beneficial. Kaczperski and Armitage [13] considered temperature to be more important than light in plug seedling storage. Plugs stored in darkness did not flower as quickly as plugs stored in a lighted storage area when the same temperatures were used in both conditions. Kaczperski and Armitage did have difficulty separating photoperiod effects from light intensity effects for some species, such as salvia.

Light is a very important factor during shipping and sales, but that aspect will be discussed in Chapter 30 on postproduction handling. Light also should be considered when bedding plants are placed in the landscape. Classification of selected bedding plant species based on suitability for sunny or shady conditions is shown in table 15.4.

Photoperiod

Carpenter and Beck [3] reported that plant height, fresh weight, and root length increased when White Cascade *Petunia hybrid*a, Moonshot

TABLE 15.4

Landscape light requirements

Sun		Shade
Ageratum (except in hot, dry areas)	Marigold	Begonia (hot, dry conditions)
Alyssum	Nasturtium	Browallia
Bachelor's button	Nicotiana	Coleus
Begonia (cool conditions)	Pansy	Dianthus (hot condition)
Calendula	Petunia	Geraniums (hot conditions)
Celosia	Portulaca	Impatiens
Cleome	Salvia	Lobelia (warm to hot conditions)
Cosmos	Snapdragon	Vinca (hot conditions)
Dahlia	Thunbergia	
Dianthus (cool conditions)	Verbena	
Dusty miller	Verbena	
Geraniums (cool to warm conditions)	Vinca (cool condition)	
Lobelia (cool conditions)	Zinnia	

Tagetes erecta (marigold) and Peter Pan Pink *Zinnia elegans* were subjected to continuous lighting after transplanting. Plants that were lighted for four weeks after transplanting flowered nine to 23 days earlier than plants grown under natural daylengths. Scarlet Elfin impatiens did not respond to supplementary light. Merritt and Kohl [17] compared the effects of nine-hour and 13-hour photoperiods on petunia plant growth.

Plants exposed to the shorter photoperiod had more lateral shoots but the dry weight was less than for plants grown under the 13-hour photoperiod. Leaf area and leaf number were greater under the longer photoperiod. Flower buds were evident after 11 to 19 days at the 13-hour photoperiod, while no flower buds were evident after 25 days at the nine-hour photoperiod. The classification of bedding plants based on photoperiodic response is shown in table 15.5.

Knowledge of daylength impact on flowering enables growers to control growth and/or flowering, if such control is desired, and to predict the flowering season for bedding plants. Temperature and photoperiod do interact, and unusually high or low temperatures can affect the flowering response.

Temperature

Temperature has a major impact on growth rate and the plants' morphological development. Many chemical processes occur simultaneous-

TABLE 15.5

Bedding plant photoperiodic response

Short day	Day neutral	Long day
Basil	Alyssum	Ageratum
Celosia	Begonia (fibrous)	Feverfew
Cleome	Dianthus	Gaillardia
Coleus	Gomphrena	Geranium
Cosmos	Impatiens	Gypsophila
Dahlia	Lobelia	Hollyhock
Marigold (African)	Marigold (French)	Marigold (African)
Morning glory	Pansy	Nicotiana
Rudbeckia	Pepper	Petunia
Salvia	Tomato	Phlox
Zinnia	Vinca	Salpiglossis
		Scabiosa
		Snapdragon
		Verbena

Source: Data from W.H. Carlson, M.P. Kaczperski, and E.M. Rowley, 1993, Bedding plants, in *Introduction to floriculture*, 2nd ed., ed. Roy Larson, Orlando, Fla.: Academic Press.

ly in a plant. The optimal temperatures for these processes vary, and it is difficult to identify the optimal temperature for plant growth. Optimal temperatures also vary with plant species and the desired morphological characteristics of the produced plants. Recommendations for production temperatures are also dependent on the growth stage.

Most bedding plants require a higher temperature for optimal germination than for the continued development. Recommended temperatures for germination vary from 65 F to 80 F (18.3 C to 26.7 C) for most bedding plants [15]. The recommended temperatures for the stem growth stage and cotyledons emergence vary among bedding plants from 62 F to 75 F (16.7 C to 23.9 C), for the growth and development of true leaves from 60 F to 72 F (15.6 C to 22.2 C), and for the final development prior to transplanting or shipping from 58 F to 66 F (14.4 C to 18.9 C) [15].

In the past, only night temperatures were indicated in grower recommendations since they usually were easier to control. Increased knowledge of temperature effects on plant growth and development has prompted a demand for growing facilities that allow better temperature control. Although temperature interacts with many other factors in controlling plant growth, many research results indicate that specific growth processes are primarily determined and controlled by average daily temperature, temperature maintained during specific periods of the 24-hour daily cycle, or the relationship between day and night temperatures. Implementing these research findings allows bedding plant growers to control crop development by maintaining and adjusting production temperatures.

Average daily temperature

The overall growth and maturation rate of plants is determined by the average daily temperature. Appearance of leaves and nodes on a plant is one way to follow the rate and progression of vegetative growth. Determining and controlling the rate of leaf unfolding has successfully been used for many years to schedule Easter lily production.

The temperature where no growth or leaf unfolding is expected to occur is called the base temperature (fig. 15.1). As the temperature increases from the base temperature, the leaf unfolding rate increases with the same amount for each degree of temperature increase in the linear range. The leaf unfolding rate continues to increase proportionally until the optimal temperature has been reached. Increasing the temperature beyond the optimal temperature will result in slower growth rates.

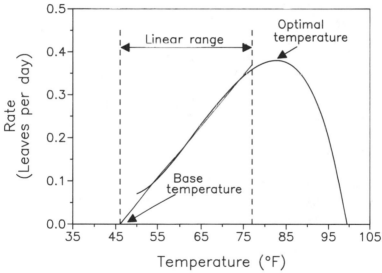

Fig. 15.1. Generalized growth rate response to average daily temperature.

The base temperature and the temperature producing the maximum leaf unfolding and growth rates vary among plant species. Plants from cooler climates usually have lower base and optimal temperatures than those from warmer climates. Base temperatures range from 32 F to 50 F (0 C to 10 C) and optimal temperatures for vegetative growth from 65 F to 85 F (18.3 C to 29.4 C) among commonly grown bedding plants [7].

Photosynthesis rate and dry weight accumulation are affected in some plants by the temperatures maintained during the day and night. During the day, a higher temperature may result in faster photosynthetic rate especially at high light conditions. Respiration or carbon depletion rate increases in plants with increasing temperatures.

During the night there is no photosynthesis, and a low temperature can be expected to result in slow respiration. High day temperature in combination with a low night temperature increases dry weight accumulation in tomatoes, peas, chrysanthemums, and peppers.

Flower initiation

Flower initiation process may be controlled by temperature. A temperature outside the optimal range for flower initiation can inhibit, delay or reduce the number of initiated flowers. Flower formation may be sensitive to the temperature maintained only during the day or during the night period or to temperatures maintained during any period of the 24-hour daily cycle [7].

High night temperatures have been known for years to cause delayed flower initiation in poinsettia. New Guinea impatiens and geraniums have a day and night temperature sensitive flower initiation process. If either the day or night temperature is lower than 63 F (17.2 C) or exceeds 76 F (24.4 C), very few New Guinea impatiens flowers are initiated.

The number of initiated zonal geranium flowers decreases rapidly as the temperature increases above 50 F (10 C). Fuchsia is a day sensitive plant, and flower initiation will not occur if the day temperature exceeds 68 F (20 C). African marigold will not initiate flowers if the night temperature is higher than 74 F (23.3 C). In respect to flower initiation, African marigold is a night temperature sensitive plant.

The rate of many bedding plants' flower bud development is an average daily temperature response. The rate of flower development increases with temperature to about 75 F (23.9 C) in several bedding plant species including geranium, New Guinea impatiens, and fuchsia. Higher temperatures than 75 F (23.9 C) will only result in slower flower development and increase the number of aborted flower buds.

DIF

During recent years, the relationship between day and night temperatures, referred to as reverse temperatures or the difference between day and night (DIF), has been utilized to control plant height. The initial DIF research was done on flowering potted plants at Michigan State University, but it has been found to work also on bedding plants [8].

The difference between day and night temperatures is **positive** when the day temperature is higher than the night temperature, **zero** when day and night temperatures are the same, and **negative** at lower day than night temperatures.

The length of stems is determined by the number of internodes and the length of each individual internode. The rate and number of nodes and internodes formed on a plant are determined primarily by the average daily temperature. The lengths of the internodes are determined by DIF.

As DIF increases from a negative difference to a more positive difference, the length of the internodes increases (fig. 15.2). The internode

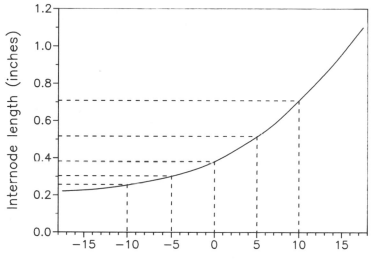

Fig. 15.2. *Generalized internode elongation response to the difference between day and night temperature.*

elongation response to DIF is not, however, linear. Changing DIF from a positive value such as 10 F or 5 F (5.6 C or 2.8 C) to zero will result in a larger decrease in internode elongation than changing DIF from zero to a negative value such as -5 F or -10 F (-2.8 C or -5.6 C) (fig. 15.2).

Growing conditions with a large negative DIF may result in severe chlorosis and slow young seedling growth. Erwin et al. [8] recommend a -2 F or -3 F (-1.1 C or -1.7 C) difference for young seedling height control (one to three weeks old). A larger negative DIF may be used for more mature bedding plants.

Photoperiod and light conditions during the day influence the response to DIF. Short day conditions and high light intensities appear to stimulate the response to DIF. A larger response can therefore be expected during sunny days compared to cloudy days.

Greenhouse temperature control is more difficult during sunny days and maintaining a zero or negative DIF may not be feasible. Under such circumstances, the original DIF technique can be modified. Internode elongation is most sensitive to temperatures during the first two to three hours after sunrise. Dropping the temperature in the morning is almost as effective as maintaining a lower temperature during the entire day.

Growers have received good height control on bedding plants by dropping the temperature immediately before sunrise to 45 F to 50 F (7.2 C to 10 C) for two to three hours or as long as a lower temperature can be maintained [7]. Average daily temperature will not be greatly impacted by a drop in temperature for a few hours each morning and overall growth rate can be maintained.

Plug storage temperature

Plug produced bedding plants sometimes need to be stored at the transplanting stage. The conditions required during storage and shipping to maintain acceptable plant quality have been studied at Michigan State University [11]. The optimal temperature range during storage varies with the bedding plant species and whether storage is in darkness or low light (5 to 50 f-c).

In general, plugs store better and can tolerate higher temperatures if lighted. Pansy plugs can be stored satisfactorily for up to 16 weeks at 32 F or 36.5 F (0 C or 2.5 C) in low light or darkness. In contrast, impatiens plugs will develop chilling injury or die when stored for more than three weeks at temperatures below 45.5 F (7.5 C).

A recommended compromise temperature range for acceptable storage up to four weeks in a lighted environment is from 45.5 to 50 F (7.5 C to 10 C) for eight bedding plant species (ageratum, fibrous begonia, geranium, impatiens, marigold, pansy, petunia, and salvia). After storage, the plugs should be allowed to warm up in a low light environment at 60 F to 70 F (15.6 C to 21.1 C) and provided with adequate media moisture [12]. Watering may also be required during storage beyond one week at low humidity conditions.

Many plant species are often grown together in a bedding plant operation. Since the optimal temperatures will vary among plants, decisions on suitable production temperatures can be a challenge. Temperature, however, can be a powerful tool to achieve desired plant growth and development. A prerequisite for using temperature to manage bedding plant production is a basic knowledge of temperature effects on different plant characteristics.

Carbon dioxide

Carbon dioxide (CO_2) is a raw material in photosynthesis for forming a plant's carbohydrates and other components. In a greenhouse or growth room filled with plants, the ambient CO_2 levels can be depleted especially with limited venting. Supplementing with CO_2 may then improve photosynthesis, overall growth, and the dry weight accumulated in the plants. The greenhouse temperature and light levels interact with the CO_2 availability in determining photosynthesis rate. At higher temperature and light levels, photosynthesis can be faster, and more CO_2 is required.

Efforts to increase CO_2 in a greenhouse during the spring can be a frustrating and expensive event when venting is required for temperature control. Producing bedding plants from plugs and using growth rooms provide opportunities to increase the CO_2 concentration to a large number of plants in a confined area. Although plants will accumulate more dry weight, they may not develop faster and have the desired morphological characteristics such as height, branching, and flowering at marketing time. Recent studies on supplementing CO_2 for a limited time are showing promising results, however, in increasing growth rate and producing high quality bedding plants.

University of Georgia studies [1] showed pansy plugs grown at an elevated CO_2 concentration could be transplanted earlier and required fewer days to flower than pansy seedlings grown at ambient CO_2 levels (about 350 ppm). The CO_2 application timing, duration, and concentration were all important for the resulting seedling development as well as the light conditions when CO_2 was applied.

CO_2 applications initiated at the cotyledon stage seven days after sowing more effectively reduced the number of days to transplant and pansy flowering than applications initiated 14, 21, 28 or 35 days after sowing. The optimum duration at elevated CO_2 was 14 to 21 days.

CO_2 applied for only seven days gave marginal growth improvements compared to ambient levels. At least 1,000 ppm of CO_2 wererequired at a 1,450 f-c light level. Growing conditions with 1,000 or 1,500 ppm CO_2 for 14 to 21 days at a 1,450 f-c light level resulted in 14 days earlier transplanting and more than 10 days faster flowering. Similar results have also been observed using CO_2 during geranium seedling development [14]

References

[1] Armitage, A.M. 1993. CO_2 decreases plug and bench time. *Greenhouse Grower* 11(11):36, 38-39.

[2] Carlson, W.H., M.P. Kaczperski, and E.M. Rowley. 1993. Bedding plants. In *Introduction to floriculture*. 2nd ed. Ed. R.A. Larson. Orlando, Fla.: Academic Press.

[3] Carpenter, W.J., and G.R. Beck. 1973. High intensity supplementary lighting of bedding plants after transplanting. *HortScience* 8(6):482-483.

[4] Dreesen, D.R., and R.W. Langhans. 1989. Let there be light (and heat). *Greenhouse Grower* 7(8):62-64.

[5] Dreesen, D.R., and R.W. Langhans. 1991. Uniformity of impatiens plug seedling growth in controlled environments. *J. Amer. Soc. Hort. Sci.* 116:786-791.

[6] Dreesen, D.R., and R.W. Langhans. 1992. Temperature effects on growth of plug seedlings in controlled environments. *J. Amer. Soc. Hort. Sci.* 117(2):209-215.

[7] Erwin, J.E., and R.D. Heins. 1993. *Temperature effects on bedding plant growth*. Minnesota Commercial Flower Growers Assn. Bul. 42(3):1-11.

[8] Erwin, J.E, R.D. Heins, W.H. Carlson, and J. Biernbaum. 1989. Do cool days/warm nights work with plugs? You bet! *GrowerTalks* 52(11):46, 48-50, 52.

[9] Graper, D.F., and W. Healy. 1991. High pressure sodium irradiation and infrared radiation accelerate petunia seedling growth. *J. Amer. Soc. Hort. Sci.* 116(3):435-438.

[10] Graper, D.F., and W. Healy. 1992. Modification of petunia seedling carbohydrate partitioning by irradiance. *J. Amer. Soc. Hort. Sci.* 1117(3):477-480.

[11] Heins, R., and N. Lange. 1992. Plug storage. One temp can fit all. *Greenhouse Grower* 10(4):30, 32-33, 36.

[12] Heins, R., W. Carlson, and N. Lange. 1991. Plug into storage. *Greenhouse Grower* 9(11):72-73.

[13] Kaczperski, M.P., and A.M. Armitage. 1992. Short-term storage of plug-grown bedding plant seedlings. *HortSci.* 27(7):798-800.

[14] Kaczperski, M.P., and A.M. Armitage. 1993. Accelerating growth of geraniums in plugs with light and carbon dioxide. *HortSci.* 28(5):520.

[15] Koranski, D. 1989. How to grow 32 plug crops. *GrowerTalks* 53(4):197-200.

[16] Koranski, D., and P. Karlovich. 1989. Plugs: problems, concerns and recommendations for the grower. *GrowerTalks* 53(8):28, 30, 32, 34.

[17] Merritt, R.H., and H.C. Kohl, Jr. 1982. Effect of root temperature and photoperiod on growth and crop productivity efficiency of petunia. *J. Amer. Soc. Hort. Sci.* 107(6):997-1000.

[18] Shoemaker, C.A., and W.H. Carlson. 1992. Temperature and light affect seed germination of *Begonia* x *semperflorens-cultorum*. *HortSci.* 27(2):181.

CHAPTER 16

Bedding Plant Height Control

James E. Barrett and John E. Erwin

Bedding plant height and size control are important components in producing plants that withstand shipping and handling stresses and have greater aesthetic appeal. Proper height control is achieved through cultural practices, environmental conditions, variety selection, and growth-regulating chemicals. Growers' methods to control plant growth vary widely for different climates and crops. Growers in cool, sunny climates can produce crops outdoors and take advantage of high natural light levels. In areas with low light and cool temperatures, temperature regulation and watering and fertilization practices are more important. In warm, humid climates growth regulators are more important.

Growth retardants

Growth retardant chemicals produce shorter plants by blocking the plants' natural production of gibberellin, which results in reduced internode elongation. The plants also have smaller, darker green leaves and use less water. Thorough reviews of growth regulators have been published by Larson [14] and Davis et al. [11].

Growth-regulating chemicals have basic characteristic differences that affect the grower's choice of chemicals, as well as determining when and how to apply. These decisions are increasingly important because stronger chemicals are available, and newer cultivars and production practices often reduce the amount needed. Additionally, growth regulators are covered by the U.S. Environmental Protection Agency regulations governing pesticide use. They can only be used on crops specifically listed on the label and must be applied as described on the label.

TABLE 16.3

Bedding plant response to DIF[a]

Common name	Scientific name	Response to DIF
African daisy	*Dimorphotheca aurantiaca*	2
Ageratum	*Ageratum houstonianum*	3
Alyssum	*Lobularia maritima*	1
Aster	*Callistephus chinensis*	3
Astilbe	*Astilbe x arendsii*	2
Baby's breath	*Gypsophila elegans*	3
Basil	*Ocimum basilicum*	3
Bean	*Phaseolus vulgaris*	0
Begonia (fibrous)	*Begonia semperflorens*	1
Begonia (tuberous)	*Begonia socotrana x Begonia tuberhybrida*	1
Broccoli	*Brassica oleracea*. Italica group	3
Browallia	*Browallia speciosa*	2
Brussels sprouts	*Brassica oleracea*. Gemmifera group	3
Cabbage	*Brassica oleracea*. Capitata group	3
Calendula	*Calendula*	2
Campanula	*Campanula isophylla*	3
Cantaloupe	*Cucumis melo*	3
Cauliflower	*Brassica oleracea*. Botrytis group	3
Celosia (crested)	*Celosia cristata*	2
Celosia (feathered)	*Celosia cristata*. Plumosa group	2
Cleome	*Cleome spinosa*	2
Coleus	*Coleus blumei*	2
Columbine	*Aquilegia*	2
Cosmos	*Cosmos bipinnatus*	2
Cucumber	*Cucumis sativus*	1-2
Dahlia	*Dahlia pinnata*	3

Table 16.3 continued

Common name	Scientific name	Response to DIF
Dusty miller (large leaf)	*Centaurea candidissima*	1
Dusty miller (feather leaf)	*Cineraria maritima*	1
Eggplant	*Solanum melongena*	3
Geranium	*Pelargonium x hortorum*	2
Gerbera	*Gerbera jamesonii*	1
Gomphrena	*Gomphrena globosa*	2
Hibiscus	*Hibiscus moscheutos*	1
Impatiens	*Impatiens wallerana*	2
Lobelia	*Lobelia erinus*	1
Marigold (African)	*Tagetes erecta*	1
Marigold (French)	*Tagetes patula*	0
Morning glory	*Ipomoea purpurea*	3
Moss rose	*Portulaca grandiflora*	2
New Guinea impatiens	*Impatiens x hybrida*	1
Pansy	*Viola tricolor*	2
Pea	*Pisum sativum*	0-1
Pepper	*Capsicum annuum*	0-1
Petunia	*Petunia x hybrida*	1-2
Pink	*Dianthus chinensis*	3
Salvia	*Salvia splendens*	2-3
Snapdragon	*Antirrhinum majus*	1
Squash	*Cucurbita*	2
Tomato	*Lycopersicon esculentum*	2
Verbena	*Verbena x hybrida*	1-2
Vinca	*Vinca rosea*	1-2
Watermelon	*Citrullus lanatus*	3

Source: Data from J.E. Erwin and R.D. Heins, 1993, *Temperature effects on bedding plant growth,* Bulletin 42:1-18, Minnesota Commercial Flower Growers Association [13].

[a] Response is indicated on a scale of 0 to 3, where 0 indicates no response and 3 indicates strong response.

TABLE 16.4

Different day-night temperatures effects on internode elongation

	Internode length		
	Day temperature: 63 F	68 F	74 F
Crop	Night temperature: 68 F	68 F	68 F
Snapdragon	1.2 cm	—	1.6 cm
Salvia	1.2 cm	2.0 cm	3.5 cm
Geranium	3.2 cm	4.5 cm	5.8 cm
Petunia	5.8 cm	6.9 cm	7.8 cm

Source: Data from J.E. Erwin and R.D. Heins, 1993, *Temperature effects on bedding plant growth,* Bulletin 42:1-18, Minnesota Commercial Flower Growers Association [13].

Environmental factors affect response to DIF. Stem elongation response to DIF is greater as day length decreases and as light intensity increases. Therefore, response to DIF is greater under short days than long days. For instance, with a crop growing under natural day length, the plant response to DIF will be greater in January than April under full-sun conditions. Similarly, a greater response to DIF occurs on sunny days than cloudy days.

Temperature drop has become widely used because stem elongation is most sensitive to temperature during the first two to three hours of the morning. Dropping temperatures during those hours can result in almost as much stem elongation reduction as if temperatures were reduced all day. Conversely, increasing temperature can stimulate stem elongation significantly. Keep temperatures cool for as long in the day as possible. In addition, do not let temperatures increase immediately in the morning.

Most growers find that using the temperature drop is the most practical aspect of using temperature to control plant height. Often controlling temperatures during the latter part of a day is more difficult than controlling temperatures during the morning. This technique is particularly useful in climates with cool nights and warm days and is even referred to as a "California DIF." Growers in cool climates may drop temperatures to 45 F to 50 F (7.5 C to 10 C) for the first two to three hours on a bedding plant crop.

Dropping temperatures for two to three hours does not affect average daily temperature in most cases. So crop schedules will not be

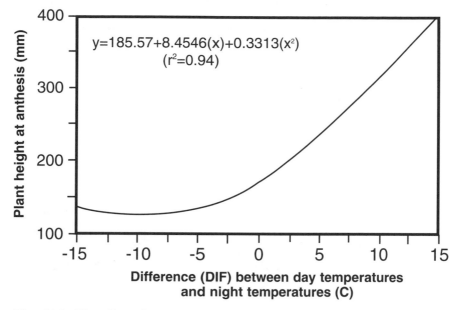

$$y=185.57+8.4546(x)+0.3313(x^2)$$
$$(r^2=0.94)$$

Fig. 16.8. The effect of increasing DIF on Dark Red Annette Hegg poinsettia plant height at flowering [13].

greatly delayed if this technique is used rather than cool temperatures all day.

The stem elongation reduction due to a temperature drop is greatest when the drop is rapid, occurs at sunrise, and light intensity is high. Alternative ways to drop temperatures can be to simply water plants overhead with cold water at sunrise. The cool water and evaporation reduces plant temperature much as a drop in air temperatures does. Fans can also drop temperatures quickly.

Leaf color or greenness increases as DIF increases. Leaf chlorosis induced by temperature is generally temporary. More severe chlorosis can occur when day temperatures are less than night temperatures. In contrast to leaf greenness, geranium leaf zonation increases as the average daily temperature under which plants are grown decreases.

Future techniques

Scientist are studying other methods for controlling plant development that have important potential in commercial bedding plant production. Light is a major factor in plant growth. High light levels produce shorter bedding plants, and photoperiods can affect time of flowering and

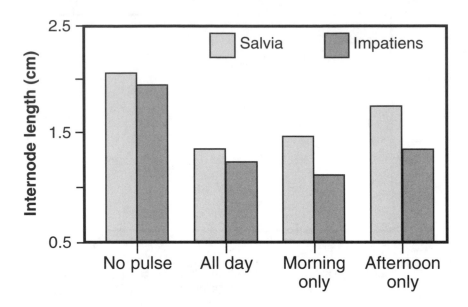

Fig. 16.9. Effect of cool temperature drop at different times of day [13].

size of several crops, such as salvia and marigolds. However, recent studies with light quality and the balance of far-red and red light show that light quality manipulation may be important in bedding plant production [12]. High far-red light causes plants to be taller, and, conversely, high red light causes them to be shorter. Also, red light given at the end of the day can produce shorter plants. Narrow spectrum light sources or filters built into greenhouse coverings can manipulate red light.

Another exciting development is using mechanical conditioning to produce compact crops [15]. Plants growing in greenhouses are frequently taller than similar plants produced outdoors and plants near doorways are often shorter. One of the reasons for this is the wind movement in open areas. Research shows that greenhouse crops that are shaken slightly for brief periods during the day will be often shorter. As with DIF, success is more likely at the beginning of the light period. Mechanical conditioning may be done by vibrating benches, brushing plants, or blowing air over them.

Note: The mention or exclusion of any product or brand name in this chapter is not intended as the author's or publisher's endorsement or lack thereof. Any mention is for illustrative purposes. Growers are advised to apply all chemicals according to manufacturers' instructions.

References

[1] Barrett, J.E. 1982. Chrysanthemum height control by ancymidol, PP333, and EL-500 dependent on medium composition. *HortSci.* 17:896-897.

[2] Barrett, J.E., C.A. Bartuska, and T.A. Nell. 1987. Efficacy of ancymidol, daminozide, flurprimdol, paclobutrazol, and XE-1019 when followed by irrigation. *HortSci.* 22:1287-1289.

[3] ———. 1994. Application techniques alter uniconazole efficacy on chrysanthemums. *HortSci.* In press.

[4] Barrett, J.E., and E. Jay Holcomb. 1993. Growth regulating chemicals. In *Geraniums IV*. 4th ed. Ed. J.W. White. Batavia, Ill.: Ball Publishing.

[5] Barrett, J.E., and T.A. Nell. 1987. Efficacy and phytotoxicity of paclobutrazol and XE-1019 on vinca. In *Proceedings*, Fla. State Hort. Soc. 100:382-383.

[6] ———. 1992. Efficacy of paclobutrazol and uniconazole on four bedding plant species. *HortSci.* 27:896-897.

[7] ———. 1990. Factors affecting efficacy of paclobutrazol and uniconazole on petunia and chrysanthemum. *Acta Horticulturae* 272:229-234.

[8] Barrett, J.E., T.A. Nell, and R.K. Schoellhorn. 1994. Effect of paclobutrazol drench on hanging basket impatiens. *HortSci.* In press.

[9] Carlson, W.H. 1993. Tree geraniums. In *Geraniums IV*. 4th ed. Ed. J.W. White. Batavia, Ill.: Ball Publishing.

[10] Davis, T.D. 1991. Post-production performance of uniconazole-treated zinnia and marigold plugs. *HortTechnology* 1:49-53.

[11] Davis, T.D., G.L. Steffens, and N. Sankhla. 1988. Triazole plant growth regulators. In *Horticultural Reviews*. Vol. 10. Ed. J. Janick. Portland, Ore.: Timber Press.

[12] Decoteau, D.R., H.A. Hatt, J.W. Kelly, M.J. McMahon, N. Rajapaske, R.E. Young, and R.K. Pollock. 1993. Applications of photomorphogenesis research to horticultural systems. *HortSci.* 28:974, 1063.

[13] Erwin, J.E., and R.D. Heins. 1993. *Temperature effects on bedding-plant growth*. Bulletin 42:1-18. Minnesota Commercial Flower Growers Association.

[14] Larson, R.A. 1985. Growth regulators in floriculture. In *Horticultural Reviews*. Vol. 7. Ed. J. Janick. Westport, Conn.: AVI Publishing Company, Inc.

[15] Latimer, J.G., and R.B. Beverly. 1993. Mechanical conditioning of greenhouse-grown transplants. *HortTechnology* 3:412-414.

CHAPTER 17

Greenhouse Structures

William J. Roberts

A greenhouse structure is designed to provide an enclosure where crops can be economically produced at optimum environmental conditions. The structure must withstand wind, rain, snow, the stress of hanging baskets and other crop loads, and be able to provide sufficient PAR (photosynthetically active radiation) through the glazing for plant growth.

The structure must also be designed so that a crop can be handled efficiently, with minimum labor and management. The cropping system, environmental control system, and materials handling features must be integrated into an effective greenhouse production facility. Considering one piece of the puzzle without the others can only lead to an ineffective and uneconomical operation.

Today's structures are made of steel, aluminum, or wood, and some designs incorporate all three materials. Anchoring and bracing are important design features to prevent wind damage. Structural members and connections should meet the standards published in the National Greenhouse Manufacturers Association's *Standards—Design Loads in Greenhouse Structures*.

Many municipalities require a licensed architect's or professional engineer's seal to ensure that the greenhouse design is adequate for the location. Human safety and fire protection are important considerations also. Recent efforts have been made to evaluate greenhouses based on their own special needs and not the needs of agricultural buildings in general.

Local governing bodies normally control the construction of new facilities. Be sure to check with these building officials when considering new construction.

Wood used in new greenhouses should be pressure-treated with copper napthanate, CCA, wolmanizing, or other non-toxic treatments.

Creosote and Penta-Chloro-Phenol are not suitable for greenhouse use. Foundations should penetrate below the frost line, usually 30 inches (750 cm), and foundation materials should be impervious to insect damage. Concrete is the normal choice, although pressure-treated wood is appropriate for wooden frame greenhouses. Footings for post construction should be designed to handle the snow's downward load and the wind's vertical uplift load.

Greenhouse orientation

Greenhouse orientation has long been debated. A free-standing greenhouse will receive more total light on a year-round basis when oriented with the long dimension in the north-south direction. The east and west roofs act as receiving surfaces for light, and the sun is directly overhead from April to October—so large amounts of light enter the greenhouse. However, only one-third of the light available in mid-June is available in mid-December at 40 degrees N latitude, and because of the low sun angle, more light enters the greenhouse during the winter if the ridge line orientation is east-west.

We normally need to shade in the summer because of excess light, so orientation should be based on light requirements during low-light periods. A free-standing greenhouse at latitudes of 40 degrees (or more) north or south of the equator should be oriented east-west.

Another debate concerns the orientation of large, gutter-connected greenhouses. The gutter structure, which is designed to support the building and carry off rain water, produces significant shadows in direct sunlight. Normal recommendations are to orient large gutter-connected greenhouses in the north-south direction, allowing the shadow pattern to move from the gutter's west side in the morning to the gutter's east side in the afternoon, so that no part of the greenhouse will be in total shade all day.

With an east-west orientation, the shadow pattern remains on the gutter's north side. The shadow's intensity and width will change with time of day and time of year, but a portion of the greenhouse production area is in total shade all day. To make better use of the light energy that enters the greenhouse, the recommended orientation for gutter-connected greenhouses at latitudes of 40 degrees (or more) north or south of the equator is north-to-south.

Roof angle

Roof angle also affects light entering the greenhouse. Flat roof angles tend to reflect light when the sun is lower in the sky and light is most critical. Roof designs should have an angle of at least 27 degrees, or a slope of 1 elevation unit for each 2 horizontal projection units. A 20-foot-wide (6 m) greenhouse should have a 5-foot (1.5 m) distance to the ridge bar (fig. 17.1). Construction designs with a wide arch should be avoided because it tends to create a large flat area at mid-span reflecting valuable light energy. This flat area can fail in heavy snow if inadequately supported. Excessive condensation dripping can also occur in the span's center area (fig. 17.2).

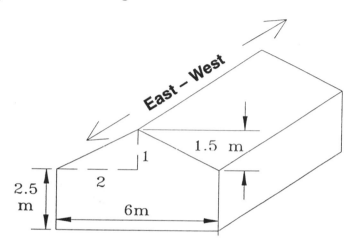

Fig. 17.1. Roof designs should have a 27-degree angle or a slope of 1 elevation unit per 2 horizontal projection units.

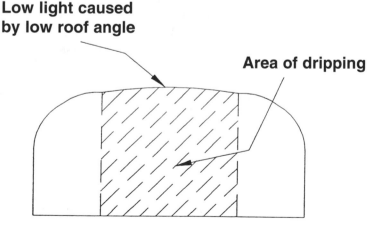

Fig. 17.2. Avoid a wide arched greenhouse roof because of low light and dripping.

If using a double glazing polyethylene air-inflated covering, minimize the structural design's horizontal purlins. Purlins tend to intercept condensate moving down the film and create drip lines in the greenhouse, a cause of uneven watering and possible disease outbreak. Designs that only use bows tend to reduce condensation drip.

Bedding plant growers often have difficult decisions to make concerning what type of structure to build. Greenhouses used only in the spring are more difficult to amortize, making costs very important. Another difficult decision involves single, free-standing versus gutter-connected greenhouse designs. Single greenhouses can be less expensive initially; the difficulty comes in predicting the size the operation will grow into.

Gutter-connected designs, although initially more expensive, allow for simple expansion, provide greater energy savings, and much greater labor efficiency. Most growers who opt for a more expensive, small gutter-connected greenhouse are more satisfied later when their operation has grown.

Snow is a consideration for some growers, but with stronger structural designs, it is no longer mandatory that a greenhouse be free-standing to withstand heavy snow weight. Gutter-connected designs are more versatile, provide simple installation of thermal screens for energy conservation and shading, and greater opportunities for improved materials handling systems.

Glazings

Greenhouse glazings provide a translucent barrier between the environment outside and an atmosphere conducive to plant growth inside the greenhouse. The glazing must allow PAR (photosynthetically active radiation) to pass into the greenhouse to provide energy for crop growth by photosynthesis. It must also provide a barrier that helps maintain appropriate temperatures inside the greenhouse.

Light is a paramount consideration when selecting a glazing material. Test results performed on three glazing systems at a Connecticut rose growing facility are presented in table 17.1. PAR transmission measured at the glazing level represents the material's effects. PAR measured at the canopy level includes the structure's influence. Canopy and glazing PAR levels are nearly the same for all treatments. The single glass was made of small panes with closely spaced wooden sash bars. The double glass system used larger panes, but the lower glass panes were set loosely into the sash bars, allowing significant condensation to form between the two panes. The acrylic panels were supported by aluminum bars spaced 4 feet (101 mm) on centers, causing minimum structural shading. Unfortunately, polycarbonate panels and polyethylene greenhouses of similar construction at the same location could not be tested.

TABLE 17.1

Percent PAR transmission

Sensor location	Single glass (%)	Double glass (%)	Acrylic (%)
At glazing	.60	.58	.58
At canopy	.56	.56	.55

Types of glazings

Several glazings are used successfully on commercial greenhouses, including glass, polycarbonate and acrylic panels, fiberglass reinforced panels, and specially-designed polyethylene film for greenhouse applications. Glass is the original and perhaps most reliable glazing for light transmission. Double-wall panel configuration and polyethylene film using the air-inflation technique have energy conservation advantages. Conservatively estimated, 30% of the heating energy can be saved with double glazing.

Glass greenhouses are popular, and most new construction is the Dutch type, imported from the Netherlands. These greenhouses feature gutter-connected construction and large glass panes that help eliminate shadows. These panes are supported on all four edges and eliminate lapping panes, a common source of air infiltration and energy loss. Energy saving blankets or thermal screens are used in most new greenhouses and reduce the energy required for heating glass structures, allowing them to be more competitive when energy costs and concerns are important.

Polyethylene film applied in a double layer is currently the most popular greenhouse glazing. Most films are carefully engineered and contain a UV inhibitor to reduce deterioration from the sun and an EVA (ethyl vinyl acetate) component to add strength at the folds. They have a three-year effective service life. In addition, IR barriers are available that can effectively reduce nighttime radiation from the greenhouse, a previous disadvantage to polyethylene greenhouse glazing, and anti-fog additives that reduce condensation drip, an undesirable feature of some film coverings.

Polyethylene film is available up to 50 feet wide (15 meters) and in the high cost of other components—the heating, ventilation, and cooling system, bench and irrigation systems, energy conservation, and shading systems.

Controlled environment

Heating

The photosynthetic process is most efficient at specific temperatures for particular crops. Night temperatures are also important for plant growth and must be maintained within specific ranges for most crops. At 40 degrees N latitude during the winter, heat energy needs to be added to the greenhouse to maintain desired temperatures. On clear days in double glazed houses, solar energy can maintain desired temperatures most of the time. In single glazed structures, however, supplemental energy is required both day and night.

Heat energy is supplied to the greenhouse in several ways. Unit hot air heaters, hot water or steam heat distributed in a pipe network, or warm floors are common methods. Many heating systems utilize one or more of these methods for effective temperature control. Unit heaters provide the least uniform temperature distribution, since the energy is being produced and released in a small box and must be distributed. Hot water or steam pipe loop systems are very efficient in distributing heat uniformly throughout the greenhouse, especially if the water temperature is controlled with mixing valves.

Floor heating or soil heating systems give the slowest response time but provide the best uniformity because the heat transfer area is large and temperature differences throughout the facility are very small. Floor or soil heating systems are not sufficient to supply all the heat necessary in cold weather, so hot air unit heaters or hot water pipe loop systems are used in conjunction with the floor heating system.

Hot water systems. Steam systems are the most difficult to control and are not used in new commercial installations. Hot water systems using mixing valves and variable pipe loop temperatures are very popular and energy efficient. A temperature control sensor monitors the system and adjusts the water temperature and the pumping mechanism. As the greenhouse temperature nears the setpoint, the pump stops, and the pipe loop system is filled with 90 F (32 C), not 160 F (70 C) water, avoiding temperature overrun and wasted energy.

Floor heating systems. These systems use 90 F to 120 F (32 C to 50 C) water and supply 40% to 50% of the required heat. Higher water temperature raises soil temperature too high and increases evaporation and energy losses. Soil heating systems are used mostly for floor growing systems. Peninsula (movable or transportable) bench systems are normally heated by a steel pipe loop under the bench or an EPDM flexible pipe system on the benches under the crop. Uneven heat distribution leads to uneven drying and to significant irrigation management problems.

Hot air unit heaters. These are the least expensive heating systems to purchase and install but give the greatest vertical and horizontal temperature gradients in a greenhouse. Unit heaters are particularly ineffective with a floor growing system. With a unit heater, the greenhouse often has to be maintained at an air temperature 15 F (8 C) higher than usual to provide proper soil temperature.

A floor heating system is the opposite; cooler temperatures can be maintained at the 6 feet (2 m) level because soil temperatures are naturally warmer. Some growers using a floor system operate the greenhouse 5 F to 10 F (3 C to 6 C) lower than normally recommended night temperature. These lower temperatures often result in 15% to 20% overall energy savings for heating.

Venting is required for all unit heaters, and an unrestricted screened inlet area of 50 square inches (310 cm) per 100,000 Btu per hour (30 kW) heater capacity is required to provide oxygen to the heating unit. Failure to vent the heater or provide air inlet can cause human and plant safety problems in the greenhouse. New greenhouse construction is extremely airtight, and you cannot assume that sufficient air intake is provided by door and vent openings.

Heating requirements. These requirements are a function of greenhouse glazing, desired night operating temperature, outside design temperature, and greenhouse wall and roof surface area. For single-glazed structures, the heating coefficient is 1.2 Btu per hour per square foot per degree F (6.8 watts/m^2/C) and 0.8 Btu per hour per square foot per degree F (4.5 watts/m^2/C) for double glazed structures. Multiplying the surface area by this coefficient by the design temperature difference for a particular location will give the heating load in Btu per hour (watts).

A single-glazed glass greenhouse in Philadelphia with a 64,585 square foot (6,000 m^2) surface area and a 60 F (33 C) design temperature difference requires a 4,595,500 Btu per hour (1,346 kW) boiler rating. This is equivalent to approximately 137 boiler horsepower. The same greenhouse with double-glazing would require only 3,063,666 Btu per hour (897 kW) and a 91 boiler horsepower.

A traditional hot water design would use 2-inch (5 cm) pipe, which fan's high cost and electrical wiring installation are drawbacks. Operating costs are reasonable, considering the system's reliability. Systems are normally designed for one volume change per minute. In houses equipped with shading and thermal screens, two-thirds of a volume change per minute is adequate.

Ventilation stages are created by using a computer or mechanical control that monitors the size of the window inlet. The greenhouse temperature determines the number of fans needed. The window vent opening is matched to the air volume to provide the optimum 700 feet per minute (3.6 m/sec) air velocity for mixing. A computer calculates the window opening by the length of time it takes to achieve the opening. A controller uses a mechanical switching system to sense window position to give appropriate vent window opening.

Air inlets are the most important ventilation system parts. During some of the growing season, cold air entering the greenhouse may cause localized subcooling and damage the crop adjacent to the inlet. Figure 17.4 illustrates a window vent where the opening is programmed to match the required fan volume at a particular moment. This high velocity creates an effective jet action, which causes the incoming air to mix

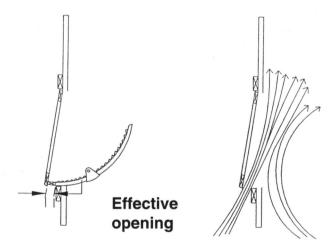

Effective opening

Fig. 17.4. Window vent is programmed to give high velocity and good mixing in cold weather.

well with greenhouse ambient air, very important when ventilating during colder days.

However, mixing during warmer weather is also important to eliminate stagnant locations in the growing area. The air jet mixing action is like placing a high volume water hose in a 50-gallon (200 l) drum— the jet of water thoroughly mixes the drum's contents.

Shading

Traditionally, shading is done by applying a white compound to the glazing material during warm periods when light is most intense. The compound limits the heat energy amount coming into the greenhouse while allowing enough PAR to enter to not limit photosynthesis. At latitude 40 degrees N, applications are normally made in early May on glass greenhouses. By October, the white compound has weathered off so that light is not limited during the darker period. Glass should be washed if it is not clean. Because white shading compound is difficult to remove, it is not normally applied to either film or rigid plastic greenhouse glazings.

Plastic netting and shading materials last for many years and are used on plastic glazed greenhouses and are applied easily over the glazing. Screen materials commonly use alternating strips of aluminized and white porous polyester materials. The strip arrangement determines shading percent. Polypropylene shade materials, available in a variety of shading percentages, are a common choice. Shading percentages range from 10% to 90% with 50% to 55% being most popular at 40 degrees N latitude.

The difficulty with the shading systems mentioned is that they are essentially fixed. Once they are applied, they remain on the greenhouse until removal in the fall. In conjunction with energy saving blankets or thermal screens, materials have been developed that are both winter energy savers of heating fuel and summer thermal screens to reduce the greenhouse's radiant heat load. The advantage of these systems is that they are movable and can provide shading as needed throughout the growing season.

Evaporative cooling

Evaporative cooling takes place in a greenhouse when plants transpire and the energy to evaporate water is taken from the greenhouse environment, cooling it. Evaporating additional water vapor in the air increases cooling.

The potential for cooling incoming air is the wet-bulb depression, which can be determined from a psychometric chart based on the incoming air's temperature and humidity. The system works very well in dry, desert-like climates. In more humid climates, wet-bulb depression is reduced and cooling potential is limited. However, even in warm tropical climates, in the heat of the day, wet-bulb depression can be between 5 F to 9 F (3 C and 5 C).

A fan and pad system is an excellent way to cool a greenhouse. This system, in addition to the crop's transpiration, can create good growing conditions in very warm climates. In a fan and pad system, air from outside the building is passed through a wall of pad material that is wet by running water. The pad is designed so that the water and air paths cross, providing good evaporation. The pad is installed at one end of the greenhouse with the fan or fans at the other end.

One difficulty with the system is that cooling takes place on one side of the house, immediately adjacent to the pads. The air is warmed as it passes through the greenhouse on the way to the fan exhaust. Acme Fan Company has an engineering design manual for fan and pad systems, which lists air volume requirements and pad areas for various size greenhouses and geographical locations.

Another system that is becoming popular is the **high-pressure fog** system. A 600 psi (4,200 KPa) pressure is used to create finely atomized water particles, increasing the chances for greater water evaporation and more cooling. Misting nozzles are located strategically in the greenhouse and at the inlet window. Evaporation occurs throughout the greenhouse, which means more uniform temperatures are possible with this system, unlike the fan and pad system where a thermal gradient spans wide greenhouses.

The high-pressure fog system requires a high investment. High-pressure pipe and fittings have to be used and the water filtered and treated so that chemical and biological buildup does not foul the small nozzle orifices. The exact water treatment required depends upon the water supply quality.

A heavy iron concentration can be handled by a relatively simple sprinkler device where the supply water is sprayed under low pressure through coarse nozzles, and the iron is separated into a collecting device. The water is then filtered, further treated, and directed into the high pressure pump.

The purpose of cooling is to control leaf surface temperature, which is controlled by the plant through transpiration and evaporation. As the greenhouse humidity increases, the potential for transpiration from leaves is reduced. When using a fogging system, the greenhouse relative humidity has to be kept as low as possible by air exchange with outside air. The exact amount of air required has not been established, but a system that has performed well uses an air exchange rate of between one-fourth and one-third volume change per minute.

Fans run constantly, and the misting system is cycled by a time clock or computer. The system must be managed to balance the possible temperature reduction with greenhouse relative humidity. Relative humidity maintained too high can be as harmful to growing plants as extremely high temperatures. Workers' comfort must also be considered in designing a fogging system.

Greenhouse environmental control for cooling is not an easy problem to solve in warm, moist climates. The best solution is rarely found in only one greenhouse cooling component. Most often the answer incorporates all three: a well-designed ventilation system for exchanging inside air with outside air, the proper amount of shading to reduce the incoming radiation and still allow plant growth, and an appropriate evaporative cooling system designed for the specific site.

Accurately determining greenhouse heating and cooling costs contributes to sound decisions and business growth. A computer model projecting monthly operational costs can assist in making decisions concerning crop selection, energy use, months during which the greenhouse remains idle, and determining an investment's economic advantages such as a thermal screen. Benefits of energy conservation systems or the cost of operation can be projected using a degree-day data evaluation (tables 17.2 and 17.3). Note that approximately one-half of the energy and operating costs occurs in winter months.

TABLE 17.2

Projected monthly heating costs/degree days [a]

	Degree days	Cost/month ($)
October	340	180
November	600	449
December	961	778
January	1,023	838
February	896	730
March	775	598
April	420	269

[a] Heating costs for a 30- by 96-foot (9.1 m by 29 m) greenhouse located in a 5,016 degree-day area.

TABLE 17.3

Projected monthly operating costs w/wo thermal screen (TS) [a]

	Degree days	Cost/month ($)	Cost/month with TS ($)
October	340	2,044	1,396
November	600	5,109	3,489
December	961	8,856	6,048
January	1,023	9,537	6,513
February	896	8,306	5,673
March	775	6,812	4,652
April	420	3,066	2,094

[a] One acre (0.4 hectare), double-glazed, polyethylene greenhouse.

CHAPTER 18

Facilities Planning and Mechanization

John W. Bartok, Jr.

Efficient facility layout and good use of labor and equipment can contribute to low bedding plant production costs. Because each flat may be handled as many as a dozen times before it is sold, it is important that you develop an efficient materials moving system.

Labor and equipment used for greenhouse crop production must be looked at as part of a system rather than as separate unrelated elements. Each task, whether performed by hand or by machine, is related to other tasks in the growing process. Consideration needs to be given to the operation's size, crops grown, production schedule, amount of capital available, and many other factors.

Analyze your operation

In analyzing an existing operation or planning a new one, many alternatives face the grower trying to develop efficient ways to handle plants and materials. With changes constantly occurring in equipment and methods, an up-to-date review is necessary. Take time to visit other growers, participate in conferences and trade shows, and contact county agents, manufacturers, and suppliers. The knowledge gained will broaden the view and make evaluation simpler. Before purchasing a piece of machinery or system consider the following:

Think simple. Systems and equipment that you understand work best. Complex equipment, although necessary for certain operations, will cost more initially and tend to need more adjustment and maintenance. It is easier to upgrade a basic system than to replace a complex one that doesn't do the job.

233

Be conservative. Have a plan for what you want to accomplish, but limit the amount of change that you institute at one time. Be conservative in what you expect pieces of equipment to do. It may take a while to get the proper adjustments and work out the bugs.

Develop a flow diagram. This diagram should show what operations are performed and the movement of materials. From this select labor intensive operations or ones that create bottlenecks to automate first.

Analyze your needs thoroughly. Because most equipment is expensive to own, consider where your resources will give the greatest return to the business. For example, an automatic watering system that can be used year-round may be a better choice than a seeder that will be used only 10 days a year.

Automate jobs that are repetitive, tedious, or time-consuming. Frequently these are the easiest to mechanize and result in a significant labor reduction. Watering, flat filling, potting, and plant spacing are good examples.

Install equipment that reduces peak period labor requirements. The spring season and holiday shipping periods are usually the busiest. Carts or conveyor systems can be used to move more plants in a shorter time than by hand labor. You are also reducing the need to hire and manage more employees.

Select equipment that will pace workers. Conveyor belts work well for potting, transplanting, and packaging and provide uniformity and consistency. A variable speed motor adjusts belt speed for different operations.

Compare equipment on performance and capacity. Use manufacturers' operating specifications to select equipment for a particular task. The equipment should meet your production capacity needs. If it is part of a production line, it should have a rate equal to other pieces in the line.

Investigate alternatives to purchasing. Renting or leasing allows the equipment to be used for short periods of time without a large investment. Sharing equipment, such as a shredder, potting machine, or pasteurizer between neighbors works well for some small growers.

Purchase from a manufacturer who has a good reputation. Check with other growers using the equipment for efficiency, problems, and service. Obtain a copy of the warranty.

Facilities planning

Planning helps to avoid costly errors and is well worth the time it takes. It can help in arranging of facilities to utilize space effectively, achieve higher production capacity, and make better use of labor. Space for layout changes and for future expansion should be included.

Planning involves looking at the overall operation—from the time materials are received until the time the plants are sold. It also includes individual tasks and ways that these can be done more efficiently. It is easier to plan on paper where different equipment arrangements can be tried and options evaluated.

Space requirements

Determine what space requirements are needed for storage, work area, and production area. These will help in evaluating the layout of existing buildings and the size of new structures. A rule of thumb for headhouse size is to provide 150 square feet per 1,000 square feet (13.9 m^2 per 92.9 m^2) of greenhouse area for operations of 10,000 to 40,000 square feet (929 to 3,716 m^2) and 100 square feet per 1,000 square feet (9.3 per 92.9 m^2) for operations of 1 to 2 acres (0.4 to 0.8 hectare).

Although it is impractical to store all growing media under cover, it is convenient to have some of it protected from rain and snow. Locate storage for bulk materials and truck loads where there is good access to an all-weather road. The storage should be located close to the work area to reduce handling.

The amount of work area needed depends on the size of the business, the amount of equipment needed, and the type of layout used. Additional space should be allowed for future expansion. The greenhouse facilities should be arranged to locate the greenhouses around the support buildings (fig. 18.1). A level area, open to the south and protected on the north, is best. Water and electricity should also be convenient.

Most bedding plants produced in flats are grown on the floor with a minimum of aisle space. This gives good space utilization. To achieve

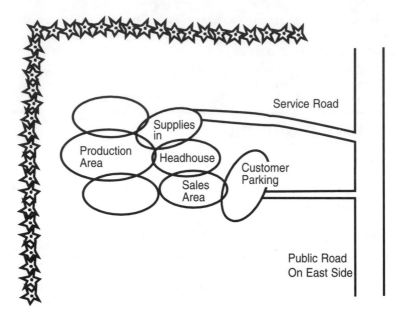

Fig. 18.1. Typical arrangement facilities for small wholesale operation.

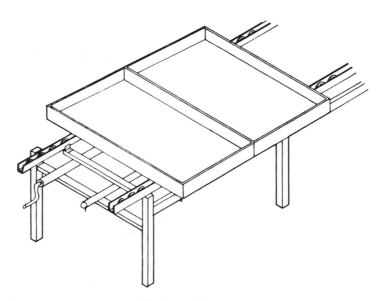

Fig. 18.2. Pallet tray system increases efficiency and space utilization.

better environment control and higher quality, install a root zone heating system.

In greenhouses used to produce potted plants when bedding plants are not grown, a movable bench system may be be more efficient. This increases growing space by eliminating all but one work aisle.

An alternate design utilizes pallet trays, 5 to 6 feet (1.5 to 1.8 m) wide by 6 to 20 feet (1.8 to 6.1 m) long that are moved on roller conveyors, tracks, or with a lift truck (fig. 18.2). Trays are moved to a work area for transplanting, potting, and shipping. Greenhouses are used only for growing.

Equipment

A large amount of equipment has been developed specifically for ornamental plant production. Equipment used in other industries, especial-

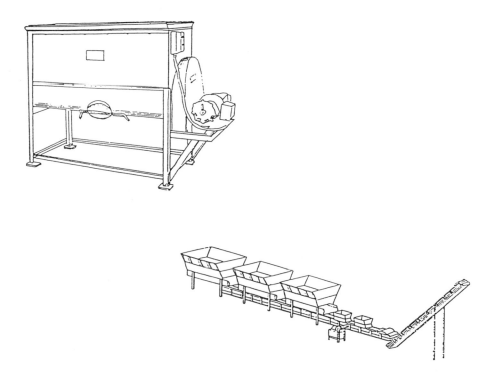

Fig. 18.3. Batch and continuous mixers.

ly for materials handling, can also be adapted. The following is a brief review of major types of equipment found in bedding plant greenhouses.

Mixing. Although many growers are purchasing premixed growing media, some growers still prepare their own or add to prepared mixes. Two types of mixers are available: batch and continuous (fig. 18.3). Concrete and drum mixers are available in capacities of 1 to 10 cubic yards (0.8 to 7 m³). A revolving drum or agitators gives the mixing action.

Features to look for include self-unloading, variable speed, and steam pasteurization injector. Care must be taken in their operation to insure a good homogenous mix without excessive pulverizing or balling. Operation time of one to two minutes is usually adequate.

To provide a continuous quantity of mix for a flat filler or potting machine, a system of feeder bins, mixing unit, and belt conveyors can be used. Flow rate is controlled by the speed of the feeder bin conveyors and the adjustable end gates. Mix components are collected on a central belt conveyor and fed through the mixing station. Rates of up to 50 cubic yards (38.2 m³) per hour are possible.

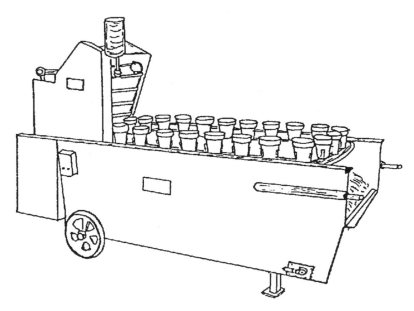

Fig. 18.4. Many potting machines can be adapted to fill flats.

Container filling. Many flat and pot filling systems are available. Most contain a soil supply hopper, metering device, leveling device, and container feed conveyor. Optional features include a soil return conveyor, pot and tray dispensers, dibble and automatic pot take-off (fig. 18.4). All filling machines can be adapted to various container sizes within certain limits. Filling rates vary but are generally in the range of 10 to 30 flats or 20 to 50 pots per minute. Most machines require two to three people to operate them efficiently.

Container filling systems range in price from $4,000 to over $30,000. For the small grower (10,000 flats/50,000 pots per year), it is

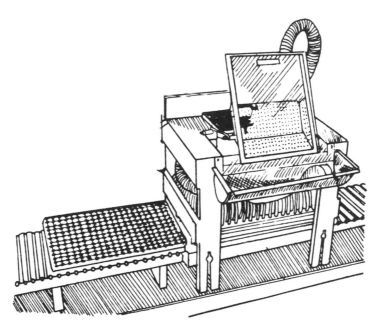

Fig. 18.5. Example of a mechanical seeder.

hard to justify purchasing this equipment when it may be used less than 12 hours per year. Consider purchasing prefilled flats or pots instead, which are available from some greenhouse suppliers. For the larger growers, container filling equipment can result in increased production rate per person and more uniformly filled containers.

Seeders. Low-cost, hand-operated, template-type seeders are available that use hand filling or a vacuum pump to pick up the seed and deposit

Fig. 18.7. Common types of materials handling equipment.

area; or 2) collectively by gathering the total day's needs of each variety, moving the plants to the shipping area, and loading them into the right truck.

Vans or box trucks fitted with shelves spaced 12 to 18 inches (30.4 to 45.7 cm) apart are suitable for shipping. Plywood or sheet metal shelves allow the containers to slide smoothly. A body holding about 200 flats can be fitted on a pickup; on larger trucks, a body holding 1,000 flats or more can be built.

Carts are becoming popular for shipping flats and pots. They are loaded in the greenhouse and rolled to the loading area to be loaded by fork lift or hydraulic tailgate onto the truck. At the garden center, they are unloaded and rolled to the holding or sales area.

CHAPTER 19

Bedding Plant Diseases

Gary W. Moorman

Bedding plant production is a specialized, carefully scheduled, labor intensive system. The short time period between rooting cuttings or seeding and selling a crop leaves little room for mistakes. Greenhouse space and time are at a premium. To produce a maximum number of salable plants in time for peak demand, plant diseases cannot be allowed to reduce plant quantity or plant quality by stunting growth or spotting the flowers and foliage.

Diseases during production reduce the number of salable plants being produced per unit area and increase the production cost of each salable unit. Time, energy, and labor are wasted on unsalable plants.

Preventing diseases of young plants helps ensure their high quality and makes it more likely that they will perform well in the customer's garden. Customers become dissatisfied when plants develop diseases because pathogens were present on the plants or in the soil at sale, or because the varieties offered were highly disease susceptible, or because plants were poorly adapted to the climate.

Five basic steps

To avoid losses due to disease, follow these five basic disease management steps in bedding plant production.

1. Select cultivars that are well adapted to the climate and resistant to common diseases.
2. Purchase seed, stock plants, and cuttings known to be free of important pathogens.
3. Prepare or purchase potting media free of disease-causing organisms, and prevent its contamination with pathogens.

4. Establish and maintain growing conditions that promote plant vigor and inhibit disease development.
5. Anticipate diseases, scout for them, and treat them promptly.

Cultivar selection

Cultivar selection requires experience. Select cultivars for production that are well adapted to the climate where they will be planted and are resistant or tolerant to diseases common to the region. Be sure to choose vegetable cultivars only after considering the diseases likely to occur.

Tomato cultivars with resistance to Fusaruim wilt, Verticillium wilt, and nematodes are available as are peppers with tobacco mosaic virus resistance and cucumbers with cucumber mosaic virus and bacterial wilt resistance. Although Verticillium wilt resistance has not been incorporated into eggplant, most hybrid varieties yield well despite infection while old, standard varieties such as Black Beauty do not [9].

Herbaceous ornamental resistance to disease is usually a secondary concern to plant breeders. Therefore, it is not possible to choose a pansy, for example, based on its resistance to anthracnose or a petunia for its Botrytis resistance.

Consider climate also. Eggplant, tomatoes, and peppers may be easy to grow in the greenhouse, but they perform poorly in cool coastal, high altitude or high latitude locations. Certain types of flowers, such as pansies, grow poorly in hot dry areas while daisies, chrysanthemums, and other plants thrive there.

Keep notes on cultivar performance in plantings you establish, and compare them with those of other growers, county agents, and members of local garden clubs to determine which cultivars do well and which do poorly in your area. If possible, visit All-America Selection trials, and make notes on the cultivars displayed.

Seed, stock plants and cuttings free of important pathogens

Many fungi, bacteria, and viruses that attack bedding plants can be carried on or inside seeds, stock plants, and cuttings. Botrytis is a fungus found on the seed coat of many composites. Pathogens such as Alternaria on zinnia, Heterosporium on California poppy, and rust on snapdragon and hollyhock have been known to be carried on seeds [3]. Certain bacteria can also be carried on seeds such as the Xanthomonas responsible for causing bacterial leaf spot on zinnia [10].

Vegetatively propagated plants commonly carry any disease occurring on the stock plant. It is the seedsman's and propagator's responsibility to ensure a high quality product. This is done by growing the seed producing plants in locations where conditions are unfavorable to pathogens.

Plants grown in areas of low rainfall and low relative humidity experience less disease from Botrytis, Alternaria, and many bacteria than when grown in wet, humid regions. Seedsmen have further control over the incidence of seedborne parasites by treating seeds with heat, disinfestants, and fungicides [10].

Vegetatively propagated bedding plants can carry any disease occurring on stock plants. For that reason, keep plants started from seed separate from vegetatively propagated plants. Bacterial blight (caused by *Xanthomonas campestris* pv. *pelargonii*) and viruses on geranium stock carry over on the cuttings. These diseases readily infect seedling geraniums, too.

The propagator must control all diseases on the stock to avoid selling those diseases to other growers and to the consumer. Geranium cuttings tested (indexed) and shown to be free of viruses, bacteria, and certain fungi are well worth the extra cost.

When cuttings arrive with a disease already on them, begin control measures immediately. Most diseases cannot be cured, only prevented from spreading to plants not already infected. Purchasing plants free of important diseases greatly reduces pesticide applications early in the production cycle.

Detecting TSWV and INSV

Two important pathogens potentially carried on a wide variety of vegetatively propagated plants are tomato spotted wilt virus (TSWV) and the closely related virus, impatiens necrotic spot virus (INSV). Diseases caused by these viruses have been widespread and devastating in the greenhouse industry [7]. Hundreds of thousands of dollars worth of crops have been destroyed after the viruses' presence has been confirmed.

However, growers aggressively attacking the problem can avoid crop losses by carefully inspecting new plants brought into the greenhouse, maintaining the health of plants already in the greenhouse, and controlling the insect (thrips) known to spread both viruses. A wide variety of symptoms develop including wilting, stem death, stunting, yellowing, poor flowering, chicken-pox-like sunken spots on leaves, and etches or ring spots on leaves.

Some plants not exhibiting symptoms have been tested and found infected with these viruses. For a positive diagnosis, submit plants to a plant disease clinic or commercial laboratory capable of either inoculating special indicator plants or running chemical tests to determine if the viruses are in the sap. Separate tests are run to detect TSWV and INSV. Plants may be infected with either or both viruses at one time.

Controlling TSWV and INSV

To control TSWV and INSV, isolate incoming plants from all other plants in the greenhouse, and inspect them for symptoms. Immediately test those found with suspicious symptoms to determine the viruses' presence or absence. Destroy infected plants since they cannot be cured and only serve as pathogen reservoirs. TSWV and INSV are carried inside cuttings taken from infected plants. If thrips, especially western flower thrips, are not present, these viruses will not spread to other plants.

Western flower thrips

The most important insect known to spread TSWV and INSV is the western flower thrips (*Frankliniella occidentalis*). Other species of thrips are much less efficient in moving these viruses from plant to plant.

Inspect all incoming plants for thrips, especially white and yellow flowered plants. Tap the plant with a pencil while holding a sheet of white paper beneath to catch any falling insects, and examine the insects with a hand lens. Since thrips are very small and stay hidden most of the time, they are difficult to detect.

Yellow or blue sticky cards placed at crop height are excellent for monitoring thrips. One to three cards per 1,000 square feet (92.9 m^2) is recommended. Effectiveness depends on the number used and their placement rather than the size of each card. Place some near vents, doors, and other openings and change cards regularly.

For handling ease, cover used cards in a cellophane layer or similar clear plastic wrap when they are removed. Record the number of thrips trapped each week to determine if the population is increasing or decreasing. If you are uncertain of the identity of the insects trapped, contact your state inspector, the Department of Agriculture, your county extension agent, or the closest university's department of entomology for assistance.

An alternative to using sticky cards is to place petunias in pots among the greenhouse crops as an indicator for thrips feeding and the presence of viruses [1]. Small leaf spots with dark margins form when plants are attacked by TSWV-carrying thrips. Replace plants on a regular basis, especially if you detect viruses, since an infected petunia will act as a source of viruses for other plants.

Follow current recommendations for thrips control in the greenhouse. Usually, a single insecticide application is not adequate. Repeated applications are necessary and must be done in a way that does not select for insecticide resistance. Maintain strict thrips control on all plants kept in the greenhouse. Eliminate all weeds and all plants not being carefully tended from the greenhouse because these plants may harbor thrips and viruses.

Potting media free of disease-causing organisms

Diseases most common in bedding plant production are carried in soil. Damping-off, cutting rot, and root rot are caused by various fungi including species of Pythium, Fusarium, and Rhizoctonia. These fungi recolonize pasteurized potting mixes if strict sanitation practices are not maintained. To prevent losses due to these and other soilborne pests, purchase or prepare pest-free mixes. The majority of commercially available mixes that lack soil are pest-free even though they are not treated to eliminate pests. However, peat and sand can be important sources of pathogens including Pythium and Thielaviopsis [6, 8]; both have been found in some commercial mixes.

Grower-prepared soil, peat, and sand potting mixes require treatment to eliminate unwanted fungi, bacteria, nematodes, insects, and weeds. Autumn is an excellent time to treat soil particularly when the soil is warm (55 F [12.8 C] or warmer) and evenly moist (50% to 85% of field capacity). Many pests in cold, dry soils are dormant and very resistant to heat or chemical treatments. Chemical fumigants in cold, wet soil require long aeration periods.

Pasteurize soil. Dry heat, steam, and aerated steam may be used to pasteurize soil for any crop. Most, but not all, organisms are killed by properly applying heat. Treated soil is said to be pasteurized rather than sterilized. The greatest mistakes with heat treatment are to use temperatures greater than 200 F (93.3 C) or to treat the soil for longer than one hour. Such treatments cause organic matter and soil structure to break down resulting in soluble salts release in amounts toxic to seedlings.

Effective pasteurization occurs when steam or dry heat is used to maintain the entire soil mass temperature between 180 F and 200 F (82.2 C to 93.3 C) for 30 minutes. Most living organisms in the soil are killed by this treatment. However, some beneficial organisms remain. If aerated steam is used, the entire soil mass temperature is kept between 145 F and 160 F (62.8 C to 71.1 C) for 30 minutes.

gence. Moderate soil temperatures and moisture levels stimulate rapid seed germination and seedling development, reducing susceptibility to damping-off. In general, overfertilizing seedlings makes them more susceptible to Pythium [5].

Damping-off rarely destroys all plants in a flat. Patches of plants are affected in flats broadcast seeded and in plug flats; in flats seeded in rows, parts of the row are destroyed. When damping-off occurs, growers may be tempted to drench the flat with a fungicide to save the remaining plants. However, fungicides are not totally effective in eliminating fungi from the soil and will not cure a root rot once it has begun.

Live fungus remains in the flat and may cause root rot in the remaining plants once the fungicide concentration declines. Infected plants never fully recover or perform well in the garden. In certain potting mixes, some soil-drench fungicides stunt seedling development [4].

When damping-off develops, it is best to discard all the plants and soil in the flat, sterilize the flat, refill it with pest-free soil (using disinfested tools), and reseed the plants. If damping-off is a recurrent problem, buy seeds that are treated with a fungicide such as captan or thiram. These materials protect the seeds against fungal infection through germination and early growth. Established plants are generally much less susceptible to damping-off.

Gray mold

The fungus Botrytis is found virtually everywhere plants are grown and causes gray mold disease. Dormant Botrytis spores can be found on the seeds' surfaces and established plants. It persists in crop debris and readily attacks fading flower parts and damaged tissues. Seedlings growing under cool humid conditions are very susceptible to gray mold. In some greenhouses seedling geranium losses from gray mold exceed losses caused by damping-off.

Sanitation is important for Botrytis control in bedding plants since crop debris serves as the fungus nutrient source. Removing crop debris and dying tissue from the greenhouse will reduce the total number of fungal spores produced. Sanitation alone will not completely eliminate the problem because even a piece of plant debris the size of your smallest fingernail can support the development of 20,000 to 60,000 Botrytis spores, each capable of causing an infection.

Reducing humidity early in the day and before sunset by venting and heating the greenhouse, combined with good air movement within the crop canopy at all times, is the most important way to manage Botrytis. Arrange plants in rows parallel to the air flow, and use fans for horizontal air movement to reduce humidity within the canopy.

Fungicides are available for Botrytis control on many bedding plants. Some product labels list a wide range of bedding plants, but frequently not all bedding plants are listed. In the United States, it is illegal to apply a chemical to a plant if the plant's name is not on the chemical label. **Always read the instructions on the label.**

Botrytis has developed resistance to important systemic fungicides like iprodione (Chipco 26019), vinclozolin (Ornalin), and thiophanate methyl (Domain FL, Topsin M, and Clearys 3336). Resistance has not developed to nonsystemics chlorothalonil (Exotherm, Termil, and Daconil), mancozeb (Dithane) or coppers (Kocide and Phyton 27) and is not expected to develop due to their less specific action.

Fungicides alone are not the answer, however. Strict humidity control is the best Botrytis control strategy, supplemented with fungicide applications and sanitation.

Phytotoxicity

Phytotoxicity refers to plant damage resulting from a chemical treatment. Young bedding plants are easily injured by sprays. Damage is usually avoided by using the concentration recommended on the product label. If a range of concentrations is suggested, use the lower rate when treating seedlings.

Evidence of phytotoxicity appears as death of young succulent tissues, stunting, death of leaf margins, dead spots on leaves or cotyledons, delayed plant development, or seedling death. Injury symptoms usually appear within 24 to 48 hours of treatment.

Damage often appears on plants at the ends of benches or in strips along the bench where the spray pattern overlapped or where a pesticide dripped excessively from the sprayer nozzle.

Phytotoxicity is influenced by many factors. Dusts and wettable powders are generally less phytotoxic than emulsifiable concentrates. Spray additives, including spreaders, stickers, and wetting agents, can cause toxicity. High-pressure sprays can cause physical damage and increase phytotoxicity by forcing the chemical into soft tissues.

High temperatures during and after application favor chlorinated hydrocarbon and sulfur toxicity, while low temperatures favor oil, carbamate, and organophosphate toxicity. Certain chemicals become phytotoxic when applied to wet foliage or when foliage remains wet for a prolonged period after application.

The application of a mixture of two incompatible chemicals or the separate application of two such chemicals within too short a period can cause damage. Product labels and supplementary literature often give steps to take to avoid phytotoxicity.

Keep records on what and how much is applied as well as the environmental conditions during and after application. This way, you can document exactly what happened when phytotoxicity occurred and avoid a similar situation in the future.

Overfertilization

Bedding plant overfertilization can cause as much crop quality damage as damping-off or gray mold. Yellowing, wilting, death of leaf tips and margins, growth slowing, and seedling death can occur with excessive soluble salts levels. Harmful fertilizer concentrations can develop if too much fertilizer is applied at one time, if soluble fertilizers are applied several times with little or no leaching, if slow-release and soluble fertilizers are used in improper combinations, and if plants are watered insufficiently in relation to the fertilizer amount present in the soil.

Use a conductivity meter to measure the total soluble salts level in a potting mix water extract. The extract can be prepared in one of two ways: a 1:5 dilution or a saturated paste. To prepare the 1:5 dilution, air-dry some potting mix and then weigh a small sample. To the sample, add five times its weight of water. Stir the mixture intermittently for 30 minutes. Decant the water into a clean container, and measure conductivity with the meter.

Prepare a saturated paste by adding just enough water to the soil so that the soil glistens but does not puddle. Stir the sample intermittently for 30 minutes. To extract liquid, dump the saturated soil into two layers of paper towels, wrap the soil and towels with cheesecloth, and then squeeze gently while catching the liquid in a clean container. Measure the liquid's conductivity. One part of dry soilless mix wet with 5 parts water is very close to being a saturated paste.

The pour-through method is useful if equipment for preparing a soil extract is not available. In this method, clear water is carefully applied to the potting mix surface until some water begins to flow from the pot

TABLE 19.1

Conductivity readings

| | Conductivity (mmhos/cm = mS/cm) | |
Extraction	Mix with 25% or more soil	Soilless mix
1 part air-dry soil:		
5 parts water (by weight)	7.5	10.0
Saturated paste extract or pour-through	40.0	10.0

bottom. Test the liquid caught from the pot for total soluble salt contents with a conductivity meter.

You can expect seedling damage if conductivity readings exceed those listed in table 19.1.

When salts become excessive because of soluble fertilization or excessive steaming, leach the potting mix. Six inches (15.2 cm) of clear water applied with a hose will reduce salts by 50%. Twelve inches (30.5 cm) of water will reduce salts by 80%. Remeasure conductivity after leaching.

If salts are excessive because too much slow-release fertilizer was used, little can be done short of repotting. Leaching only releases more salts.

References

[1]   Allen, W.R., and J.A. Matteoni. 1991. Petunia as an indicator plant for use by growers to monitor for thrips carrying the tomato spotted wilt virus in greenhouses. *Plant Disease* 75:78-82.

[2]   Averre, C.W., J.C. Wells, and S.F. Jenkins. 1977. Lettuce seed test for checking residual soil fumigant in soil. Information Note 160. Department of Plant Pathology. North Carolina State University.

[3]   Baker, K.F. 1952. Seed-borne parasites. *Seed World* 70:38-47.

[4]   Bolton, A.T. 1982. Toxicity of fungicide drenches. *Florists' Review* 169:29, 48, and 50.

[5]   Gladstone, L.A., and G.W. Moorman. 1989. Pythium root rot of seedling geraniums associated with various concentrations of nitrogen, phosphorus, and sodium chloride. *Plant Disease* 73:733-736.

[6]   Graham, J.H., and N.H. Timmer. 1991. Peat-based media as a source of *Thielaviopsis basicola* causing black root rot on citrus seedlings. *Plant Disease* 75:1246-1249.

[7]   Hausbeck, M.K., R.A. Welliver, M.A. Derr, and F.E. Gildow. 1992. Tomato spotted wilt virus survey among greenhouse ornamentals in Pennsylvania. *Plant Disease* 76:795-800.

[8]   Kim, S.H., L.B. Forer, and J.L. Longnecker. 1975. Recovery of plant pathogens from commercial peat products. In *Proceedings*. Am. Phytopath. Soc. 2:124.

[9]   Moorman, G.W. 1982. The influence of black plastic mulching on infection rates of Verticillium wilt and yield of eggplant. *Phytopathology* 72:1412-1414.

[10]   Strider, D.L. 1979. Detection of *Xanthomonas nigromaculans* f. sp. *zinniae* in zinnia seed. *Plant Disease Reporter* 63:869-873.

[11]   Strider, D.L. 1980. Control of bacterial leaf spot of zinnia with captan. *Plant Disease* 64:920-922.

CHAPTER 20

Insect and Mites

James R. Baker

Aphids, whiteflies, and fungus gnats are the principal bedding plant insect pests during production. If a resident western flower thrips population has not been eliminated from the previous year's crops, this pest may cause serious problems to tomatoes and peppers. Two-spotted spider mites also infest bedding plants, and slugs are an occasional nuisance.

Excluding pests by screening greenhouse ventilation openings and doorways can help manage aphids and fungus gnats on early bedding plants and thrips and whiteflies on later crops. Screening, if retrofitted properly, will not excessively increase greenhouse temperatures or stress to ventilation fans.

Insects, mites, and slugs

Aphids

Green peach aphids and melon aphids have acquired resistance to many pesticides. Aphids are small, fragile insects that feed by sucking plant sap through slender mouthparts. Aphids excrete honeydew and molt as they grow. Infested plants are often disfigured by the honeydew, by the molted skins adhering to the honeydew, and by sooty molds (dark fungi) that grow in the honeydew.

In greenhouses, aphids give birth to live young. Aphids are often wingless, but when the population becomes dense or the host plant becomes unsuitable, young aphids can develop wings and fly elsewhere.

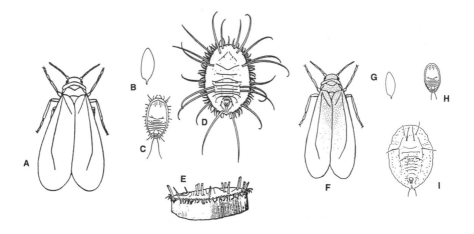

Fig. 20.3. Greenhouse whitefly. A, adult. B, egg. C, crawler. D, pupa (top). E, pupa (side) shown with long setae truncated. Sweet potato whitefly. F, adult. G, egg. H, crawler. I, pupa (top).

pupae 13 days later. Then 10 days later, new adults emerge from a slit in the pupa top. Adults are pale green to yellow at first but soon secrete a white, waxy bloom.

Adult and immature whiteflies suck sap from the phloem and excrete honeydew, a sweet, sticky substance that drips down and disfigures infested plants. Sooty molds and other fungi often grow in the honeydew causing infested plants to become dark and unsightly. The commercial value of heavily infested plants is destroyed long before they decline in vigor and die.

Whitefly Control. Lower greenhouse temperatures used in the culture of some bedding and potted plant varieties tend to encourage whitefly infestations, because a naturally occurring parasitic wasp, *Encarsia formosa*, is reproductively inhibited at temperatures below 75 F (23.9 C). These wasps sometimes stabilize greenhouse whitefly populations, but the wasps are more sensitive to insecticides than whiteflies, so using synthetic petrochemicals may worsen whitefly problems.

Most insecticides used in the greenhouse are toxic to newly-hatched whitefly nymphs. However, whitefly eggs, older nymphs and pupae are fairly resistant to pesticides. In our demonstrations, Talstar and an insecticidal soap (M-Pede) gave very good control although the populations seemed to rebound rapidly after soap treatments.

Kinoprene (Enstar II) is toxic to whitefly nymphs and pupae at the 8 ounces (226.8 g) per 100 gallons (378.5 l) of water rate and is toxic to all stages at 20 ounces (567 g) per 100 gallons (378.5 l). The combination of Tame plus Orthene as a tank mix is also effective for whitefly management (found on the Tame label).

Darkwinged fungus gnats

Darkwinged fungus gnats are small (about .1 inch [2.5 mm] long), dark, slender flies with comparatively long legs and antennae (fig. 20.4) and are found throughout the United States. Females lay 100 to 150 yellowish-white eggs in soil usually near the plant. Maggots have shiny black heads and white bodies. Mature larvae are about .22 inch

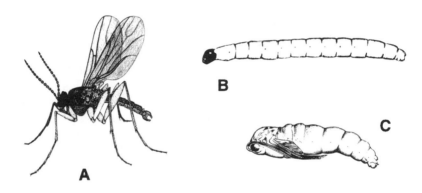

Fig. 20.4. Darkwinged fungus gnat. A, *adult.* B, *larva.* C, *pupa.*

(5.5 mm) long. Maggots feed on fungi and yeasts but may attack the roots and stems of bedding plants causing wilting.

Maggots mature in about 14 days, and the pupal stage lasts about 3½ days. Fungus gnat adults are usually noticed before maggot-caused injury is apparent. Generally, fungus gnats are most abundant in greenhouses in the winter and spring. Adults and larvae inhabit moist, shady areas. Adults live about one week. They are weak fliers but often run rapidly on the soil surface.

Darkwinged fungus gnat control. Clean cultural practices and no excessive watering help prevent fungus gnat infestations. Since fungus gnats prefer potting mixes containing peat moss and abundant moisture, consider using bark mixes and avoid overwatering ornamental plants. Remove organic matter that collects on and under benches.

Decoy pots of sprouting grain are attractive for egg-laying females. Afterwards, the pots should be submerged in hot water or the contents sterilized every two weeks to destroy the eggs and maggots. Darkwinged fungus gnats have few natural enemies. In mushroom houses, some species have developed up to a 47-fold pyrethroid insecticide resistance.

A *Bacillus thuringiensis* var. *israelinsis* (Gnatrol) formulation is a biological control organism that infests darkwinged fungus gnat maggots. A predaceous nematode, *Steinernema feltiae*, is available in the product ScanMask. The advantage of these nematodes is that they attack darkwinged fungus gnat pupae as well as maggots. Pyrethrin (X-Clude), resmethrin (SPB 1382), oxamyl (Oxamyl 10G and Vydate), and diazinon formulation Knox-Out are all labeled for fungus gnat control. When applied carefully, these pesticides give adequate control.

Western flower thrips

Thrips are active insects and fly readily in warm, bright weather (fig. 20.5). These insects are repelled by certain pesticides, especially pyrethroids. When a grower sprays only part of his greenhouse crops, thrips can fly to nearby unsprayed plants. Some of the thrips will return to the sprayed plants shortly after the residue dries, and the population will hardly seem to have been affected.

Western flower thrips control. Western flower thrips management is complicated because of thrips physiological and behavioral resistance to an array of insecticides. Thrips wedge down deep into blossoms and buds and avoid pesticide residue. Because systemic insecticides do not readily translocate into ornamental plant buds and flowers, growers cannot protect the blossoms by applying Oxamyl 10G or Orthene to the growing medium.

Robb and Parrella [14] reported that Dibrom as a fumigant provided 95% control of western flower thrips. Dursban (89% to 95% control), Dycarb (80% to 90% control), and Carzol (84% control, 24[c] registration for western flower thrips on greenhouse ornamentals in some states) are pesticides labeled for greenhouse thrips control. Avid (84% to 95% control) is labeled for leafminer and spider mite greenhouse control. Diazinon (Knox-Out), Orthene, sumithrin, and Thiodan sprays provided fair control [14].

Growers should treat all plants in a greenhouse in order to suppress

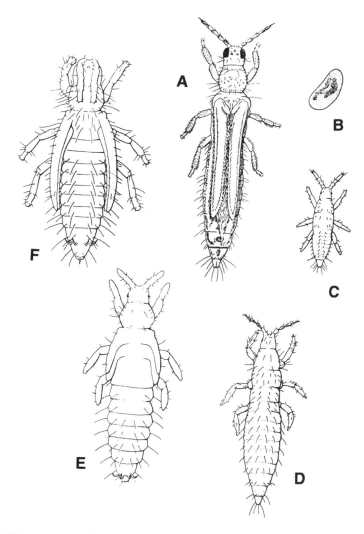

Fig. 20.5. *Western flower thrips.* A, *adult.* B, *egg.* C, *first larva.* D, *second larva.* E, *pre-pupa.* F, *pupa.*

thrips population. Unfortunately, western flower thrips control is likely to be difficult and costly in the near future.

The following guides should help to control western flower thrips:
1. Do not wear light blue, white, or yellow clothing into the greenhouse.
2. Use sticky traps or cards to determine if thrips are increasing.
3. Screen greenhouses to exclude thrips.
4. When roguing plant material, be sure to transport it far from the greenhouse, or cover it with clear plastic.

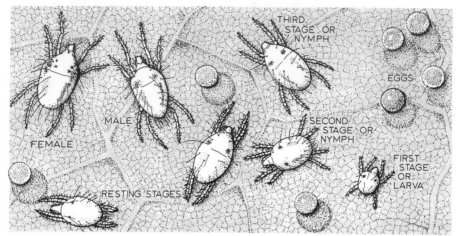

Fig. 20.6. Various stages of the two-spotted spider mite.

5. Pesticide treatments should be scheduled twice a week or no further apart than five days.
6. Use pyrethrum or a pyrethroid insecticide as a flushing agent.
7. Use normal insecticde rates and treat more often rather than heavy rates less often.
8. Use a variety of insecticides rather than using only one pesticide year in and year out.

Two-spotted spider mites

Two-spotted spider mites are tiny, spiderlike, green to yellowish arthropods usually having two (sometimes four) black spots on top (fig. 20.6). Two-spotted spider mites pierce the host plant leaf's epidermis with sharp, slender mouthparts. As they extract the sap, the leaf's mesophyll tissue collapses in the area of the puncture, and a pale spot forms at each feeding site. After a heavy attack, an entire plant may become yellowed, bronzed, or even killed. Mites may spin so much webbing over the plant that it becomes entirely covered.

In mild winter weather, two-spotted spider mites continue to feed and lay eggs, although winter development is much slower than summer (20 days compared to five days). After each larval and nymphal stage, there is a resting stage. Females lay over 100 eggs (up to 19 eggs per day).

Two-spotted spider mites have been reported on over 300 host plants, including over 100 cultivated species. Spider mites overwinter on common weeds like violets, chickweed, wild mustard, henbit, vetch, and blackberry, then later infest nearby crops.

Spider mite control. Two-spotted spider mite's resting stages and eggs are more pesticide-tolerant than motile forms. So a second pesticide application may be necessary at four- or five-day intervals in hot weather (seven to 10 days in cool weather) to kill those mites that survived the first application.

Also a fungal pathogen, *Neozygites floridanus*, attacks spider mites in cool, damp weather. Although spider mites have become resistant to many traditional pesticides, Avid, Talstar, Pentac, and insecticidal soaps (M-Pede), all give adequate control.

Fig. 20.7. Lehmannia slug.

Slugs

Slug are light brown to yellowish gray or gray animals with spots or dark lines along the body top (fig. 20.7). Some slugs grow to about 2.4 inches (60 mm) long and can stretch to 3 inches (75 mm)! Slugs feed readily on living bedding plants. Slugs require high moisture and tend to burrow into soft soil or rest under boards, logs, flats, pots, and other debris whenever the temperature is rising. As temperatures start to fall, slugs actively begin foraging.

Slug control. First, remove places where slugs can hide. Picking up flats, boards, pots, and debris will force slugs to look elsewhere for a suitable resting spot. Metaldehyde baits have attracted slugs up to 3.3 feet (1 m) away. Metaldehyde's toxic effects seem to be primarily due to dehydration as metaldehyde elicits excessive mucus production (mucus is 98% water and 2% mucoproteins). Thus metaldehyde is more effective in dry weather.

In wet weather, slugs can sometimes absorb enough moisture to compensate for water lost in mucus production and can recover from metaldehyde effects. As they mature, slugs become more susceptible to carbamate pesticides such as Sevin and methiocarb (Grand Slam, Mesurol, Pt 1700) pesticides. Copper sulfate is toxic to slugs, and slugs will not crawl across a barrier of copper metal or wooden surfaces treated with copper sulfate. Deadline, a metaldehyde formulation, seems to be the slug bait most resistant to weathering away.

Screening is part of insect and disease management

Pesticide resistance has made insect and mite pest control increasingly difficult in the greenhouse. An obvious way to reduce pesticide exposure is to lessen the need for pesticides by reducing the numbers of pests entering a greenhouse. However, if you start with pests already inside or bring pests in on plants or clothing, screening will retain them as well.

Robb and Parrella [14] grew a chrysanthemum crop without a single pesticide application by screening the entire greenhouse. Baker and Jones [1, 2] reported that screening reduced thrips, aphids, and whitefly numbers entering screened structures and reduced the tomato spotted wilt virus amount inside screened structures.

Bethke and Paine [3] found that screen openings not larger than .1 inches (0.34 mm) would exclude melon aphids and sweetpotato whiteflies.

Non-woven screen materials. Spunbonded materials are materials that are extruded and stuck together to form a fabric. FlyBarr is a spunbonded fabric with a plastic mesh that gives it strength. FlyBarr is available from Hydro-Gardens, P.O. Box 9707, Colorado Springs, CO 80932.

Typar is a spunbonded polypropylene material that is very resistant to ultraviolet light degradation. It is also resistant to air, so growers using Typar must use a relatively large screen area.

Remay is a spunbonded polyethylene material that breaks down in a matter of months outdoors. On the other hand, Remay has much less resistance to air. Remay screens may function well with a much smaller area.

Typar and Remay are manufactured by Remay, Inc., 70 Old Hickory Blvd., Old Hickory, TN 37138. These fabrics are also sold in various greenhouse supply catalogs.

Woven materials. Woven materials include ordinary window screening, available at many hardware and building supply houses. Chicopee 32 and Chicopee 52 fabrics are available from various greenhouse supply catalogs and from Lumite, 6525 The Corners Parkway, Suite 115, Norcross, GA 30092.

Pak 32, 52, and 87 fabrics are also carried by various greenhouse suppliers and Pak Unlimited Inc, 3300 Holcomb Bridge Road, Suite 215, Norcross, GA 30092. The Pak 87 material is woven polyethylene coated with acrylic for ultraviolet light resistance.

Bed Bug 123 and 85 materials are available from the Green Thumb Group, 3380 Venard Road, Suite 2, Downers Grove, IL 60515. Econet is available from L.S. Americas, 1813-E Associates Lane, Charlotte, NC 28215.

Static pressure. When exhaust fans are running, air pressure drops inside the greenhouse. Growers then notice doors are harder to open, and gusts of air whoosh through open doors as pressure inside equalizes with pressure outside.

Air pressure inside a greenhouse is called static pressure. If one end of a U-shaped tube filled with liquid (manometer) were inserted into the greenhouse, the level of the liquid inside the house would rise as the fans come on and static pressure drops like sucking soda up a straw. A relatively inexpensive manometer (Mark II, model 25) is available from Dwyer Instruments, Inc., P.O. Box 373, Michigan City, IN 46360.

Static pressure is usually measured in inches of water (kilopascals). If static pressure drop is too great, the fans will not be able to move enough air to properly ventilate the greenhouse and will use excessive power [11], or the covering plastic film may pull loose from the staples. In either case, the greenhouse will become too hot during bright summer days. Johnson [9] suggested not using screening materials that create a static pressure over 0.05 inches of water (inchH$_2$O) (0.0124 kiloPascal [kPa]) at 250 feet per minute (127 centimeters/second [cps]) air velocity.

Sase and Christianson [15] recommend 0.032 inchH$_2$O (0.008 kPa) pressure drop for clean screening materials and total pressure drop should not exceed 0.1 inch (0.0249 kPa) with dirty screening. Since the pressure drop inside an unscreened greenhouse may approach 0.095 inchH$_2$O (0.0236 kPa) [7], screening may increase total pressure 0.145 inchH$_2$O (0.0361 kPa) to 0.195 inchH$_2$O (0.0485 kPa) as the screen gets dirty. (In North Carolina, we rarely measure pressure drops in unscreened greenhouses above 0.03 inchH$_2$O [0.0075 kPa]). The Green Thumb Group recommends a maximum of 0.15 inchH$_2$O [0.373 kPa]) total static pressure drop (screening and all) so as not to overload the fans.

Volume of air needed for adequate cooling. Nelson [12] suggests 8 cubic feet per minute (cfm) (3.8 liters per second [l/s]) for each square foot (0.929 m^2) of greenhouse space as the optimal minimal requirement for air exchange. Thus for a 30- by 100-foot (9.1 by 30.5 m) greenhouse, the optimal minimal air exchange is 8 cfm/square foot times 3,000 square feet which equals 24,000 cfm (44.6 l/s per m^2 times 277.6 m^2 equals 11,330 l/s).

Willis [16] recommends 11 to 17 cfm for each square foot (55.9 to 86.4 l/s) for each square meter (1 to 1½ air exchanges per minute). Thus for a 30- by 100-foot (9.1 by 30.5 m) greenhouse, the optimal air exchange at 11 to 17 cfm per square foot times 3,000 square feet equals 33,000 to 51,000 cfm (55.9 to 86.4 l/s per m² times 277.4 m² equals 15,600 to 24,100 l/s).

How to retrofit screening on a greenhouse

Caution: Any screening retrofitted to a greenhouse without other changes will decrease airflow and increase greenhouse temperatures. The following procedure should help avoid serious ventilation problems.

Step 1. Measure the pressure drop inside the greenhouse by using a manometer: _____ inchH$_2$O. (If the pressure drop is close to 0.1 inch (0.0249 kPa) without screening, consider enlarging the ventilation window. If the fans stay the same, enlarging the ventilation windows will reduce static pressure.)

Step 2. Subtract the pressure drop in Step 1 from 0.1 inch (0.0249 kPa): _____ inchH$_2$O (kPa). This difference is a guide to how much additional resistance to air movement can be tolerated. For example, if your pressure drop in Step 1 is 0.025 inch (0.0062 kPa), you can use a screen that adds up to an additional 0.075 inch (0.0187 kPa) of pressure drop without exceeding the maximum recommended pressure drop of Sase and Christianson [15].

Step 3. Use the fan performance chart given in most greenhouse supply catalogs to roughly estimate the total air exchange. You can interpolate between the 0.0 inch, 0.05 inch (0.0124 kPa), and 0.1 inch (0.0249 kPa) volumes given for the various fans and motors. (For example, if your pressure drop is 0.025 inch [0.00062 kPa] that is halfway between 0 inch and 0.05 inch [0.0124 kPa], then the air volume moved by your fans would be about halfway between the volumes given for 0 inch and 0.05 inch [0.0124 kPa]). Total air movement: _____ cfm (l/s).

Step 4. Calculate an estimated total air movement at 0.1 inch (0.0249 kPa): _____ cfm (l/s).

Now you can check if the air volume being moved through the house after screening exceeds Nelson's [12] or Willits' [16] recommendations. If not, your houses may become too hot during July and August. Consider using larger motors on the fans or adding additional fans.

Suggested air exchange per minute

Nelson's: Area of greenhouse x 8 cfm/square foot (40.6 l/s/m^2) = _____ cfm (l/s).

Willits' low: Area of greenhouse x 11 cfm/square foot (55.9 l/s/m^2) = _____ cfm (l/s).

Willits' high: Area of greenhouse x 17 cfm/square foot (86.4 l/s/m^2) = _____ cfm (l/s).

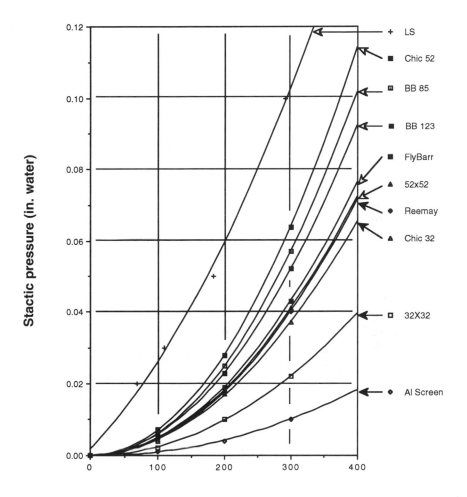

Fig. 20.8. Resistance factors for 10 screening materials shown as functions of velocity in feet per minute and static pressure in inches of water.
Al = aluminum window screen.   *BB = Bug Bed.*   *LS = Econet.*
32x32 = Pak 32x32.   *Chic = Chicopee.*   *52x52 = Pak 52x52.*

Step 5. Calculate the area of the ventilation windows. Total ventilation window area (length x width): _____ ft² (m²).

Step 6. Calculate the air's approach velocity moving through the ventilation windows. Total air volume (after screening) divided by ventilation window area: _____ ft/min.

Step 7. Examine the chart (fig. 20.8), and find the approach velocity from Step 6 on the horizontal axis. Those fabrics whose curves do not exceed the pressure drop level calculated in Step 2 at the approach velocity from Step 6 can be used directly over the ventilation window.

If the resistance curve for the fabric you wish to use exceeds the pressure drop level from Step 2, then move to the left along the velocity axis until you reach a velocity at which the resistance does not exceed Step 2 pressure drop. Then divide the velocity through the ventilation window in Step 6 by the lower velocity on the chart and the quotient is the number you must multiply the ventilation window's area to arrive at the screening material area: Multiplication factor: _____.

References

[1]   Baker, J.R., and R.K. Jones. 1989. *Screening as part of insect and disease management in the greenhouse.* Bul. 34(6):1-9. North Carolina Flower Growers.

[2]   ——. 1990. *An update on screening as part of insect and disease management* in the greenhouse. Bul. 35(6):1-3. North Carolina Flower Growers.

[3]   Bethke, J.A., and T.D. Paine. 1991. Screen hole size and barriers for exclusion of insect pests of glasshouse crops. *J. Entomol. Sci.* 26(1):169-177.

[4]   Butler, G.D., Jr., S.N. Puri, and T.J. Henneberry. 1991. Plant-derived oil and detergent solutions as control agents for *Bemisia tabaci* and *Aphis gossypii* on cotton. *Southwestern Entomol.* 16:331-337.

[5]   Dickson, R.C. 1959. Aphid dispersal over southern California deserts. *Ann. Entomol. Soc. Amer.* 52:368-372.

[6]   Grafton-Cardwell, E.E. 1991. Geological and temporal variation in response to insecticides in various life stages of *Aphis gossypii* (Homoptera: Aphididae) infesting cotton in California. *J. Econ. Entomol.* 84(3):741-749.

[7]   Green Thumb Group. *Greenhouse ventilation and screening.* Downers Grove, Illinois.

[8]   Halbert, S.E., and T.M. Mowry. 1992. Survey of *Myzus persicae* (Sulzer) (Homoptera: Aphididae) infestations on bedding plants for sale in eastern Idaho. *Pan-Pacific Entomol.* 68(1):8-11.

[9]   Johnson, G.B. 1990. Insect barrier. Amer. Coolair Bul. 90-6. Jacksonville, Fla.: American Coolair Corp.

[10]   Kennedy, J.S., C.O. Booth, and W.J.S. Kershaw. 1961. Host finding by aphids in the field. III. Visual attraction. *Ann. Appl. Bio.* 49:1-21.

[11]   National Greenhouse Manufacturers Association. 1993. Recommendations for using insect screens in greenhouse structures. Addendum to NGMA ventilation and cooling standards.

[12]   Nelson, P.V. 1985. *Greenhouse operation and management.* 3rd ed. Virginia: Reston Pub.

[13]   Robb, K.L., and M.P. Parrella. 1988. Chemical and non-chemical control of western flower thrips. In *Proceedings.* Fourth Conf. on Insect and Disease Management on Ornamentals.

[14]   ——. 1989. An integrated approach to preventing western flower thrips and TSWV in the greenhouse. *GrowerTalks.* March 1989: 26-30, 32.

[15]   Sase, S., and L.L. Christianson. 1990. Screening greenhouses—some engineering considerations. Paper No. NABEC 90-201. Northeast Agr./Bio. Eng. Conf. Penn. State Univ.

[16]   Willits, D.H. 1993. *Greenhouse cooling.* Bul. 38(2):15-18. North Carolina Flower Growers.

[17]   Yokoyama, V.Y. 1978. Relation of seasonal changes in extrafloral nectar and foliar protein and arthropod populations in cotton. *Environ. Entomol.* 7:799-802.

CHAPTER 21

Weeds

Larry J Kuhns

Unless you take the right precautions, weeds can be your most difficult and costly item to control in a plant production system. Weed seeds can blow into an area at any stage of crop growth or can be introduced as seeds, rhizomes, stolons, or nutlets in soil used for potting. Once established, weeds compete with bedding plants for water, mineral nutrients, light, and space. Most weeds' vigorous nature enables them to crowd out and overrun crop plants.

Weed control program

Too many people look at weed control as a fire fighting measure—when weeds appear, kill them. It is much easier and cheaper to prevent weed growth than to kill existing weeds. Preventive measures are safer and longer lasting.

Anyone growing bedding plants should think in terms of a weed control program. This means planning how you are going to control weeds in your crop **before** planting. A good program has three parts:

1. Eliminate weeds in and around the growing area, and kill seeds or vegetative parts prior to planting. It is especially important to kill all perennial weeds or their parts because they are not controlled by mulches or preemergence herbicides. Postemergence herbicides that can be used freely prior to planting must be used with extreme caution after planting.
2. Prevent weed growth in and around the growing area. Mulches and/or preemergence herbicides work very well for controlling weeds from seed.
3. Eliminate weeds as they appear. Few preventive methods provide total control, so hand weeding or careful spot treating with a postemergence herbicide may be necessary.

Weed control methods

Weeds can be controlled by physical and chemical methods. Generally speaking, the physical methods are the safest while the chemical methods are the least expensive. Physical weed control methods include proper selection of a growing medium, steam pasteurization, mulches, and hand weeding.

Growing medium. By selecting a growing medium that is naturally and consistently weed-free, most weed problems can be avoided. Vermiculite and perlite are weed-free because of the way in which they are produced. Most peat contains very few, if any, weed seeds. Organic matter that has been properly composted will be weed free because the high temperatures reached during composting kill weeds and their seeds. Composted bark, sawdust, leaves, or sewage sludge may be used.

Steam pasteurization. This is an effective way of controlling weeds and most soil-borne insects and pathogens. Media should be heated to between 160 F and 180 F (71.1 C and 82.2 C) and held for 30 minutes. Steamed media should be covered or used within a week or so because it can be reinfested while being stored. Portable steam generators are available for steaming outdoor beds.

Mulches. Mulches can effectively control weeds from seeds that germinate at or near the soil surface. Organic mulches such as wood chips, shredded bark, or other plant residues can be applied to weed-free soil soon after planting. To be most effective they should be applied at least 2 inches deep. Avoid covering bedding plant stems and leaves. The primary inorganic mulches used are black polyethylene film and many types of geotextile weed barriers that allow air and water exchange.

Use only black films. Clear or white films allow weeds to grow under them. Black film increases soil temperature and, like the other mulches, maintains high moisture levels at the growing medium's surface.

Hand weeding. This is a high-cost, last-resort method. It always seems that some weeds manage to evade or survive the best weed control program. Hand weeding is not only expensive in terms of labor costs, but if weeds are allowed to grow out of control for a short time, the crop may be damaged during the pulling operation. Stems may be broken or roots severely damaged.

Chemical methods

Chemicals used to control weeds are classified as:

Selective versus nonselective. Selective herbicides kill some plants with little or no damage to others; nonselective are toxic to all plants.

Contact versus translocated. Contact herbicides kill only that part of the plant with which they come in contact. Translocated herbicides move within the plant and kill all parts of it. Perennial weeds usually regrow following contact herbicide application.

Preemergence versus postemergence. Preemergence herbicides control weeds at the seed germination stage. For best results, apply to weed-free soil before weeds emerge. Postemergence herbicides control existing weeds.

Fumigants. Fumigants may kill all living things in the soil including weeds, weed seeds, insects, and disease organisms.

The following herbicides are registered for use on annual and perennial flowers, groundcovers, and vines. The plants for which they are registered follow a brief description of the herbicide. Application rates are presented in pounds of active ingredient per acre (lbs. AIA) and pounds or volume of product per acre.

Preemergence herbicides

All preemergence herbicides must be applied and activated with rainfall or irrigation prior to germination of weed seeds. Very few of preemergence herbicides provide control of existing annual weeds or perennial weeds growing from established vegetative parts, such as roots, rhizomes, or tubers.

Bensulide (Betasan, Betamec, Lescosan, others). Available in granular or sprayable formulations. It controls many annual grasses and some broad-leaved weeds for six to eight weeks. Apply at 7.5 to 12.6 lbs. AIA (82-13.9 kg/ha) (107 to 180 lbs. Betasan 7-G or 7.5 to 12.5 qts. Betasan 4-E). Bensulide is recommended for use on mineral soils only, as it is bound and inactivated by organic matter.

> *Herbaceous plants:* alyssum, aster, bachelor's-button, calendula, campanula, candytuft, coralbells, daffodil, dahlia, daisy, daphne, freesia, gazania, gladiolus, marigold, narcissus, pansy, periwinkle, primrose, ranunculus, sedum, star jasmine, stock, sweet pea, tulip, wallflower, wild strawberry, zinnia.

Ground covers and vines: ajuga, hypericum, ice plant, ivy, juniper, myrtle, pachysandra.

DCPA (Dacthal). Available only in sprayable formulations. It will control most grasses and some broad-leaved weeds (spurge, purslane, chickweed, and carpetweed) for six to eight weeks. DCPA is recommended for use only on mineral soils, and it should be applied at the rate of 10 to 12 lbs. AIA (11.0-13.2 kg/ha) (7 to 8 qts. Dacthal 6-E or 14 to 16 lbs. Dacthal W-75). Cultivation following application will reduce its effectiveness.

Herbaceous plants: African violet, ageratum, alyssum, aster, baby's-breath, bellflower, bleeding-heart, bugloss, calliopsis (coreopsis), candytuft, chrysanthemum, coleus, columbine, coneflower, coralbells, cosmos, dahlia, delphinium, feverfew, forget-me-not, four-o'clock, foxglove, gaillardia, geranium, gladiolus, gold-dust, goldentuft, honeysuckle, iris, lantana, larkspur, lavendercotton, lily, lupine, marguerite, marigold, morning glory, moss rose, mother-of-thyme, mourning-bride, nasturtium, peony, petunia, poker plant, rose, sedum (stonecrop), snapdragon, spiderwort, strawflower, sundrops, sunflower, sweet pea, wormwood, yarrow, zinnia.

Ground covers and vines: euonymus, heath, ivy, pachysandra.

The label warns against use on the following plants: bugleweed, button pink, carnation, germander, geum, ice plant, Joseph's coat, mesembryanthemum, pansy, phlox, sweet William, telanthera.

EPTC (Eptam). Available only in granular formulations. It is highly volatile and must be incorporated 2 to 3 inches immediately after application. It will kill some tough-to-control perennial weeds as well as provide some preemergence weed control. For control of quack grass, Bermuda grass, or mugwort, incorporate 6 inches.

Existing stands of these weeds should be thoroughly chopped up before application. Apply EPTC at the rate of 5 lbs. AIA (5.5 kg/ha) (200 lbs. Eptam 2.3-G or 100 lbs. Eptam 5-G) to dry soil that permits thorough incorporation. Though it kills some difficult-to-control weeds, it only provides four- to six-weeks' preemergence weed control. This and its requirement for mechanical incorporation limit its use.

Herbaceous plants: ageratum, alyssum, amaranthus, aster, balsam, begonia, chrysanthemum, dahlia, daylily, dianthus, gazania, marigold, nasturtium, pansy, petunia, sedum, strawberry (ornamental), sweet alyssum, zinnia.

Ground covers and vines: ajuga, ice plant, ivy, pachysandra, periwinkle, St.-Johns-wort.

The label warns against use on the following plants: allium, crocus, daffodil, hyacinth, iris, lily, narcissus, ornamental pepper, phlox, salvia, snapdragon, tulip.

Isoxaben (Gallery). Available alone only as a sprayable formulation. It provides excellent, long-term control of broad-leaved weeds but is weak on grasses. Apply at a rate of 0.5 to 1.0 lb. AIA (.6-1.1 kg/ha) (0.66 to 1.33 lbs. Gallery 75DF).

> *Herbaceous plants:* African daisy, blue fescue, daffodil, daylily, eulalia grass, gardenia, gazania, heather, hibiscus, hosta, hyacinth, iris, jasmine, tulip.

> *Ground covers and vines:* ice plant, English ivy, liriope, pachysandra, periwinkle, St.-Johns-wort.

The label warns against use on the following plants: ajuga, hydrangea, iberis, sedum, yucca. Do not use on tulip plants that have emerged more than 0.75 inch, gladiolus prior to emergence if the corms are less than 1 inch in diameter, or to any bulbs while they are flowering. Do not use on bedding plants or areas in which bedding plants will be planted within one year following application or to ground covers until they are established and well rooted.

Isoxaben + oryzalin (Snapshot 80DF). Available only as a sprayable formulation. It provides excellent, long-term control of broad-leaved weeds and grasses growing from seed. Apply at a rate of 2 to 4 lbs. AIA (2.2-4.4 kg/ha) (2.5 to 5 lbs. Snapshot 80DF). See precautions for isoxaben and oryzalin.

> *Herbaceous plants:* African daisy, bottlebrush, gardenia, gazania, hosta, mondo grass, nandina, pampas grass.

> *Ground covers and vines:* bougainvillea, cape marigold, daylily, honeysuckle, ice plant, English ivy, liriope, periwinkle, plumbago, St.-Johns-wort.

Isoxaben + trifluralin (Snapshot TG). Available only as a granular formulation. It provides excellent, long-term control of broad-leaved weeds and grasses. Apply at a rate of 2.5 to 5 lbs. AIA (2.8-5.5 kg/ha) (100 to 200 lbs. Snapshot 2.5TG). See precautions for isoxaben and trifluralin.

Herbaceous plants: beach grass, blue fescue, bottlebrush, camellia, daylily, gardenia, gazania, hakonecloa, heather, hosta, miscanthus, mondo grass, nandina, plumbago, ribbon grass, snow-in-summer.

Ground covers and vines: cape marigold, carex, descampsia, honeysuckle, ice plant, ivy, jasmine, liriope, pachysandra, periwinkle, St.-Johns-wort.

Metolachlor (Pennant). Available as a granular or sprayable formulation. It controls most grasses and some broad-leaved weeds. It is also the best material currently available for controlling nutsedge. Apply at 2 to 4 lbs. AIA (2.2-4.4 kg/ha) (2 to 4 pts. Pennant Liquid). Use the higher rate for fine-textured or high organic soils, including container media, and where yellow nutsedge is expected. Do not use Pennant in greenhouses or other enclosed structures.

Herbaceous plants: African lily, allium, alyssum, aster, bellflower, chrysanthemum, columbine, coreopsis, crocus, daylily, delphinium, gaillardia, gazania, geranium, hibiscus, hosta, hydrangea, impatiens, Leopard's-bane, lupines, marigold, nandina, pansy, petunia, phlox, primrose, Queen-Anne's lace, sedum, snapdragon, statice, sweet William, tulip, veronica, zinnia.

Ground covers and vines: ajuga, dusty miller, English ivy, ice plant, liriope, pachysandra, periwinkle, St.-Johns-wort.

Metolachlor + simazine (Derby). Available only as a granular formulation. It provides excellent control of broad-leaved weeds, grasses, and nutsedge. Apply at 3 to 5 lbs. AIA (3.3-5.5 kg/ha) (60 to 100 lbs. Derby 5G). Use the higher rate for fine-textured or high organic soils, including container media and where yellow nutsedge is expected. Do not use in greenhouses or other enclosed structures.

Herbaceous plants: hosta, hydrangea, marigold, nandina.

Ground covers and vines: English ivy, euonymus, liriope, pachysandra.

Napropamide (Devrinol). Provides excellent long-term control of most grasses and some broad-leaved weeds from seed. It is available in sprayable formulation and may be available in granular formulation. Apply at a rate of 4 to 6 lbs. AIA (4.4-6.6 kg/ha) (8 to 12 lbs. Devrinol 50 DF). Napropamide is not stable on the soil surface in bright sun and warm temperatures. Cover with a mulch or incorporate into the soil mechanically or with irrigation or rainfall soon after applying.

Herbaceous plants: ageratum, African daisy, aster, bird-of-paradise, dahlia, daisy, eucalyptus, gardenia, gazania, geranium, heather, hibiscus, hosta, lantana, nandina, narcissus, petunia, sedum.

Ground covers and vines: ajuga, bougainvillea, carpobrotus, delosperma, dichondra, erysimum, English ivy, euonymus, ice plant, liriope, osteospermum, pachysandra, St.-Johns-wort, vinca.

Oryzalin (Surflan). Available only in a sprayable formulation. Apply oryzalin only to established plants. It provides excellent control of most annual grasses and some broadleaved weeds. It resists leaching and is non-volatile, so that it can be applied during any season. If weeds begin to emerge prior to rainfall, shallow cultivate (1 to 2 inches) (2.5 to 5 cm) to destroy existing weeds and to incorporate oryzalin into the weed germination zone. Oryzalin should be applied at the rate of 2 to 4 lbs. AIA (2.2-4.4 kg/ha) (2 to 4 qts. Surflan 4 A.S.). Do not apply oryzalin in greenhouses or enclosed greenhouse-type structures. Do not apply to plants within three weeks prior to enclosing in structures.

Herbaceous plants: aster, astilbe, baby's-breath, bellflower, bird-of-paradise, bleeding-heart, bottlebrush, caladium, campanula, cape marigold, chrysanthemum, coneflower, coreopsis, daisy, daylily, eucalyptus, gardenia, gazania, geranium, gladiolus, hibiscus, honeysuckle, impatiens, iris, marigold, moss rose, nandina, pansy, petunia, rose, sage, sedum, sweet William, yarrow, yucca, zinnia.

Ground covers and vines: ajuga, euonymus, ice plant, ivy, liriope, periwinkle, vinca.

Oryzalin + benefin (XL). Available only as a granular formulation. It controls most grasses and a few broad-leaved weeds from seed. Apply at a rate of 4 to 6 lbs. AIA (4.4-6.6 kg/ha) (200 to 300 lbs. XL 2G). Follow the same use guidelines as for oryzalin. Do not apply to tulip plants that are more than three-fourths-inch tall.

Herbaceous plants: bird-of-paradise, blue fescue, bottlebrush, cape marigold, capeweed, chrysanthemum, daisy, eucalyptus, gardenia, gazania, geranium, gladiolus, hibiscus, honeysuckle, impatiens, iris, marigold, nandina, narcissus, pansy, petunia, rose, sedum (stonecrop), tulip, zinnia.

Ground covers and vines: euonymus, Algerian and English ivy, ice plant, periwinkle, St.-Johns-wort.

mended rates, there is little chance of weed or desirable plant root uptake.

Bentazon (Basagran). Contols nutsedge and some broad-leaved weeds. It can be applied over tops of ground covers listed below, but it will injure most herbaceous plants contacted. Apply at a rate of 0.75 to 1.0 lb. AIA (.82-1.1 kg/ha) (1.5 to 2.0 pts. Basagran 4E). Add a crop oil concentrate to the spray solution to improve control.

Ground covers and vines: English ivy, liriope, pachysandra.

Fenoxaprop (Acclaim). Selectively controls annual and perennial grasses. Young, actively growing grasses are more easily controlled than larger grasses. Apply at 0.17 to 0.35 lbs. AIA (.19-.38 kg/ha) (23 to 45 oz. Acclaim 1E). Adding a surfactant improves coverage and weed control.

Herbaceous plants: African daisy, astilbe, baby-blue-eyes, baby's-breath, bachelor's-button, begonia, bellflower, black-eyed Susan, bleeding-heart, bluebells, blue flax, California poppy, caliopsis, candytuft, catchfly, chrysanthemum, coleus, columbine, coneflower, coreopsis, cosmos, daisy, dame's-rocket, daylily, English wallflower, forget-me-not, gaillardia, gayfeather, gazania, geranium, gilia, hosta, iris, leopard's-bane, liatrus, lily, liriope, maiden pinks, phlox, peony, petunia, pimpernel, poppy, red yarrow, Shasta daisy, Siberian wallflower, snapdragon, snow-in-summer, soapwort, statice, sundrops, sweet alyssum, sweet William, wild thyme, yarrow, zinnia.

Ground covers and vines: ajuga, ivy.

Precaution: Fenoxaprop may injure juniper, philodendron, salvia, podocarpus, and pittosporum.

Fluazifop-butyl (Fusilade, Ornamec). Selectively controls annual and perennial grasses. Ornamec is a systemic herbicide that moves from the treated foliage into grasses' rhizomes, stolons, and growing points. Treated grasses stop growing soon after application, but injury symptoms may not be seen for several weeks. Apply 0.25 to 0.37 lb. AIA (.28-.41 kg/ha) (32 to 48 oz. Fusilade 1E or 64 to 96 oz. Ornamec 0.5 E). Use a nonionic surfactant to improve treated weed coverage and control. Fluazifop may be applied over the plant tops in Group 1. Apply as a directed spray to prevent contact with plant foliage in Group 2.

Group 1:

Herbaceous plants: ageratum, alyssum, bellflower, bird-of-paradise, calendula, campanula, candytuft, chrysanthemum, coleus, coreopsis, crownvetch, daisy, daylily, dusty miller, eucalyptus, fountain grass, gardenia, gay feather, gazania, geranium, hibiscus, hollyhock, hosta, iris, lantana, lavendercotton, liriope, marigold, mesembryanthemum, periwinkle, petunia, rose, salvia, sedum, statice, ornamental strawberry, sweet William, yarrow, yucca, zinnia.

Ground covers and vines: bougainvillea, bearberry, cotoneaster, Algerian and English ivy, grape ivy, myrtle, pachysandra.

Group 2:

Herbaceous plants: bleeding-heart, cinquefoil, fountain grass, gazania, gladiolus, lantana, mondo grass, primrose.

Ground covers and vines: ajuga, honeysuckle, juniper.

Glyphosate (Roundup). This is a nonselective, systemic herbicide that is absorbed through the foliage and translocated to all plant parts. It kills below-ground plant parts so it effectively controls perennial weeds. For best results, Roundup should be applied to actively growing, well developed weeds. Use the rate specified on the label for the weeds present.

Do not apply Roundup if rainfall is imminent. Allow 24 hours for absorption, but some control is obtained if only six hours elapse between application and rainfall.

Roundup requires three to 10 days to kill effectively, depending on weed species and growing conditions. It is inactivated rapidly in the soil, so it can be safely used as a preplant application for any species.

It can also be used to control weeds growing in greenhouses with certain limitations. Remove any desirable vegetation before applying, and turn off air circulation fans. Roundup is not labeled for use around any existing bedding plants.

Potassium salt of fatty acid (Sharpshooter). This is a nonselective contact herbicide that kills only small weeds. It does not effectively control perennial weeds or large annual weeds. Do not spray over the top of any desirable plants.

Sethoxydim (Vantage). Sethoxydim selectively controls annual and perennial grasses. Vantage is a systemic herbicide that moves from the treated foliage into the grasses' rhizomes, stolons, and growing points. Treated grasses stop growing soon after application, but injury symptoms may not be seen for several weeks. Apply 0.28 to 0.47 lb. AIA (.31-.52 kg/ha) (36 to 60 oz. Vantage 1E). Vantage contains a wetting agent so no additional surfactant needs to be added to the spray solution. Vantage can be applied over plant tops.

Herbaceous plants: alyssum, asparagus fern, aster, begonia, bird-of-paradise, bleeding-heart, blue fescue, butterfly weed, camellia, candytuft, canna, capeweed, carnation, chrysanthemum, cockscomb, coleus, coralbells, crownvetch, dahlia, daisy, daylily, dusty miller, euonymus, gardenia, gazania, geranium, gerbera daisy, gladiolus, heather, hibiscus, honeysuckle, hosta, hydrangea, impatiens, iris, Jack-in-the-pulpit, jade plant, jasmine, lantana, lavender, lily-of-the-valley, liriope, lobelia, purple loosestrife, marigold, mondo grass, moneywort, moss rose, nandina, nicotiana, pampas grass, pansy, ornamental pepper, periwinkle, petunia, phlox, plumbago, sage, salvia, sedum, snapdragon, speed well, statice, stock, sweet William, verbena, zinnia.

Ground covers and vines: ajuga, bittersweet, bougainvillea, capeweed, grape ivy, heather, honeysuckle, hypericum, ice plant, ivy, pachysandra, periwinkle, plumbago, St. Johns-wort, trumpet vine, vinca, wisteria.

Integrating a weed control program

1. **Eliminate weeds prior to planting.** If plants are to be grown in containers, either use a soilless medium free of weed seeds, or steam pasteurize the medium prior to use. If plants are to be grown in the field, either fumigate the area, or apply glyphosate to kill all existing vegetation prior to planting.

2. **Prevent weed growth.** Bedding plants grown in containers in a soilless or pasteurized medium should not require any preventive measures. They should be ready for sale before any weed problems develop. Apply mulch and/or a preemergence herbicide to plants grown in the field. Repeat preemergence herbicide applications may be necessary.

3. **Eliminate weeds as they appear.** In many cases, the most efficient way to remove weeds that escape preventive measures is to simply hand-pull them. Where high-density grasses are the primary problem, use Acclaim, Ornamec, or Vantage to kill them. If weeds get out of control and grow 4 or more inches taller than the crop, use Roundup with wick applicators.

CHAPTER 22

Pesticide Application

Richard K. Lindquist and Charles C. Powell

Pesticides, including fungicides, insecticides, and miticides, are an important part of bedding plant pest and disease management programs. The most important pesticide application objective is delivering the pesticide in sufficient concentration to control a pest or pathogen.

The target may be an entire plant, specific area on the plant, growing medium, or the pest or pathogen. Defining the target is important for proper pesticide application.

Is the objective to hit airborne pests? Pests on or in leaf surfaces? Are the pests on all plant parts or only certain areas? Are pests in the growing medium or under benches? Bedding plants produced on greenhouse floors can have coverage and deposition problems because of thick foliage canopies.

Appropriate pesticide selection based on mode of action is crucial to any application's success or failure. Does the pesticide have vapor or systemic activity? If so, it will redistribute from the deposition point to reach other areas.

Many fungicides are preventive; they prevent a pathogen from becoming established. Most insecticides are eradicative; they eradicate a pest that is present, but do not prevent future infestations.

Deposition and distribution

Pesticide application is a two-step process: deposition and distribution. Deposition is applying the pesticide to the target area, and distribution is getting the material to the correct area in the required, effective amounts. With any applicator, you must first distribute the pesticide to the area, then deposit it onto the target.

Spray drop size affects deposition and distribution with any application. Table 22.1 shows the number of spray drops per square centimeter that can be produced from 1 liter (about 1 quart) of liquid based

TABLE 22.1

Theoretical spray coverage [a]

Drop diameter (microns)	No. drops/cm^2
10	19,099.00
20	2,387.00
50	153.00
100	19.00
200	2.40
400	0.30
1,000	0.02

[a] In drops/cm^2, applying 1 liter/hectare with different drop sizes.

on drop size. It is easy to see that small drops will *potentially* increase coverage.

Laboratory research indicates that large numbers of small drops usually give better pest and disease control than fewer, larger drops, if deposition proceeds properly. However, in practice, this may not always be true for bedding plants. Deposition of small droplets depends greatly on target characteristics (foliage canopy thickness, plant height, bed, floor, or bench-grown plants) and equipment characteristics (air-assisted movement, flow rate).

High-volume sprays

High-volume sprays (HV) are the traditional method of applying pesticides to bedding plants in greenhouses and outdoors. Equipment and methods have not changed much over the years. These sprays involve mixing a certain pesticide quantity with a large water volume and spraying the plants or growing medium to some wetness point. Water is used to dilute the pesticide concentrate. It serves as a carrier to deliver the material to the target and deposit it on the target.

High-volume sprays can be inefficient. For instance, when the target is a small flying insect, only about 2% to 6% of the pesticide applied actually reaches its intended target, and the remaining material is lost through evaporation, drift, or runoff. Spray inefficiency in such cases relates to spray drop size. Most of the volume in HV sprays consists of large drops (100 to 400 microns diam.); however, there are also significant numbers of very small drops. Neither extreme will deposit effectively on target surfaces. Efficiency of HV sprays can be significantly increased if proper application techniques are used. Consistent use of high pressure, getting close to plants, and moving the spray nozzle in an arc can result in effective, uniform foliage canopy penetration and leaf surface coverage.

High-volume spray equipment is widely available, relatively inexpensive, and remains the only legal way to apply many pesticides. Every greenhouse operator should have an HV sprayer and should properly train employees applying the sprays.

Low-volume sprays

Low-volume applications are not new. Various LV equipment types have been in use for decades. These sprays often utilize specialized equipment, including thermal pulse-jet foggers, mechanical aerosol generators, and electrostatic mist sprayers. They are designed to eliminate many of the disadvantages of conventional HV applications.

They often take less time, use less water or oil to dilute and carry the pesticide (no runoff), may use less pesticide, and produce most of the spray volume in small spray drops, which are supposed to be more efficient. Advantages and limitations of using certain types of presently available low-volume equipment follow.

Thermal pulse-jet foggers

Thermal foggers have been in use for more than 30 years. Originally, foggers were used to apply vapor-active fumigants and are still very effective for this. However, thermal foggers are effective also when applying residual pesticides, often depositing as much pesticide as an HV application. A thermal fogger's primary advantage is the short time required to apply a pesticide to a large greenhouse area.

Most thermal foggers will disperse both liquid or wettable powder formulations. A carrier or dispersal agent, to be mixed with or used in place of water, may be specified by the manufacturer to help ensure a persistent fog. Using a pesticide that redistributes after application through systemic or vapor action can be very effective. Pesticide deposition within the plant canopy and on leaf undersides is often poor, so using thermal pulse-jet applicators with certain pesticide/pest combinations will not be successful.

Thermal foggers produce very small drops, mostly 10 to 50 microns in diameter, that are able to move rather long distances from the applicator. With some of the larger units available, the drops will travel more than 200 feet (65 meters). Liquid flow rates also vary with the unit size. For example, a small fogger will disperse 10.6 quarts (10 l) in 30 minutes, and the largest model will disperse 21.1 quarts (20 l) in 30 minutes. The area covered will depend on whether a wettable or liquid formulation is applied. Obviously, foggers are not used to apply pesticides to small areas for spot treatments. They are designed to treat large areas quickly.

Aerosol generators

There now are several different aerosol generators being sold. These sprayers use air pressure, supplied by a compressor, to break up the spray liquid into small drops—sometimes less than 5 microns in diameter. Air also is the primary method of moving the spray around the greenhouse and onto the foliage. Much of the spray movement is accomplished by the greenhouse air circulation system, e.g., horizontal air flow or overhead convection tubes. Aerosol generators are supposed to disperse both liquid and dry pesticide formulations.

The flow rate from these sprayers is less than 2 fluid ounces (59.1 ml) per minute, so it will take about $2\frac{1}{2}$ hours to apply 7.4 quarts (7 l) of spray. Our results in commercial greenhouses, using fluorescent tracer material as well as non-systemic insecticides, have shown that deposition and distribution can vary quite widely, and that deposition on upper leaf surfaces was much higher than on undersides. However, in smaller research greenhouse experiments, control of greenhouse whitefly larvae on leaf undersides with bifenthrin was excellent. Similar results have been obtained against two-spotted spider mites and melon aphids.

The obvious advantage of using this sprayer type is that the application can be made without anyone being in the greenhouse. The pesticide can be mixed with water in the tank and applied when no one is present. Ventilation must be thorough before any workers reenter the greenhouse.

Questions that remain are largely safety-related, such as the amount of off-target pesticide deposition on benches, fans, walls, and equipment surfaces. Some growers have experienced nozzle clogging problems with oily, liquid, and wettable powder formulations.

Air-assisted electrostatic sprayers

Using electrical charging of spray drops to achieve better leaf underside coverage and to reduce spray drift is a concept that has been around for many years. We have evaluated three types of electrostatic low-volume applicators. In general, our results showed that air-assistance from a fan on the sprayer or an air compressor gave better pest and disease control than non-air-assisted sprayers.

The air-assisted electrostatic sprayer commonly sold in the United States produces drops with a median volume diameter of about 30 microns. Between 4 to 16 gallons of spray are applied per acre (6.1 l to 24.5 l/ha), depending on pressure and walking speed. Either liquid or powder formulations can be applied.

Sprays are applied by walking through the greenhouse, aiming the spray ahead and slightly downward toward the crop with a sweeping motion. Practice is necessary to obtain even coverage and deposition. The time required to treat an area is between that of using a thermal fogger and high-volume spray. One acre (.4 ha) can be treated in about one to two hours.

We have conducted several experiments in commercial and research greenhouses with the air-assisted electrostatic sprayer. Figure 22.1 summarizes fluorescent tracer deposition within a potted geranium plant canopy after electrostatically charged and uncharged sprays using three spray volumes. Total fluorescent tracer deposition was related to spray volume, as might be expected.

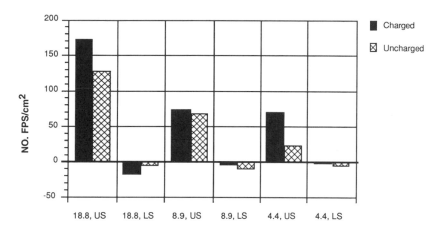

Fig. 22.1. Fluorescent tracer deposition (FPS) on upper (US) and lower (LS) leaf surfaces using charged sprays at three spray volumes 18.8, 8.9 and 4.4 gallons per acre (28.8 l, 13.6 l and 6.7 l/ha).

However, insect and disease control have also been related to spray volume; i.e., the dosage-per-area effectiveness was related to the spray volume in which the product was applied. Higher volumes generally resulted in better control. This was true especially for plant pathogens and insects on the leaf underside.

Also, the difference between electrostatically charged and uncharged applications was most pronounced at the lower spray volumes. Most of the deposition was on upper leaf surfaces. However, excellent control of greenhouse whitefly nymphs has been obtained

Clothing. A cotton T-shirt and shorts do not provide adequate protection when applying pesticides. Protective clothing should include a clean, long-sleeved shirt and long trousers made of a tightly woven fabric or a water-repellent material. Wearing an undershirt adds protection. Additional clothing layers help to absorb pesticides and reduce the amount that reaches the skin. Avoid pants with cuffs to prevent collecting granules or powder in the cuff. When a granular pesticide is used, shake clothing and empty pockets and cuffs outdoors.

Disposable coveralls are available that are laminated with other fabrics to increase wearer protection from chemicals. Different brands vary in their comfort, durability, and the degree of protection they provide. Throw away used disposable clothing—do not attempt to clean and reuse. Be sure the protective suit's elasticized sleeves and legs are sufficiently tight to prevent pesticides from reaching exposed arms and legs.

A liquid-proof, solvent-resistant apron or rainsuit should be worn when pouring and mixing concentrates. Porous coveralls do not provide adequate protection against spills and splashes. An apron should cover the body from your chest to your boots. Waterproof clothing should also be worn whenever mist or spray drift occur.

Gloves. Wear unlined, waterproof rubber gloves when handling or applying pesticides. Nitrile, butyl, and neoprene rubber provide the best protection for both liquid and dry pesticide formulations. Natural rubber gloves are recommended only for dry formulations. Never use leather or fabric gloves because they absorb pesticides and transfer them to the skin.

Be certain gloves are approved for use with the chemicals you intend to use. Some rubber products react with certain solvents and become sticky as the rubber dissolves. If this occurs, dispose of those gloves. Check gloves frequently to be sure there are no holes—fill them with water and squeeze—and discard any damaged or leaking gloves.

Gloves should be long enough to cover the wrist and should not have a fabric wristband. For most jobs, shirt sleeves should be worn on the outside of the gloves to keep pesticides from running down the sleeves into the gloves. However, when working with hands and arms overhead, sleeves should be tucked into the gloves with the glove cuffs turned up to catch any material that might run down.

Wash off chemicals with soap and water before removing gloves to avoid contaminating your hands when you remove gloves.

Hats. Wear a waterproof head covering when handling pesticides. A nonabsorbent hood, hard hat, or wide-brimmed rain hat protect the head, face, and neck. Hats should be either disposable or easy to clean with soap and water. Get rid of used disposables—do not attempt to clean and reuse.

Shoes/boots. Wear boots made of unlined nitrile, butyl, or neoprene rubber. Do not wear absorbent leather, canvas, or cloth shoes or boots when handling pesticides. Wear trouser bottoms outside boots to prevent pesticides from running down the leg and into the boot.

Goggles/face shields. Wear tight fitting, nonfogging goggles or a full face shield if there is any chance of getting pesticide in the eyes. This is especially important when pouring or mixing concentrates or when handling dusts or toxic sprays. If you wear contact lenses, consult an eye doctor before using pesticides.

Keep goggles and face shields clean at all times. Wash with soap and water, and sanitize by soaking for two minutes in a mixture of 2 tablespoons (30 ml) chlorine bleach in a gallon (3.7 l) of water. Rinse thoroughly with clean water to remove soap and sanitizer. Wipe with a clean cloth and allow to air dry. Replace absorbent goggle headbands after each use.

Respirators. For many toxic chemicals, the respiratory (breathing) system is the quickest and most direct entry route into the circulatory system. If inhaled into the lungs, pesticides can enter the bloodstream and be transported rapidly throughout the body.

Respiratory protective devices vary in design, use, and protective capability. Different respirators are needed for different chemical applications. Select a respirator that is designed for the intended use, and follow the manufacturer's use and maintenance instructions. Select only equipment approved by the National Institute of Occupational Safety and Health (NIOSH), and the Mine Safety and Health Administration (MSHA). The NIOSH/MSHA approval numbers begin with the letters TC.

Mix and load pesticides safely

The highest risks in using pesticides occur during mixing and loading of concentrates. Always have adequate protective clothing and equipment available, and put them on before handling or opening a pesticide container. Before opening the container, **read the label** so you are familiar with mixing and usage directions. Wear a respirator and appropriate eye protection if there is any chance of pesticide inhalation or eye exposure.

Carefully choose the pesticide mixing and loading area. It should be located outside, away from other people, livestock, and pets. Pesticides should not be mixed where a spill could contaminate a water supply. If the mixing area is unavoidably near a well, pond, or stream bank, grade the area to slope away from the water.

Lengthen the water hose to permit filling and mixing as far away from the water source as possible. Mixing chemicals on a concrete pad facilitates cleanup and prevents spilled pesticides from contaminating the soil. **Never leave a spray unit unattended while it is being filled.**

If you must work indoors or at night, be sure you have adequate ventilation and light. Have a supply of clean water and soap available. If possible, do not work alone.

Use a sharp knife or a scissors to open—do **NOT** tear—paper containers. When pouring from a container, keep the container below eye level to avoid splashing chemical on your face. Always stand upwind, so the wind does not blow the pesticide towards you. Never use your mouth to siphon a pesticide from a container. If an accident does occur, attend to it immediately. Remove any contaminated clothing, and wash thoroughly with soap and water.

Read the label, and follow label instructions. Mix only what you plan to immediately use. Measure accurately! The application will not be effective if too much or too little chemical is used. Measuring devices such as "tip and pours" are a great help in handling small concentrate amounts. Keep all measuring devices (spoons, cups, scales) in the pesticide storage area and never use them for other purposes. Label them "FOR PESTICIDE USE ONLY" to prevent any other use.

Rinse measuring cups after using and put rinsate into the spray tank. Triple rinse pesticide containers as soon as they are emptied. Dried residues can be difficult to remove later. Pour the rinsate into the spray tank to avoid disposal problems and to avoid wasting product.

Check and calibrate equipment prior to filling and use. The spray tank must also be clean since oil, grease, and chemical residues can cause incompatibility problems. The agitation system should be running, and the spray tank about half-filled with water before adding any pesticide.

Keep your head out of the tank and above the fill hole. Do not spill or splash any chemical when putting it into the tank. If two or more pesticides are to be mixed, they must be compatible and mixed in the correct order. Small quantities of wettable powders often mix more easily if a slurry is made first.

Back-siphoning pesticide into a water system is a very costly mistake that can be easily avoided. When adding water to the spray mixture, leave an air gap between the hose end and the top of the mix. Install antibackflow check valves. Fill the spray tank from a nurse tank that contains only water. If possible, add the pesticide in the field after the tank has been filled with water.

Water quality influences some pesticides' effectiveness. Alkaline spray water promotes chemical breakdown of many organophosphates and carbamates. Recommended water pH for mixing most pesticides is between 5.0 and 7.0. Buffers and acidifying agents can be used to adjust the water pH if necessary. Water high in suspended solids (silt or organic matter) can render certain pesticides completely ineffective, because the pesticides bind to the contaminants in the water.

Closed handling systems minimize user exposure to pesticide concentrates. A closed handling system has interconnected equipment that allows the applicator to remove a pesticide concentrate from its original container, rinse the empty container, and transfer the pesticide and rinsate to the spray tank without the applicator being exposed to the chemical.

Apply pesticides safely and effectively

Employers must comply with all aspects of the revised Environmental Protection Agency Worker Protection Standard (WPS). The new WPS includes requirements intended to reduce illness or injury risks to agricultural workers and pesticide handlers from occupational or accidental exposure to pesticides in the production of agricultural plants on farms, nurseries, greenhouses, and forests. All bedding plant growers will probably be impacted by this regulation.

A pesticide application's safety and effectiveness depends largely on using the correct pesticide amount and an appropriate application method. This assumes, however, that the pest problem has already been correctly diagnosed and the pesticide carefully selected to consider performance, worker safety, cost, compatibility with other chemicals, preharvest and reentry intervals, carryover, and nontarget exposure.

Before application. Before making a pesticide application, READ THE PRODUCT LABEL! Correct handling procedures require that clean clothing and proper protective equipment be worn. Respiratory protection may be essential if the application is made indoors or if the applicator is in an enclosed cab without air filters. Check application equipment carefully, particularly for leaking hoses and connections and plugged or worn nozzles. Applicators should plan to work in pairs when applying highly toxic pesticides. Never let an inexperienced person apply pesticides alone.

Never eat, smoke, or drink while handling pesticides—do not even carry food or smoking items with you. Carry fresh water, soap, and paper towels in a protected container to allow for quick removal of pesticide contaminants from the body in case of a spill or exposure to spray drift. A first aid kit and an eyewash bottle are also good precautions, particularly in service vehicles.

Remove livestock, pets, and farm equipment from the area to be treated. Any persons not involved in the application should leave the treatment area. Post placards to keep unauthorized or unprotected persons from entering the area.

During application. During the pesticide application, monitor the weather carefully. Apply pesticides only under favorable weather conditions. Do not apply pesticides during high winds—as wind velocity increases, drift and volatilization also increase.

Do not apply pesticides just before a heavy rain—rain can wash the chemicals off treated surfaces and cause pesticide runoff from a treated area. Apply pesticides in the early morning or early evening when wind speeds are usually low, and protective clothing and equipment can be worn with less discomfort.

Guard against pesticide drift onto nearby water bodies, crops, pastures, livestock, or residential areas when making outdoor applications. Spray drift is any movement of airborne pesticides (particles, spray droplets, or gases) beyond the intended contact area.

By keeping your application equipment in good condition and operating properly, you can avoid unnecessary personal hazards as well as possible crop damage. While spraying, if you have to stop to fix and adjust equipment that is in poor condition, you may be excessively exposed to the chemical.

Minimize your exposure to the chemical when working on equipment. If a nozzle becomes clogged while making an application, stop the sprayer and move to an untreated area before correcting the problem. Never touch your mouth to a spray nozzle or a clogged pump part.

Be sure that you are using the recommended type of equipment. Never attempt to use a powder that is intended to be mixed in water in a dust applicator. The label explains what types of applications are permissible.

After application. Never reenter a recently sprayed or fumigated greenhouse unless you are wearing proper protective clothing and equipment. Do not handle treated plants until the spray has dried. Post appropriate warning signs at each entrance during and immediately after an application to reduce the possibility of someone accidentally walking into a treated area.

Immediately following application and equipment cleaning, wash thoroughly and change to all clean clothing. Spray residue must be removed from contact with the skin. In the past, applicators who delayed bathing and changing to clean clothing have become extremely ill because of toxic residues on the skin and in clothing.

To increase a pesticide application's efficacy and safety, be sure to follow any postapplication procedures listed on the label, such as reentry periods and incorporation procedures if the pesticide was applied to the soil. Never leave equipment unattended at the application site.

Clean all equipment after pesticide application. Follow any cleaning recommendations on the label. Clean equipment in a designated area away from water supplies. Wear the appropriate protective equipment and clothing, and remember that the pesticide has contaminated all equipment parts (pumps, tanks, and hoses). Exercise extreme caution if you plan to use a herbicide sprayer to apply another type of agricultural chemical.

After cleaning application equipment, clean your protective equipment. Personal cleanup is next. Wash your hands and face thoroughly with soap and water before eating, drinking, or smoking. Shower and change clothing as soon as possible. Be sure to scrub your scalp, neck, behind your ears, and clean under your nails.

Pesticide poisoning

Symptoms of poisoning may appear almost immediately after exposure or may be delayed for several hours depending on the chemical, dose, exposure time, and the individual. Symptoms are headache, giddiness, nervousness, blurred vision, cramps, diarrhea, "numb-all-over" feeling, or abnormal pupil size. In some cases, there is excessive sweating, tearing, or mouth secretions.

Severe poisoning cases may cause nausea and vomiting, fluid in the lungs, changes in heart rate, muscle weakness, breathing difficulty, confusion, convulsions, coma, or death. However, pesticide poisoning may mimic brain hemorrhage, heat stroke, heat exhaustion, hypoglycemia (low blood sugar), stomach and intestinal disorders, pneumonia, asthma, or other severe respiratory infections.

If a poisoning occurs or is suspected, regardless of how trivial the exposure may seem, get medical advice at once. If a physician is not immediately available by phone, take the person directly to the nearest hospital's emergency room. Take the pesticide label and telephone number of the closest Poison Control Center with you.

If first-aid treatment is necessary, read the pesticide container label and carefully follow first-aid instructions. If two people are present, one should give first aid and the other should retrieve the pesticide container and call a physician. Tell the doctor the name of the pesticide, the symptoms, and ask for instructions.

If a pesticide has been ingested: Call a physician or emergency room immediately. Have the pesticide label available. You will need instructions on whether or not to induce vomiting.

Equipment rinsates

Equipment rinsate comes from washing and rinsing spray application equipment after use. Rinsates must be handled carefully to avoid water contamination or injury to nontarget plants and animals.

When possible, rinse your equipment at the application site and spray the rinsate on the treated area. This is feasible only if a water source is available at the application site. A more practical option for most pesticide users is to rinse equipment at the mixing site and then apply the rinsate to a crop listed on the product label.

Another option is to collect and store the rinsate for future use. Collection and storage systems usually consist of a concrete pad or platform on which equipment is washed, a drainage system that connects to a holding tank, and a pump to dispense the liquid from the holding tank into the sprayer. Aboveground holding tanks are usually preferred over buried tanks because they can be more easily monitored for leaks.

These systems can be very useful in managing pesticide wastes, but must be used responsibly. Careful records must be kept of all pesticide rinsates put into the holding tanks to avoid subsequent plant injury or illegal residues on a crop when the rinsates are used.

Do not allow equipment rinsate to enter a sewer or a drain that leads to a water/sewage treatment system. Also, remember that repeated application equipment cleaning on bare ground in the same location can lead to pesticide levels in the soil that exceed the soil's capacity to bind or degrade the chemical. Pesticide leaching from such areas can lead to groundwater contamination.

Pesticide containers

Properly rinsing glass, metal, plastic, and even some heavy paper containers effectively removes most pesticide remaining in the container. Rinsing not only saves the applicator money by using the rinsate in the spray tank, but also allows container disposal as nonhazardous waste.

Rinse containers as soon as they are empty. Some pesticide residues become very difficult, if not impossible, to remove after drying. Rinse containers using either the triple rinse method or its equivalent such as pressure rinsing.

Triple-rinsed or pressure-rinsed containers that are being held for disposal later should be marked to indicate that rinsing has been done and the date. Pierce or crush containers that cannot be recycled through a recycling facility or a dealer. Never reuse pesticide containers for any purpose.

All used containers should be kept in a locked storage facility until disposal, and away from all possible contact with children and animals.

Few disposal options exist for empty pesticide containers. Municipal sanitary landfills are not required to accept pesticide containers, but at this time, **rinsed** containers are still being accepted at many licensed municipal landfills. It is a good policy to check with your local solid waste authority prior to discarding pesticide containers in this way. Triple-rinsed or pressure-rinsed containers should be recycled whenever feasible. For information on recycling facilities, consult your state or local solid waste disposal authorities.

Never leave pesticide containers in fields, unlocked sheds, or buildings, even after they have been rinsed. Properly rinsed containers can be buried on your own property, but the site should be located away from houses, crop growing areas, livestock areas, farm ponds, irrigation channels, wells, and streams. For your own protection, keep a map and a burial site list.

Combustible containers can be burned only if permitted by label instructions on the label and by local and state ordinances and policies. Contact the Bureau of Air Quality at a state or regional EPA office if you plan to burn combustible containers.

Remove as much residue from combustible containers as possible; triple rinse containers if feasible. Burn pesticide containers in an approved site, away from residential areas or where people might come in contact with the smoke.

Always stand upwind when burning pesticide containers. Pesticide smoke may be toxic. Herbicide vapors, particularly those from growth-regulating herbicides such as 2,4-D and dicamba, can cause injury to nearby plants.

Transport pesticides safely

Once a pesticide is in your possession, you are responsible for its safe transportation. Accidents can happen even when transporting pesticides a short distance. Know how to prevent transportation problems. Be prepared in case of an emergency.

Transport vehicle. The safest way to carry pesticides is usually in the back of a truck. Steel beds are preferable since they can be more easily cleaned if a spill occurs. Flatbed trucks should have side and tail racks. Any vehicle used to transport pesticides should be in safe driving condition. In particular, check the tires, brakes, and steering.

Never carry pesticides in a vehicle's passenger compartment because spilled chemical and hazardous fumes can cause serious injury to the occupants. Also, spilled pesticides can be very difficult, if not impossible, to remove from upholstery. If pesticides must be transported in a station wagon, windows should remain open, and permit no one to ride near the containers.

Serious accidents. Serious accidents involving chemicals present unusually hazardous conditions—perhaps a major spill has occurred, or the chemical is particularly dangerous to handle.

To protect the public and to assist public agencies in handling such mishaps, the chemical industry has in place an emergency response system. Here is how this response system works:

1. Caller reports an incident to CHEMTREC in Washington, D.C., using the telephone number 1-800-424-9300. CHEMTREC will ask the caller for information about the incident being reported and to identify the chemical(s) involved.
2. CHEMTREC will then provide basic emergency information on the chemical(s) reported.
3. CHEMTREC will contact the manufacturer(s) of the chemical(s) involved so that the company can initiate its own technical assistance and response procedures. Pesticide manufacturers have technical staff skilled in dealing with emergencies involving their products.

Emergency telephone number on pesticide labels. An additional and *very important* number to remember is the emergency telephone number found on many product labels and on transportation shipping papers. The lines are answered 24 hours per day by people who are prepared to handle pesticide emergencies involving their products.

Follow up. For legal protection, keep records of your activities and conversations with regulatory authorities, emergency response personnel, and the general public when dealing with a pesticide spill. Photographs help to document any damage, as well as the clean-up process.

Be sure the spill has been reported to the appropriate regulatory agencies. SARA Title III also requires the reporting of certain pesticide spills if the amount spilled is greater than the "reportable quantity" for that chemical. Discharge of chemical substances into waterways must also be reported to the U.S. Environmental Protection Agency under the authority of the Clean Water Act.

Spill prevention and preparation. A key to preventing pesticide spills is to properly maintain all vehicles and application equipment. Leaks and drips from cracks or loose fittings in equipment are indications of potential trouble. An understanding of how spray equipment works, especially a pumping system, is often essential to controlling a product's flow and minimizing equipment damage should a problem occur. Safe driving and other good operating habits further reduce the likelihood of a spill.

Knowing how to safely handle pesticide spills and leaks is as important as knowing how to correctly apply the material. All facilities in which pesticides are handled should have a complete listing of emergency telephone numbers readily available. Always have the product label with you!

A Material Safety Data Sheet (MSDS) for every pesticide on the premises is a must. Proper equipment and supplies for cleaning up spills are essential in every storage establishment.

All persons using or transporting pesticides and other hazardous chemicals have a responsibility to protect the public and the environment. Doing everything possible to avoid spills and adhering to a few basic guidelines when handling spills and leaks can go a long way toward meeting that responsibility.

CHAPTER 24

Price and Market Analysis

Alvi O. Voigt

An understanding of prices and markets is somewhat elusive, primarily because prices and markets depend upon supply and demand factors, which in turn are elusive because they depend upon people: producers, consumers, and those in the market structure or environment.

The profit equation

Pricing should be placed in perspective as part of the profit equation:

PRICE × QUANTITY – COST = PROFIT

Pricing (with the quantity to sell and the cost incurred) is a means to the profit objective. Profit not only has varying degrees of importance, depending on one's business/personal circumstances and objectives, but profit can be viewed in different ways as well.

Profit can be considered in absolute dollars and/or as percentages. Owners of small unincorporated businesses may consider profit as their wages, with little or no regard to a return on investment. Family businesses may be content with a dollar profit (wages) sufficient to meet family expenses. Incorporated businesses, on the other hand, include owner-operator compensation as an expense. Profits tend to be considered a return on investment. As a percentage of current net worth, this return allows a reasonable comparison with returns on other investments. If a competitive return on investment is a major business objective, then the business should earn what represents a reasonable alternative financial market return.

less of low price. However, some minimum number of plants is required; and they will pay a nickel, dime, or quarter more to get the plants if they are scarce.

One strategy could be to sell more individual—rather than pack— vegetable plants of larger size and higher price with varying types and varieties. The basic strategy for inelastic products is to try to restrict supply (do not overproduce), because any oversupply will sell at drastically lower prices. A smaller crop is worth more than a bumper crop.

The strategy for flowering potted crops and flowering bedding plants (elastic demand) is to increase volume to generate profit, rather than restrict volume. Flowering plants have a much greater unit sales potential. Some minimum number of flowering plants could be inelastic ("must have"); however, additional sales will result (elastic, "luxury type") providing that consumers have the income, time, and space for gardening, as well as the willingness. Usually, limited time and space for gardening will not deter sales if items are priced and merchandised attractively.

Market control characteristics

Price behavior is explained also by the market structure that exists. Table 24.1 indicates pertinent market control characteristics for markets varying from highly competitive to monopoly, or from price takers to price makers.

TABLE 24.1

Market control characteristics

	Example	Type of market	Number of firms	Type of produce	Entry
Smaller control (Price takers)	Agriculture	Competitive	Many	Homogeneous (H)	Easy
	Retailing	Monopolistic-competitive	Many	Differentiated (D)	Easy
Greater control (Price makers)	Large mfgr.	Oligopoly	Few	Either H or D	Restricted
	Public utility	Monopoly	One	No substitutes	Restricted

Businesses with smaller control (competitive) are characterized by the many agricultural production firms that produce homogeneous products (milk, wheat, beef, eggs, flowers) and are a relatively easy occupation to enter. Retailing offers somewhat more control over price. Retailing, like agriculture, has many firms and is easy to enter, but it offers the possibility of differentiating the product line. Through product differentiation, bedding plant retailers can have more influence on price. Oligopolists and monopolists have even greater control, chiefly because of restricted entry and the existence of only a few firms (or sometimes only one firm) in the market. Entry is restricted, of course, because of the monstrous amount of capital necessary to become a General Electric, a General Motors, an IBM, or Xerox.

Market emphasis

The pricing model (fig. 24.1) indicates that the primary demand factor the bedding plant industry should focus on is consumer tastes and preferences. This is consumer willingness (or reluctance) to buy bedding plants. The remaining two demand factors—number of customers and their incomes, and prices of substitutes—cannot be influenced unless drastic individual action is taken, such as relocating to an area with more customers or taking on a broader product mix that includes substitutes.

Know your customer

Customer knowledge—their characteristics, tastes, and preferences— can improve customer satisfaction and loyalty and create greater demand, potentially influencing prices. The Nursery Marketing Council of the American Association of Nurserymen researched homeowners' purchasing motivations and practices and identified three distinct groups based on the amount each is likely to spend on outdoor living plants and related products.

The top group of homeowners, who would spend $50 or more a year on living plants for their yards and gardens, represented 18% of the homeowners and accounted for almost as much nursery expenditure as the remaining 82%! This group averages $97 a year on living plants in the yard and $90 for related materials (mulch, fertilizer, insecticides, etc.); has an average household income of $25,000 or more per year; an average age of 25 to 34; a college-educated husband and wife; considers installation and care of living plants outdoors as a positive experience to be enjoyed as a family an average seven hours a week; plans their

TABLE 24.2

Customer survey results

A. Is this where you buy most of your plants and garden supplies?

Yes: 48   **No**: 23

B. What facts about this garden center influenced your decision to shop here today? (Check as many as you wish.)

Closest, most convenient	40
Service	44
Wide selection of products	44
High quality products	37
Saw advertising	7
Hours of service	9
Prices	16
Overall appearance of our center	32
Just wanted to come in	21

C. Your rating of our facilities and service can help us improve. Don't be afraid to offend us, but don't avoid praise either. Just check off each item to let us know how we are doing.

	Poor	Average	Good	Great
Display of plants				
Inside	—	5	34	29
Outside	—	10	24	27
Labeling of plants—price and type				
Inside	1	11	41	12
Outside	—	10	36	7
Wide selection of plants				
Inside	—	4	34	31
Outside	—	6	29	24
Layout of our garden center	—	5	39	26
Quality of our products[a]	—	2	31	32
Price of our products	7	23	17	3
House plants	8	29	15	3
Outside plants	8	25	15	2
Hardware	7	26	14	3
Pots	10	29	10	5
Our hours of operation	—	4	32	24
Courteous salespeople	—	—	12	53
Knowledgeable salespeople	—	—	12	39

D. How do you think our prices compare to those at other garden centers?

Good: 18   **Average**: 28   **Poor**: 5

E. Have you ever compared our prices elsewhere?

Yes: 59   **No**: 6

[a] Note price is rated last but salespeople first!

Future market prospects

Pricing and market analysis are not the ends but the means to achieving business as well as personal objectives. These objectives are variable for different people in different circumstances; they can complement or compete with personal objectives, and they change over time. Some common objectives might be to provide the family with a good income; to leave the business, perhaps the world, a little better; to serve the community; to retire with a suitable income; to own a business, debt-free; to be the best (bedding plant) grower; to have leisure time; to expand; to be your own boss; to have a good place to live and work; to be regarded as fair by customers; to be respected by rivals; and so on. Identifying and establishing objectives—a far-from-easy task—is the starting point for dealing with pricing and marketing methods.

The bedding plant industry had a 16.27% compounded annual growth rate from about $94 million (wholesale) in 1976 to $1,049 million (wholesale) in 1992. An 11-times increase in size from 1976 to 1992 and more than a billion dollars in sales last year, even with weather adversity, provide a solid history of our society's interest in bedding plants and gardening.

Exciting market prospects are expected because of higher disposable incomes, projected higher market prices for substitutes, a continued emphasis on gardening and landscaping, and a higher demand and usage possibility than we are experiencing today.

Bedding plant prices may only increase at the same rate as the country's average price inflation. Volume sales and cost efficiency—along with product differentiation and a customer orientation—will be the keys to increased profit. Management and market analysis can help you determine what types of bedding plants to produce, how much to produce, when to sell, to whom and at what price!

TABLE 24.3

Suggestions for product differentiation

How nurserymen can better serve homeowners through improved merchandising	Total responses
Check to see what people need or want	39
Do not misrepresent themselves and their products	24
Advertise more	22
Guarantee and replace plants	20
Do not try to high-pressure people	13
Be better staffed with trained men	13

TABLE 24.3 continued

More salesmen and door-to-door work	9
Service throughout year—not just on holidays	9
Be more prompt—do things when promised	8
Local nurserymen should sell rather than have out-of-town salesmen come around	8
Be more interested in people	5
Draw plan, leave catalog, let people think about it without trying to sell them	4
Be reliable	3
Work with builder—set up a package deal	3
More and better displays	3
Bring plants to show when selling	3
Be more ready to take on small jobs	2
Landscape a home free in neighborhood to advertise	2
Be more courteous, congenial	2
Be available at nurseries to give prices and information	2
Have more help	2
Other	7
Subtotal	**203**

How nurserymen can better serve homeowners with better information and services	Total responses
More advice on trees and shrubs	63
Come back and check on jobs	19
More pamphlets and catalogs	16
Draw up plans without charge	15
More information and more pictures	7
Monthly or seasonal planting guides	4
Inform public of products and services	4
Plan better. Know local conditions	4
Better literature	3
Speak at garden clubs	3
Work with schools	3
Take time to talk over problems	3
Monthly flyer to introduce one or two well-chosen plants	2
Have local shows and clinics	2
Demonstrate on television	2
Educate people	2
Sponsor courses in landscaping	3
Other	14
Subtotal	**166**

TABLE 24.3 continued

Miscellaneous comments

Lower prices—prices too high	40
Sell healthier, stronger plants	5
Do a better job of landscaping	3
Adapt plants to area	2
Miscellaneous responses	14
Total, all responses	**433**

CHAPTER 25

Cost Accounting

Robin G. Brumfield

The bedding plant industry has changed rapidly in recent years. Plug technology has been widely adapted, and specialty producers and prefinishers have entered the market. Several options exist for bedding plant production. Growers can still produce bedding plants from bare-rooted seedlings or buy flats of seedlings. Bedding plants can also be produced using plugs, which can be either grower-produced or purchased from another wholesale grower or distributor. Many growers combine purchasing and producing plugs. Prefinished bedding plants are also an option.

The mass market's growing importance has pushed bedding plant prices down. The mass market has also moved to a higher quality product. As a result, a 36-cell flat is becoming the standard on the East and West Coasts. This larger plant holds up longer in the mass market than plants in 72- or 48-cell flats, requires little watering in the retail store, and provides instant color for the consumer. However, a 72-cell flat is still the standard in the Colorado area. Different products in different regions result in different cost and pricing structures. Marketing costs vary with the market channel and type of distribution and add to the total production costs.

Questions producers face

With so many options, what should you as a producer do? Should you buy plugs or produce your own? Should you consider producing plugs and selling them? How much does it cost to produce a flat of bedding plants or a flat of plugs? Should you produce in a 288-cell flat, a 512-cell flat, or some other size? How many plants should go in the finished flat?

Answering these questions requires that you know the costs of producing each crop. Most greenhouse operators produce many different crops and numerous types of bedding plants, all requiring different production schedules and different lengths of production time. So, while you know the profit for the entire business, it is difficult to know each crop's costs and returns.

Every greenhouse firm has a unique set of circumstances and unique costs. Costs can vary from firm to firm because of size, location, managerial practices, time of year, market channel, number of flats produced, the options for use of greenhouse space, the permanent work crew size, part-time labor availability, type of heating system, greenhouse efficiency, supply sources, how quickly you pay for supplies (financing and credit costs), and investment level in overhead facilities. Essential to profitable bedding plant production is an available market willing to purchase bedding plants at a price that is higher than production costs.

This chapter can serve as a guide in calculating costs for a specific greenhouse firm and provide information on average costs. Looking at industry averages, however, is no substitute for doing your own cost analysis. Every producer's costs are different! Do not assume that your costs are the same as those in the example; but comparing these averages to those actually incurred by your operation will enable you to identify cost items that are low and can be used to your advantage and items that are high and need to be reduced.

You can determine the costs of producing each crop you grow with a simple cost accounting method, using existing records and cost allocation techniques. Use your income statement and balance sheet as starting points. A simple computer program using Lotus 1-2-3 or a compiled version can make these calculations easier [1].

In the following tables, each cost is categorized into overhead and variable types because each needs to be treated differently. Variable costs vary as the number of units produced changes. Overhead costs don't vary directly with the number of units produced but are incurred regardless of output.

Overhead costs

Total overhead costs, or fixed costs, remain constant regardless of which crop or how many units are produced. Overhead costs per unit, however, decrease as more units are produced. Overhead costs include managerial salaries, depreciation, interest, insurance, repairs and other items that cannot be easily allocated on a per-flat basis to a particular bedding plant variety or other crop, but are available as a total for the year. They must be allocated on some other basis, such as cost-per-square-foot-week of bench area.

Even though heating fuel costs vary depending on greenhouse temperature, it's difficult for most managers to calculate the heating fuel consumed to produce a flat of bedding plants, so it is considered an overhead cost in these examples.

The annual income statement includes all overhead costs as well as variable costs. To calculate overhead costs, first allocate as many costs as possible to specific bedding plants and to other crops. After you have subtracted all variable costs that can be allocated to a specific crop, treat the remaining costs as overhead costs. Divide that number by the number of weeks you use the greenhouse for production to give an annual overhand cost per week.

Next, divide that number by square footage of greenhouse space actually utilized to determine the cost per square foot per week. This has been done for a typical, 20,000 square foot (1,858 m²), double-layer, polyethylene greenhouse producing in the mass-marketing channel (table 25.1).

Overhead costs presented here were derived from previous studies [2, 3, 4, 5]. In these studies, the average greenhouse used 77% total floor area as production area. Overhead costs were updated using Producer Price Indices and Employment Cost Indices.

These overhead costs begin with the managerial salaries, office and sales staff salaries, unemployment insurance, worker's compensation, and social security. For a 20,000-square-foot greenhouse, the overhead staff consists of one general manager, 0.8 salesperson, and 0.4 secretary-bookkeeper. If you don't know how much time is spent on each production task, leave those wages as an overhead cost and allocate them on a per-square-foot-week basis.

Depreciation, interest, insurance, repairs, and taxes on the greenhouses, facilities, and equipment are considered overhead costs. Other overhead expenses include utilities, advertising, dues and subscriptions, travel and entertainment, office expense, professional fees, truck expenses, land use cost, contributions, and bad debt. Overhead costs do not include hourly wages, which will be added later as a variable production cost.

Overhead costs per square foot-week of bench space are calculated by dividing the total overhead costs by 52 weeks and dividing by 15,400 square feet (14, 306.6 m²) (77% of the floor space) to determine a cost of $0.200 per square foot-week of bench space for small firms. Overhead costs for medium and large firms were derived by multiplying $0.200 per square foot by 74% and 71% to obtain $0.148 and $0.142 for medium and large firms, respectively. This ratio came from Brumfield et al. [4].

must purchase supplies and pay for labor before you sell plants and collect accounts receivable, so you must calculate an interest cost for materials and labor.

First, determine the annual interest rate and divide it by 52 to obtain the weekly interest rate. Then multiply that by the number of weeks that your money is tied up for bedding plants. The interest rate is assumed to be 9% for the example here and is assumed to be required for six months. Other variable costs were derived from previous studies [3, 5, 7, 8] and were updated using Producer Price Indices and Employment Cost Indices and by contacting supply companies to obtain 1993 costs (table 25.5).

Impatiens are used in the examples presented here because they are the best selling bedding plant in the United States [10]. Many other types of bedding plants are grown. The production costs and the sales price depend on the types and sizes of bedding plants with other products being more or less costly than the examples shown here.

Producing seedlings

Many systems exist for producing seedlings, and costs vary depending on the system, size of firm, and technology level. While plug production has increased rapidly, many growers still use barerooted seedlings for some or all of their bedding plant production. In the examples shown in tables 25.2, 25.3, 25.4, and 25.5, small greenhouses are 20,000 square feet (1,858 m²), medium are 100,000 square feet (9,290 m²) and large greenhouses are 400,000 square feet (37,160 m²).

Production labor inputs for the seedling and finished flat stages for greenhouses producing barerooted seedlings and plugs were obtained from Jenkins [7]. In all greenhouses, flats were filled and seeds sown in a central work area or headhouse and then moved into the greenhouse until they were ready for transplant. The seedling flats were moved back to the central work area where seedlings were transplanted into finishing flats.

Some large greenhouses used systems similar to other size greenhouses for transplanting. The operations were staged in different locations within the headhouse but weren't automated. In large automated greenhouses, transplanting took place on a conveyor belt so that all operations took place smoothly in an assembly line with considerably reduced labor. Plants were hand watered an average of four times per week. A growth regulator was applied once and pesticides twice.

TABLE 25.2

Labor inputs for seedling production

	Time (seconds per flat)						
					Plug		
	Barerooted			Small	Medium	Large	
Seedling stage	Small	Medium	Large			Nonauto	Auto
Fill flat	35	37	22	24	49	47	47
Seed and move to germination area	144	162	85	103	140	81	81
Move to greenhouse	16	40	33	36	29	14	14
Irrigate	14	14	6	14	7	5	5
Move to work area	40	30	67	46	51	25	25
Total	**249**	**283**	**213**	**223**	**276**	**172**	**172**
Finished flat stage							
Fill flat	45	120	35	36	44	66	4
Transplant and move to greenhouse	209	180	191	76	187	137	108
Irrigate	99	78	62	84	66	53	53
Spray growth regulator	14	10	2	14	10	2	2
Spray pesticide	14	2	2	14	2	2	2
Total	**381**	**390**	**292**	**224**	**309**	**260**	**169**

In general, the labor inputs per flat were reduced as the greenhouse size increased (table 25.2). Moving required more time in the medium-size plug producing greenhouses than in small or large greenhouses. Many medium-size greenhouses began smaller without a plan for growth; expansion often did not result in large, labor-efficient greenhouse blocks. Labor inputs were slightly less in greenhouses that used plug technology than in same size greenhouses that used barerooted seedlings.

Producing barerooted seedlings

A germination rate of 90% is assumed, so 555 seeds are sown to yield 500 seedlings. In the past, many seeds were sold by weight, but plug production has made germination percentages more critical, and many seed suppliers now list seed count as well as germination percentage on the package. This makes calculating the cost per seed much easier. A higher germination percentage would reduce the cost per seed. This is especially important since the seed cost is often the largest input in producing both barerooted and plug seedlings (table 25.3).

In these examples, barerooted seedlings are produced in open plastic flats by the production crew. The flats are used only once and then discarded. If the tray were to be reused, its cost would be cut in half for seedling production.

The seeds are sown by hand in flats filled with a peat lite mix that

TABLE 25.3

Seedling production costs

	Conventional			Plug		
	Small	Medium	Large	Small	Medium	Large
Seeds [a]	$12.50	$10.80	$10.00	$3.60	$3.11	$2.88
Tray	0.47	0.42	0.38	0.59	0.32	0.47
Medium	0.46	0.42	0.37	0.15	0.14	0.14
Fertilizer	0.01	0.01	0.01	0.01	0.01	0.01
Labor	0.55	0.61	0.46	0.48	0.60	0.37
Interest on variable costs [b]	0.63	0.55	0 50	0.22	0.19	0.17
Overhead costs [c]	0.98	0.73	0.70	2.95	2.18	2.10
Total per flat	**$15.60**	**$13.54**	**$12.42**	**$8.00**	**$6.55**	**$6.14**
Total per seedling	**$0.03**	**$0.03**	**$0.02**	**$0.03**	**$0.03**	**$0.02**

[a] 555 seeds planted per conventional flat and 288 per plug flat. Germination rate is assumed to be 90%.

[b] Interest rate is assumed to be 9% for six months.

[c] Overhead costs are calculated using $0.200, $0.148, and $0.142 per square-foot-bench-week, respectively for small, medium, and large greenhouses. It is assumed that a flat uses 1.64 square feet x three weeks for bareroot seedling flats and nine weeks for plug flats.

costs $8.80 (including shipping) for a 3-cubic-foot (.085 m³) bag for small quantities and 20% less for large quantities. A 3-cubic-foot bag will fill 19 flats. Thus a large firm spends $0.46 per flat on growing media. The growing medium's cost varies depending on the quantity and the supplier. Freight can become a substantial cost if the greenhouse is located a considerable distance from the supplier.

The average time in the seedling flats for barerooted impatiens was estimated to be three weeks by Jenkins [7] and seed suppliers. The seedling flat occupies 1.64 square feet (.15 m²) of bench space. At a cost of $0.200, $0.148, and $0.142 per square foot of bench area per week, the overhead costs are $0.98, $0.73, and $0.70 per flat for small, medium, and large firms, respectively. The cost of producing a flat of 500 seedlings ranges from $12.42 to $15.60 or $0.02 to $0.03 per barerooted seedling.

Producing plugs

Plug production has been adopted rapidly by bedding plant producers in the past few years, probably because it promises several economic benefits over barerooted seedling production. Plug production also allows the seeding operation to be mechanized. Transplanting plugs is faster than transplanting barerooted seedlings because of ease of handling plugs. Plug production offers managerial flexibility because plugs can be held in seedling flats longer than barerooted seedlings. Time from transplant to finishing is reportedly less than with barerooted seedlings.

Many systems exist for producing plugs. Plugs can be produced in plug trays with 50 to 648 plugs per tray. Growers who produce their own plugs are moving to a larger plug flat, which requires more time in the plug flat, but less time in the finished flat than production using small plugs. In this scenario, 288 plugs will be produced per plug tray. A germination rate of 90% would yield 259 finished plugs.

Assume that the plug flats are used only once and then disposed of. At a cost of $8.80 for a 3-cubic-foot (.085 m³) bag of root medium that can fill 57 plug flats, the medium, including shipping, costs $0.15 per flat for small producers. Large producers receive a discount and pay $0.14 per plug flat.

As with barerooted seedling production, labor inputs tend to decline as the operation's size increases. The exception to this is the medium-sized greenhouse, which for both plug and seedling production used more labor for moving flats than small and large firms. Medium-sized greenhouses are apparently not large enough to take full advantage of automation available to large producers, but are too large to operate as efficiently as producers who do not have to transport the plants far in the greenhouse.

The flat occupies 1.64 square feet (.15 m²) of bench area for nine weeks. Using the same overhead costs per bench square foot of $0.200, $0.148, and $0.142 used for barerooted seedling production, overhead costs per plug flat (288 count) are $2.95, $2.18, and $2.10 for small, medium, and large firms, respectively.

Although the overhead cost of producing plugs was greater than for barerooted seedlings, since the seed costs were less, the per seedling cost is ultimately the same for plugs and barerooted seedlings under the assumptions in these examples.

Producing transplants from plugs

Numerous options exist for producing or buying barerooted seedlings or plugs in various sizes. Plug production has exploded since plugs were introduced. Often greenhouse managers who purchase plug production equipment produce more plugs than are required for his or her own use and sell plugs to other growers. There are many specialist propagators giving bedding plant producers a choice of producing their own plugs or purchasing plugs from another producer. Plugs may be grown locally or in another part of the country.

Let's assume for now that the barerooted seedlings are produced in a 555-seedling tray, and plugs produced in a 288-cell tray in table 25.3 then become an input costing $0.02 to $0.03 per seedling in transplant production. Also assume that both types of seedlings are transplanted into plastic flats with inserts containing 36 cells per flat. The transplants are grown in soilless root medium that costs $7 (including shipping) per 3-cubic-foot (.085 m³) bag for small growers and $6.60 for large growers.

The transplants are fertilized with every watering, treated with a growth regulator twice and pesticides once. The amount of labor required to produce a finished flat was determined from a study by Jenkins [7]. Finished flats using barerooted seedlings are on the bench for eight weeks; finished flats using plugs from a 288-cell plug tray are on the bench two weeks. The flats occupy 1.64 square feet (.15 m³) of bench area.

Most of the inputs involved in producing transplants from plugs are the same as those used to produce transplants from seedlings, but the finished flats using plugs require only two weeks on the bench versus eight weeks for finished flats using barerooted seedlings. The other difference is that flats using plugs require less transplanting labor (table 25.2).

TABLE 25.4

Finished flat production costs using grower produced plugs

Variable costs	Barerooted			Plug produced in 288-cell tray			
	Small	Medium	Large	Small	Medium	Large Nonauto	Large Auto
Seedlings [a]	$1.08	$1.08	$0.72	$1.08	$1.08	$0.72	$0.72
Flat	0.47	0.42	0.38	0.47	0.42	0.38	0.38
Insert	0.29	0.25	0.23	0.29	0.25	0.23	0.23
Rooting medium	0.37	0.36	0.35	0.37	0.36	0.35	0.35
Label	0.15	0.13	0.12	0.15	0.13	0.12	0.12
Fertilizer	0.03	0.02	0.02	0.03	0.02	0.02	0.02
Growth regulator	0.03	0.02	0.02	0.03	0.02	0.02	0.02
Pesticide	0.01	0.01	0.01	0.01	0.01	0.01	0.01
Labor	0.85	0.87	0.65	0.50	0.69	0.58	0.38
Interest onvariable cost	0.15	0.14	0.11	3.06	3.11	2.54	2.33
Total variable costs	**$3.42**	**$3.30**	**$2.61**	**$3.06**	**$3.11**	**$2.54**	**$2.33**
Overhead costs [b]	2.62	1.94	1.86	0.66	0.49	0.47	0.47
Loss allocation [c]	0.32	0.28	0.24	0.20	0.19	0.16	0.15
Total per flat	**$6.37**	**$5.52**	**$4.71**	**$3.91**	**$3.79**	**$3.16**	**$2.94**

[a] 36 seedlings per finished flat.

[b] Overhead costs are calculated at $0.200, $0.048, and $0.142 per square-foot-bench-week for small, medium, and large greenhouses respectively. It is assumed that a flat uses 1.64 square feet of bench area per week, and production takes eight weeks for barerooted flats and two weeks for plug flats.

[c] Based on a 5% loss.

Loss

Some of the crop invariably will not be sold due to a variety of circumstances, including the weather. To calculate the cost of these losses, add all costs per unit and multiply by the number of unsold units. Then divide by the number of flats sold. Losses in these examples were assumed to be 5% of plants produced.

For example, the sum of variable costs ($3.42) and overhead costs ($2.62) is $6.04 for the small greenhouse finishing a flat from barerooted seedlings (table 25.4). If you start with 100 flats and do not sell five of them, multiply $6.04 cost per flat by five unsold flats and divide by 95 sold flats to yield a loss of $0.32 to be assigned to each finished flat.

Producing versus buying plugs

While a producer can produce impatiens plugs currently in a 288-flat for $0.02 to $0.03 per plug, the cost of buying plugs is $0.07, $0.06, and $0.055 for small, medium, and large firms respectively, based on information from greenhouse suppliers. To reduce the plug's cost, many greenhouse managers buy smaller plugs. The trade-off is that the finished flat will require more time on the bench than one using larger plugs. If we assume that all costs are the same except for plugs and overhead, we find that finished flats using larger plugs cost less to produce than those using smaller plugs (table 25.5).

The extra overhead cost of requiring five weeks for finished flats using plugs produced in a 512-cell tray versus two weeks for finished flats from plugs produced in a 288-cell tray is larger than the amount saved by purchasing the less expensive plugs. However, this assumes that all greenhouse bench space is being fully utilized. If part of the greenhouse is unused, it may be more cost-effective to purchase smaller plugs and more fully utilize existing space. Take those considerations into account when you are developing bedding plant budgets for your particular operation.

In all of the alternatives presented in table 25.5, producing impatiens in 36-cell finished flats is profitable using the 1992 national average wholesale price of $7.10 per flat [9]. As with costs, however, prices vary by region. Small Michigan growers who face a statewide average wholesale price of $5.35 per flat would not operate profitably under the assumptions presented in table 25.5. They could, however, make a profit by producing their own plugs and finishing them in a flat of 36 plants. This cost was $3.91 (table 25.4). They could also consider retailing and capturing some of the marketing margin.

As the bedding plant industry becomes more competitive, produc-

TABLE 25.5

Finished flat production costs using purchased plugs

Variable costs	Plug size							
	288-cell plug tray				512-cell plug tray			
	Small	Medium	Large		Small	Medium	Large	
			Nonauto	Auto			Nonauto	Auto
Seedlings a	$2.52	$2.16	$1.93	$1.98	$1.80	$1.62	$1.44	$1.44
Flat	0.47	0.42	0.38	0.38	0.47	0.42	0.38	0.38
Insert	0.29	0.25	0.23	0.23	0.29	0.25	0.23	0.23
Rooting medium	0.37	0.36	0.35	0.35	0.37	0.36	0.35	0.35
Labels	0.15	0.13	0.12	0.12	0.15	0.13	0.12	0.12
Fertilizers	0.03	0.02	0.02	0.02	0.03	0.02	0.02	0.02
Growth regulators	0.03	0.02	0.02	0.02	0.03	0.02	0.02	0.02
Pesticides	0.01	0.01	0.01	0.01	0.01	0.01	0.01	0.01
Labor	0.50	0.69	0.58	0.38	0.50	0.69	0.58	0.38
Interest on variable costs	0.20	0.18	0.17	0.16	0.16	0.16	0.14	0.13
Total variable costs	**$4.46**	**$4.24**	**$3.85**	**$3.64**	**$3.81**	**$3.67**	**$3.29**	**$3.08**
Overhead costs b	0.66	0.49	0.47	0.47	1.64	1.21	1.16	1.16
Loss allocation c	0.27	0.25	0.23	0.22	0.29	0.26	0.23	0.22
Total per flat	**$5.50**	**$4.97**	**$4.55**	**$4.32**	**$5.74**	**$5.15**	**$4.61**	**$4.47**

a 36 seedlings per finished flat.
b Overhead costs are calculated at $0.200, $0.048, and $0.142 per square-foot-bench-week for small, medium, and large greenhouses respectively. It is assumed that a flat uses 1.64 square feet of bench area per week, and production takes two weeks for flats using plugs from a 288-cell tray and five weeks for flats using plugs from a 512-cell tray.
c Based on a 5% loss.

There are many factors affecting morale. It's inconceivable that good morale can be developed among unhappy, discontented people without first ridding them of their unhappiness and discontent. Any number of events, occurrences, or actions can make people unhappy or discontented.

Some people seem to be discontented and unhappy all the time. They can have a negative impact on the entire work group's morale. These people may need to be reassigned. It's possible, of course, that we're wrong about them. Perhaps we don't know enough about their individual needs or expectations to understand how they feel or what might be bothering them. We may be misinterpreting the signals they are sending.

Factors causing low morale don't all occur at the place of employment. They may not be under a work-place supervisor's control and perhaps can't be overcome by any on-job actions a supervisor might take. However, if the causes of unhappiness are associated with the job and those causes can be eliminated without too high a cost, then it's good business to do it.

Some articles dealing with employee-employer relations provide lists of what supervisors should or shouldn't do. Presumably, if you faithfully follow their suggested recipes, all will be well, but usually such lists are of limited value.

Instead of using a recipe approach, the following discussion will provide supervisors with some basic concepts that bear on human relations. Consideration of the concepts and ideas behind them should allow each reader to self-evaluate his or her supervisory skills, methods, and techniques. Self-evaluation may reassure some supervisors who think they are doing pretty well. Others may need to improve by altering their beliefs about employees or by making changes in their management styles.

What makes people happy?

First let's discuss the linkages between a person's happiness, his or her morale, and goal achievement. What is motivation? How are people motivated, and why do they take action to achieve whatever it is they wish to gain? We begin by developing a working definition of motivation.

Happiness and morale

If happiness is defined as the feeling that one is in a state of well-being, comfortable, at peace, and perhaps even joyous then it's evident that achievement of your desired goals plays a significant role in determining your level of happiness or morale. Goals that are not met or needs that aren't satisfied are failures from a person's point of view. Failure to achieve goals may not be the only reason for unhappiness, discontent, and low morale, but it is difficult to imagine a situation where failure of any kind would contribute to happiness and high morale. Achievement of goals and satisfaction of wants are important to a person's self-esteem, morale, and happiness.

Some employee needs can be met at work and some can't. If they can't, employees may look elsewhere. That in itself isn't bad, but it may be bad if the employer could meet some of the employee's needs at work and doesn't. It can be bad because the employee will tend to focus on off-job activities at the expense of the job. Of course, if the costs of changes that would enable a person to meet more of his or her individual needs on-the-job are too high in either financial or human relations terms, then it may be advisable to let the employee satisfy those goals outside the work place.

It seems reasonable to conclude though, that goal achievement, happiness, and high morale go hand-in-hand. The relationship between high morale and productivity is well established and obtaining higher levels of productivity is important. Many managers gain a great deal of personal pleasure and pride from the knowledge that they have developed a happy, highly motivated team.

Once managers believed they could motivate people and get more output per employee by using either the carrot or the stick. Those approaches may still work in some cases but are not likely to be entirely satisfactory ways of motivating subordinates, at least not in our society. A little praise or a small pay raise might once have been enough to encourage a worker to increase productivity, but in today's world of social safety nets these methods don't have as great a motivating value.

By the same token, firing (the stick) isn't so easy anymore either. It can be quite costly when you consider unemployment insurance assessments, the costs associated with litigation that might result, and the money spent on finding and hiring a replacement. Today, different motivational techniques and motivating methods must be found and used.

Motivating associates

Dozens of attempts to define or explain human motivation have been made. The following is one of them. It provides important insights into the nature of human motivation. It also suggests reasons that may help to explain why some supervisory techniques are likely to succeed while others are just as likely to fail.

MOTIVATION IS THAT INNER FORCE WHICH CAUSES AN INDIVIDUAL TO RELEASE HIS OR HER OWN UNIQUE RESOURCES TOWARD THE ACCOMPLISHMENT OF PERSONAL AND ORGANIZATIONAL GOALS!

If you subscribe to this definition, several observations logically follow. If motivation is an *inner force*, then it is within the individual and can't be augmented much from outside sources, such as from a supervisor's pep talks or threats. Motivation is self-induced for the most part and attempting to motivate others may not be very successful. People must motivate themselves.

Secondly, that inner force is what causes a person to release or unleash his or her mind and body to do useful work. Release! Release what? The answer, of course, is the person's own unique resources. Each person is different from all others, which implies that different people will react differently to the same stimuli. The end results can be good in any case.

What inner force would cause a person to release his or her own unique resources to accomplish some goal the business has set for itself? The motivation or inner force causing that release, it seems, is the individual's desire to achieve some *personal goal*. If this is a goal that can be achieved on the job, then the employee and the business can reach or partially reach their respective goals together.

This does not imply that fear and reward or even motivational talks have no effect on people. Clearly they do, but the impact of actions or events tends to be immediate and not very long lasting. For instance, a coach's half-time theatrics may be inspiring, but their impact may last only until a player takes the first "hit."

Some people seem to be unresponsive to outside stimuli of any kind and appear void of that inner force that would cause them to take action. A few unfortunate experiences with these people may cause supervisors to generalize about other or potential employees. These generalizations influence supervisors' methods. In turn, these methods impact productivity.

Management styles

Douglas McGregor, professor of management at the Massachusetts Institute of Technology, once said that the management style a supervisor adopts is in part dependent upon that person's views of the people supervised [3]. The old conventional style of personnel management is employed by those who think that, for the most part, people consider work bad and try to avoid it, are lazy and must be prodded to accomplish, are incapable of making decisions and must be directed in minute detail, are motivated primarily by a pay check or fear of job loss, avoid responsibility, are unwilling to learn, and are generally functioning at full capacity. McGregor labels people with these beliefs as being **Theory X** supervisors.

Those who believe people find work neither inherently good nor bad, but think that most want to work because it fulfills a basic human need to achieve, that people want more from their jobs than just a paycheck and economic security, are capable of self-direction and self-control, may even seek responsibility, sometimes want to and can learn and, in general, are underutilized by their employers, are referred to as **Theory Y** supervisors.

McGregor didn't label either set of beliefs good or bad. However, each of these views requires a different management style. The style employed is dependent upon the supervisor's beliefs about the people in the work team. A Theory X manager tends to employ an autocratic or dictatorial style, and a Theory Y manager tends to use a participatory style of management. An autocratic style of management can be characterized as a top-down flow of decisions, precise instructions, and close supervision of employees. A participatory style features work-group decision making and team work.

Autocratic versus participatory

Theory X managers tend to be autocratic because, they see it, it's the only way that their people can be directed to accomplish useful work. A Theory Y manager believes, however, that better results come from allowing workers to participate in decision making, at least to the extent that decisions concern how the group should proceed to do a specific job. It requires many fewer specific instructions and releases some of the supervisor's time for other things since it reduces the amount of direct supervision required. Theory X and Theory Y beliefs represent extreme positions among the many that supervisors hold about employees. They are but two, one at each end of a spectrum that probably encompasses many intermediate views.

McGregor did not advocate either one of these styles. Nor did he infer that a participatory management style is better or that to use it is an abdication of management responsibility. Supervisors practicing participatory management needn't feel they aren't doing their jobs. It is probably the preferred management style today.

By contrast, there are situations where it would make sense for a Theory Y manager to use an autocratic style. An emergency threatening the business or the life of a person calls for an autocratic style since there would be no time for discussion, and discussion is a necessary ingredient of a participatory style.

One of the primary differences between an autocratic management style and a participatory style is the way decisions are made and translated into action. The autocratic manager makes the decision without consultation or receives it from some higher level of the business and translates it into action by giving orders to subordinates. The participatory manager includes the work force in decision making and implementation. Implementation is nearly automatic after consensus is reached as to how and by whom work should be done.

Management style relates to people beliefs

The supervisor's style of management is directly related to his or her beliefs about the people supervised, and the workers themselves have little to say about it. It makes no difference that the work group may be entirely different from the image the supervisor has of them. In other words, the Theory X manager adopts an autocratic style because he or she thinks it is the one that is necessary to get the work done.

It's what the supervisor believes is most important when choosing a management style, and it is not necessarily a malicious belief. The work force may actually possess Theory X characteristics, and an autocratic management style may be the only one that makes sense.

If the work group doesn't have those attributes and is treated as if it does, then unhappiness and discontent are likely to result. In these cases, employees don't have the same personal expectations of the job that the supervisor believes they have. These people will quite likely leave the job and seek satisfaction of personal goals elsewhere. Supervisors will eventually have the kind of work force they believed they had in the first place, because those types of employees are the only ones who will stay with the firm or come to work for it. Business firms get reputations as good or bad places to work. Thus a supervisor's view of employees, even if incorrect, may become a self-fulfilling prophecy.

An autocratic manager pays little attention to an individual's needs and may even thwart a worker's attempts to achieve or satisfy them. A participatory style used by a supervisor with strong Theory Y convictions can, on the other hand, open up opportunities for individual workers and allow them to satisfy their perceived needs as well as those of the busine

Maslow's hierarchy of human needs

Nearly 40 years ago Abraham Maslow developed the idea of a hierarchy of human needs or wants [2]. He believed human wants and needs could all be grouped into general categories, and these groupings could then be ranked according to the order in which most people strive to satisfy them.

Starting with the most basic group of wants or needs (physiological) and progressing into higher levels (safety, social, ego and self-fulfillment) in the hierarchy, Maslow places all wants or needs of human beings into one or another of the five strata. Presumably most people would attempt to satisfy the more basic needs first and then proceed to satisfy higher level needs. Needs motivate people to take action. The employee's actions can be channeled in ways that will satisfy his or her needs and, at the same time, those of the business.

After some level of need satisfaction has been achieved, that particular need is no longer a very strong motivator and won't encourage a person to release much more of his or her unique resources to obtain more of it. Thus, when some basic need such as the need for food is partially satisfied, it isn't a very strong motivational force anymore. Perhaps that's why carrot or stick approaches don't work as well continuously. After a big meal a person may be more interested in satisfying some other need rather than obtaining more food.

It might be some other physiological need such as obtaining better housing or more clothing, or it might be more important to the person to seek satisfaction of some higher level need such as for safety or to participate in social activities. The opportunity to satisfy this other need will then become a stronger motivating force.

Some needs such as food, shelter, and clothing are necessary to sustain life. Others, such as social interaction and self-esteem, may not be essential for life but are important needs in Maslow's hierarchy. Many people try to satisfy them to some degree. If an individual's needs can't be satisfied on the job, either because it is not possible within the work environment or because a supervisor's style frustrates attempts, people will turn away from their jobs and try to meet their needs away from the workplace.

Needs motivate action

Needs motivate people to take action. A partially satisfied need is no longer as strong a motivator as it formerly was and some other, perhaps less basic need, may become the preeminent one.

Maslow's hierarchy is illustrated with the most basic needs at the base and successively higher needs as one moves up the pyramid towards its apex (fig. 26.1). Most people will fulfill those basic, physiological needs first before moving on to satisfying those at higher levels—safety, social, ego, and self-fulfillment. Not all workers strive to reach the very top or are likely to place equal importance or emphasis on those at intermediate levels. The needs that motivate a person will quite likely change as lower level needs are satisfied and over time, particularly as that person gets older. Safety or security become much more important to people as they get older, for example.

If a supervisor can identify the motivating needs each worker is striving to satisfy, then he or she can adjust work assignments and his or her management style to enhance job satisfaction. In the process, morale and productivity are likely to improve.

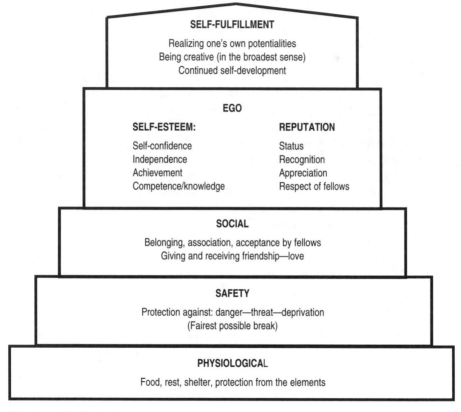

Fig. 26.1 Maslow's "Pyramid of Human Needs"

The supervisor's role

Supervisors must ask themselves, "Am I a Theory X or Theory Y supervisor? Do I generally agree with the Theory X supervisor's view of employees, or am I in stronger agreement with the Theory Y manager's views?"

Theory X manager

If you are a Theory X manager and utilize an autocratic or dictatorial management style, there is little to do except continue as in the past. If you supervise a work force that exhibits the attributes a Theory X manager believes them to have, it may be the only way such people can be directed. This supervisor may never have the opportunity to employ workers who have Theory Y attributes unless his or her management style changes. If a person is or wants to be a Theory Y manager—employing a participatory style of management and through it assisting workers to achieve their personal goals and to be more productive—then there are necessary steps to take.

To a degree, the approach a supervisor uses is defined for him or her at some higher management level. If the supervisor's boss holds a view of his or her subordinates similar to that of a Theory X manager and deals with them in an autocratic manner, it may be impossible for lower level supervisors to do otherwise. After all one might be thought incompetent if he or she were to manage in a way different from that of his or her superiors. A Theory X boss would not understand.

Theory Y manager

If free from such constraints, a supervisor may alter his or her style in ways that would also be expected to increase worker morale and productivity. If a supervisor subscribes to Maslow's theories about human needs and how they motivate and is willing to use them in day-to-day supervision, that person has taken the first step to becoming a Theory Y manager.

You must know enough about each individual employee to gain insights into each one's needs. These needs may in turn serve as motivators. A supervisor should ask, "How well do I know each of the people who work for (or preferably *with*) me? What needs and expectations does each person have?" The participatory supervisor must answer such questions.

The second step is to make the effort to learn more about each person and what his or her needs are. Further steps, directions, or actions that should be taken are much less precise. What can be done to achieve supervisory goals requires a great deal of thought about alternatives, whether or not contemplated changes would conform with the firm's policies and be in its best interests, and about the acceptability of possible changes to employees. To be successful, any changes that are considered must meet and pass those tests.

Employees must not perceive changes as job loading efforts—trying to get them to do more for the same monetary or other rewards. Discussion with employees, alone and together, is essential before major changes are made! A supervisor wishing to employ a more participatory style must approach such discussions with caution and an open mind. Any impression that the supervisor's mind is already made up, will label the supervisor as autocratic in employees' eyes. It could delay shifting to a participatory work style. Go slowly and let the idea grow.

So, what should be done if the work group dismisses efforts to make desired changes in style? If they resist it for a long period of time, it may simply mean that the group is a Theory X work force, and change will not be possible with these people unless you can inspire them to seek higher goals. And that is worth a try!

One initial change to consider is to gradually reduce the number of unnecessary rules in the work place. Some may have served useful purposes once and may even have been necessary with an autocratic style but may not be any longer. As you move toward more work force participation, group or peer discipline begins to take over and formal rules, at least older ones, are no longer as necessary.

Dissatisfiers/Satisfiers

There are no particular prescriptions for success when changing to a more participatory management style. Action indicators that might prove successful are provided by a worker study conducted by Herzberg [1]. After investigating the impacts a number of different factors have on workers' attitudes and performance, he divided them into two categories. He called one group **dissatisfiers.** These factors tended to cause poor attitudes among the workers and poorer performance. The second group he called **satisfiers**. They led to better attitudes and higher levels of performance.

Some factors fall in both categories. Satisfiers are considered good motivators. On the other hand, dissatisfiers are not. Improvement of a dissatisfier will not necessarily translate into better performance until some acceptable level is reached. At an unsatisfactory level it causes poor attitudes and low performance and will continue to do so until it reaches a level considered appropriate.

Making it super good doesn't have much of an impact either. Such things as cleanliness or housekeeping in the work place might be examples—if it isn't up to some expected level, low morale and productivity will result, but making it as clean as a hospital operating room will not inspire greater effort on the employee's part.

Technically inept supervisors, archaic or senseless company policies or administration, poor interpersonal relations with supervisors, poor working conditions, or inadequate salaries are dissatisfiers. At very unsatisfactory levels these factors can seriously affect attitudes and performance. As they are improved, significant changes in attitudes and productivity will not be observed until they reach the acceptable level.

Surpassing that acceptable level will not necessarily continue to improve productivity, but it will establish a supervisory foundation from which to operate. It will allow maximum attitude gains when using or increasing the use of satisfiers.

Salary can serve as either a satisfying or dissatisfying factor. If it isn't up to an acceptable level when compared to similar employment in the area, it is a dissatisfier and will continue to be until salaries are raised to a satisfactory level.

Employees may believe that the loss of their job provides them with an opportunity to get a better one. Such a view would not be likely to make working people happy or highly productive. Unlike other dissatisfiers, salaries that are above the acceptable level can be satisfiers and motivate people.

Satisfiers lead to higher productivity

Herzberg measured the importance of a change in attitude accompanying a change or improvement in each of the factors. In addition he measured the length of time the attitude change would persist. Some of his results provide clues to changes that could be made that would allow employees to fulfill more of their individual higher level needs.

Among the **satisfiers** leading to higher morale and productivity were: achievement, recognition, work itself, responsibility, advancement, and salary. These are listed in declining order of importance in motivating people. It doesn't mean that salary level is unimportant but only that after a certain level is attained on any particular job, it becomes relatively less important as a motivator than other aspects of the work or environment.

Interestingly, it was found that responsibility, the work itself, and advancement seemed to have the longest lasting impact on improved attitude and performance. Each suggests opportunities for implementing a participatory management style. For example, giving an employee the authority to establish a way of doing a job and making that person responsible for developing a good solution may satisfy his or her need for greater self-esteem and help develop a participatory management style within the work group.

A supervisor must decide which of the various management styles he or she wishes to use. An autocratic supervisor must be willing to rule in a pressure relationship where workers' actions can be controlled but their attitudes, beliefs, and understanding cannot. It is a relationship that tends to inhibit output and seldom uses a worker's full potential.

When a worker is hired, the worker's intellect as well as his or her hands, arms, legs, and back comes along. If you hire that intellect, why not use it?

An autocratic management style provides little opportunity for using a worker's mind. If employees become very unhappy with supervisors or their management styles, they may retaliate or leave the business. On the other hand, the supervisor is in a position of complete control—which may be ego-satisfying. The autocratic approach is simple to administer and will give immediate results. It works well with large numbers of employees and in emergency situations. It requires very precise directions and a tremendous amount of a supervisor's time to ensure that the job is done, done correctly, and that something productive is engaged in when each project is finished.

The participatory supervisor's role is a bit different. It is one of providing leadership, guidance, and encouragement for the work team. Power flows both up and down. The supervisor may sometimes feel like the man or woman in the middle, but utilizing the wisdom, training, and skills of the entire group usually results in better decisions about how work should be done. This is particularly true for non-routine decisions.

Authority, responsibility, and accountability are shared with all members of the team. It takes more of a supervisor's time as a coach or teacher, and this is particularly true when starting to develop a participatory work team. The result may be a much more highly motivated work force, increased productivity, and a more pleasant work environment.

A final word

Much of this discussion is based on research that sheds light on this very important area of human relations. No one need subscribe to all the concepts suggested here. Think about each of them, try them on, and experiment with them in your own work environment. They might just work and pay big dividends. At most they require little more than some of your time.

The author subscribes to the philosophy put forth here: I am convinced that managers holding rigid Theory X views about employees will soon become extinct in this society. Also, a participatory management style is the only effective style if most employees fit the Theory Y manager's beliefs about workers. For a manager there is no sense of achievement that can top that of being captain of a championship team! The 10 commandments of motivation sum it up quite well [4].

The 10 commandments of motivation

1. Share responsibility with your subordinates, remembering that as you take credit for their success you must also share their failure.
2. Understand that as a manager you can give authority to your subordinates and allow them to contribute to their own and your success.
3. Constantly remind yourself that only through participation can your subordinates make their jobs more meaningful.
4. Communicate the why, as well as the what, to ensure that under standing and cooperation become a habit.
5. Evaluate accomplishment on the basis of the results achieved rather than on the activities engaged in.
6. Sincerely be humble, knowing that most people would rather succeed than fail at their jobs.
7. Seek always to set a good example, and through expecting good performance, reap great rewards.
8. Force yourself to set goals and priorities for your job, so that your subordinates can build their goals toward these.
9. Unceasingly seek to be objective, fair, and honest in your act and deed, realizing the mantle of leadership is yours.
10. Light the way for change, knowing that being able to put yourself in the other person's shoes is the greatest gift of a manager.

References

[1] Herzberg, F. 1966. *Work and the nature of man*. Cleveland, Ohio: World Publishing Company.
[2] Maslow, A. 1967. *Motivation and personality*. 3rd ed. Ed. R. Frager and J. Fadiman. New York: Harper and Row Publishing Company.
[3] McGregor, D. 1960. *The human side of enterprise*. New York: McGraw Hill Publishing Company.
[4] Trocke, J. 1972. *Motivation for modern managers*. Cooperative Extension Service. Michigan State University.

CHAPTER 27

Vegetable Transplant

Charles S. Vavrina

Almost any vegetable crop can be grown as a transplant, but only a handful are traditionally grown in this manner. A "good" transplant is usually defined by consumer specifications. Home gardeners may favor robust, succulent plants while commercial farmers may want yellowed, more hardened plants. Such differences in consumer requisites emphasize the need for proper transplant crop management. No simple procedure can be followed in growing vegetable transplants, and only through experience can one begin to produce a consistent product.

In general, a good vegetable transplant should be stocky, green, and pest-free, with a well-developed root system. The ideal technique for growing transplants would be to raise a plant from start to finish by slow, steady, uninterrupted growth with minimal stress to the plant. Because ideal growing conditions rarely exist, the grower must control plant growth by manipulating water, temperature, and fertilizer.

This chapter's purpose is to discuss some of the factors involved in vegetable transplant production. It's a good idea for a first-time grower to visit several major transplant production facilities to develop his/her own management philosophies.

Media

Most growers are encouraged to use a commercial, pre-mixed, soilless mix. Self-prepared media often result in an uneven distribution of the component materials, which may affect germination and plant growth and lead to non-uniform plants. Once seeded, the planting container may be top-dressed with vermiculite to hold in water and prevent large temperature shifts in the germination environment.

351

Containers

Seeding directly into the container that will be sold to the customer is the preferred method in today's market. However, the old-fashioned method of pricking seedlings from heavily seeded flats into final containers will produce high quality plants and good yields [10].

Containers other than styrofoam or molded plastic—clay, wood, peat pots, etc.—are not recommended for large scale commercial production. In general, research indicates that larger cell sizes result in greater yields (particularly early yield) in the field. This is especially true for longer cycle vegetable transplants (greater than five weeks) such as peppers [22] and tomatoes [23]. For short cycle crops (less than four-week-old transplants), smaller cells may be the better choice. In these crops, root growth may not completely fill a large cell, and damage may occur when pulling crops as soil falls away and exposes roots.

Cell size may become an economic matter in crops such as onions or lettuce, where plants per acre number in the thousands. Small cells (i.e., more cells per tray) are preferred in these crops since more plants can be grown in less space.

Seed and seed germination

Quality seed ensures good germination, rapid emergence, and vigorous growth. Poor quality seed results in skips or requires excessive seeding to compensate for low germination, either of which diminishes profitability. Purchase only certified seed that is disease-free or has been treated to eliminate disease-causing organisms.

Extremes in water and/or temperature can result in poor germination. A moist but well-drained medium is best for maximum germination. Many producers prefer a controlled temperature germination room, where the flats are stacked on pallets. This arrangement will help resist additional moisture, as well as overcome thermodormancy, which refers to a germination inhibition brought on by high soil temperature that affects many vegetable species. This phenomenon is mostly a problem in fall-grown transplants but can occur in the winter in crops such as celery and lettuce if bottom heat is applied. Tropical crops, such as tomatoes and peppers, exhibit thermodormancy in southern climates when grown for fall and winter container production.

Fertilization

The goal in vegetable transplant production is to produce a sturdy, compact plant that will grow quickly when transplanted and yield well. A good rule of thumb is to begin fertilization only after the first true leaf has expanded from one-half to three-quarters of an inch (1.3 to 1.9 cm) long.

Fertilizers used for transplant crop liquid feeding should be 100% water soluble. Application rate depends on the application method; for example, on nozzle size and trolley speed in automatic watering systems. In general, 50 parts per million of a totally water-soluble fertilizer applied on a daily basis should adequately meet most crop nutrient demands. Frequency of fertilizer application varies from grower to grower. Some growers prefer to deliver 250 to 400 ppm nitrogen once weekly, rather than 50 ppm N daily.

Water

When watering, the soil should be moistened thoroughly until water runs through the plug. Water only when needed, and allow the plug to dry sufficiently before additional watering. The media should be kept moist but not continually wet. Under cloudy conditions, maintaining low soil moisture is preferred. Irrigate in the morning to allow foliage to dry off before night. Prolonged periods of wet foliage encourage disease.

Other Factors

Sanitation. Strict sanitary practices should be followed: Use clean tools, sterilize trays for reuse, and store transplant materials (trays, media, seed, fertilizer) separate from contaminating compounds (herbicides, growth regulators, insecticides, fungicides). Do not touch plants unless necessary. Use alcohol spray bottles to sterilize hands if plants and flats need to be moved.

Environmental conditions. Do not grow summer crops (e.g., tomatoes, watermelons) and winter crops (e.g., cabbage, lettuce) in the same greenhouse. Conditions, such as temperature, that are ideal for one crop may be detrimental to another.

Supplemental light. Research from Canada [11] has shown that supplemental lighting can increase celery, lettuce, broccoli, and tomato transplant quality by increasing shoot and root weights. Only tomato exhibited field yield enhancement from transplant supplemental lighting [12].

Transplant age. Information presented in table 27.1 suggests how long a particular transplant crop may be expected to stay in the greenhouse. These data are provided to help schedule successive crops. The ideal age for vegetable transplants has eluded researchers for years. For example, good commercial tomato yields have occurred with transplants ranging from two to 13 weeks old [21]. Studies with other crops (broccoli, pepper, watermelon) have shown similar results [8, 22, 21].

Transplanting in the greenhouse. The practice of germinating seedlings in flats and transplanting them to containerized trays is a time-honored one. In general, this process is best accomplished when the first true leaf is one-fourth to one-half inch (.6 to 1.3 cm) long. Prick the plants from the flat using a small tool (pot stake, small knife, etc.) to support the stem's hypocotyl section and adjacent root system. Transfer the seedling to the new container (well-drained media) and, for support, set slightly deeper into the media than originally placed. Shade may be required to protect newly potted seedlings from wilting. Water lightly. ***Do not use this process with cucurbit crops.***

The plug transfer method involves transferring a small plug to a larger sized plug. Less damage occurs with this technique, but it may still be harmful to vine crops. Either procedure is labor intensive and may not work in large scale operations, since quality transplants can be grown in containerized trays from seed to maturity.

Plant height. With the loss of Alar for tomato transplants in 1989, growers were deprived of the only chemical tool available for controlling plant height. Other plant growth regulating chemicals can accomplish the same result [19], but none is registered with the Environmental Protection Agency for use on vegetable crops at this time.

Hardening. Most transplants will be sufficiently hardened for field setting if compact plant height is strictly maintained. Gradually increase light intensity, reduce irrigation inputs, or lower the greenhouse temperature by 5 to 10 degrees F (2.7 C to 5.5 C) for additional hardening.

Shipping

Shipping factors, such as mechanical injury, environmental conditions, and length of storage, can affect plant vigor and establishment. Mechanical injury most often occurs if the plants are pulled from trays and packed in boxes. Leskovar and Cantliffe [9] showed that tomato transplants shipped in the tray yielded more extra-large fruit than transplants pulled from the tray and packed in boxes. Risse et al. [18] found densely packed transplants fared poorly compared to loosely

TABLE 27.1

Vegetable transplant production in containerized cells

Crop a	Cell size (diameter in inches)	Seed required for 10,000 transplants	Seedling depth (inches)	Optimum germination temperature (F)	Days to germination b	Optimum growing temperature (F) Day	Night	pH tolerance c	Time required in weeks
Broccoli	0.8–1.0	2 oz	1/4	85	4	60–70	50–60	6.0–6.8	5–7
Brussels sprouts	0.8–1.0	2 oz	1/4	80	5	60–70	50–60	5.5–6.8	5–7
Cabbage	0.8–1.0	2 oz	1/4	85	4	60–70	50–60	6.0–6.8	5–7
Cauliflower	0.8–1.0	2 oz	1/4	80	5	60–70	50–60	6.0–6.8	5–7
Celery	0.5–0.8	1 oz	1/8–1/4	70	7	65–75	60–65	6.0–6.8	10–12
Collards	0.8–1.0	2 oz	1/4	85	5	60–70	50–60	5.5–6.8	5–7
Cucumber	0.5–0.8	1¼ lb	1/2	95	3	70–75	60–65	5.5–6.8	2–3
Eggplant	1.0	4 oz	1/4	85	5	70–80	65–70	6.0–6.8	5–7
Lettuce	0.5–0.8	1 oz	1/8	75	2	55–65	50–55	6.0–6.8	4
Muskmelon	1.0	1¼ lb	1/2	90	3	70–75	60–65	6.0–6.8	4–5
Onion	0.5–0.8	3 oz	1/4	75	4	60–65	55–60	6.0–6.8	10–12
Pepper	0.5–0.8	7 oz	1/4	85	8	65–75	60–65	5.5–6.8	5–7
Squash	0.5–0.8	3¾ lb	1/2	95	3	70–75	60–65	5.5–6.8	3–4
Tomato	1.0	3 oz	1/4	85	5	65–75	60–65	5.5–6.8	5–7
Watermelon	1.0	3¾ lb	1/2	95	3	70–80	65–70	5.0–6.8	3–4

Source: Adapted from Knott's handbook for vegetable growers [7].

a Other crops can be grown as transplants by matching seed types and growing according to the above specifications (examples: endive=lettuce). Sweet corn can be transplanted, but tap root is susceptible to breakage.

b Under optimum germination temperatures. Primed seed will germinate more rapidly than unprimed seed under most conditions.

c Plug pH will increase over time with alkaline irrigation water.

packed transplants both in field survival and yield. These researchers also showed that plants held at 50 F (10 C) had greater field survival than plants held at 70 F (21.1 C) or higher during shipping.

Ethylene exposure can also damage vegetable transplants. Ethylene is, in fact, a plant hormone, but exposure to high levels can cause leaf abscision, senescence, or chlorophyll loss. Ethylene gas sources include exhaust from propane-powered forklift trucks or heaters and senescing fruits and plants.

Individual crops

The following information is specifically for plants raised in trays from seed to maturity. Generalized conditions for crop production are outlined in table 27.1.

Cole crops. Hot-water treated seed should be used for all cole crops to combat seed-borne diseases, specifically black rot. Cold frames may be used to grow and harden cole crops; however, excessively cold temperatures can cause premature bolting (flower stalk production) in these plants [4, 6].

Several factors are involved in floral initiation, for example, chilling is required for cole crops, floral initiation. Plant age [5], variety, and light conditions [16] may also play a role. As cole crops age (from one to five weeks) their receptivity to chilling usually increases. In general, if cole crops are raised at temperatures above 50 F (10 C) (optimum 70 F to 80 F or 21.1 C to 26.7 C), premature bolting in the field will not be a problem. Also note that Chinese cabbage, kohlrabi, and mustard seed can receive the chilling stimulus, so cold storage of these seeds is not advised.

Lamont [8] showed that transplant age alone does not influence broccoli head weight or diameter. Broccoli transplants held 31 weeks in standard container trays yielded the same as plants held only six weeks. This raises questions about traditional thinking that checked growth in transplants produces "buttons" (small heads) in the field. While these data cannot be directly extrapolated to other cole crops, similar thinking about other species could be questioned.

Cole crops can be grown successfully in both the spring and fall. Brussels sprouts, however, should be grown in the fall since a frost improves firmness and flavor. Summer cole crop transplant production is often subject to extremes in soil temperature, so shade cloth may be necessary to ensure good germination. Remove shade cloth before plants become spindly.

Adequate boron is suggested for cole crops, as deficiencies in B may result in hollow heart (broccoli, cabbage), unacceptable curd formation (cauliflower), and other maladies. A complete analysis fertilizer should provide sufficient B.

Cucurbit crops. Cucurbits, such as cucumbers and squash, can be direct-seeded in the field and be market-ready about the same time as a crop grown from transplants. This is not the case with watermelon and cantaloupe, which have long maturation periods. With these crops, transplants are recommended to shorten the time from planting to market. Any time cucurbit transplants are used, they should be transported to the field in the container in which they were seeded. Cucurbit root damage is the primary cause of transplant loss.

These crops traditionally have the least amount of greenhouse time of any transplant crop. Cucumbers, for example, generally require less than three weeks from seed to setting. The higher temperatures needed to grow these crops produce a leggy plant that complicates field setting, so a shorter greenhouse time is recommended. It is best to field-set cucurbit transplants with a maximum of two true leaves, before the plant gets much larger than a silver dollar. Cucurbits are fleshy, succulent plants, and the natural environmental rigors (heat, cold, wind, abrasion, etc.) easily take their toll on leggy plants.

The hardest cucurbit to grow is the triploid (seedless) watermelon. Seedless watermelons are inherently weaker than standard genetic watermelons, so take extra care through all production stages. With high germination seed (preferably over 90% emergence), sow one seed per container or cell. Growers should never grow more than one plant per container because the plant will stretch in competition for light and will become root-bound quickly.

Sow seedless watermelon in media that is moist but not wet (saturate, then drain for 24 hours). Seed should be sown one-fourth to one-half inch (.6 to 1.3 cm) below the media surface. Seedless watermelons may drown if overwatered before or during the germination phase, because morphologically these seeds have greater air space (that can fill with water) within the seed coat.

Containers should not be irrigated again until the vermiculite (or soil surface) is dry, and the soil media is barely moist. This practice requires experience, and it reduces hypocotyl stretch during the germination stage. Hypocotyl stretch refers to excessive growth of the node between the root and the cotyledons (seed leaves). Excessive growth or stretch in this area will result in weak, spindly plants that are difficult to transplant and susceptible to wind damage. Maintain low moisture in the media until the cotyledons are fully expanded, and the first true leaf is one-half to three-quarters of an inch (1.3 to 1.9 cm) in diameter. Once true leaves develop, begin the fertilization program.

One difficulty with seedless watermelon is that the seed coat often adheres to the cotyledons, resulting in deformed seedlings. To correct this, the seed's pointed end should be planted up or at a 45-degree angle to the tray surface. This causes the radical (first root) to emerge and hook downward. The increased drag placed on the seedcoat from the resulting hook-shaped radical during emergence will usually free the seed coat [13].

A common problem in watermelon transplants is rat-tailing. If seeds are planted too shallowly, the radical will push out of the soil, exposing a portion of the root to the air and producing a weak plant. Plant seed at an appropriate depth to prevent this condition.

Many new hybrid watermelons may flower during their stay in the greenhouse. Because these hybrids have been bred for increased productivity, this problem may become more prominent in the future as our use of hybrid watermelons increases. Preliminary research shows that these seedling male flowers do not affect subsequent field production (Vavrina, unpublished).

Solanaceous crops. Production procedures for Solanaceae crops are similar (table 27.1); however, several differences are worth mentioning. Pepper and eggplant seeds germinate more slowly than tomato, so these crops are excellent priming candidates. Pepper and egglant primed seeds germinate in two days as opposed to the seven to 10 days required under ideal conditions with nonprimed seed. This should advance scheduling by at least one week. Pepper seed is probably the most variable in emergence and growth compared to tomato and eggplant. Pepper varieties are much more diverse (bell, banana, hot, etc.), and even cultivars within a specific type can vary widely in emergence time.

None of the Solanaceous crops can tolerate low temperatures. Below 50 F (10 C), all growth stops, and chilling injury can occur with prolonged exposure. Eggplant and pepper grow more slowly than tomato, so slightly higher night growing temperatures are necessary. Jalapeno varieties are extremely variable in their growth. You may need to hold some jalapeno varieties as long as 10 weeks to get sufficient growth before going to the field. Bar-Tal et al. [1] reported that the larger the pepper is at transplanting, the earlier the crop yields; however, total fruit yield (after several harvests) was unaffected by a range of greenhouse nutritional regimens.

Irrigation scheduling is more critical in pepper and eggplant than in tomato. Pepper and eggplant will react more quickly to irrigation deficits and recover more slowly. Neither eggplant nor pepper recover readily from any serious shock or stunting.

Research on tomato transplants is abundant, since this crop is perhaps the most widely grown from transplants. Concerning nutrition, Melton and Dufault [14] found nitrogen to be the driving force in tomato transplant growth and recommended at least 225 ppm N feedings weekly. They noted phosphorus was only minimally involved and potassium did not impact the growth parameters measured. Widders [24] found higher growth rates five days after field setting when higher N rates were used in the plant house.

In the past it was believed that tomato transplants should be grown at 80 F (26.7 C) or above, but this has been challenged by Dufault and Melton [3] and Melton and Dufault [15]. They found that tomato seedlings exposed to warm days and cold nights showed no decrease in earliness, yield, or quality. Bugbee and White [2] showed that hydroponically grown tomatoes' optimum root growth during the first four weeks occurred at 77 F to 86 F (25 C to 30 C). In weeks five and six, the best root growth occurred between 68 F to 77 F (20 C to 25 C).

Lettuce. In the spring, long day light conditions contribute to lettuce bolting. Because of this, spring-grown lettuce is best started from transplants. Iceberg lettuce, grown predominantly in California, typically spends 28 days in the greenhouse and 28 days in the field. Leafy types mature earlier, though four weeks in the greenhouse is still a good rule of thumb.

Lettuce seed requires light to germinate. While adequate germination occurs under normal daylight conditions, continuous supplemental light (300 foot-candle/.32 klux, cool-white, fluorescent light) can hasten establishment. As mentioned earlier, supplemental lighting can increase lettuce transplant quality by increasing plant mass, but no benefit is noted in the field (e.g., pounds per acre, size of head, etc.).

Due to the large number of plants per acre required for commercial lettuce production, it may be necessary to plant these crops in very small cells; otherwise, greenhouse space will be used inefficiently. Establish lettuce at 70 F to 75 F (21.1 C to 23.9 C) early (weeks one and two), then drop the temperature for the remaining time. Lettuce can be grown in the same greenhouse as cole crops.

Onion. Onions can also be produced in containers. Due to the enormous number of plants per acre required for commercial production, it is necessary to grow onions in small plugs. Onions, like celery, will remain in the greenhouse longer (10 to 12 weeks) than most other crops, so consider this if space is limited.

After germination (75 F/23.9 C), best results will be produced by growing onions at cooler temperatures (50 F/10 C at night and 60 F to 70 F/15.6 C to 21.1 C during the day). Harden onions by lowering the growing temperature to 40 F to 45 F (4.4 C to 7.2 C) at night and reducing water. Onions can be grown with cole crops as well, although the tips of older onion leaves often yellow. This seems a normal occurrence and generally poses no problem with a proper fungicide program to prevent secondary fungal tissue infection.

Onion roots are poor at best, so over-watering can cause more harm than good. Onion leaves can be clipped to about 4 inches (10.2 cm) to prevent the tops from becoming tangled and to facilitate planting later. Onions are also salt intolerant, so watch your fertilizer's salt index.

Celery. Celery seed germinates slowly and is an excellent candidate for priming. Primed celery seed should advance scheduling by one week. Most celery seed provided by reputable seed companies will be certified Septoria-free, which indicates this foliar disease is not likely to occur and alleviates the need for seed sanitation procedures. Germination percentage is generally low in celery, but seed companies should provide seed of 90% germination.

After seed is sown, keep soilless mixes moist but not waterlogged. Presoaking seed may produce a better stand [17]. Celery seed requires continuous light for best germination. Supplemental lighting can increase plant mass in the greenhouse, but yields are not increased in the field. Researchers have found that alternating celery germination temperatures from 77 F (25 C) during the day to 59 F (15 C) at night produces the best results. Growing temperatures of 55 F (12.8 C) or greater lessens bolting. Trim tall plants to harden them as well. Low temperature hardening may predispose celery to bolting.

Celery needs high levels of nitrogen, calcium, magnesium, and boron. Make certain that soilless media and a constant feed program supply these nutrients adequately and in proper balance.

References

[1]   Bar-Tal, A., B. Bar-Yosef, and U. Kafkafi. 1990. Pepper transplant response to root volume and nutrition in the nursery. *Agron.* J. 82:989-995.

[2]   Bugbee, B., and J.W. White. 1984. Tomato growth as affected by root-zone temperature and the addition of gibberellic acid and kinetin to nutrient solutions. *J. Amer. Soc. Hort. Sci.* 109:121-125.

[3]   Dufault, R.J., and R.R. Melton. 1990. Cyclic cold stresses before trans-
        planting influence tomato seedling growth but not fruit earliness, fresh-
        market yield, or quality. *J. Amer. Soc. Hort. Sci.* 115:559-563.
[4]   Fontes, M.R., J.L. Ozbun, and S. Sadik. 1967. Influence of temperature
        on initiation of floral primordia in green sprouting broccoli. In
        Proceedings, Amer. Soc. Hort. Sci. 91:315-320.
[5]   Guttormsen, G., and R. Moe. 1985a. Effect of plant age and temperature
        on bolting in Chinese cabbage. *Sci. Hort.* 25:217-224.
[6]   ———. 1985b. Effect of day and night temperature at different stages of
        growth on bolting in Chinese cabbage. *Sci. Hort.* 25:224-233.
[7]   Knott, J.E. 1988. *Knott's Handbook for vegetable growers.* 3rd ed. Ed. O.
        Lorenz and D. Maynard. New York: Wiley Interscience Publication.
[8]   Lamont, W.J. 1992. Transplant age has little effect on broccoli head
        weight and diameter. *HortScience* 27:848.
[9]   Leskovar, D.I., and D.J. Cantliffe. 1991. Tomato transplant morphology
        affected by handling and storage. HortScience 26:1377-1379.
[10]   Marr, C.W., and M. Jirak. 1990. Holding tomato transplants in plug
        trays. *HortScience* 25:173-176.
[11]   Masson, J., N. Tremblay, and A. Gosselin. 1991a. Nitrogen fertilization a
        nd HPS supplemental lighting influence vegetable transplant production.
        I. Transplant growth. *J. Amer. Soc. Hort. Sci.* 116:594-598.
[12]   ———. 1991b. Effects of nitrogen fertilization and HPS supplemental
        lighting on vegetable transplant production. II. Yield. *J. Amer. Soc. Hort.
        Sci.* 116:599-602.
[13]   Maynard, D.N. 1989. Triploid watermelon seed orientation affects
        seedcoat adherence on emerged cotyledons. *HortScience* 24:603-604.
[14]   Melton, R.R., and R.J. Dufault. 1991a. Nitrogen, phosphorus, and
        potassium fertility regimes affect tomato transplant growth. *HortScience*
        26:141-142.
[15]   ———. 1991b. Tomato seedling growth, earliness, yield, and quality
        following pretransplant nutritional conditioning and low temperatures.
        J. Amer. Soc. Hort. Sci. 116:421-425.
[16]   Moe, R., and G. Guttormsen. 1985. Effect of photoperiod and temperature
        on bolting in Chinese cabbage. *Sci. Hort.* 27:49-54.
[17]   Nonnecke, I.L. 1989. *Vegetable production.* New York: Van Nostrand
        Reinhold.
[18]   Risse, L.A., D.W. Kretchman, and C.A. Jaworski. 1985. Quality and field
        performance of densely packed tomato transplants during shipment and
        storage. *HortScience* 20:438-439.
[19]   Vavrina, C.S., and K. Armbrester. 1990. Performance of plant growth
        regulators on tomato transplants and subsequent field production. In
        Proceedings, Nat. Symp. Stand Estab. Hort. Crops. April, 1990.
[20]   Vavrina, C.S., and M. Orzolek. 1993. Tomato transplant age: A review.
        HortTechnology 3(3):313.
[21]   Vavrina, C.S., S. Olson, and J.A. Cornell. 1993. Watermelon transplant
        age: Influence on fruit yield. *HortScience* 28:789-790.
[22]   Weston, L.A. 1988. Effect of flat cell size, transplant age, and production
        site on growth and yield of pepper transplants. *HortScience* 23:709-711.

Layering is used commercially to propagate vining crops and/or ground covers in the bedding plant industry. Some species of nepeta, sedum, veronica, and thymus are typically propagated through layering.

Tissue culture. Widespread commercial propagation of bedding plants through tissue culture is in the beginning stages. Tissue culture propagation of gerbera, hosta, hemerocallis, and liatrus has been successful. However, the cost of tissue-cultured materials can be prohibitive. Two of the greatest benefits of tissue culture propagation are: 1) use in developing virus-indexed (disease free) plant material, and 2) rapid initial regeneration of an individual plant into a population.

Stock plant management

Stock plants are the source of cuttings, or vegetative tissue, used to propagate new plants. A stock plant's productivity is directly related to a plant's leaf unfolding rate. The faster the leaf unfolding rate, the more frequently cuttings can be harvested.

Leaf unfolding rate is dependent on the average daily temperature that plants are grown under, preferably 50 F to 77 F (10 C to 25 C) for most crops. Leaf unfolding rate usually decreases when temperatures exceed 76 F (24 C) with many plant species (fig. 28.1). Remember that on a sunny day leaf temperature can be 5 to 8 degrees F (2.7 C to 4.2 C) warmer than the air temperature. Therefore, leaf unfolding rate is regularly slowed during the warmer periods of the year because the plant temperature exceeds 76 F to 78 F (24.4 C to 25.6 C). Either cool or shade the crop if possible during warm periods of the year to reduce temperature and increase leaf unfolding rate.

Flowering on stock plants is not desirable since vegetative and not reproductive tissue is required. The energy expended by the plant should promote cutting production (leaf and stem) and not flower development. Flowers should be removed mechanically or chemically from stock plants. Mechanically remove flowers early in development. Ethephon, or florel, can be used to abort flowers early in development and/or increase branching on stock plants.

Application of florel will have the side effect of reducing leaf area slightly. Dr. Peter Konjoian has conducted significant research on using florel for hanging basket production. Florel effectively eliminated flowering and increased branching early in development. Flowering occurred normally on most crops no earlier than 30 days after the last growth regulator application.

Total daily light (accumulated radiance) affects stock plant vigor.

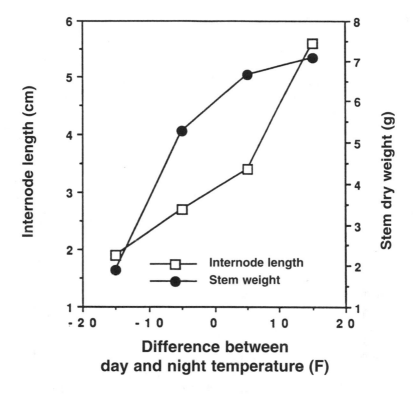

Fig. 28.1. The effect of the difference between day and night temperature (day temperature minus night temperature) on New Guinea impatiens internode length and stem dry weight.

Supplemental lighting of stock plants during low light periods of the year increases stock plant productivity, cutting quality, and the degree to which cuttings root.

Nutritionally stressed stock plants produce nutritionally stressed cuttings. Stock plants should be nutrient tested regularly to ensure that plants are healthy. Both soil and tissue tests should be conducted.

Cutting quality

A cutting should snap from the stock plant. Cuttings are most turgid in the morning, so that is the best time to take cuttings. An ideal cutting is approximately 3 to 4 inches (7.6 to 10.1 cm) long and has three to five leaves. A cutting's caliper, internode lengths, and stem weight are primarily dependent on the difference between day and night temperature (DIF). Stem caliper, internode length, and stem weight increase as DIF increases (fig. 28.1). Cutting quality for many species is highest when plant day and night temperatures are 76 F and 68 F (24.4 C to 20 C), respectively.

Light intensity interacts with temperature to affect cutting quality. Light intensity also affects cutting weight. Stem weight is closely associated with a cutting's rootability. In general, stock plants should be grown at a cooler temperature under lower light intensity to maintain high quality cuttings.

High temperatures in conjunction with low light intensity decreases cutting quality. The reason for this drop in cutting quality is that the high leaf unfolding rate in conjunction with low light levels result in cuttings with thin stems and low overall dry weight. Maintain light intensity ranging from 200 to 600 μmol m^{-2} s^{-1} during the day for growing stock plants. Light intensity does not affect leaf unfolding rate.

Rooting cuttings

Factors that affect the ability of cuttings to root include: 1) the stock plant's condition, 2) cutting tissue age, 3) presence or absence of rooting hormone, 4) degree of cutting dehydration, 5) shoot and medium temperature, 6) medium structure and pH, 7) light quality in the propagation environment, and 8) the presence or absence of disease.

Condition. A cutting's ability to root is directly related to the stock plant's vigor. Factors that increase stock plant vigor, such as supplemental lighting and adequate nutrition, affect a cutting's vigor and subsequent rooting. For instance, the number of roots increased 130% when the stock plants received 500 foot-candles (.54 klux) supplemental lighting compared to natural daylight on zonal geraniums cuttings harvested in March [2].

Tissue age. In general, the most rapid and complete rooting occurs on cuttings that originate four to six leaves from an actively growing meristem; in other words, tissue that is finished or almost finished elongating but is not too old. Not only does older tissue root more slowly, if at all, but branching is usually decreased on older tissue versus younger tissue.

Rooting hormone. Application of rooting hormone can result in earlier and/or more complete rooting in many species. In general, rooting hormone is most beneficial when applied to difficult-to-root species. For instance, IBA had no effect on the easy-to-root Gypsy Queen *Clematis* x *hybrida* but increased rooting on the difficult-to-root cultivar Jackmanii [1]. Overapplication of rooting hormone can burn a cutting's base. Bedding plants require lower IBA rates than woody plant materials. The more tender the cutting, the less hormone is needed.

Hydration. It is essential that cuttings not dry out. Plant tissue is most turgid, or filled with water, immediately after sunrise, so take cuttings first thing in the morning. Shade cuttings, and wrap them in moist newspaper until they can either be placed in the propagation area or in a holding cooler. Do not hold cuttings for more than three days in the cooler.

Spray cuttings with a wetting agent immediately after placing them in the propagation area. Wetting agents help limit water loss from the cutting immediately after placing them in a sunlight environment by coating the leaf more completely with water. The propagation area should be shaded (usually saran) to limit high light intensity early in development. Often shading can be removed after the first week.

When cuttings are under mist for prolonged periods of time, nutrients may leach from the leaves. When this occurs, leaf color becomes more chlorotic or yellow. Fertilize cuttings through the mist line using 100 to 300 ppm N and K no more than once per week if cuttings require an extended rooting time.

Temperature. Media and air temperatures should be maintained between 70 F and 78 F (21.1 C to 25.6 C), depending on the crop. Rooting is enhanced when the medium temperature is the same or slightly higher than the air temperature. Cooler or warmer temperatures will delay rooting and will often increase root rot at the cutting base. Warmer temperatures can also encourage bacterial disease spread among cuttings.

Media characteristics. The propagation medium should allow for good aeration. Heavy media with poor aeration will delay rooting and encourage root rot. For this reason, a soilless medium should be used. Soilless media are generally sterile and have good aeration. Do not propagate in soil- or sand-based media, as the potential for pathogens is much greater and aeration is reduced compared to soilless media.

Different species have a different optimal pH for rooting. Many species have an optimal media pH of 5.8 to 6.5 for rooting. In contrast, some plants, such as clematis, appear to have an optimal pH of 7.0 to 8.0 for rooting. Make sure media pH are in the recommended levels prior to sticking cuttings.

Light intensity. Cuttings should receive bright but not direct light. Ideally, light intensity should be maintained at 500 to 1,500 foot-candles (.54 to 1.6 klux). More or less light may stress cuttings and reduce rooting. Some species can be rooted at higher light intensities after the first week.

Disease. Any disease on a cutting can reduce rooting. Some diseases, such as Botrytis, may only affect an individual leaf on a cutting. In contrast, bacterial diseases, such as Erwinia, will destroy the entire cutting rapidly. Disease can easily spread among cuttings.

Common diseases in asexual propagation: Botrytis is a common problem during propagation. The most effective method of control is to remove of all debris in the propagation area. Chemical spray applications are also effective. Lastly, good air movement is critical. When cuttings are spaced tightly, the risk of Botrytis increases substantially.

Bacterial soft rot (Erwinia) is a common problem in unsanitary rooting environments. Poor air movement, warm temperatures, and splashing water contribute to the spread of the disease throughout the propagation area. If soft rot is found, destroy infected plants and isolate healthy plants from the infected region immediately. Remember that bacterial soft rot can be spread by hand contact. Therefore, sterilize hands periodically when touching plants if soft rot is evident.

Pythium and Rhizoctonia are root diseases that can attack cuttings during propagation. Symptoms usually move from the root system up and are characterized by wilting of the cutting and a black soft region on the stem's lower part.

Postrooting care

Following rooting, take care not to stress rooted cuttings. Typically, rooted cuttings are potted and placed in an open greenhouse. During the first three to five days, it is critical not to expose cuttings to direct sunlight. In addition, do not apply strong fertilizer and/or acid solutions over the cuttings. When strong fertilizer or acid solutions are applied overhead, young leaf distortion can occur.

Specific crop recommendations

Specific recommendations will be discussed for geraniums, New Guinea and double impatiens, and basket and patio crops. Tables 28.3 and 28.4 include specific recommendations for propagation techniques for perennials and ground cover crops.

Pelargonium. Geraniums have been vegetatively propagated for centuries, and sexually propagated geraniums are a recent development. The most common geraniums propagated asexually are zonal geraniums and regal pelargoniums. The zonal geranium, or *Pelargonium* x *hortorum* is a hybrid between *P. inquinans* and *P. zonale*.

TABLE 28.2

Expected cutting yield per zonal geranium plant[a]

Month	Yield
June	50 cuttings (100%)
July	45 cuttings (90%)
August	40 cuttings (80%)
September	33 cuttings (65%)
October	25 cuttings (50%)
January	10 cuttings (20%)

[a] Zonal geranium stock plants planted at different times of the year. A stock plant that produces a maximum of 50 cuttings is used, as an example.

Geranium stock plants are started at different times of the year. The earlier stock plants are started, the more cuttings a stock plant will produce over the plant's life. Regal pelargonium stock plants should be started one month earlier than zonal geranium stock plants. Table 28.2 shows the expected yield per zonal geranium stock plant planted at different times of the year.

Zonal geraniums are day-neutral plants. In other words, day length does not affect flower initiation in zonal geraniums. In contrast, regal pelargoniums are long-day plants—days longer than nights will promote regals' flowering. Days shorter than nights will promote vegetative growth. During summer months, temperatures are so warm that flowering is generally inhibited in regal pelargoniums. However, if stock plants receive light pollution or night interruption lighting during cooler periods of the year, flowering may be promoted. During cooler periods of the year, pull shade cloth to limit photoperiod length to aid in maintaining vegetative plants.

Plant cuttings in a 6- to 8-inch (15.2 to 20.3-cm) pot. Final spacing should be approximately one plant per square foot (.09 m²) on plants started in June. Pinch plants three to five weeks after planting when the stem is approximately 4 to 6 inches (10.1 to 15.2 cm) high. There should be at least four to five internodes on the mother stem when plants are pinched. Pinch plants by removing the uppermost two to three leaves.

Pinch as needed after the initial pinch. Harvest or take cuttings periodically when at least three to five leaves can be taken with a cutting and still leave three to four nodes on the stock plant from which new lateral shoots can develop. Apply florel to stock plants to increase

TABLE 28.3

Preferred perennial asexual propagation methods

Crop	Preferred method of commercial propagation	Crop	Preferred method of commercial propagation
Achillea	cutting	Lavender	cutting
Aegopodium	division	Ligularia	division
Ajuga	division	Lythrum	cutting
Alchemilla	division	Mentha	cutting
Artemisia	cutting	Monarda	cutting
Aruncus	cutting	Nepeta	cutting
Aster	cutting	Peony	division
Astilbe	division	Penstemon	cutting
Boltonia	cutting	Phalaris	division
Brunnera	division	Phlox	cutting
Convallaria	division	Physostegia	cutting
Dianthus	cutting	Polemonium	division
Dicentra	division	Salvia	cutting
Galium	cutting	Sedum	cutting
Geranium	division	Sempervivum	division
Gypsophilia	cutting	Tiarella	division
Hemerocallis	division	Teucrium	cutting
Heuchera	division	Tradescantia	division
Hosta	division	Thymus	cutting
Iris	division	Veronica	cutting
Lamium	cutting	Viola	division

branching and decrease leaf size. Do not apply florel after October 15, as cutting quality can decrease substantially under low light conditions during the winter.

The most critical factor in producing geraniums from cuttings is maintaining disease-free stock plants. Geraniums are particularly susceptible to bacterial diseases such as Xanthomonas after propagation. Infection of propagation stock has resulted in enormous losses throughout the geranium industry. Often infection symptoms are not evident until the spring of the year following propagation, when temperatures increase. Symptoms may also appear in the greenhouse or after planting by the consumer.

It is essential that stock plant cuttings be purchased from a reputable source who supplies culture-virus indexed stock plants. Remember to have cuttings tested for Xanthomonas regardless of the cutting source! Universities often have a disease testing laboratory that can test for Xanthamonas. In addition, diagnostic kits allow growers to easily use immunoassay techniques at a significantly reduced price. Even if cuttings are certified "disease-free," you should grow the crop as

TABLE 28.4

Preferred asexual propagation techniques and time for ground cover crops

Genus	Common name	Time of year	Propagation method
Aegopodium	Goutweed	spring or fall	division
Ajuga	Bugleweed	spring or fall	division
Cerastium	Snow in summer	spring or fall	cuttings, division
Convallaria	Lily of the valley	early spring	division
Epimedium	Barrenwort	spring	division
Euonymus	Winter-creeper	June to August	cuttings, root layering
Hedera	English ivy	July to September	cuttings, root layering
Hemerocallis	Daylily	spring or fall	division, tissue culture
Hosta	Hosta	spring or fall	division, tissue culture
Iberis	Candytuft	June to August	cuttings, division
Lonicera	Japanese honeysuckle	summer	cuttings, division
Pachysandra	Japanese spurge	late June	cuttings, division
Sedum	Stonecrop	midsummer	cuttings, division
Thymus	Creeping thyme	spring or fall	division, cuttings
Vinca	Periwinkle	spring	division, cuttings

if there may be some infected plants. In other words, plants should be grown to limit potential disease spread.

1. Limit water splashing between plants. The best way is to water plants using trickle irrigation instead of overhead watering.
2. Clean benches with a 10% Clorox solution prior placing stock plants on them.
3. Regularly dip all tools used for pruning or taking cuttings in alcohol or 10% Clorox solution.

Grow stock plants at temperatures between 65 F and 76 F (18.3 C to 24.4 C). The warmer the average daily temperature (when day and night temperature fall within this temperature range), the more rapid the leaf unfolding rate. Cutting production increases as average daily temperature increases up to 76 F on zonal geraniums (fig. 28.2).

In general, zonal geranium cuttings do not need rooting hormone to promote rooting. Cuttings taken at the appropriate time in development and placed on a bench with bottom heat (70 F to 74 F/21.1 C to 23.3 C) will root in seven to 10 days. However, if cuttings are taken when tissue is harder, rooting hormone may be necessary. If rooting hormone is applied, use liquid formulations at low rates or talc (Hormex #1).

Generally, regal pelargoniums require rooting hormone application for rooting to occur. It is especially important that medium temperature

TABLE 28.5

Cultural information for common spring hanging basket/container crops

Crop	Planting time	Plants per pot	Number/time of pinches	Crop time (weeks)
Anigozanthos (Kangaroo Paw)	February through March	3-5 per 6" pot; 4-5 per 8-10" pot	None	10-14
Achimenes hybrids	Plant rhizomes February through April	8 per 8" pot; 6 per 6" pot	As needed	10-14
Abutilon Apricot Glow	Mid-December to late February	3-4 per 8-10" pot; 1 per 4-6" pot	Two: pinch at planting and 6 weeks later	14-16
Argeranthemum frutescens (Marguerite daisy)	Mid-December to late February	3-4 per 8-10" pot; 1 per 4-6" pot	One pinch 2 weeks after planting	12-14
Astericus Gold Coin	Mid-December to late February	3-4 per 8-10" pot; 1 per 4-6" pot	Soft pinch at planting, additional for shaping	12-14
Bacopa Snowflake (*Sutera diffusus*)	January through February	3-4 per 8-10" pot; 1-2 per 4-6" pot	One soft pinch at planting	12-14
Begonia Looking Glass	Mid-December to late February	3-4 per 8-10" pot; 1 per 4-6" pot	Once 2 weeks after planting	12-14
Brachycome melanocarpa Pink Swirl	Early December to early February	3-4 per 8-10" pot; 2 per 6" pot; 1 per 4" pot	Once 4 weeks after planting liners	14-16
Geranium Sugar Plum	Mid-December to late February	3-4 per 8-10" pot; 1 per 4-6" pot	One soft pinch 2 weeks after planting	10-14
Helichrysum bracteatum Golden Beauty	January through March	3-4 per 8-10" pot; 1 per 4-6" pot	Once, 2 weeks after planting	12-14
Ivy geranium	Mid-December to late February	3-5 per 8-10" pot; 1 per 4-6" pot	Two to three times. Do not pinch after March 15	12-16
Lantana camara	Mid-December to February	4-5 per 8-10" pot; 1 per 4" pot	Pinch as needed for stem elongation	12-16
Lobelia Royal Jewels	Mid-December to late February	3-4 per 8-10" pot; 1 per 4-6" pot	Twice, 2 weeks after planting and as necessary	14-16
Lotus	Mid-December to early February	3-4 per 8-10" pot; 1 per 4-6" pot	2 weeks after planting and 5 weeks later	14-16
Lysimachia Golden Globes	Mid-December to late February	3-4 per 8-10" pot; 1 per 4-6" pot	Once, 2 weeks after planting	12-14
New Guinea impatiens	Mid-January to early April	3-4 per 8-10" pot; 1 per 4-6" pot	No pinch	8-12
Osteospermum Sparkler	January through February	3-4 per 8-10" pot; 1 per 4-6" pot	Two weeks after planting and again 5 weeks later	12-14
Passiflora	December through March	3-5 per 8-10" pot	As needed	15-18
Pseuderanthemum Amethyst Star	Mid-April to mid-June for late summer finish	3-4 per 8-10" pot; 1 per 4-6" pot	Twice, once at planting and again 6 weeks later	14-18
Ranunculus asiaticus	Mid-February to early March	3-5 tuberous roots per 5-6" pot	No pinch	10-12
Scaevola aemula Blue Wonder	January to April	3-4 per 8-10" pot; 1 per 4-6" pot	2-3 times: 2 weeks after planting until 4 weeks before finish	12-14
Scaevola Petite	Mid-December to late February	3-4 per 8-10" pot; 1 per 4-6" pot	Once at planting	14-16
Supertunias Sunlovers	Mid-February to late March	3-4 per 8-10" pot; 1 per 4-6" pot	Once, 2 weeks after planting	5-6

Conclusions

The primary concern when asexually propagating plant material should be bacterial and viral disease control. Monitoring for these diseases regularly and roguing infected plants throughout the propagation industry and within your greenhouse will greatly decrease the spread of these diseases. When in doubt—test!

References

[1]   Nilsen, J.H. 1976. Effects of irradiation of the motherplants on rooting of *Pelargonium (hortorum)* cuttings. *Acta Horticulturae* 64:65-69.
[2]   Erwin J.E, and D. Schwarze, 1992. *Factors affecting clematis rooting* Bulletin 41(4):1-7. Minnesota Commercial Flower Growers Association.

but are more often grown for another year before being sold. When perennials are grown by traditional perennial growers, plants will be propagated and grown in a variety of ways, including seed propagation, but most are vegetatively propagated to maintain cultivar purity. (See table 29.8 for herbaceous perennial propagation methods.) Perhaps the biggest difference between the perennial specialist and other growers is the number of taxa grown, sometimes more than 4,000 cultivars by a single nursery.

Definition of a perennial

The traditional definition of an herbaceous perennial is a plant that has non-woody, above-ground parts that die back to an underground, over-wintering storage organ. They also normally require an exposure to cold each year to renew the flower. However, herbaceous perennials sold by the industry are somewhat more variable than the strict definition would imply. Some, like Asarum or Epimedium are evergreen, but others, like Perovskia or *Paeonia suffruticosa,* are technically sub-shrubs. Some species, for example Echeveria, grown by perennial growers in the South, may be produced as a vegetatively-propagated annual by bedding plant growers in the North.

Popularity of perennials

There are several reasons for herbaceous perennials' continuing rise in popularity. They do not require replanting each year, although some like Aquilegia or Lupinus may require replanting every three to four years. In comparison, Dictamnus or Paeonia may live for decades.

Perennials enhance the beauty of woody plants, but their principle landscape contribution is their diversity of heights, foliage types, flower color, and bloom times. Perennials like Hosta and Artemisia, however, are grown for their foliage. Also, many perennials bloom in mid to late spring, well before most annuals make much of a show.

Perennials have been mistakenly touted as low- or no-maintenance plants. While some are lower maintenance than annuals, few plants—either annual or perennial—are truly zero maintenance. All gardens require periodic maintenance to realize their aesthetic potential.

Problems that limit or modify production

Several problems face the prospective perennial grower who wants to produce a wide variety of perennials as bedding plants. First, most perennials require exposure to cold in order to flower. Second, high quality, true-to-type seed has not been generally available, and third, many desirable cultivars are vegetatively propagated, and the knowledge of their production methods has not been generally known.

Perennials live from year to year, and most require cold to renew their growth and bloom cycle. Knowledge of this cold requirement is critical to successful plant production, especially in producing seed propagated perennials as bedding plants. If a cold period is required, plants must be started the previous summer or fall, grown until they can initiate flower buds, then held in an unheated greenhouse or other cold structure to complete the cold requirement until the following spring. The cold exposure time may be several hundred hours at temperatures below between 35 F and 40 F (1.7 C and 4.4 C).

Obtaining true-to-name, high-quality seed is a constant problem. There are several thousand taxa of seed propagated perennials, and no single seed source is adequate to supply a grower's needs. Seed suppliers rely on dozens of sources, including seed that they produce, as well as seed purchased from other producers, nurseries, or even homeowners.

Because some seeds come from so many sources they are sometimes produced under unregulated conditions and packaged without viability or purity tests. Fortunately, with increasing popularity of perennials and the accompanying competition, several reliable seed sources have emerged. Seed companies have also learned how to produce and store seed more efficiently.

Another problem limiting the production of perennials is that most cultivars are vegetatively propagated. Most of the knowledge about how to propagate these cultivars has been proprietary—it has resided in the skills of a few propagators and is not generally available. Another problem with perennials is that some plants—for instance Moonbeam Coreopsis—do not produce viable seed. Moonbeam must be propagated by stem cuttings the previous summer, then held in an unheated greenhouse.

Many newly introduced herbaceous perennial cultivars have come from amateur breeders or from nurserymen. Although new Hosta and Hemerocallis cultivars may be expensive—some cost more than $200 each—the prices seldom repay the breeder for his time and effort. It's a labor of love that has produced such popular, re-blooming, daylily cultivars like Stella D'Oro and Happy Returns and Frances Williams hosta.

Production systems

The methods used to produce herbaceous perennials depend on several factors: 1) propagation method; 2) plant growth rate; 3) minimum plant size required to end the juvenile phase; 4) photoperiod requirement; 5) whether plants require vernalization for flowering; 6) salable plant size; and 7) available facilities including growth rooms, greenhouses, and cold storage.

Most growers use variations of three basic production systems:
- Seed propagated in spring; plants will flower without vernalization.
- Summer or fall propagated, either by seed or vegetatively; vernalized prior to spring sales or potting up.
- Field-grown, dug in the autumn or early spring, divided and re-established in cells or small containers for sale.

Seed propagated in spring; plants will flower without vernalization. Several perennials will flower from seed (table 29.1) without being exposed to cold. The grower can use the same production facilities and methods that are used for annuals.

Summer or fall propagated, either by seed or vegetatively; vernalized prior to spring sales or potting up. The majority of perennials (table 29.2) require exposure to cold (vernalizing) temperatures in order to flower. Seed propagated selections are handled much in the same way as spring propagated ones except they must be sufficiently large so that they pass through the juvenile growth stage and will flower once they overwinter. For instance, Shedron [3] found that Aquilegia require at least 15 leaves and Aurinia require 10 or more shoots in order to flower.

When plants are overwintered, larger plug or cell sizes are used—

TABLE 29.1

Perennials that flower first year without a cold requirement

• Achillea ptarmica	• Delphinium elatum	• Platycodon grandiflora
• Anchusa spp.	• Gypsophila paniculata	(dwarf cultivars)
• Anemone x hybrida	• Helenium autumnale	• Rudbeckia fulgida
• Aquilegia x hybrida	• Heliopsis spp.	• Sagina subulata
(Songbird series)	• Heuchera sanguinea	• Salvia superba
• Aster novae-angliae	(some cultivars)	• Sedum spectabile
• Aster novi-belgii	• Lupinus spp.	• Solidago spp.
• Campanula carpatica	• Lychnis arkwrightii	• Veronica spp.
• Chrysanthemum	• Lychnis chalcedonica	• Viola tricolor
morifolium	• Phlox paniculata	• Viscaria oculata
• Coreopsis lanceolata	• Phlox subulata	
• Coreopsis verticillata	• Physostegia virginiana	

TABLE 29.2

Overwintering bare-root perennials [a]

• Achillea	• Erysimum	• Rudbeckia
• Anthemis	• Eupatorium	• Salvia
• Aster	• Helenium	• Scabiosa
• Astilbe	• Heliopsis	• Sedum
• Centaurea	• Lamium	• Stachys
• Ceratostigma	• Lychnis	• Stokesia
• Chrysanthemum	• Nepeta	• Thymus
• Coreopsis	• Oenothera	• Tiarella
• Dianthus	• Phlox subulata	• Tradescantia
• Echinaceae	• Polemonium	• Veronica

[a] These perennials are easy to overwinter and can be further subdivided.

48s or 72s—so that plants are sufficiently well established and will not be harmed by freezing temperatures. Likewise, plants that were propagated by cuttings or division must have a well established root system before being stored in overwintering structures.

When cell or plug-sized perennials are overwintered, provide protection. Root systems are vulnerable to damage by excessively low temperatures or desiccation from heaving. Plants can be held in minimal heat greenhouses where the temperature is not allowed to go much below freezing. Once their chilling period has been completed, however, many perennials will grow, even at low daytime winter temperatures. Fit greenhouses with ventilation systems that maintain daytime temperatures below 40 F (4.4 C) to suppress growth, so plants do not grow excessively or bloom before the sales season begins.

Field-grown, dug in the autumn or early spring, divided and reestablished in cells or small containers for sale. Although most perennials are sold at retail in small containers, large numbers of perennials—especially those produced in the Netherlands—are field grown, dug in the fall, and overwintered bare-root in common storage. After completing their cold requirement, they are potted directly or further divided and established in cells or small pots.

Several perennials are difficult to reestablish if they are harvested as bare-root plants. Examples include Aquilegia, Asarum, Asclepias, Delphinium, and Gypsophila. These plants are most successfully produced if they are grown in containers and transplanted as few times as possible. When possible, these should be propagated into the final sales container.

Propagation methods

Seed. Seeds can be sown using a variety of methods and container sizes. They can be sown directly into small cells or plugs and, when established, either sold or transplanted to larger sized containers. Seed can be sown into flats then transplanted into the sale container. Seeding machines are used to sow into small cells. When sown into flats, even rows are sown either by hand or by using a battery-powered vibrator.

Row placement physically separates groups of seedlings so that if damping off does occur, spread is reduced. In addition, seedlings are easier to remove for transplanting. When small numbers of seed are to be germinated, or where seed testing is to be done, seeds can be wrapped in moist paper towels and placed in glass jars for germination.

Timing seed sowing is important. Fall sowing must be done early enough to allow the plants to reach sufficient size to easily overwinter. Spring-sown seed must be started in time to flower for spring sales. For instance, Heuchera and Campanula require up to 20 weeks from sowing to sale. Timing should also include stratification requirement. In general, the stratification time for most perennials is relatively short— one to four weeks—compared to that required for woody perennials.

If large numbers are to be propagated, seeding machines are helpful, although not all perennial seeds are the correct size or shape for machine sowing. For instance, Digitalis and Lobelia seed are too small for most seeding machines. Seeds can be coated with clay or other substances, but the value of these crops does not warrant seed coating, so the propagator must contend with hand sowing and wasting some seed.

The seed of another plant, *Pulsatilla vulgaris*, has a long projection on the seed, which requires clipping in order to properly size the seed for a seeding machine. Again, the value of this crop is not high enough to warrant further seed processing, so seeds are sown by hand.

Seed scarification. Some perennials, particularly members of the pea family like Baptisia and Lupinus, have hard seed coats and require scarification. Scarification weakens the hard seed coat by puncturing or thinning. For small seed lots, seeds can be rubbed between sheets of sandpaper.

Spread a small quantity of seeds on one sheet of sandpaper and cover with another. Do not scarify too many seeds at once, because seeds that are missed will not germinate.

Larger seed quantities may require acid scarification for uniform results. Soaking Baptisia or Lupinus seed in concentrated sulfuric acid for 15 minutes followed by a water rinse results in significantly improved germination. When acid is used, always wear eye protection.

If you have no experience with scarifying a particular seed variety, **always** test small lots before scarifying the entire group.

Germination. Producing perennials from seed depends on vigorous seed that germinates at high percentages and is influenced by many factors (table 29.3). Preharvest growing conditions, thorough cleaning, and correct storage conditions have the greatest effect but must be coupled with a correct germination environment for efficient production. Some seeds can be sown and germinated in the greenhouse; others should be held in germination cabinets or controlled environment growth rooms.

Few, if any, perennials are germinated with the precision of impatiens seed. This reduces but does not eliminate the opportunity for mechanization. Several European growers have successfully applied high-technology methods to germinating and growing perennials. As their popularity continues, American growers will adopt these methods.

Overwintering. Overwintering perennials can present major problems to growers. First, the small plant size necessitates a greenhouse that can be maintained at near freezing temperatures. Secondly, once the cold requirement of perennials has been completed, many begin to grow, even at cool temperatures. Thus the greenhouse must have sufficient ventilation so that during the sunny days of late winter and early spring, low temperatures can be maintained to suppress growth until the selling season begins.

Asexual propagation

Perennials have traditionally been propagated by dividing and potting-up (or just potting-up) for spring sales of field-grown plants that were dug and stored over the winter. Plants with a multi-stemmed growth habit can be further divided while others cannot. For instance, Tiny Rubies Dianthus or Moonbeam Coreopsis purchased as a bare-root field division can be divided several times and sold in 3- or 4-inch (7.6- or 10.2-cm) pots. In contrast, tap-rooted plants like Platycodon cannot be further subdivided.

Perennials are also propagated from stem and/or root cuttings. This propagation method is very similar to vegetative propagation of annuals, with similar requirements for sanitation, timing, and maintenance, although it is not always necessary to maintain the propagation stock in a greenhouse or controlled environment. It is critical that propagation stock be healthy for successful/economical reproduction.

Table 29.3

Optimum seed germination conditions for perennials

Name	Seeds/oz. (x 1,000)	Germination temp. (F)	Days	Cold (C) Light (L) Dark (D) requirement	Seed to sale (weeks)[a]	Comments
Achillea millefolium	173	65-70	3-10	L	7	—
Achillea ptarmica	—	65	6	L	7	—
Aconitum napellus	—	55-60	30	L	—	stratify 6 wks.
Alcea rosea	32	65-70	10-14	—	6	—
Alchemilla spp.	—	60-70	21-30	—	12+	—
Allium spp.	—	65-70	14-21	L	—	stratify 4 wks.
Anaphalis spp.	600	55-65	10-14	C	—	—
Anchusa italica	—	65-85	14-21	—	9	alternate temp./ possible low germination
Anemone spp.	—	70-75	21-28	—	14+	use fresh seed
Anthemis spp.	45-85	70	8-14	—	9	—
Aquilegia x hybrida	17	65-70	14-21	L	18	stratify 3 wks.
Arabis alpina	105	70	15-25	L	9	cover seeds lightly
Armeria maritima	12-18	70	10	—	12+	stratify seeds 2 wks.; water soak
Aruncus spp.	—	55-65	30-90	—	—	—
Asclepia tuberosa	—	65-75	10	—	11	fresh seed
Aster alpinus	12	70	15	—	6	—
Aster novae-angliae	76	65	7	—	7	water soak
Aster novi-belgii	—	65-75	10-14	—	—	stratify 2 wks.
Astilbe spp.	350	60-70	21-28	—	13	—
Aubretia deltoidea	85	65-75	14-21	L, C	9	—
Aurinia saxatilis (Alyssum)	30	55-65	7-14	L	9	—
Baptisia spp.	1-2	70-75	5-10	—	15	water soak 24 hrs.
Bellis perennis	160	70	6-15	L	8	—
Bergenia spp.	—	60-70	15-20	C	16+	stratify 2 wks.
Brunnera spp.	—	55	15-20	—	11	fall seed outside
Buphthalum spp.	30	70-75	14-30	L	—	—
Campanula carpatica	300	60-70	14-28	L	22	50 F after 3 wks. at 70 F
Campanula medium	105	70	15	L	22	see C. carpatica
Campanula rotundifolia	700	70	5-10	L	7	—
Catanache spp.	—	65-75	21-25	—	—	—
Centaurea spp.	4-7	60-70	7-14	D	11	—
Centranthus spp.	175	65-70	14-21	—	13	—
Cerastium spp.	39	65-75	5-14	L	8	—

Name	Seeds/oz. (x 1,000)	Germination temp. (F)	Days	Cold (C) Light (L) Dark (D) requirement	Seed to sale (weeks)[a]	Comments
Cheiranthus spp.	19	55-65	5-10	L, C	—	—
Chelone spp.	45	55-65	14-42	—	—	—
Chrysanthemum leucanthemum	20	60-65	10	—	10	—
Cimicifuga spp.	—	65-70	21-28	—	16+	use fresh seed
Coreopsis spp.	13	55-70	7-21	L	10	—
Cynoglossum amabile	—	65-75	5-10	D	—	—
Delphinium spp.	13	65-75	8-18	D	10	stratify 2 wks., grow on 45 F
Dianthus spp.	23	60-70	7-14	—	10	grow on 45 F
Dicentra spp.	6	55-60	30	—	15	stratify 6 wks.
Dictamnus spp.	1-2	55-60	30-180	C	—	fresh seed or stratify old 4-6 wks.
Digitalis spp.	300	60-75	7-21	L	9	grow on 45 F
Dodecatheon spp.	—	60-75	30	—	—	stratify 3 wks.
Doronicum caucasicum	17	70	15-20	L	9	—
Echinacea purpurea	73	70-75	10-20	—	7	—
Echinops ritro	2	65-75	15-20	L	9	—
Erigeron spp.	100	55-60	15-20	C	9	—
Eryngium spp.	6	65-80	14(5-90)	—	10+	use fresh seed
Erysimum spp.	—	65-70	2-3	—	7	—
Eupatorium spp.	—	65-70	2-3	—	13	—
Euphorbia myrsinites	3	65-70	15-20	L	9	stratify 4-6 wks., water soak
Gaillardia aristata	8	70-75	10	L	6	—
Gaillardia x grandiflora	10	65-75	5-15	L	9	—
Gentiana spp.	133	70-85	14-180	D	16+	stratify 3 wks.
Geranium spp.	—	70	20-41	—	12+	—
Geum spp.	7	65-75	20-28	L	9	—
Gypsophila paniculata	35	70-75	10-15	L	9	—
Helenium spp.	18	70	7-10	L	8+	—
Helianthemum spp.	15	70-75	15-20	—	—	—
Heliopsis spp.	8-9	70	15-20	—	8+	—
Helleborus spp.	3-4	70-75	30-60+	—	16+	fresh seed or stratify old 3-6 wks.
Hemerocallis spp.	0.8	60-70	10-21	—	16+	stratify 2-4 wks.
Hesperis matronalis	18	65-85	5-21	L	7	—
Heuchera sanguinea	700	55-70	14-21	L, C	22	prefers peat-lite mix, cool to 50 F after 3 wks.
Hibiscus spp.	2	70-75	15-30	—	—	water 24 hrs., scarify

TABLE 29.3 continued

Name	Seeds/oz. (x 1,000)	Germination temp. (F)	Days	Cold (C) Light (L) Dark (D) requirement	Seed to sale (weeks)[a]	Comments
Hosta spp.	5-6	70	15-20	—	16+	no pre-treatment
Iberis sempervirens	10	55-65	5-20	C	10	grow on 45 F
Incarvillea delavayi	6	55-65	25-30	C	—	—
Inula spp.	40	68-86	6-14	L	—	alternate temps
Iris spp.	—	60-70	21-45	—	16+	water soak; stratify 6 wks.
Jasione perennis	300	70	10-21	—	—	—
Kniphofia uvaria	20	65-75	10-20	—	9	—
Lavandula spp.	32	65-75	14-21	—	—	fungicide soak
Leontopodium alpinum	268	55-65	10-14	L, C	9	stratify 3 wks.
Lewisia spp.	—	70	30	—	—	stratify 3 wks.
Liatris spp.	7-9	55-75	10-25	—	7	fall direct seed outside
Ligularia spp.	—	55-65	14-42	—	—	—
Limonium spp.	—	70	15	—	9	—
Linum spp.	18	65-70	14-18+	—	9	self-sows
Lobelia spp.	700	70	15-20	L	12+	stratify 3 months
Lunaria biennus	1-2	65-70	10-14	—	7	self-sows
Lupinus spp.	1-2	55-75	7-21	D	10	water soak 24 hrs., or scarify
Lychnis chalcedonica	64	65-70	9-14+	L	9	stratify 2 wks., no bottom heat
Lysimachia spp.	—	55-65	30-90	—	9	—
Matricaria spp.	145	70	14-21	L, C	9	—
Meconopsis spp.	—	65-70	20-25	—	—	—
Mertiensia spp.	—	55-60	4-8	—	12+	can fall sow
Monarda didyma	56	60-70	5(15-20)	—	7	—
Myosotis spp.	44	65-70	14-21	D	7	self-sows
Nepeta spp.	52	60-70	7-21	—	—	—
Oenothera missouriensis	54	70-85	6-20	—	7	can direct fall sow
Papaver nudicaule	165	65-70	14	L, C	9	difficult to transplant
Papaver orientale	110	70	12	L, C	9	grow on 45 F
Penisetum spp.	—	70	15-20	—	—	—
Penstemon confertus	—	55	10-15	L, C	—	—
Penstemon strictus	37	60-75	7-14	C	11	—
Phlomis spp.	—	60	14-42	—	—	—
Phlox spp.	2-3	70	25-30	D, C	11	stratify 3-4 wks.

Name	Seeds/oz. (x 1,000)	Germination temp. (F)	Days	Cold (C) Light (L) Dark (D) requirement	Seed to sale (weeks)[a]	Comments
Physostegia spp.	16	65-75	20-25	—	9	—
Platycodon spp.	28	60	15-30	L	9	—
Polemonium spp.	—	70	20-25	—	—	—
Polygonum spp.	30	70-75	21-60	—	—	—
Potentilla atrosanguinea	—	65-70	15-20	—	—	—
Potentilla tridentata	—	65-70	10-30	—	—	acid soil, stratify 2-4 wks.
Primula spp.	25-35	65-75	14-40	L	23	stratify 3-4 wks.
Pulmonaria spp.	—	65-70	14-21	—	11	—
Pyrethrum spp.	18	60-70	14-28	L	9	—
Ranunculus spp.	5-42	70	10-15	—	16+	—
Rudbeckia hirta	61	65-70	14-21	L	7	self sows, no bottom heat
Salvia sclarea	—	75	4-10	—	9	—
Salvia superba	26	70	12-15	—		stratify 3-4 wks.
Saponaria spp.	5-6	70	10-15	D	9	—
Saxifraga spp.	445	65-70	15-20	—	11	—
Scabiosa spp.	2-3	65-70	14-21	—	9	—
Sedum spp.	260	60	14-21	L	8+	—
Sempervivum spp.	400	50	15-30	—	12	—
Senecio spp.	—	65-75	10-15	—	—	—
Silene maritima	61	70	15-20	—	9	—
Sisyrinchium spp.	—	50	30-180	—	—	—
Stachys lanata	70	70-80	15-21	—	9	—
Stipa spp.	—	70	30	—	—	—
Stokesia spp.	—	70	25-30	—	11	—
Thalictrum aquilegifolium	12	70-80	15-30	—	14	—
Thermopsis caroliniana	6	70-80	15-21	—	—	scarify
Thymus spp.	224	55	15-20	C	9	—
Tradescantia spp.	10-11	70	30	—	—	water soak 24 hrs.
Trollius spp.	8	50	30+	—	9	stratify 2 wks., July sow fresh seed
Verbascum spp.	125	55-65	14-30	—	9	—
Verbena spp.	—	70-75	20-25	D	—	—
Veronica longifolia	225	70	15-20	—	9	—
Viola tricolor	22	70-75	10-20	D	11	bottom heat or fall seed outside

Cuttings may be stuck directly into prepared medium in the finishing container and placed under mist in propagation facilities until the root system is sufficiently established to allow the plant to be shipped or moved to the sales area. Another form of asexual propagation is shoot tip culture, the regeneration of a plant from a microscopic shoot in the laboratory. This is used primarily for disease prevention. It is necessary for species such as Gypsophila and is particularly suited for mass stock propagation when introducing new cultivars.

Media

Several propagation growing media are suitable for perennials. Many commercial preparations are based on either bark or peat as the organic component (table 29.4). It is especially important that propagation media be free of weed seeds and pathogens. For germinating and growing seedlings or for propagating in small cells, field soils are generally not suitable because they tend to reduce aeration and remain too wet.

TABLE 29.4

Peat-lite medium for perennials

Ingredient	For 1 cubic yard
Sphagnum moss peat	15 cu. ft.[a] or 13 bushels[a]
Perlite-horticultural grade	15 cu. ft.[a] or 13 bushels[a]
Vermiculite #3 for seed germ	
Vermiculite #2 for transplanting	
Dolomitic lime[b]	1 to 5 lb.
Gypsum	2 lb.
Treble superphosphate	1 lb.
Seedlings/newly potted cuttings	
CaNO$_3$ or KNO$_3$	0.5 lb.
Slow-release fertilizer[c]	Follow manufacturer's instructions
AquaGro 2000G	5 oz.
Fritted Trace Elements (FTE)	2 oz.

[a] Increase volume of raw ingredients to account for shrinkage due to mixing.

[b] For plants that prefer acidic soils, like Astilbe or Pulmonaria, reduce or eliminate.

[c] Some slow-release fertilizers (such as Osmocote) should only be added just prior to potting.

For pot sizes 4-inch (10.2 cm) and larger, however, many growers prefer some soil in their growing mix because it provides a buffering action, and it requires less frequent watering. For seed germination, media that are fine-textured are preferred because they result in better seed-medium contact. As plant and container size increase, the aerated pore space should also increase. If plants are to be overwintered in larger containers in unheated houses, media that do not contain vermiculite are best. Under freeze/thaw conditions vermiculite's plate structure is destroyed, and aeration is reduced, resulting in root problems.

Fertilization

Perennials are fertilized using one of three methods: incorporating fertilizers into the growing medium prior to transplanting or potting; application of liquid feed fertilization after planting; or a combination of liquid feed and preplanting incorporation of slow release fertilizers.

Most perennials prefer a medium pH of 5.5 to 6.0; some prefer higher and some lower (table 29.5). Therefore, water supply and media acidity should be tested prior to propagation and planting, and the results must be considered when determining which crops to produce, fertilization regimes, and lime applications. Water testing is especially important in limestone regions, where the water may contain large amounts of dissolved calcium that result in very high water pH. If this is encountered, the grower should reduce preplant lime incorporation and may consider injecting an acid into the irrigation water.

TABLE 29.5

Preferred pH conditions for selected perennials

Examples of crops preferring acidic conditions	Examples of crops preferring alkaline conditions
Astilbe	Gypsophila
Iris ensate	
Pulmonaria	

In practice, each grower develops his own liquid feed program. However, a complete, general-purpose fertilizer, such as 20-20-20 or 21-17-11, injected into the irrigation water at 100 to 150 ppm-nitrogen at each watering has proved satisfactory for many growers. Growers should monitor the fertilizer levels in their crops by using a solubridge (table 29.6).

TABLE 29.6

Solubridge readings for two extraction methods

Extraction method	Solubridge reading (mhos)
Saturated paste	
Low	0 to 740
Medium	750 to 3490
High	above 3490
Pour through (suggested)	
Low	0 to 400
Medium	400 to 2000
High	above 2000

Pot configuration

The stored plant's root size defines pot size chosen for sale. Many perennials have a fibrous root system, so they can occupy cells and pots that are shaped like those used for annuals. However, many perennials, especially those with tap roots like lupines and Baptisia, or with larger fleshy roots that have been grown in the field like Dicentra or Hemerocallis, will not fit into cells and even require a deeper or larger pot. Pot and cell configurations where the container depth is $1^{1}/_{2}$ times that of the width are available. Most perennials are transplanted to gallon containers.

Marketing

Selling perennials as bedding plants requires considerable skill and knowledge by the retailer, because most perennials are sold when they are not in bloom. Today, colorful posters, display cards, and pot tags are available for most common perennials. They also contain a picture, a brief description of the plant, and some information on cultural requirements.

The best sales aid, however, is a knowledgeable salesperson. Although there are many more booklets and brochures available covering perennials, retailers sometimes have difficulty educating their staffs. Fortunately, nursery organizations are devoting more program time to perennial education, and professional organizations like the Perennial Plant Association in Hilliard, Ohio, are devoted exclusively to this crop area.

TABLE 29.7

Flowering herbaceous perennial and ornamental biennial photoperiodic responses

Condition	Example
Short day plants	
Plants requiring short days	*Chrysanthemum* x *morifolium* (chrysanthemum)
Plant flowers faster in short days	*Chrysanthemum* x *morifolium* (chrysanthemum)
Short day response accelerated after low temperature vernalization	*Chrysanthemum* x *morifolium* (chrysanthemum)
Long day plants	
Plants requiring long days	*Chrysanthemum maximum* (Shasta daisy)
	Phlox paniculata (Summer phlox)
	Rudbeckia hirta (Black-eyed Susan)
	Sedum telephium (Stone crop)
	Sedum spectabile (Stone crop)
Long day response accelerated after low temperature vernalization	*Dianthus caesius* (Cheddar pink)
	Oenothera spp. (Evening primrose)
	Aquilegia x *hybrida* (Columbine)
	Aurinia saxitilis (Basket of gold)
Long day at low temperature, day neutral at high temperature	*Delphinium* x *cultorum* (Larkspur)
	Rudbeckia bicolor (Coneflower)
Flowering speeded up by long days	*Dianthus barbatus* (Sweet William)
	Dianthus caryophyllus (Carnation)
Flowering speeded up by exposure to long days following low temperature vernalization	*Campanula persicifolia* (Peach-leaf bellflower)
	Dianthus caryophyllus (Carnation)
	Dianthus barbatus (Sweet William)
	Digitalis purpurea (Foxglove)
	Lupinus x Russell Hybrid (Lupine)
	Lychnis coronaria (Rose campion)
Flowering speeded up at high temperature, no effect at low temperature	*Centaurea cyanus* (Cornflower)
Short/long day plant; low temperature substitutes for the short-day effect and responds as long-day plant after low temperature exposure	*Campanula medium* (Canterbury bells)

TABLE 29.8

Propagation methods for herbaceous perennials[a]

Name	Seed	Stem cutting	Root scuttings	Division	Shoot tip culture
Acanthus spp.	□		□	○	
Achillea spp. (Yarrow)	□	□		□	
Aconitum spp. (Monkshood)	□			○	
Aegopodium podagraria (Goutweed)			○	□	
Ajuga spp. (Bugleweed)		○		□	
Althaea rosea (Hollyhock)	□				
Anemone x hybrida (Japanese anemone)	○		□	○	
Anthemis tinctoria (Golden Marguerite)	○	□		□	
Aquilegia spp. (Columbine)	□				
Arabis spp. (Rock-cress)	□	○	○		
Armeria spp. (Sea pink)	□	□		□	
Artemisia spp. (Artemisia)		□		□	
Asarum europeaum (Ginger)	○			○	
Asclepias tuberosa (Butterfly weed)	○		○		
Asperula odorata (Woodruft)		□		○	
Aster spp. (Hardy aster)	○			□	○
Astilbe spp. (False spirea)	○			□	○
Aubrietia deltoides (Rock-cress)	□				
Aurinia spp. (Alyssum)	□	○			
Baptisia australis	□		□		
Bellis perennis (English daisy)	○				
Bergenia cordifolia (Bergenia)	□		□	○	○
Brunnera macrophylla (Siberian bugloss)	○	○	□		
Campanula carpatica (Carpathian harebell)	□	○			
Campanula medium (Canterbury bells)	□				
Catanache caerulea (Cupid's dart)	□			○	
Centaurea spp. (Cornflower)	□			○	
Cerastium tomentosum (Snow-in-summer)	□	○		○	
Ceratostigma plumbaginoides (Plumbago)		□		○	
Cheiranthus spp. (Wallflower)	□				
Chrysanthemum coccineum (Painted daisy)	□	○			○
C. x morifolium (Garden chrysanthemum)		□		○	
C. x superbum (Shasta daisy)	□			○	○
Convallaria majalis (Lily-of-the-valley)				□	
Coreopsis spp. (Coreopsis)	□	□		○	
Delphinium spp. (Larkspur)	□	○		○	

[a] Methods accented with squares are preferred commercial methods.

Name	Seed	Stem cutting	Root scuttings	Division	Shoot tip culture
Dianthus barbatus (Sweet William)	☐				
Dicentra spp. (Bleeding heart)	○	☐	○	○	
Dictamnus albus (Gas plant)	☐	○			
Digitalis purpurea (Foxglove)	☐				
Dodecatheon spp. (Shooting star)	☐			○	
Doronicum spp. (Doronicum)	☐			○	
Echinacea purpurea (Purple coneflower)	☐			☐	
Echinops exaltatus (Globe-thistle)	☐		○	○	
Echinops ritro (Small globe-thistle)	○		☐	○	
Erigeron spp. (Fleabane)	☐	○		○	
Eryngium spp. (Sea holly)	☐		○		
Euphorbia spp. (Spurge)	○	☐			
Filipendula spp. (Filipendula)	○		○	○	
Gaillardia x *grandiflora* (Blanket flower)	☐		○		
Gentiana spp. (Gentian)	☐				
Geranium spp. (Crane's bill)	☐	☐	○	○	
Geum spp. (Geum)	☐			○	
Gypsophila spp. (Baby's breath)	☐	○	☐		☐
Helenium spp. (Helen's flower)		☐		○	
Helianthemum spp. (Sun rose)		☐			
Heliopsis spp. (Heliopsis)			☐	○	
Helleborus spp. (Hellebore)	☐			○	
Hemerocallis (Daylily)	○			☐	☐
Heuchera spp. (Coral bells)	☐	☐		○	○
Hibiscus moscheutos (Hardy hibiscus)	○			○	
Hosta spp. (Plantain-lily)	○			☐	☐
Iberis spp. (Candytuft)	○	○			
Kniphofia uvaria (Red-hot-poker)	○			○	
Lamium maculatum (Dead nettle)		☐		○	
Lavandula angustifolia (Lavender)	☐	☐		○	
Liatris spp. (Blazing star)	☐			☐	
Limonium spp. (Hardy statice)	☐		○		
Linum perenne (Flax)	☐	○			
Lobelia spp. (Cardinal flower)	☐			○	
Lunaria annua (Moneyplant)	☐				
Lupinus spp. (Lupine)	☐	○			
Lychnis spp. (Maltese cross)	☐			○	
Lysimachia clethroides (Goose loosestrife)	○	☐			
Lythrum salicaria (Purple loosestrife)		☐			○
Matricaria spp. (Feverfew)	○	○		○	
Mentha spp. (Mint)		☐		○	
Mertensia virginica (Bluebells)	☐		☐	○	

Name	Seed	Stem cutting	Root scuttings	Division	Shoot tip culture
Monarda didyma (Beebalm)	○	□		○	
Myosotis spp. (Forget-me-not)		□		○	
Nepeta cataria (Catmint)		□		○	
Nepeta x *fussenii* (Catnip)		□			
Oenothera spp. (Evening primrose)	□				
Pachysandra terminalis (Pachysandra)		□			
Paeonia lactiflora (Herbaceous peony)			○	□	
Papaver orientale (Oriental poppy)	○		□	○	
Penstemon spp. (Beards tongue)	□	□		○	
Phlox paniculata (Summer phlox)		○	○	○	
Phlox subulata (Creeping phlox)		□		○	○
Physostegia virginiana (False dragonhead)	○	□		○	
Platycodon grandiflorum (Balloon flower)	□	○			
Polemonium coeruleum (Jacob's ladder)	□			○	
Polygonum cuspidatum (Mexican bamboo)			□		
Potentilla spp. (Cinquefoil)	□			○	
Pulmonaria spp. (Lungwort)	○		□	○	○
Pulsatilla vulgaris (Windflower)	□		○	○	
Rudbeckia spp. (Coneflower)	□		□	□	
Salvia spp. (Sage)	○	□		○	
Santolina spp. (Santolina)		□			
Saponaria ocymoides (Soapwort)	□	□	○	○	
Saxifraga spp. (Saxifrage)				□	
Scabiosa caucasia (Pincushion flower)	○	□		○	
Sedum spp. (Stonecrop)	○	□		○	
Sempervivum spp. (Hens and chicks)				□	
Solidago spp. (Goldenrod)		○		□	
Stachys lanata (Lamb's ear)				□	
Stokesia laevis (Stokes aster)	□		□	○	
Teucrium chamaedrys (Germander)		○		○	
Thalictrum aquilegifolium (Meadowrue)	□	○		○	
Thymus spp. (Thyme)		□		□	
Tradescantia x *andersoniana* (Spiderwort)		□		□	
Trollius spp. (Globe flower)	□		○		
Verbascum spp. (Mullein)	□		○		
Veronica spp. (Speedwell)	○	□		○	
Viola spp. (Violet)	□			○	
Waldsteinia ternata (Barren strawberry)		□		○	
Yucca filamentosa (Spanish bayonet)	□		□	○	

Lighting and photoperiod

Many perennials are sensitive to photoperiod and most benefit from the use of high intensity discharge (HID) lamps to accelerate seedling growth. Manufacturers can assist growers in choosing efficient HID lights, but lamp output of 25 watts per square foot (.09 m²) results in good seedling growth in most instances. Cool-white fluorescent lamps are most often used in germination chambers or in growth rooms. For photoperiod control (night-break), place 100 watt incandescent lamps 3 feet (.9 m) above the crop, on 3-foot centers.

Photoperiod is perhaps the most important environmental influence on floral initiation. Plants are categorized by their photoperiodic reaction; such as short day (SD), long day (LD), short day/long day (SDLD), long day/short day (LDSD) or day neutral (DN) (table 29.7). These terms refer to the day length or more correctly, the length of the dark period required for floral initiation.

Some plants, however, require one photoperiod for initiation and another for development to flowering. These are referred to as dual day length plants, such as the LDSD or SDLD types. If plants are unresponsive to any photoperiod, they are considered day neutral. Within each group, the response can be either qualitative or quantitative; and in some plants, photoperiodic requirements can be modified by temperature.

Many seed-propagated perennials are heterogeneous, and the critical photoperiod (and cool temperature) requirement for one plant may not be applicable to the whole population. For instance, Sheldron [3] found vast differences in a seedling population of Shasta daisy (*chrysanthemum* x *superbum*). From the cultivar G. Marconi five different photoperiod/chilling temperature types were identified. These clones reacted as follows:

Clone A   no vernalization, 14-hour photoperiod
Clone B   no vernalization, 18-hour photoperiod
Clone C   four weeks at 4.5 C (40 F) followed by 10-hour photoperiod
Clone D   eight weeks at 4.5 C (40 F) followed by 10-hour photoperiod
Clone E   12 weeks at 4.5 C (40 F) followed by 10-hour photoperiod

Similar differences, although not as dramatic, have been reported for *Campanula pyramidalis* and Goblin *Gaillardia aristata*. In Campanula seedling populations, Zimmer [5] found some seedlings require no chilling for flowering, while others require up to 15 weeks at 4 C (39 F) to complete vernalization.

Also, the ability to respond to the vernalization stimulus depended on seedling age. Among five-month old seedlings, only 30% bolted when vernalized, while 90% bolted when they were nine months old. In

Gaillardia, King [1] reported that from a seedling population, 30% flowered as annuals. In addition, he identified numerous differences in leaf shape, size, and color.

References

[1]   King, J. 1983. Evaluation of *Gaillardia aristata* 'Goblin' as a container-grown crop. Undergraduate research paper. The Pennsylvania State University
[2]   Rhodus, T. 1993. Views on management. *Perennial Plants* 1(3):26-34.
[3]   Shedron, K. 1980. Regulation of growth and flowering of four herbaceous perennials: *Aquilegia* x *hybrida* Sims, *Aurinia saxatilis* (L.) Desv., *Chrysanthemum* x *superbum* Bergmans, and *Lupinus* spp. Russell. Master's Thesis. Purdue University.
[4]   Voigt, A. 1991. Sales were strong for the 1990 bedding plant season, despite adverse weather—An increase of 6.4% expected. *PPGA News* 22(1):1-19.
[5]   Zimmer, K. 1983. *Campanula pyramidalis* IV: Cold requirement. *Gartenbauwissenschaft* 48(1):23-27.

CHAPTER 30

Bedding Plant Performance

Production and Postproduction Factors

Terril A. Nell, Ria T. Leonard, and James E. Barrett

Unlike many other floriculture crops, bedding plants are expected to do most of their growing and flowering after, rather than prior to, point of sale. High quality bedding plants are associated primarily with green leaf color, plant size, stage of flowering, and type and size of the container as well as overall appearance. Unless bedding plants perform satisfactorily in the landscape, however, grades and standards are of little value.

Successful postproduction performance depends on production practices, transport, and retail conditions, as well as continued sound maintenance practices if plants are to achieve optimal results. The large, diverse number of bedding plant genera, species, and varieties make it difficult to establish universal recommendations for this important floriculture segment. However, a number of principles can be used to assure that good quality plants are available for garden use. Armitage [2] has developed a comprehensive review of bedding plant longevity that should be considered by anyone involved in bedding plant production or handling.

Production factors

Fertilization

Fertilization practices during production have a significant influence on bedding plants' garden performance. Plants receiving high fertilizer levels often have large, dark green succulent leaves compared to plants receiving recommended fertilizer levels. Flowering may be delayed, and plants may be more sensitive to transport and retail conditions when they receive high fertilizer levels. Sensitivity to transport and retail stresses may result from high soluble salt levels in the growing medium or elemental toxicity in the leaves, leading to leaf yellowing or brown leaves in extreme cases. Soluble salt problems are exacerbated if plants dry out during transport or during the retail phase. Leaching prior to shipment may minimize soluble salt problems, but few growers find it convenient to leach plants prior to sale.

For some crops, proper fertilizer levels may be the most important factor affecting postproduction performance. For instance, potted mums grown with low fertilizer levels (150 parts per million N) lasted seven to 14 days longer than plants receiving high fertilizer levels (450 ppm N) at each watering [4]. Terminating fertilizer three weeks prior to flowering increased longevity of plants grown with high fertilizer levels. Similarly, foliage plant leaf drop is reduced significantly when plants are grown with low fertilizer levels or when fertilizer is terminated prior to transport.

Armitage [2] has shown that increasing fertilizer level during production decreased marigolds' survival in simulated retail conditions. However, bedding plants react differently to fertilizer termination, as demonstrated in a recently completed University of Florida postproduction study.

Geraniums, vinca, salvia, and impatiens were grown with 150 ppm N until flowering or fertilizer was terminated one, two, three, or four weeks prior to marketable stage (flowering). Plants were transplanted to outdoor beds and grown from six to 14 weeks. Geraniums were least affected by the fertilizer treatments.

At flowering, plants were slightly larger with increased fertilizer applications, but leaf color was not affected (table 30.1). After six weeks growth in landscape conditions, plant size was similar for all fertilizer treatments (table 30.1). The number of flowers produced was 31% higher in plants that received fertilizer until one or two weeks before planting outdoors. However, plants that were fertilized until one week of flowering or fertilized continuously produced more flowers in the landscape (table 30.1).

Among the other bedding plants evaluated, growth was reduced or plants were stunted when fertilizer was terminated for more than two weeks. Vinca plants overcame the effects of reduced fertilizer during production by the sixth week in ground beds (table 30.2). However, the injurious effects of terminating fertilizer three or four weeks before flowering lasted throughout the outdoor trial for salvia and impatiens (tables 30.3 and 30.4). Salvia plant dry weight was reduced 36%, and

TABLE 30.1

Fertilizer termination effects on Kim geranium postproduction performance

| Fertilizer termination prior to flowering | Days to flowering | Plant height (cm) | | Plant width [a] (cm) | | Plant size [b] (cm) | | Total number of flowered stalks | Plant dry weight [c] (g) |
		At flowering	After six weeks in landscape	At flowering	After six weeks in landscape	At flowering	After six weeks in landscape		
0 weeks	31	24.5	26.5	26.0	26.0	25.5	23.5	21	21.1
1	31	25.5	26.5	25.0	25.5	25.5	25.5	21	20.4
2	27	23.5	26.0	25.5	25.5	24.5	25.5	19	19.0
3	34	26.0	24.0	24.0	23.5	25.0	26.5	16	16.4

[a] Average of two width measurements per plant.

[b] Size = (width + flower height/2).

[c] Plant dry weight, excluding roots, after six weeks in landscape.

impatiens dry weight was reduced three to seven times when fertilizer was terminated four weeks before marketing.

These results demonstrate that bedding plant fertilizer can be terminated one to two weeks prior to marketing without affecting some plants' landscape performance. However, earlier termination may severely limit landscape growth on plants such as vinca, salvia, and impatiens.

TABLE 30.2

Fertilizer termination effects on Cooler Blush vinca postproduction performance

| Fertilizer termination prior to flowering | Plant height (cm) | | | Plant width (cm) [a] | | Plant size (cm) [b] | | Plant dry weight [c] (g) |
	At flowering	After six weeks in landscape	After 14 weeks in landscape	At flowering	After six weeks in landscape	At flowering	After six weeks in landscape	
0 weeks	14.0	32.0	53.0	17.5	41.5	15.5	36.5	117.5
1	13.5	31.5	50.0	17.5	37.0	15.5	34.0	76.0
2	14.0	31.5	50.5	17.0	38.0	15.5	35.0	97.5
3	12.5	29.0	46.5	17.0	32.0	15.0	30.5	41.5
4	11.0	29.5	47.5	15.0	33.5	13.0	31.5	80.5

[a] Average of two width measurements per plant. Unable to get accurate widths after six weeks in landscape.

[b] Size = (width + flower height/2).

[c] Plant dry weight, excluding roots, after 14 weeks in landscape.

TABLE 30.3

Fertilizer termination effects on salvia postproduction performance

Fertilizer termination prior to flowering	Plant height (cm)			Plant width [a] (cm)			Plant size [b] (cm)			Plant dry weigh[c] (g)	Total number of flowered stalks
	At flowering	After 6 weeks in landscape	After 14 weeks in landscape	At flowering	After 6 weeks in landscape	After 14 weeks in landscape	At flowering	After 6 weeks in landscape	After 14 weeks in landscape		
0 weeks	33.5	41.0	35.0	27.5	24.0	23.5	30.5	32.5	29.0	11.7	64
1	33.5	39.5	37.5	27.0	23.0	24.0	30.0	31.0	30.5	13.4	60
2	31.5	39.5	37.0	22.5	20.5	22.0	27.0	30.0	29.5	8.9	53
3	32.5	35.5	35.5	18.5	17.5	19.5	25.5	26.5	27.5	7.3	48
4	33.0	31.5	35.5	11.5	11.5	16.0	22.5	21.5	25.5	5.3	31

[a] Average of two width measurements per plant.

[b] Size = (width + flower height/2).

[c] Plant dry weight, excluding roots, after 14 weeks in landscape.

Based on results with other plants, growers should restrict ammonium to no more than 30% of the total nitrogen used on bedding plants. High ammonium levels can cause leaf yellowing and reduced growth of geraniums and other bedding plants. Also, high ammonium levels may increase the transport sensitivity and reduce bedding plants' landscape performance.

Irrigation practices

Wilting of bedding plants, often referred to as "toning," has been used by growers for many years to acclimatize plants for the transition from the greenhouse to the landscape. Eakes et al., [3] found that salvia adapted to water stress after four wilting periods, but results were related to potassium concentration. Using wilting to acclimatize plants must be done cautiously since soluble salts increase significantly in the growing medium with decreasing soil moisture. Also, vinca exhibits cultivar differences when wilting is used.

Transport conditions

When not produced locally, bedding plants must be transported to market. During transport, bedding plants can be affected by darkness, temperature, drying out, mechanical shaking (vibration), and ethylene. Extended transport periods are undesirable. Improper conditions during transport can cause leaf yellowing and drop, bud drop, flower shat-

TABLE 30.4

Fertilizer termination effects on Showstopper impatiens postproduction performance

Fertilizer termination prior to flowering	Plant height (cm)		Plant width [a] (cm)		Plant size [b] (cm)		Plant dry weight [c] (g)
	At flowering	After 6 weeks in landscape	At flowering	After 6 weeks in landscape	At flowering	After 6 weeks in landscape	
0 weeks	21.0	30.5	42.0	46.5	31.5	38.5	28.9
1	17.0	23.5	38.0	39.0	27.5	31.5	16.1
2	15.5	23.0	33.5	34.0	25.0	28.5	11.1
3	16.0	21.5	30.0	31.0	23.0	26.0	9.8
4	11.5	18.0	23.5	28.0	17.5	23.0	3.9

[a] Average of two width measurements per plant.

[b] Size = (width + flower height/2).

[c] Plant dry weight, excluding roots, after six weeks in landscape.

tering, or a plant's failure to grow vigorously in the landscape. Production conditions, such as overfertilization and excessive watering, can predispose plants to increased sensitivity and plant degradation during transport. Effects of transplant may not be evident until four to seven days after shipping.

Many transport problems can be eliminated or minimized by maintaining appropriate temperatures to reduce respiration and minimize harmful gases' effects. Many different kinds of bedding plants are generally transported on a single vehicle, and optimum transport temperatures for each type of plant cannot be maintained. So keep transport time as brief as possible.

Another problem associated with transporting bedding plants involves ethylene's damaging effects. Ethylene is a colorless, odorless gas that may cause bud drop, flower shattering, leaf drop, and leaf yellowing. Ethylene injury can be reduced by maintaining cool transport temperatures, but use of differential transport temperatures is not currently feasible.

Spraying plants with silver thiosulfate (STS), an ethylene inhibitor, reduced flower shattering and leaf yellowing in geraniums and may be beneficial on other bedding plants. However, STS is not labeled by the Environmental Protection Agency for this purpose, and local water ordinances may limit disposal of heavy metals, such as silver. Other non-silver ethylene inhibitors are being evaluated for use in preventing ethylene injury.

Retail conditions

Ideal retail settings offer bedding plants moderate light and cool temperatures with no drying out. However, many bedding plants offered for sale suffer from bright light, high temperatures, and frequently wilt prior to watering. Bedding plants subjected to these conditions can deteriorate rapidly, resulting in leaf damage, bud drop, stunting, and ultimately may fail to grow in the landscape. Retailers should provide both a pleasing display and an environment that prolongs plants' longevity and promotes continued growth after transplant.

A common problem, particularly in mass market outlets, is allowing plants to dry out and wilt before watering. Plants grown in larger containers are less likely to wilt, since they have a larger water reservoir. Sales personnel should be trained to water plants properly, and sufficient staff should be available to assist customers as well as maintain the plants during busy periods. While growers can acclimatize plants for retail markets and landscape conditions, no procedures or products have been developed that significantly reduce the time between waterings for plants on display.

Many research projects have investigated the use of water absorbing gels and antitranspirants. In theory, gels wer designed to be incorporated into the growing medium, increasing the amount of water available to the plant and delaying the time between waterings during retail display. In practice, however, enhanced availability of water has not been demonstrated consistently across a variety of growing media, fertilization practices, water sources, or a large assortment of plants.

Anti-transpirants are sprayed onto plants to close stomates and reduce moisture loss. In some cases, water loss has been reduced 20% to 30%, but the delay is not sufficient to justify the materials' expense. Using a wetting agent several days prior to marketing has proved equal to using gels or anti-transpirants, due to increased uniformity in wetting the medium.

Consumer care

The finest, freshest, and highest quality bedding plants must be properly cared for in the garden, or performance will be less than satisfactory. Growers and retailers should provide care tags on every plant sold. Sales staffs should tell customers how plants should be fertilized and watered in that area.

Most universities have bulletins outlining bedding plant care and handling procedures for consumers. Innovative garden centers and mass markets are providing free educational programs for consumers about bedding plant use and maintenance. Some retailers use point-of-purchase videos to educate customers.

Proper watering practices are essential. Consumers and commercial landscapers need to realize that lawn sprinklers may not deliver sufficient water to moisten the small bedding plant root area adequately for the first few weeks after transplant. Hand-watering directed at the root area is often necessary at first. Otherwise, plants may experience periodic wilting that limits growth and flowering. Incorporating peat moss into the growing area will increase the soil's moisture-holding ability in most cases and adding mulch to the planted bed will minimize water loss from the soil surface.

Bedding plants add color to residential and commercial landscapes and can offer a rewarding gardening experience to consumers. Properly produced, transported, marketed and maintained, bedding plants provide sufficient enjoyment to bring consumers back each season for the newest plants for their landscapes.

References

[1]   Argo, W.R., and J.A. Biernbaum. 1990. *Factors affecting garden performance of flowering plants in hanging baskets.* Research Report F-061. Bedding Plants Foundation, Inc. Lansing, Mich.

[2]   Armitage, A. 1993. *Bedding plants, prolonging shelf performance.* Batavia, Ill.: Ball Publishing.

[3]   Eakes, D.J., R.D. Wright, and J.R. Seiler. 1991. Water relations of *Salvia splendens* 'Bonfire' as influenced by potassium nutrition and moisture stress conditioning. *J. Amer. Soc. Hort. Sci.* 116:712-715.

[4]   Nell, T.A. 1991. How to make long-lasting, top performers out of your pot mums. *GrowerTalks* 54(9):67-80.

[5]   Virk, S.S., and O.S. Singh. 1990. Osmotic properties of drought stressed periwinkle (*Catharanthus roseus*) genotypes. *Annals of Botany.* 66:23-30.

CHAPTER 31

Breeding Improved Cultivars

Richard Craig

The modern bedding plant industry is approaching its first half-century of existence and, by all measures, it represents the greatest revolution in commercial horticulture's history. Bedding plants include plants for gardens, hanging baskets, window boxes, and specimen planters. Bedding plants can be flowers, vegetables, herbs, and small fruits.

Bedding plants are propagated by seeds or through various asexual methods. Bedding plant producers range from part-time local retail growers to large corporate interstate enterprises.

There are many reasons for the the bedding plant industry's commercial success, but the premier reason is supply and demand, where the grower has been able to supply high quality products through an organized marketing structure to consumers who have an insatiable demand for beauty.

If we focus on the equation's supply side, we see that growers have been well served by both academic and industry researchers and information transfer specialists (extension specialists, technical advisors, salespersons, etc.), as well as an aggressive trade press and trade organizations, which have provided significant benefits to the whole industry. Important discoveries related to bedding plants' growth and flowering as affected by irrigation, fertilization, growth regulators, environmental factors, and innovative production containers—cell paks to plug trays—have provided the technological advancements that have spurred industry growth. Technology, when coupled with advanced marketing systems, has provided high quality products to consumers at appropriate costs.

On the demand side, observe the significant effects of All-America Selections, Fleuroselect, All-Britain Trials, and Florastar on consumer bedding plant education. Professional Plant Growers Association (formerly Bedding Plants Inc.) and the Garden Writers Association have

TABLE 31.1

Steps for successful cultivar development

VISION: Ideal profile development
- Most important phase of a plant breeding program.
- Requires collaboration among breeders, propagators, producers, marketers, and consumers.
- A profile or list of criteria is developed to describe the envisioned cultivar.
- All progress in the breeding program is measured in comparison to the profile.

VARIABILITY: Germplasm/gene collection
- Usually a collection of cultivars and species of the genus.
- Can be living plants, seeds, or tissue culture.
- Collecting the genes (genetic variability) that are used in the breeding program.
- Additional variation may be created through directed mutations.

BREEDING TECHNOLOGIES: Production of progeny
- Sports or mutation breeding.
- Pollination protocols: selection and/or hybridization.
- Biotechnological protocols: transformation, somaclonal variation, somatic hybridization.

SELECTION PRESSURE: Genetic expression
- The unique environmental and cultural conditions the progeny will be grown in which to express the envisioned traits.

EVALUATION PROTOCOLS: Discernment of phenotypes
Discerning phenotypes is based on genes expressed at various levels:
- Visual
- Anatomical
- Biochemical
- Molecular
- Morphological
- Physiological
- Enzymatic
- DNA

COMMERCIALIZATION
- Clean stock: propagules that are disease- and insect-free.
- Intellectual property protection: plant patents, plant variety protection certificates, utility patents or trade secrets.
- National competitive trials: All-America Selections, Fleuroselect, Florastar.
- Distribution: wholesale and retail channels.
- Marketing: creating a market for your new product.

---

had a substantial impact on marketing new products to consumers; however, marketing alone cannot be successful if quality products are not available. Improvements in bedding plant quality would not have been possible without the development of new cultivars, which is the point of this chapter.

Breeding is an art, science, industry

Improved cultivars are the products of innovative plant breeding research programs. Plant breeding is an art, a science, and an industry. Art involves the ability to envision improved cultivars and to utilize various protocols for their development. The science of plant breeding is primarily genetics; however, many other sciences are critical to the success of breeding programs—statistics, physiology, plant pathology, botany, biochemistry, entomology, and engineering.

Modern breeding programs also are strongly impacted by computer science and information technologies. It is important to note that many bedding plants—zinnias, geraniums, marigolds, petunias, and snap-dragons—have been scientifically investigated by academic researchers. Much of this information—botanical, genetic, cytological, and physiological—has been useful in applied breeding programs.

Professional plant breeders develop the majority of new bedding plant cultivars and are employed by seed companies or by commercial propagators. These organizations are located throughout the world but are more often found in Western Europe, Japan, or the United States. Many of the corporations are international, so the breeding/research responsibilities may be a division of a larger organization. Also, some cultivar development is conducted at public—state or federal—institutions; often academic institutions are responsible for the initial new crop introduction. Examples are the Catharanthus program at the University of Connecticut and the Pelargonium program at The Pennsylvania State University. Academic institutions are primarily responsible for training plant breeders and for research projects.

Developing improved bedding plant cultivars results from planned breeding programs; these programs require substantial funding over a long period of time. There are six steps involved in every successful breeding program: vision, variability, breeding technologies, selection pressure, evaluation, and commercialization. Each step is summarized in table 31.1 and each will be discussed in detail.

Developing successful cultivars

Vision

A breeding program's most important phase is envisioning the traits that will characterize an improved cultivar. These traits can be listed in general terms, but ultimately they must be developed very specifically. The term "profile" could be used to describe the ideal traits required in a specific new cultivar. The more specific the profile, the better the chance of developing a specific cultivar (table 31.2).

General traits for a bedding plant cultivar are:
1. Efficient source of high quality, uniform propagules—seeds, plugs, and/or cuttings
2. Cultural requirements that coincide with other bedding plant species
3. Ability to be produced in an efficient time from plugs or seedlings
4. Availability of an efficient height control and branching method—genetic, chemical, or environmental
5. Limited disease/insect/mite problems and physiological disorders
6. Ability to withstand hardening stress
7. Ability of finished plants to be shipped long distances

TABLE 31.2

A profile, including specific traits, for _Petunia hybrida_

Objective: To develop an improved F$_1$ hybrid multiflora, royal-blue-flowered petunia with Botrytis resistance under field conditions.

TRAIT	CRITERIA
A. Aesthetic qualities:	
Flower color	Cobalt Blue (HCC44, RHSCC 101A)
Flower type	Single
Flowering class	Multiflora
Flower size	5.5 cm
B. Propagation: high seed germination potential; especially for plug production	
C. Pack performance:	
Growth habit	Compact (10 cm x 10 cm x 10 cm at six weeks after transplant) Self-branching
Flowering time	First flower at 30 days after transplant; uniform flowering—75% of plants in flower at 40 days after transplant
Host plant resistance	Botrytis resistant under production conditions
D. Shipping	Ability to be stored in a warehouse for 12 hours, shipped via truck for 24 hours, restored in a warehouse for 12 hours and transshipped to market
E. Shelf life	Ability to be maintained with minimum care in a market environment for four days
F. Garden performance:	
Stress tolerance	Ability to reflower after a significant rainfall Resistance to _Botrytis cinerea_ greater than some standard cultivar
Heat tolerance	Ability to withstand 10 consecutive days above 95 F
Drought tolerance	Ability to withstand 21 days without irrigation at 75 F

8. Ability to tolerate marketing stresses
9. Garden performance

Our vision of specific traits could be affected by several factors:

1. Is this the first cultivar of a species (new crop) or the first of a new series (such as dwarf)? If so, color and other traits may not be critical.
2. Is this cultivar being developed to complement a series already on the market? Some traits must then be similar to match the series.
3. Is this cultivar a replacement for an existing cultivar—yours or your competitors'? Is the replacement an improvement, or is it simply to fill a product line?

For all F$_1$ hybrid cultivars, it is assumed that the proper inbred (parent) lines are available, that the seed parent is capable of profitable seed production, that some pollen control mechanism is available, and that the pollen parent produces an adequate amount of viable pollen. It is crucial that F$_1$ hybrid seed can be efficiently produced.

Variability

Variability in a narrow sense refers to the collection of genes, usually in the form of a plant collection—called germplasm—that is used in cultivar development programs. Germplasm is the raw material from which plant breeders create new cultivars. Plant breeding is essentially the manipulation of genes and their deliberate assemblage into improved cultivars. I wish to take a broad view of genetic variability because we are describing a myriad of plant genera and species. Two issues are critical. One is the collection and long-term storage of germplasm collections of species that represent the major bedding plant types. The second is protecting natural environments from which new bedding plants may emerge in the future.

To obtain new germplasm, there are several important factors: identification, collection, and maintenance of clean stock of species, cultivars, and breeding lines of bedding plants. A United States Department of Agriculture sponsored committee—The Herbaceous Ornamental Crop Advisory Committee—has determined priorities for collecting and preserving floricultural genera, which includes bedding plants. Several of their priorities are begonia, impatiens, petunia, zinnia, ageratum, catharanthus, verbena, pelargonium, and dianthus.

Seed storage is well-organized by the National Seed Laboratory at Fort Collins, Colorado. Maintenance of asexually propagated plant material collections is more problematic and needs attention. Of course, this implies that there are specimens to be collected in the wild. Again, this area is of great concern in many developing countries for two reasons: destruction of natural forests and landscapes, and political policies that inhibit germplasm exchange.

Genetic variability is a difficult concept with respect to bedding plants. First, bedding plants are diverse in their botanical origins. Plant families, represented by commercial bedding plants, are outlined in table 31.3; you can see that botanical diversity abounds. Within plant families only a relatively few genera and even fewer species of each genus have been developed into commercial bedding plants.

Adri van der Walt states that of the over 250 species of pelargonium, only three to five have been improved as commercial plants—bedding and pot geraniums, ivy geraniums, regal pelargoniums, and a few major scented species for oil and horticultural uses. Much potential variability has never been utilized even when available in plant collections.

Several interesting vignettes illustrate the germplasm issues. Geraniums are mostly native to South Africa; parental species were collected and transported to Europe by the Dutch East India Company as early as the 1600s. The germplasm (genes) transfer has never ceased, and it is this genetic variability that is used today to improve geranium cultivars.

Australia New Guinea impatiens are relatively recent, having been collected by a Longwood Gardens/USDA-sponsored plant exploration team in 1970. The discovery was serendipitous—impatiens were not among the taxa expected to be collected. (Information provided by H.F. Winters, USDA, and R.J. Armstrong, Longwood Gardens.) In less than

TABLE 31.3

Bedding plants by botanical family and cultivar propagation method

Species	Seed propagated				Asexually propagated
	Inbred	F$_1$	F$_2$	Mixture	
Ageratum (Asteraceae)	✓	✓			✓
Alyssum (Brassicaceae)	✓			✓	
Aster (Asteraceae)	✓			✓	
Balsam (Balsaminaceae)	✓			✓	
Begonia (Begoniaceae)	✓	✓		✓	✓
Brachycome (Asteraceae)	✓			✓	
Browallia (Solanaceae)	✓			✓	
Calceolaria (Scrophulariaceae)	✓	✓	✓	✓	
Calendula (Asteraceae)	✓			✓	
Carnation (Caryophyllaceae)	✓	✓		✓	
Celosia (Amaranthaceae)	✓			✓	
Chrysanthemum (Dendranthema) (Asteraceae)		✓		✓	✓
Cleome (Capparaceae)	✓			✓	
Coleus (Lamiaceae)	✓			✓	✓
Cosmos (Asteraceae)	✓			✓	
Dahlia (Asteraceae)				✓	✓
Dianthus (Caryophyllaceae)	✓	✓		✓	
Digitalis (Scrophulariaceae)				✓	
Dusty miller (Senecio) (Asteraceae)		✓			
Eustoma (Lisianthus) (Gentianaceae)		✓		✓	
Fuchsia (Onagraceae)				✓	✓
Gazania (Asteraceae)	✓	✓		✓	
Geranium (Pelargonium) (Geraniaceae)		✓	✓	✓	✓
Gerbera (Asteraceae)	✓	✓		✓	✓
Gomphrena (Amaranthaceae)	✓			✓	
Gypsophila (Caryophyllaceae)	✓				✓
Helichrysum (Asteraceae)	✓			✓	
Heliotrope (Heliotropium) (Boraginaceae)	✓				
Iberis (Candytuft) (Brassicaceae)	✓			✓	
Impatiens (Balsaminaceae)	✓	✓	✓	✓	✓
Kochia (Chenopodiaceae)	✓				
Lantana (Verbenaceae)					✓
Larkspur (Delphinium) (Ranunculaceae)	✓			✓	
Lobelia (Lobeliaceae) (annual)	✓			✓	
Marigold (Tagetes) (Asteraceae)	✓	✓		✓	
Melampodium (Asteraceae)	✓				
Mimulus (Scrophulariaceae)	✓	✓		✓	
Morning glory (Ipomoea) (Convolvulaceae)	✓			✓	
Nasturtium (Brassicaceae)	✓			✓	
Nemesia (Scrophulariaceae)	✓			✓	✓
New Guinea impatiens	✓	✓		✓	✓
Nicotiana (Solanaceae)		✓			
Ornamental pepper (Capsicum) (Solanaceae)	✓	✓			
Pansy (Viola) (Violaceae)	✓	✓	✓		
Petunia (Solanaceae)		✓	✓	✓	
Phlox (Polemoniaceae)	✓			✓	
Poppy (Papaver) (Papaveraceae)	✓	✓		✓	✓
Portulaca (Portulacaceae)	✓	✓	✓	✓	
Salpiglossis (Solanaceae)		✓		✓	
Salvia (Labiatae/Lamiaceae)	✓	✓			
Sanvitalia (Asteraceae)	✓				
Scabiosa (Dipsacaceae)	✓			✓	
Snapdragon (Antirrhinum) (Scrophulariaceae)		✓	✓	✓	
Statice (Limonium) (Plumbaginaceae)	✓			✓	✓

| Species | Seed propagated | | | | Asexually propagated |
	Inbred	F_1	F_2	Mixture	
Stocks (Matthiola) (Brassicaceae)	✓			✓	
Sweet pea (Lathyrus) (Fabaceae)	✓			✓	
Thunbergia (Acanthaceae)	✓			✓	
Torenia (Scrophulariaceae)	✓				
Verbena (Verbenaceae)	✓			✓	
Vinca (Catharanthus) (Apocynaceae)	✓			✓	
Zinnia (Asteraceae)	✓	✓		✓	

20 years, this crop has become immensely popular among growers and consumers.

A third interesting story involves eustoma or lisianthus. A native American plant growing wild in the U.S. Great Plains, eustoma was introduced into Europe in about 1835 and was listed in the export catalog of T. Sakata and Company in 1934. Following decades of culture and breeding in Japan, Sakata introduced the first F_1 hybrids, the Yodel series, to the U.S. market in the early 1980s.

Breeding technologies

A breeding program is a strategic plan for developing a new cultivar. Breeding technologies are specific protocols resulting in the production of progeny that are evaluated within the breeding program.

Breeding programs can include multiple technologies. Such programs are often dependent on whether the species is naturally self- or cross-pollinated. One example of a breeding technology to develop improved bedding plants is F_1 hybridization. This technology requires developing two specific parental lines that, when cross-pollinated, will produce an acceptable F_1 hybrid. In truth, many inbred lines and many test F_1 hybrids are evaluated in most breeding programs. In this example, the breeding technologies are self- and cross-pollination. Selection is also critical and can be based either on mass selection or pedigree selection strategies. In mass selection, progeny in various generations are bulked and not identified. In pedigree selection, seed from individual plants are maintained as separate breeding units.

Other breeding technologies that are used include backcross breeding, where a single trait is incorporated from a nonrecurrent (donor) parent into an otherwise acceptable line or cultivar (recurrent parent) through pollination techniques. The same result could be accomplished through gene insertion or transformation techniques.

One should view plant breeding technologies as a selection of tools that are utilized in developing improved cultivars. In other words, technologies are protocols that allow breeders to manipulate genes (variability) that condition envisioned traits into commercially acceptable progeny.

Broadly, the technologies can be segmented as classical versus biotechnological. Biotechnology can infer only molecular genetic manipulation or can also include other tissue-culture-based protocols. Classical technologies include selection, pollination techniques including hybridization, mutation breeding, and manipulation of ploidy levels. Biotechnology includes genetic transformation, somatic hybridization (protoplast fusion), antisense technology, and somaclonal variation.

Associated techniques, such as apomixis, embryo rescue, somatic embryogenesis, and anther/ovule culture, can be used in concert with both classical and biotechnological approaches. All of these technologies, whether used alone or in combinations, have one final objective—the production of progeny.

Classical breeding technologies

Selection. This is the earliest breeding method. Essentially it involves selecting acceptable progeny (positive selection) from a population and using the selection(s) as a cultivar or for breeding purposes. Conversely, negative selection would mean roguing undesirable plants from a cultivar and not allowing these plants to be used for either propagation or breeding purposes. In our petunia example, selection is practiced in every generation for those traits included in the specific profile, i.e., blue flower color, compact, multiflora, etc.

Pollination techniques. Only two types of pollinations are possible: self-pollination, which also includes sib (sister/brother) mating; and cross-pollination (hybridization). Self-pollination results when the pollen and seed parents are identical—either the same plant or clonal/inbred propagules of a single genotype. Cross pollinations that result in hybrid progeny imply that the pollen and egg parents are genetically different. The term hybrid may be used to identify any progeny resulting from cross-pollination; however, F_1 hybrid is the term reserved for a cross of two true-breeding or inbred lines.

Most breeding programs combine self- and cross-pollinations; however, many species of naturally cross-pollinated plants exhibit mild to severe inbreeding depression when self-pollinated. This is usually expressed as reduced vigor or reduced fertility among self-pollinated progeny. Initial or continued self-pollination is difficult, if not impossible, for these species.

Factors that limit self-pollination are self-incompatibility, pollen or egg sterility, dioecy, and various forms of functional sterility such as an extremely double flower, differential timing of anthesis and stigma receptivity, etc. When self-pollination is possible, it leads to homozygosity (genotypic uniformity) and homogeneity (phenotypic uniformity) of the resulting progeny.

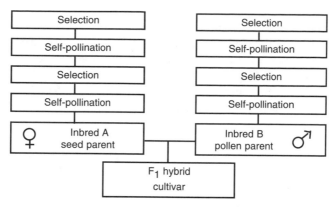

Fig. 31.1. F_1 hybrid cultivar resulting from two inbred lines.

Self-pollination is requisite for the production of F_1 hybrid parents. Also, many cultivars result from controlled self-pollination, which is accomplished usually by natural self-pollination or open pollinations in an isolated (from other pollen sources) environment.

Hybridization greatly benefits plant breeding because it allows for recombining genes from two sources. Since F_1 hybrids are so important among bedding plant cultivars, hybridization is actually the technology of choice. Hybridization also can result in two associated benefits. First, in many crops, hybridization results in heterosis (hybrid vigor), a condition where the hybrid/F_1 hybrid is superior to both of its parents for general or specific traits. Second, F_1 hybridization results in unique intellectual property protection termed trade secret. Plant breeders maintain complete control of F_1 hybrids as long as they have exclusive control of the parental inbreds.

Example: our petunia cultivar is an F_1 hybrid; it therefore must result from two inbred lines. Each contributes traits to the F_1 hybrid. In addition, we might expect the F_1 to display hybrid vigor (fig. 31.1).

Mutation breeding. This is often used for improving asexually reproduced plants. Mutagens can be either radiation- or chemical-based. The most often used radiation mutagens are acute doses of gamma and x-rays; however, other classes have been used under research conditions.

When treating plant material—seeds, seedlings, cuttings, bulbs, tissue culture, pollen, etc.—with gamma or x-rays, both the total dose and the dose per minute are important factors. The goal of mutation breeding is to create useful mutations and to maintain some degree of egg and pollen fertility.

Ploidy manipulation. The general chromosome condition for non-gametic (somatic) cells of most plants is diploidy (one pair of each chromosome that is characteristic of the species). Diploids are usually effectively and efficiently used in cultivar development programs.

However, some bedding plant species (zonal geraniums—especially those that are asexually propagated) are polyploids—that is, they have more chromosomes than usual. The most frequent condition is tetraploidy, where four (two pairs) of each chromosome exist in each somatic cell.

Tetraploidy usually results in a plant having enhanced size of various organs (thicker leaves, larger flowers, etc.), but often it is also associated with reduced fertility. It should be noted that other ploidy conditions exist within cultivated plants. Increases in ploidy levels occur spontaneously. For example, the first tetraploid geranium was observed ca. 1880 in France and led to many of the asexually propagated cultivars available today.

Increases in ploidy level can also be induced. The normal method of inducing polyploidy is by using the chemical colchicine. Colchicine causes the chromosome number of treated cells to double. In a breeding program, ploidy reduction (complement reduction) is sometimes utilized, usually through producing progeny from anthers (pollen) in tissue culture.

Biotechnological breeding technologies

Biotechnological protocols are usually performed using tissue culture. One prerequisite for using these procedures is that cells, organs, and/or tissues of a given species must be able to be grown in artificial culture. More specifically, single cells are often required that ultimately can be regenerated into a whole plant.

An excellent review of recent advances in flower crops is presented by Dr. Robert Griesbach [3]. He notes that protoplasts of 18 flower crop genera, including several important bedding plants such as snapdragons, geranium, and petunias, have been regenerated into whole plants.

Protocols classified under biotechnology include recombinant DNA technologies (molecular genetics). Genes are borne linearly on chromosomes, a unique DNA sequence. Since genes are unique, they can be isolated from chromosomes and are virtually interchangeable among organisms. Genes can be cloned to produce millions of copies. When genes are physically inserted into an alien organism, this is called transformation. When an inserted gene produces an effect in the new plant, it is called expression. Transformation is valuable for adding one or more genes to a plant that is commercially acceptable, except for the trait(s) conditioned by the gene(s) in question. See Moe, et. al., [5] for a review of molecular flower breeding [5].

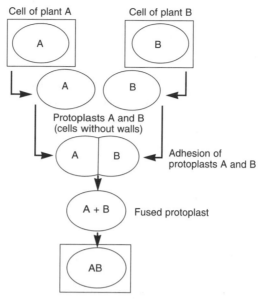

Fig. 31.2. An example of protoplast fusion.

Somatic hybridization (Protoplast fusion). To combine the chromosomes and/or cytoplasm of two disparate organisms, take protoplasts (cells without cell walls) of each organism and place them in an environment where they can fuse into one unit. In this way all of the two organisms' genes would now exist in a single organism (fig. 31.2).

The final step would be to generate a cell wall around this new product and to cause the fused cell to form a complete organism. Petunia has been the model plant for much of the research on somatic hybrids. Although this appeared to be a promising breeding technology, its practical use has been very limited to date.

Somaclonal variation. Often cells cultured on artificial media mutate at an enhanced frequency. The word somaclonal is derived from "soma" = somatic cells, such as those from leaves, and "clonal" = from clonal or asexual propagation. A somaclonal variant would be a cell, or its tissue, or the derived whole plant that is a variant (mutant) of the original cell, tissue, or plant. Somaclonal variants may vary in flower color, plant form, fertility, disease resistance, or any other trait.

Why cells in culture have an enhanced mutation rate is not known. The number of mutation events is increased in proportion to the number of progeny observed, and we can grow thousands of progeny (cells) in a single Petri dish or flask. We cannot yet direct specific mutations;

however, by clever screening (selection) strategies, we can increase the opportunity to detect specific mutations.

Associated technologies

Apomixis. While not a breeding technology, apomixis can be important in an overall cultivar development program. Apomixis, or the production of seed entirely of maternal origin, is essentially cloning through "artificial" seed produced on whole plants in a similar manner to normal seed production. Certain plants, such as bluegrass cultivars and some citrus, are propagated in this way. Researchers know there is a genetic basis for apomixis; however, they have not yet discovered the mechanism controlling apomixis. If the production of apomictic seed could be controlled, virtually any plant could be cloned through seed and grown efficiently through plug culture.

Embryo/ovule rescue. Many times during classical breeding protocols, certain desired cross-pollinations (especially hybridizations between different species) can be made; however, no seed are developed due to abortion of the developing embryo. Embryo rescue is a term that describes the removal of the fertilized embryo from the plant while it is still viable and the culture of that embryo into a whole plant in a tissue culture environment. At times, only the embryo is cultured; at other times the ovule containing the embryo is removed and placed into culture.

Anther/ovule culture. While embryo/ovule rescue infers rescuing and culturing individual progeny from a self- or cross-pollination, anther/ovule culture infers developing whole plants or viable tissues from gametes—pollen or eggs. In this sense, its use in plant breeding is more narrowly delimited so that reducing chromosome number is usually the objective. Note that chromosome number can be subsequently restored by the use of colchicine.

Somatic embryogenesis. Embryo production from somatic tissue such as leaves, petals, stems, roots—virtually all plant tissues except pollen and eggs—is termed somatic embryogenesis. Scientists have observed the production of somatic embryos in many flower crops. An exciting series of papers resulted from research conducted at the University of Guelph in Ontario, Canada (Marsolais et al, [4]; Slimmon et al., [6]; Wilson, [7]). The result is the production of "artificial seeds" without seed coats.

Scientists have managed to desiccate the embryos (it is expected that artificial seed coats can be applied), germinate them efficiently, and produce whole plants. Somatic embryogenesis is under strict genetic control since major differences exist among cultivars of a single species; thus, incorporating this trait into desirable cultivars will be accomplished in the future. One major constraint to this technology's broad utilization will be the requirement for genetic uniformity among the somatic embryo-generated progeny.

Selection pressure

Once progeny have been developed in sufficient numbers, they must be grown and evaluated under specific conditions termed "selection pressure". This is the pressure—environmental, pathological or cultural—to which a progeny population is subjected during the evaluation/selection process. Examples would be low temperature, absence of chemical growth regulators, *Botrytis cinerea*, mites, low fertility, heat stress, simulated consumer environment, garden conditions, etc.

This is a critical phase of every cultivar development program. A well-planned selection pressure can greatly increase the effectiveness and efficiency of the total plant improvement (cultivar development) effort. In simple words, selection pressure is the "environment" that will allow us to accurately identify the unique combination of genes as embodied in a whole plant (genotype) that we envisioned in our profile for the specific cultivar.

It is obvious that for the same group of progeny, multiple environments may be experienced during a crop's various phases of growth: propagation, plug stage, greenhouse/pack trials, marketing, and garden environments. It is the composite environment—propagation to garden—that constitutes the selection pressure. Within this composite, many climatic, cultural, and other factors must be included. In addition, for biotechnological protocols, selection pressures may be imposed in a Petri dish or flask.

Evaluation protocols

Once progeny are subjected to the unique selection pressure, each plant must be evaluated and either retained or discarded from the breeding program. Plants that are retained—"selections"—can be used as a new cultivar and/or for further breeding purposes. Perhaps the best benchmark that can be used in a breeding program is comparison to cultivars that are currently available. Plants of standard cultivars are usually included in a plant breeding trial. It is important that these controls be treated exactly like the breeding plants. When breeding for plant quality, such head-to-head comparisons are particularly effective.

By referring to the profiled petunia, you can see the traits that are of primary interest to a plant breeder. Now, how and when does the plant breeder evaluate the various traits? Evaluation methods can include visual assessment of traits, anatomical or morphological determinations, biochemical or physiological protocols, or even DNA/RNA fingerprints.

An example that illustrates the various levels of phenotypic evaluation would be floral color. In the petunia example, we selected a blue color, referenced as Royal Horticultural Society Color Chart 101A (Cobalt Blue, HCC44 under an older system). Visually, you could compare the flower of each progeny to the color chart and select progeny that match the profile.

At a biochemical level, you might be able to determine that cobalt blue results when the floral tissue contains a specific concentration of one or more anthocyanin pigments such as delphinidin, petunidin, etc. So you could assay flowers from each progeny with a High Pressure Liquid Chromatograph and match biochemical concentrations with a desired profile.

Environmental variation could certainly affect both of the evaluation methods. A method that is both environmentally insensitive and age-of-tissue insensitive is to determine if the gene(s) conditioning cobalt blue/specific pigment concentrations exist(s) in a particular progeny. A DNA fingerprint could be used. Since DNA is the same in every cell and at all ages of the plant, such an assay could be conducted on seedlings prior to flowering; thus, selection could be accomplished on thousands of progeny grown in a relatively small space.

A second example would be resistance to *Botrytis cinerea*. Here the selection pressure could be controlled inoculation of progeny with Botrytis spores under standardized conditions. You could visually evaluate each progeny for resistance/susceptibility, based on the signs or symptoms (presence and/or intensity) of disease. However, if you could determine the resistance mechanism—for example, cuticle thickness—then progeny could be evaluated for resistance vicariously by measuring cuticle thickness. Of course, you could proceed all the way to the DNA fingerprint for this trait, also.

It is possible to devise some very creative methods to evaluate certain traits that might add to the effectiveness and efficiency of a cultivar development program.

Often we picture the plant breeder with a large notebook diligently collecting data on the progeny from his/her breeding research. This is certainly one method to record results. Other methods include photo-documentation—still and video, audio tape recordings, environmental sensors with data loggers, and more recently, bar code instruments and computers. Computers will be used more in the future, especially when voice input is perfected and available at an affordable price.

To experienced plant breeders who evaluate progeny in the greenhouse or trial garden, the mention of standardization is unnecessary. However, the inherent value of experimental design and statistics is often overlooked; "if you can't see it, it isn't important." The proper use of statistics can improve the efficiency, the economics, the effectiveness, and the overall integrity of breeding evaluations.

Commercialization

Nothing is accomplished in a cultivar development program until the improved cultivar is available to the grower, marketer, and consumer. Commercialization involves a series of steps that must occur after a new cultivar is developed (fig. 31.3):

1. Intellectual property protection; select and trademark name
2. Regional cultural/marketing trials
3. Establishing clean stock
4. Propagating new cultivar
5. Marketing propagules
6. Distributing propagules
7. Commercial production

Intellectual property protection. Intellectual property protection to most growers means patents; however, only asexually propagated cultivars are protected by plant patents. Plant patents are only one method of protecting the products of plant breeders. A full review of this topic is available in the July/Sept. 1993 issue of *HortTechnology* [2].

Products of a plant breeding program are in a sense horticultural inventions. They have resulted from expensive and time consuming breeding programs. Some "sports" or simple mutations result almost serendipitiously and involve minimal cost—these also are protectable. In order to recover costs invested in a breeding/research program, you may obtain various types of legal protection (intellectual property rights) and limit the use, sales, or propagation of a protected cultivar to those people who are willing to pay a royalty.

Three types of protection are currently used for bedding plants: asexually propagated plants may be protected with plant patents; seed produced inbred cultivars may be protected with Plant Variety Protection (PVP) legislation; and F_1 hybrids are protected as Trade Secrets (if the parents are kept secret, then no one else can produce the unique F_1 plant) (fig. 31.4). Royalties are specifically attached to plant patents; however, assessments are applicable any time that there is an effective legal monopoly on a cultivar. At the present time it is possible to protect any cultivar—regardless of propagation method and type of product—with a utility patent (Sec. 101 patent).

One of the more interesting parts of developing a new cultivar is in naming the plant. Often a name does not become part of a patent or PVP certificate since a time limitation (17 years) applies; usually the official document includes a working name. The commercial name is usually protected by registering it as a trademark or by copyrighting.

Develop new
cultivar

Protect/
name

Used by
consumer

Regional
trials

Production **Commercialization
of improved cultivars**

Clean stock

Distribution

Propagate

Marketing

Fig. 31.3. Necessary steps in new cultivar development.

There are no time limitations for such marks/names, thus they can out-live the limitations of patent or PVP certificate protection.

The name can be almost anything; however, there are rules that theoretically apply [1]. Also, for many species there are official regis-tration groups that have some status. It is important to follow the rules and to prevent the use of duplicate, misleading, or previously registered names. Gertrude Stein said "A rose is a rose is a rose," but in commerce, this isn't true. There has been a huge commercial difference between Peace rose (PP591, June 15, 1943) and Waves rose (PP638, Sept. 5, 1944).

A name is often the secret to marketing success, such as Envy zin-nia, with green flowers; Carefree, one of the earliest F_1 hybrid seed propagated geraniums, and Firechief, the first red-flowered petunia.

Regional cultural/marketing trials. The official trialing of bedding plants is international in scope and highly organized by the seed indus-try in cooperation with public institutions—university, botanical gar-dens, city gardens, etc. The most prestigious North American trials are conducted by All-America Selections (see Chapter 2); these trials have been active for almost 60 years and their success has paralleled the suc-cess of the bedding plant industry. AAS evaluates bedding plants in several categories; however, their focus is the identification of cultivars that are excellent for garden use. Other international trialing organi-zations are FloraStar, Fleuroselect and the All Britain Trials.

Establishment of clean stock. Clean stock production refers to developing propagules—seeds, plugs, cuttings, etc.—that are free of disease organisms and arthropod pests. Disease organisms include fungi, bacteria, and viruses, and arthropod pests include insects and mites. Weeds can also be a possible seed contaminant in certain crops.

Freedom from diseases and pests just does not happen; it is part of a planned program to produce quality products. It is also the law in many areas of the United States and the world.

Most potential problems are readily controlled by disciplined production techniques such as sanitation, exclusion and biological or chemical therapies. The major, difficult-to-control situations are related to systemic bacterial and viral diseases. These can only be controlled by two methods: genetically conditioned host plant resistance and/or culture and virus indexing programs for the production of clean mother plants (plants that provide seeds or cuttings for sale).

It is obvious that improved cultivars of bedding plants, whether sexually or asexually propagated, are more valuable, more predictable, and of higher quality when they are distributed and marketed as clean stock.

Propagation. Propagation refers to the scaling up of a new cultivar to the number required for commercial sales. Again, it is important to propagate from a clean stock base. The most critical steps are in estimating the number of propagules required for a given season and coordination of propagation with marketing efforts.

Marketing. This infers creating a demand for the new or improved cultivar through advertising and public relations. Of course, regional and national trials and awards could be critical to the overall marketing success of bedding plant cultivars.

Distribution. Distribution of improved cultivars to plug or seedling producers, prefinishers, or to commercial bedding plant growers is the final stage of commercialization under a breeder's control. Distribution is usually accomplished through brokers, but some organizations maintain their own sales division. It is critical that quality plants be distributed; this will hopefully affect repeat sales. One item not discussed is distributing a new cultivar in consumer trade (seed) packets. This is a separate but tremendously large industry.

Production and use. New bedding plant cultivars are produced by professional flower growers. Bedding plant growers may wholesale or retail specific items; but the final consumer is either a homeowner or private or public organization.

Conclusions

We have followed the development of an improved cultivar of a bedding plant from its initial visualization to the ultimate use by the consumer.

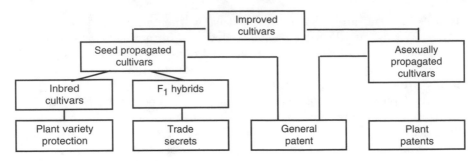

Fig. 31.4. Intellectual property protection for bedding plant cultivars.

A fascinating series of events must occur for the successful introduction of new cultivars into horticulture. The time period for development could range from five to 15 years, depending on the species. We have not discussed all of the associated research that may need to be conducted for the described process to be successful; such research can be tremendously time consuming and costly over a long period of time. The final return on an investment occurs many years after a breeding program is initiated.

New and improved cultivars are the lifeblood of the bedding plant industry; this has been true in the last five decades and will be even more important as we approach and enter into the 21st century.

References

[1] Brickell, C.D., ed. 1980. *International code of nomenclature for cultivated plants—1980*. Utrecht, The Netherlands: Bohn, Scheltema & Holkema.

[2] Craig, R. 1993. Intellectual property protection of pelargoniums. *HortTechnology* 3(3):284-290.

[3] Griesbach, R. 1980. Recent advances in the protoplast biology of flower crops. *Scientia Horticulturae* 37:247-256.

[4] Marsolais, A.A., D.P.M. Wilson, and M.J. Tsujita. 1991. Somatic embryo genesis and artificial seed production in zonal (*Pelargonium* x *hortorum*) and regal (*P*. x *domesticum*) geranium. *Can. J. Bot.* 60:1188-1193.

[5] Mol, J., A. Stuitje, A. Gerates, A. van der Krol, and R. Jorgensen. 1989. Saying it with genes: molecular flower breeding. *TIBTECH* 7:148-153.

[6] Slimmon, T., J.A. Qureshi, and P.K. Saxena. 1991. Phenylacetic acid-induced somatic embryogenesis in cultured hypocotyl explants of geranium (*Pelargonium* x *hortorum* Bailey). *Plant Cell Reports* 10:587-589.

[7] Wilson, D.P.M. 1990. Somatic embryogenesis in *Pelargonium* x *domesticum* Bailey and *Pelargonium* x *hortorum* Bailey. Master's Thesis. University of Guelph, Guelph, Ontario, Canada.

INDEX

media
    compaction of, 136
    container size and, 134–135
    formulations, 131–133
    mixing, 133–135
    for perennials, 390
    in plug production, 122
    substrate, 127–131, 169–171
    vegetable, 351
    water, effects on, 145
merchandising
    packaging, 52
    plant labels, 53, 68
    product familiarity, 51
    product quality, 52
    for profit, 55
    promotion and presentation, 55, 57
    signage, 67–68
mites. *See* pests
motivation
    Maslow's hierarchy of human needs,
        342–343
    ten commandments of, 349
mulches. *See* weed control program

N

New Guinea impatiens
    florel, 375
    media conditions, 375
    tomato spotted wilt virus, 375
nutrition
    deficiencies, COLOR PLATE SECTION
        calcium, 173
        nitrogen, 171
        phosphorus, 172
        potassium, 173
    monitoring
        substrate testing, 169
        tissue testing, 171
        visual observation, 172–175
    See also fertilization

P

perennials
    fertilization, 391–392
    lighting/photoperiod, 397–398
    marketing, 392
    media, 390
    propagation, 384–390, 394–396
    propagation time, 382–383

pesticides
    clothing. *See* protective clothing
    concentrates, 301
    containers, 302–303
    disposal, 300
    emergencies, 305–307
    equipment rinsates, 302
    mixes, 301
    mixing and loading, 295–297
    poisoning, 299–300
    precautions, 293, 297–299, 304–305
    sprays
        aersol generators, 288
        air-assisted electrostatic,
            288–290
        high volume, 286–287
        low volume, 287–290
        thermal pulse-jet foggers, 287
    transporting, 303–304
pests
    aphids, 257–259
    biological control, 262
    fungus gnats, 261–262
    screening, 266–267
    slugs, 265
    spider mites, 264–265
    western flower thrips, 248, 262–264
    whiteflies, 259–261
plant production
    beginnings of, 3
    cuttings, care of, 370
    equipment, production. *See*
        equipment
    Iowa State University stage
        classification, 151, 161
    irrigation differences in, 120–121
    labor, allocation of, 327
    nutrient monitoring, 169,
        171–175
    plug method. *See* plugs
    schedule, developing, 93
    seedling
        cost of production, 328, 330–331
        environment, 108–110
    sowing seed, 94–95
    space utilization, 117
    specific plants
        geranium, 370–373
        New Guinea impatiens, 374–375
        pelargonium, 370–373
        perennials, 380–384, 386–389